Animal Psychophysics: the design and conduct of sensory experiments

Animal

the design and conduct

APPLETON-CENTURY-CROFTS
EDUCATIONAL DIVISION/MEREDITH CORPORATION
New York

Psychophysics:
of sensory experiments

EDITOR:

WILLIAM C. STEBBINS

Kresge Hearing Research Institute, and Departments
of Otorhinolaryngology and Psychology, University
of Michigan, Ann Arbor, Michigan

Contributors

SUSAN BARROW
Department of Psychology, Brown University, Providence, Rhode Island.

MARK A. BERKLEY
Psychology Department, Florida State University, Tallahassee, Florida.

HARRY J. CARLISLE
Department of Psychology, University of California at Santa Barbara, Santa Barbara, California.

BEN CLOPTON
Department of Physiology and Biophysics, and Regional Primate Research Center, University of Washington Medical School, Seattle, Washington.

JOHN I. DALLAND
Division of Social Sciences, Richmond College, The City University of New York, Staten Island, New York.

EBERHARD FETZ
Department of Physiology and Biophysics, and Regional Primate Research Center, University of Washington Medical School, Seattle, Washington.

MITCHELL GLICKSTEIN
Department of Psychology, Brown University, Providence, Rhode Island.

GEORGE GOUREVITCH
Hunter College, The City University of New York, New York, New York.

JOSEPH KIMM
Departments of Otolaryngology, Physiology and Biophysics, and Regional Primate Research Center, University of Washington Medical School, Seattle, Washington.

VICTOR G. LATIES
Department of Radiation Biology and Biophysics, The University of Rochester School of Medicine and Dentistry, Rochester, New York.

ERICH LUSCHEI
Department of Physiology and Biophysics, and Regional Primate Research Center, University of Washington School of Medicine, Seattle, Washington.

RICHARD W. MALOTT
Psychology Department, Western Michigan University, Kalamazoo, Michigan.

MARILYN KAY MALOTT
Psychology Department, Western Michigan University, Kalamazoo, Michigan.

JOSEF M. MILLER
Departments of Otolaryngology, Physiology and Biophysics, and Regional Primate Research Center, University of Washington Medical School, Seattle, Washington.

W. LLOYD MILLIGAN
Psychological Research Laboratory, Veteran's Administration Hospital, Columbia, South Carolina.

DAVID B. MOODY
Kresge Hearing Research Institute, and Department of Psychology, University of Michigan, Ann Arbor, Michigan.

JOHN A. NEVIN
Psychology Department, Columbia University, New York, New York.

BARBARA A. RAY
Neurology Research, Massachusetts General Hospital, Boston, Massachusetts.

ROBERT W. REYNOLDS
Department of Psychology, University of California at Santa Barbara, Santa Barbara, California.

PETER B. ROSENBERGER
Pediatric Neurology Unit, Massachusetts General Hospital, Boston, Massachusetts.

THOMAS R. SCOTT

Psychological Research Laboratory, Veteran's Administration Hospital, Columbia, South Carolina.

JAMES SMITH

Psychology Department, Florida State University, Tallahassee, Florida.

WILLIAM C. STEBBINS

Kresge Hearing Research Institute, and Departments of Otorhinolaryngology and Psychology, University of Michigan, Ann Arbor, Michigan.

SYLVIA THORPE

Psychology Department, Brown University, Providence, Rhode Island.

BERNARD WEISS

Department of Radiation Biology and Biophysics, The University of Rochester School of Medicine and Dentistry, Rochester, New York.

DEAN YAGER

Psychology Department, Brown University, Providence, Rhode Island.

Preface

In May of 1969, the contributors to this book gathered at the University of Michigan in Ann Arbor for three days to talk about their work in the behavioral analysis of animal sensory function and to share their research experiences in the laboratory with particular emphasis on methodology in behavioral training, testing, and instrumentation. It was their feeling and mine as a consequence of this meeting that we had sufficient substance to justify a book which we hoped would be of interest and even of pragmatic value to any biologic or biomedical scientist whose work deals with sensory function.

Clearly, there is no aspect of an organism's behavior that is not to some extent controlled by environmental stimuli. In recent years, due in large part to technical advances in microscopy and histology and in electrophysiology, there have been several extremely informative published proceedings from conferences and symposia concerned with some of the early and very basic stages in the reception of environmental energy by the sense organs and its processing by the nervous system. Transduction at the receptor and stimulus coding by the nervous system, cell membrane changes, and the basic structure of the receptor and related tissue as seen through the electron and phase contrast microscope have received major attention, and exciting new discoveries in sensory function and structure have been reported.

Ultimately, such discoveries must be related to an intact behaving organism. Questions ranging from the resolving power of a sensory system (the concept of threshold) to a wide variety of complex perceptual phenomena can only be directed to such a behavioral preparation. For all of their obvious value in understanding nervous function, potentials recorded in end organ and brain take on new meaning when their relationship to behavior has been made clear and unequivocal.

Although data on sensory acuity are available for man, it is only in recent years that we have improved our techniques to be able to obtain similar data from lower animals. Since much of the research on physiologic function and anatomic structure has been done with these animals, it becomes particularly important to know in some detail their sensory and perceptual acuity as revealed by their behavioral responses to sensory stimulation.

Training and testing procedures based on the principles of operant conditioning have shown that animals can report on their sensory capabilities in as precise and reliable a fashion as humans. In the past decade in the laboratory, we have acquired considerable normative data on sensory acuity in animals. Second, developments in other areas of inquiry have reached a stage of readiness for such behavioral technology. For example, the information to be gained from electrical recording and stimulating in neural tissue and direct infusion of substances in the awake animal in neurophysiology and neuropharmacology is greatly increased if the animal has been trained as a precise observer and reporter of sensory events. The conference and the book, then, had at least two primary objectives. The first was in fact to demonstrate the efficacy of these operant conditioning methods for the analysis of sensory function in animals, and the second was to show, where possible, the use of these methods in conjunction with methods from other biologic research areas in an attempt to better understand some aspect of sensory function (normal or pathological). I think it is safe to say, in conclusion, that the success of our venture—conference and book—rests to a large extent on the data that these behavioral procedures have produced.

There did not appear to us to be any very obvious order of arrangement for the chapters in the book, although the reader will see that some attempt at grouping has been made. The introductory chapter was written primarily for our colleagues in other research areas of biology and biomedicine in the hope that our methods and our findings might be of some interest to them and even applicable to their work. In that chapter, I have tried to show some of the background for the development of animal psychophysics from both the literature of human psychophysics and animal conditioning. I have also tried to introduce some of the terminology that we use, some typical experimental designs and arrangements, and some idea of the problems encountered. All this is done far too briefly, but reference is made to other sources for more extended background and to the chapters themselves where procedures and findings are described with the same clarity, rigor, and thoroughness with which the original experiments were carried out in the laboratory. Although the chapters are based on papers presented within a somewhat formal structure at the conference, a general attitude of informality and enthusiasm prevailed at the time. Hopefully some of this attitude remains in the book, which has not been severely edited. It is an attitude which characterizes the field. We who work there have a good time doing what we do and talking with our colleagues about it.

The support for the research, the conference, and the book came from many sources. Granting agencies are appropriately listed with the individual chapters in the book. Partial support for the conference and subsequent preparation of the book came from Appleton-Century-Crofts. A contract from the Office of Naval Research (Nonr(G)-00024-67) to E. R. Galanter supported a two-day planning session in the spring of 1968 at Columbia University; unfortunately, Dr. Galanter was unable to attend our conference in Ann Arbor.

There are many people who played an important part, directly and indirectly, in putting together both the conference and the book. I would dedicate the book to the contributors who made it an exciting and rewarding conference and sent their chapters in quickly, to the students from our laboratory at the University of Michigan who were so helpful in making the conference a success: Bill Clark, Julie Costin, Doris Foster, Swayzer Green, Elbert Magoun, Dick Pearson, and Bud Wilkinson, to Karen Pritula who played a major role in taking care of all the many problems that arose between original manuscript and page proofs, to my colleague Dave Moody for keeping the lab going, to Dick Van Frank for his help as Appleton-Century-Croft's Editor-in-Chief, Scientific Books Department, to my wife and daughters who provided inspiration and rarely complained about late hours and lost weekends, and to those of my teachers from whom I learned, among many other things, that a liberal attitude may be suitable for politics but a conservative one with caution and healthy skepticism is sometimes more appropriate for science: W. W. Cumming, F. S. Keller, H. D. Patton, W. N. Schoenfeld, and A. L. Towe.

Contents

Animal Psychophysics: the design and conduct of sensory experiments

WILLIAM C. STEBBINS [1]

1

PRINCIPLES OF ANIMAL PSYCHOPHYSICS *

In the most general sense, animal psychophysics can be defined as an area of research in which the primary concern is with the behavioral analysis of sensory function. The basic data are the conditioned responses of the awake, intact organism to sensory stimulation. The properties of a sensory system—that is, its qualifications as a detector of environmental energy—are evaluated by reference to these overt behavioral responses.

The first objective of experimental inquiry has been to determine the minimum detectable energy levels of stimulation (absolute threshold) and the minimum detectable difference between values on a continuum of, for example, amplitude and wavelength of stimulation (difference threshold) to which an animal can respond. Experimental findings then permit us to make descriptive statements about the limits of resolution of an organism's sensory system. Further objectives involve an examination of some of the response characteristics of an animal when the energy values of stimulation are clearly above threshold. Stimulus magnitude estimation, perceptual phenomena, and the self-regulation of thermal and noxious stimuli are examples of research problems that lie within the domain of animal psychophysics and that require judgments about the relation between stimuli which are above minimum detectable levels.

This book (and the conference from which it came) addresses itself primarily to the methodology by which normative data on sensory function can be obtained from lower animals. This concern with questions of method, with ways to improve the validity and reliability of the findings, and with the relations to data obtained with methods from other biologic research areas represents the current stage of development of animal psychophysics. A major part of evaluating methodology is the analysis of the procedural variables themselves and the extent to which the sensory data might vary with changes in the values of these variables—that is, the extent to which the results might be a function of our procedures. The questions of what are the "best" set of procedures might be answered partly by defining the conditions for producing any or all of the following: rapid acquisition of

[1] Kresge Hearing Research Institute, and Departments of Otorhinolaryngology and Psychology, University of Michigan Medical School, Ann Arbor, Michigan.

* Preparation of this chapter was partly supported by grants (NS 05077 and NS 05785) from the National Institute of Neurological Diseases and Stroke. I am indebted to Dr. R. N. Lanson for his contributions to an earlier version of the chapter and to Drs. G. Gourevitch, D. B. Moody, and J. G. Sherman for their suggestions and criticism which led to this, the final version.

1

stable discriminative responding by the animal, stable behavioral baselines over time, replicability, and so on.

Clearly, we have not attempted to represent the entire field of study of sensory function in animals. At the same time, the behavioral analysis of sensory function overlaps many related disciplines. Researchers interested in procedures for the experimental analysis of behavior, for establishing stimulus control in animals, in the structure and function of sensory systems and their relation to sensory capacity behaviorally determined, and in comparative or phyletic study of sensory function have contributed to the literature of animal psychophysics. As evidenced by some of the contributions in this book, the methodology of animal psychophysics has found applications in the study of brain function (Glickstein's chapter), behavioral pharmacology (Weiss' chapter), inner ear function (Stebbins' chapter), cortical electrophysiology (Miller's chapter), and genetics (Ray's chapter). It becomes the responsibility of the individual contributor to make the case for the importance of the particular line of inquiry that he has chosen to follow and its relevance to sensory function. It will be the purpose of this chapter to try to provide a brief overview to this form of research and to identify the limits we have set for ourselves.

The term "psychophysics" was used historically to refer to a methodology for presenting stimuli to an organism to determine the limits and dimensions of its sensory experience. This methodology has evolved during the last century as a means of answering experimental questions about human sensory acuity. No attempt will be made to review historically a field which dates back to 1860 with Gustav Fechner's publication of *Elemente der Psychophysik*. The already large and still growing body of data obtained on human observers using psychophysical methods can at best be alluded to here, but the basic experimental aim and the procedures that have been developed for humans are germaine to the formulation of experimental questions in work with lower animals. The endpoint of the psychophysical experiment is a functional relation between environmental stimuli and behavior. The stimulus can be specified in physical units and is usually varied along a single physical dimension. The basic question concerns the ability of an organism to discriminate; that is, to respond differentially to values along this dimension.

The absolute threshold (minimum detectable energy level) can be thought of as the limiting case of a more general discrimination in which the subject is asked to judge changes in, or differences between, stimuli varying in one dimension. Difference thresholds may be exemplified by the just discriminable increment (or decrement) in light intensity, the smallest detectable change in acoustic frequency or intensity, or the change in thermal stimulation that is just noticeable. In these discriminations, the change in stimulation is made from a stimulus condition or standard whose physical composition can be specified. From the earliest investigations with man it was noted that the stimulus change detected was some function of the value of this standard stimulus. At least two suggested relations have had considerable influence on the treatment of difference threshold data: Weber's Law, which states that just noticeable differences in intensity are proportional to the standard stimulus intensity, and Fechner's Law, which proposes a logarithmic relation between sensory effect and stimulus intensity.

Another set of experimental questions concerns comparisons among supra-threshold stimuli. For instance, when do two audible tones differing in frequency "sound" equally loud, or when does one tone "sound" twice as loud as another? The specification of the pitch of a tone and the brightness of a light refer to questions that have been approached through techniques of psychophysical scaling. The subject is instructed to set two or more stimuli in a fixed relation to one another or to assign stimuli to categories (sometimes numerical) to describe their sensory magnitudes. A more detailed description of the variations in scaling procedures for human subjects can be found in Stevens (1957) and Torgerson (1958). In such studies, an important (and seldom studied) controlling variable is the role of the instructional stimuli. The impact of scaling techniques has also influenced the analysis of psychophysical data by demonstrating that a power function often best describes the relation between scaled sensory effects and stimulus intensity (Stevens, 1957).

The perceptual experiment may ask still another kind of question about sensory discriminations. Although we cannot treat here the differences that have been proposed to separate perceptual experiments from sensory experiments, in an attempt to relate such research to the sensory issues we will adopt the position of Graham and Ratoosh (1962) and Schoenfeld and Cumming (1963) that the study of perception can advance within the same systematic or theoretic framework as the study of sensation, and that perceptual experiments can be characterized as studying the effects of manipulating additional classes of variables on discriminations. In some instances, these variables are stimulus variables as in the study of brightness contrast where one assesses the effects of a surround field on the brightness of a test light. But these variables might also be instructional, historic, or training variables. The determining variables in the illusions, for example, may be shown to depend upon the discriminative history of the subject with respect to specific parts of the stimulus complex.

One distinction between perceptual experiments and sensory experiments should be emphasized. In the sensory experiment in which two stimuli differ in only one regard, the experimenter can specify à priori a unique stimulus value which is known with respect to the subject's threshold. The condition of stimulus absence in absolute threshold studies and physical equality in difference threshold studies define below threshold values. If a subject reported the stimulus as present or different, respectively, under these conditions, the experimenter would label these responses "incorrect" by definition and might suspect the presence of other controlling variables. In the perceptual experiment, no such prior specification is possible because of the existence of other controlling variables. In most instances, we cannot state a relationship between behavior and some stimulus value as "correct" or "incorrect" before we have done the experiment. The distinction is critical for animal psychophysics and creates some challenging problems for training as will become evident.

Before a sensory experiment, human subjects are usually instructed verbally for their observing task with regard to the responses permitted and the payoffs associated with "correct" and "incorrect" responses. Here "correctness" refers to reporting the stimuli when presented, and to withholding a report either in the absence of stimulation or when other than the designated stimulus is presented.

The payoffs may be monetary but often the subject is merely instructed about the degree of vigilance necessary and the savings in time if he is "careful." Manipulation of these instructional variables has been studied as the influence of determining set or tendency or the effects of "motivation" (Woodworth and Schlosberg, 1954). There is considerable current interest and already a sizeable literature based on the general theory of signal detectability and concerned with the possible confounding of threshold measures with motivational and other nonsensory effects (Galanter, 1962; Swets, 1964; Green and Swets, 1966). Variables such as payoff for correct and incorrect responses and signal presentation probability have been studied under relatively difficult discrimination conditions where subjects are asked to detect signals which are usually embedded in noisy backgrounds. Presumably, the sensory experiment can be designed in such a way as to provide a pure measure of sensitivity which is independent of effects which have been labeled motivational or even attitudinal. Based on concepts taken from engineering and mathematics, signal detection theory offers a relatively new and unique approach to the study of sensory function in man. Proponents have raised some interesting questions about the validity of the classic concept of threshold as representing a rigid partition or dichotomy on a stimulus continuum between sensation and its absence.

Clearly, threshold is not a fixed immutable point but can be shown to vary with changes in a variety of different conditions including momentary unpredicted alterations in both stimulus and subject. Repeated measurements are necessary and threshold is usually defined as some sort of average of these measurements. The reliability and small variance in most threshold experiments has been impressive and often matches that found in the measurement of physical systems.

In threshold experiments, the response class is usually binary ("Yes, I detect the stimulus [or difference between stimuli]"; "No, I do not"). The use of more than two response categories is less commonly used because of major difficulties with multiple categories in the mathematical treatment of the different responses. Scaling procedures (e.g., stimulus magnitude estimation), however, often use more than two response alternatives and sophisticated mathematical analyses have been applied to these data (Stevens, 1957; Torgerson, 1958). To determine threshold, the experimenter manipulates stimulus values along one dimension and defines a range in which one extreme is detected 100 percent of the time and the other extreme 0 percent of the time. Between these two values the subject displays some uncertainty about whether the stimulus has been presented or whether one stimulus differs from another. To further explore this range, the psychophysical methods have been developed, and those most commonly used are described below. A number of variations on these basic methods have been used and a more detailed treatment of the parameters and mathematical analyses is possible (Woodworth and Schlosberg, 1954; Green and Swets, 1966; Guilford, 1954; and Stevens, 1951).

In the *method of constant stimuli*, the experimenter chooses a fixed set of stimulus values (usually 5 to 7) delimited as described above. These stimuli are then presented to the subject in a mixed or randomized sequence. The response measure is the probability (or relative frequency) with which the subject reports each stimulus value. The form of the psychometric function relating response probability to some measure of the stimulus is often ogival, and its slope provides information about the fineness or sharpness of discrimination, a measure of sensitivity. Threshold is calculated directly from the function.

In the *method of limits*, the experimenter chooses a stimulus value at one extreme of a stimulus range of uncertainty where the probability of one response (either "yes" or "no") is 1.0, and over succeeding trials the stimulus is changed in the direction of the other end of the range until a change in the subject's response is noted. Another series of trials is then initiated with the starting point of the series at the opposite end of the range. A series of trials run in the direction of increasing stimulus difference or magnitude is referred to as an ascending series, those in decreasing magnitude as a descending series. The points of transition from one response class to another are used in the statistical computation of the threshold. Whether the experimenter chooses to use both ascending and descending series will depend to some extent on the task. The process of dark adaptation, for example, is best studied with an ascending series since the test light which is used will light-adapt the eye and hence affect the course of dark adaptation.

The method of limits, although it provides a quick estimate of threshold, is complicated by possible sequential effects on the subject's responding. The experimenter only sets the starting point and step size of the series; the subject continues to make the same response for a number of trials before shifting to the other response, presumably at threshold. Different starting points in the series are selected so that response sequences vary, and where both directions are explored, a counter-balanced order of ascending-descending-descending-ascending series is used to reduce some of the internal sequential dependencies of the task. Nevertheless, comparisons of the ascending thresholds to the descending thresholds sometimes reveal different values.

A variation on the method of limits that attempts to lessen the complications from sequential effects is called the *tracking method* (also *staircase* and *up-down*). In this method, although the initial starting point of a series of trials is set by the experimenter, and the stimuli are presented in sequential order, the direction of stimulus change is completely dependent upon the subject's response. Each correct detection is followed by a decrease in stimulus magnitude or difference; each failure to detect by an increase. There is a form of closed loop or feedback system between subject and experimenter or equipment; ideally the subject will track the stimulus continually back and forth across his threshold. Calculation of threshold is based on the average transition value between detection and failure to detect. Some sequential problems and solutions have been suggested by Cornsweet (1962). The tracking method has the advantage over the methods of limits and constant stimuli of reducing the range of stimuli to those in the immediate vicinity of the threshold. The advantage is very much an economic one since there is a greater amount of usable information per total number of trials. With the other methods only a small percentage of the data contributes to the calculation of threshold. The benefits are a savings in time which is critical in animal work where the length of an experimental session is often limited by the amount of food or water the animal will ingest. An obvious drawback of the procedure is the relative difficulty of the discriminations required of the subject with the stimulus always close to minimum detectable levels. Rosenberger has reviewed the history of the tracking procedure and discussed its use in animal psychophysics (see Chapter 7).

In the *method of adjustment*, the subject is allowed to present himself with a range of stimuli and to search this range until he finds the stimulus value that is just discriminable. Here, in a single trial, the threshold is specified directly as the subject's choice. Over multiple trials, some measure of central tendency among these response settings is used to characterize the threshold. One of the drawbacks to this method is that the experimenter has no control over the rate at which the subject presents himself with the stimuli. There are also sequential dependencies as in the method of limits.

With any of the psychophysical methods, there is concern that the subject's behavior may be under the control of variables other than the properties of the stimulus. To determine the extent of stimulus control, "catch" trials for which the stimulus has been turned off are presented. Catch trials used in difference threshold experiments usually represent the condition of physical equality of the stimuli to be discriminated. A stimulus-reporting response to a catch trial indicates the presence of other controlling variables.

The definition of threshold is a statistical statement. By convention, the physical stimulus which yields 50 percent detection is determined directly from the psychometric function for the method of constant stimuli. This value has been called the point of maximal uncertainty because at either extreme of the function, the subject was more certain that the stimulus was present or absent. The choice of the 50 percent value from the psychometric function is to some degree arbitrary, and in certain cases, other percentage values have been dictated from theoretic models (Hecht, Shlaer, and Pirenne, 1942). In the calculation of threshold from data obtained by other psychophysical methods, the 50 percent detection point and also the mean response transition value (between "yes" and "no") are in common usage.

The interest of the psychophysicist does not usually stop with the determination of a single threshold value. More importantly, he is interested in comparing threshold values obtained when a second dimension of the stimulus is varied (Graham, 1934; 1950; 1965). The resulting function has been variously termed a stimulus-stimulus function, stimulus-critical value function, or a perceptual function. For example, the minimum energy required to detect a tone of a single frequency is by itself a rather limited piece of information, but by determining threshold energies for tones along the auditory frequency continuum, we have discovered the frequency limits of hearing as well as the absolute sensitivity over the entire frequency range. In a sense, we have found the frequency response function for a sensory modality by determining what stimulus values are necessary to yield a constant response, which in this instance is the threshold. Such constant response contours represent the basic psychophysical functions. In the example of the threshold value, detection of the stimulus half the time is taken to be a constant response criterion. Absolute threshold functions may be considered a special case of the constant response contour. Subjects have been asked to match clearly audible tones on the basis of "loudness" or visible lights on the basis of "brightness," for example. The resultant functions are equal loudness contours for the ear and equal brightness contours for the eye. Suprathreshold matching and scaling of sensation represent a unique challenge to the animal psychophysicist since such experiments are completely based on the use of human language. In order to study such phenomena in lower animals, it is necessary to find nonlinguistic referents for the basic concepts (e.g., loudness, brightness, etc.).

With behavioral evidence of normal sensory function in hand, the psychophysicist may try to relate this evidence to other measures of sensory function. Such additional information may be behavioral (sensory deficit, perhaps drug or noise induced), electrophysiologic (evoked potential recording), or anatomic (structure of receptor tissue). Often studies are designed to answer questions, in so far as possible, about mediation of sensory process by sense organ and central nervous system. Many such questions are, of course, not appropriately directed to human subjects. With lower animals, electrodes can usually be placed nearer to the relevant anatomic structures, drugs dangerous to man can be examined, and postmortem histologic analysis of tissue can be carried out in closer temporal proximity to the treatment and to whatever related behavioral change has occurred.

In this all too brief summary of the principal issues and testing methods for sensory research on human subjects, it should be noted that there are, in addition, a number of specific procedural considerations. An experimenter works with a limited number of subjects and stimulus dimensions to the exclusion of others. The laboratory situation is both highly analytic and highly structured. To avoid the effects of additional or extraneous variables, the subject is put in a situation (i.e., soundproof, light-tight rooms) where these extraneous variables are eliminated if possible, or held at a constant value during the experiment. Those stimulus variables which are manipulated must be capable of specification in physical units and therefore great emphasis is placed on precise calibration of the physical stimulus and on its accurate and reproducible delivery to the sensory end organ under investigation. Much sensory research places a premium on subjects who must give reliable data within and across several sessions. To achieve this high level of reliability, considerable time is devoted to giving subjects practice in an attempt to reduce response variability before taking final threshold measurements. Sometimes subjects are given feedback during training as to their accuracy or variability. Usually, if a subject responds to a catch trial, he is warned that he may forfeit time or money or even be dismissed if he persists. Human psychophysical observers often represent considerable investments in training time and money.

The use of animal subjects in psychophysical experiments requires many of the same strategies that are standard for human observers. The restricted laboratory environment is used to minimize the number of controlling variables. A limited class of stimulus variables is manipulated, and their precise calibration is required. Stimulus location on the sensory receptors is as carefully controlled and specified as technologically possible. Finally, animal subjects must be put through an extensive behavioral training program to transform them into reliable psycho-physical observers.

This highly structured, laboratory oriented approach to the study of animal sensory processes might meet with objection from some on the grounds that the constraints we impose prevent us from making any statement about the behavior of the organism in its own econiche or "natural" environment. However, as with human observers, precise quantitative data on the limits of sensory resolving power are unobtainable outside of the laboratory. It may well be that certain questions raised in "naturalistic" studies might be further explored by psycho-physical methods in the laboratory. For example, Struhsaker (1967, 1970) has recorded primate calls in the vervet monkey and galago in the field. Spectral analysis of their calls indicates ultrasonic frequency components (beyond the human range of hearing). Their role in communication will of course depend upon the monkey's ability to hear and to respond to them. On the basis of laboratory evidence (Stebbins et al., 1966), we have been able to establish that, in fact, some monkeys can hear and respond to considerably higher frequencies than man. Further research might be applied to the question of whether these high frequencies are functional in communication by selectively filtering the frequency composition of the recorded primate call and observing the effects on behavior. There are clearly problem areas beginning to develop around issues which require both laboratory and field information and the experimental results may do much toward bridging the gap between these two traditionally separate areas of inquiry. The kind of basic information about sensitivity which was sought and is presented by the contributors to this book is, however, inaccessible without the procedural constraints of the laboratory.

It was an obvious fact of life to earliest man that animals could make discriminations in some sense modalities far more acute than his own. Most lower animals clearly surpass man in their olfactory acuity. The frequency range of hearing of the domestic dog and the visual acuity of the hawk are two among countless examples from the earliest recorded legends of antiquity. The data were based on simple observation, much of which was anecdotal, and interpretation based on incomplete evidence sometimes produced false conclusions which have been perpetuated and are still held as truth outside the scientific community. Many still believe, for example, that the domestic cat is color-blind, and that the snake responds to the sound of the snake charmer's music rather than to the visual cues produced by his movement. Perhaps the most formidable obstacle to a nonhuman (ergo nonverbal) psychophysics was considered insurmountable by Claude Bernard when he wrote in 1865 in his "Introduction to Experimental Medicine": "Experimental study of sense organs must be made on man because animals can not directly account to us for the sensations which they experience" (1949, p. 125). The problem becomes one of developing procedures to provide the necessary substitute for verbal instructions and thus overcome the language barrier between subject and experimenter. These procedures must insure that the animal can learn to attend to the relevant stimulus dimension and report on very small changes in the stimuli along this dimension.

The development of procedures for studying sensory function in animals by behavioral means is historically tied to the beginnings of animal psychology in the post-Darwinian period in the late nineteenth century (Boring, 1950). After a bout with anecdotalism and a philosophic concern with the mental life of animals, the study of animal behavior moved into the laboratory (Jennings, 1923; Loeb, 1918; Yerkes and Watson, 1911). The experimental studies of animal behavior began to add objective rigor to a field dominated by anthropomorphic and teleological accounts and began to reveal strong stimulus dependencies. The work of Jennings (1923) on invertebrates and Loeb (1918) demonstrated movements directed toward or away from a stimulus. These "forced movements" could take several forms. In the presence of some stimuli, certain animals would display undirected movements whose speed of locomotion or amount of turning per unit time was dependent on the intensity of the stimulus. Such movements were called "kineses." Another form of forced movement was called a "taxis" (formerly "tropism") and referred to directed orientation. Positive and negative phototaxis referred to behavior straight toward or straight away from a light. A third form of forced movement is similar to taxes but the orientation takes place at a temporarily fixed angle to the direction of the stimulus or at a fixed angle of 90°. This class of orientation is called transverse. Examples include the "light compass reaction" in which locomotion occurs at a fixed angle to the direction of stimulation, and the dorsal (or ventral) light reaction in which locomotion is not observed but the animal orients to keep a directed light perpendicular to the axis of the body. A more detailed account of this early research can be found in Fraenkel and Gunn (1961) and Crozier and Hoagland (1934).

With these techniques, the response class was specified as an approach, non-approach, or orientation of the organism with respect to the stimulus. Much of this research was conducted with a large population of animals exposed to a given stimulus condition. The number of organisms attracted (or repelled or orienting) was taken as a measure of the probability of responding from the entire population, and quantitative relations were then obtained for different stimulus conditions such as stimulus intensity. Using attraction as a response, one could also equate different stimuli on the basis of what stimuli would produce the same constant response (percent attracted). Perhaps the major disadvantage of this approach to animal psychophysics is that this reflexive behavior has to be present from the outset, and unless one is fortunate enough to find a stimulus-response correlation in the modality of interest, this restriction can seriously limit the range of questions that one can ask about the sensory process. These methods are also subject to changes in responding (possibly adaptation effects) when the organisms are exposed to continual stimulation.

The work of Pavlov (1927) opened up new possibilities for sensory research with animals. As a result of his experiments, a researcher was no longer limited by whether the reflex was already in the organism's repertoire. With Pavlov's methods, one could construct or condition a new reflex from other already present reflexes by pairing a stimulus which initially had no observable or measurable behavioral consequences (i.e., neutral) with a stimulus (unconditioned) already capable of eliciting a response. After a number of pairings, the occurrence of the response become conditional upon the presence of this once neutral stimulus, hence the name conditional (sometimes conditioned) stimulus. The method of pairing stimuli has been called, variously, Pavlovian, respondent, or classic conditioning. Pavlov further contributed a method for establishing a behavioral discrimination between stimuli. His "method of contrasts" specifies that an organism can be trained to respond differentially to different conditioned stimuli by following only one with the unconditioned stimulus (a process called reinforcement). Heart rate, respiration rate, skin resistance, eye blink, and amount of glandular secretion have been conditioned in this manner and used as indications of sensory effect.

As an example of the application of these conditioning procedures to animal psychophysics, McCleary and Bernstein (1959) paired a light with a shock delivered through electrodes placed across the body of a goldfish. The shock alone produced a decrease in heart rate. The light acquired the property of a conditional stimulus, and the effectiveness of different spectral lights in changing heart rate was compared. Ammonia is another stimulus producing decreased heart rate. Jamison (1951) studied auditory sensitivity in the rat by pairing a tone with the presentation of ammonia so that the tone alone produced a change in heart rate. Tonal frequencies were then varied to see what intensities were necessary to produce a decrement in heart rate of 10 percent or more. Brown (1936, 1937), using similar methods, paired a visual stimulus with electric shock and looked at changes in respiration rate produced by the visual stimulus. He was able to determine the sensitivity to lights of different wavelength by finding the intensity needed to bring about a change in respiration. Dalton (1967), using a measure of change in skin resistance (galvanic skin response) of the monkey, paired tones with shock and was able to derive an audiogram from changes in this response measure.

Surprisingly little evidence is available on the reliability of thresholds obtained with these techniques. Adaptation and/or habituation may be seen as decreases in magnitude of the response to the unconditioned stimulus. It is also frequently necessary to recondition the reflex by pairing the conditional stimulus with the unconditioned stimulus to prevent complete loss or extinction of the newly established reflex. Often there are severe limitations on the number of trials that can be given per day. The behavior is easily disrupted and training is apt to be lengthy and cumbersome. Perhaps the most serious handicap to the use of the Pavlovian techniques is the problem of defining a response which indicates sensory effect. Sometimes the response is an analog event and the definition of criterion response change is arbitrary. Decisions about threshold may be based on something as ephemeral as the size and shape of a waveform (galvanic skin response) reflecting a momentary voltage change. Hence, differences between experimental results may depend on the selection of the response as well as the stimulus variable. The use of the evoked cortical response (in EEG audiometry) for threshold testing, though not an example of conditioning, presents the same problem in response definition.

Unquestionably, one major line of development in animal psychophysics can be traced to Thorndike's (1911) early laboratory work with animals and his formulation of the law of effect. In contrast to the Pavlovian emphasis on antecedent eliciting stimuli, the law of effect clearly placed the major responsibility for behavioral control on the consequences of behavior. However, it was not until 1938 with the publication of *Behavior of Organisms* that the method, the systematic position, and the fruitfulness and enormous scope of operant or instrumental conditioning became apparent. Skinner (1938) clearly identified the consequences as measurable stimuli (reinforcers or reinforcements) and made precise, methodologic distinctions between the Pavlovian form of conditioning on the one hand and operant conditioning on the other.

Whether the distinction between two kinds of conditioning is more than methodologic is not a relevant issue here. The important point was that operant behavior could be modified in endless ways by the appropriate manipulation of its consequences (food, water, etc.). In comparison, the conditioned reflex was a relatively rigid and inflexible unit. The behavior was elicited in a rather invariant manner by the antecedent stimulus. It is these antecedent stimuli which are of concern to the animal psychophysicist. In operant conditioning, their function is quite different; their control over behavior is determined by the consequences (reinforcements) of that behavior. Specifically, the probability of a response to one stimulus is high relative to its probability of occurrence to a second stimulus if there has been a history of reinforcement to stimulus one and of nonreinforcement to stimulus two. Such differential responding established under conditions of reinforcement and nonreinforcement forms the major basis for the development of animal psychophysics.

There are two primary behavioral processes of concern to the animal psychophysicist. The first is the process of acquisition (operant conditioning) and the establishment of stimulus control by certain explicit training procedures. The second is the maintenance of a stable baseline of discriminative responding while the psychophysical testing methods are being applied to obtain sensory data. The attendant problems and their solutions are treated in detail in the individual chapters. Here, I will try to review very briefly some of the more commonly used procedures. For a more thorough and adequate examination of the basic principles of operant conditioning, the reader is referred to the references listed in the special appendix at the end of this chapter.

It may well be that the concept of response differentiation or "shaping" is one of Skinner's most important contributions. Certainly its application is essential in the early stages of behavioral training. Reinforcement is applied selectively to an animal's behavior until that particular response which the experimenter has chosen to study is emitted with a high degree of regularity and invariance. Where the response is not already in the animal's repertoire, a procedure is used which requires reinforcement of successive approximations to the final response form. Extinction or nonreinforcement is continuously applied to behavior other than the selected response in an effort to reduce its frequency of occurrence. The monkey's ability to fixate a visual target (see Chapter 16) or to respond in one-fifth of a second to the onset of auditory stimulation (see Chapter 13) are examples of the successful application of the "shaping" procedure.

Reinforcement (food, water, shock) may be effectively scheduled in various ways to maintain stable stimulus observing behavior over long periods of time. Although there are countless ways of devising such schedules, for our purposes they are based either on the animal's behavior—his emission of a number of responses since the previous reinforcement—or on the passage of a time interval since the previous reinforcement. The ratio schedules and the interval schedules can be either fixed or variable. A fixed-ratio (FR) requires a predetermined number of responses prior to each reinforcement; for a variable-ratio (VR) the number requirement varies from one reinforcement to the next but the schedule is often specified in terms of a mean value and range. Fixed-interval (FI) and variable-interval (VI) are defined similarly but in units of time. Any combination or mixture of the above is possible and many variants of these basic reinforcement schedules have been studied (Ferster and Skinner, 1957). It is perhaps safe to say that the variable requirement schedules are more widely used in animal psychophysics since the behavior generated is more stable, particularly between reinforcements, and a change in the behavior produced by introduction of a stimulus is therefore much more readily detected. Further discussion of the different baseline schedules and some of their unique advantages for sensory work is presented in context in the following chapters.

For classificatory purposes, we can consider two processes by which an organism's behavior comes to vary with changes in sensory stimulation. An animal trained to respond to only one value of stimulation will respond, perhaps less frequently or with longer latency, to other values on the same physical continuum when they are introduced, presumably for the first time. The process is called generalization, and the behavioral effect, the generalization gradient. The Malotts in their chapter describe a generalization procedure and discuss its merits as a behavioral baseline for psychophysical research with animals. More commonly, an animal is specifically trained to respond to one value of a stimulus (or perhaps in its absence) and to withhold responding to some other value. By selective reinforcement, the animal's behavior can be brought under stimulus control—that is, the behavior occurs with shorter latency and with greater frequency to the reinforced stimulus value. The process is called discrimination and forms the starting point for much of the work that has been done in animal psychophysics.

The effects of explicit discrimination training with selective reinforcement as opposed to the generalization procedure are seen in more powerful stimulus control—that is, a clearer change in behavior as some dimension of the stimulus is varied. For animal psychophysics, this gain in stimulus control may be the greatest benefit of the discrimination procedures, and the behavioral findings are far less equivocal.

To use the discrimination procedure, it is necessary to be able to specify à priori the basic discrimination requirements for the animal and therefore the physical stimulus conditions under which reinforcement must occur, and this of course can be done for threshold testing. For absolute threshold, the discrimination is between stimulus "on" and stimulus "off" and for difference threshold, between physical equality and physical difference. In some situations, it is not possible to specify the stimulus conditions for reinforcement in advance of the experiment without seriously altering the nature of the experiment. In fact, in these situations, the very question the experiment seeks to answer is directed at the organism's response to stimulus change where there is no stimulus "off" or equality condition, and therefore no preestablished "incorrect" response for which reinforcement can be withheld. For that reason, the extent of an illusion, the loudness of a tone, or the brightness of a light are probably not appropriate subject matter for study under the discrimination method. One alternative is the use of the generalization procedure (see Chapter 17) where reinforcement is not selective with respect to stimulus value. There are other possibilities, and Moody (see Chapter 13) has used the fact that the latency of an operant response varies inversely in an orderly way with stimulus intensity. Equal latencies are then used as a measure of equal sensory effect, and phenomena such as loudness and brightness are then amenable to experimental study. Again, selective reinforcement is not used since the appropriate conditions for reinforcement are unknown before the experiment; responses are reinforced without regard to stimulus value. Little attention has been given to the study of sensory scaling and perceptual processes in lower animals probably, in part, because of the great difficulty in specifying the conditions of reinforcement. Most of the research in these areas has been uniquely human and the concepts (e.g., loudness, brightness, etc.) have been defined entirely on the basis of human language. Direct translation into the terms of reinforcement is usually not possible, and this places serious limitations on the value of these concepts to biologic science if their study is indeed limited to verbal man. Redefinition of the concepts for use with nonverbal subjects has been the only option available and this approach is exemplified in the work of the Malotts, Moody, and Scott and Milligan in the present volume.

I have described the discrimination procedure thus far in skeletal form merely as selective reinforcement for responding to one value on a stimulus dimension. The procedure is almost never seen so simply in psychophysical experiments with animals. A number of contingencies are added in an effort to ensure ever "tighter" stimulus control, and some of these contingencies are discussed in the chapters which follow.

Perhaps one feature common to most, if not all, of these experiments in which selective positive reinforcement is used with the discrimination method is the requirement of an explicit "observing" response. Delivery of stimulation is contingent upon the emission of such a response. The response is often selected by the experimenter in such a way that it places the animal in the best possible position to receive stimulation. Thus Scott (Chapter 16) requires his monkeys to fixate a visual target; Dalland's bats (see Chapter 2) must position themselves rigidly upon a narrowly circumscribed platform before a tone is presented. In both examples, the response is one of holding still, and it is relatively difficult to condition. In the reaction time procedure (see chapters by Miller et al., Moody, and Reynolds), the observing response consists of holding down a key. Since the next response (reporting the stimulus) is key release, the observing response ensures that the animal is in the best position to respond quickly to stimulus onset. In other situations, the observing response may be repetitive (see chapters by Gourevitch, Nevin, Stebbins, or Yager and Thorpe). The presentation of the stimulus is response contingent and scheduled on variable interval or ratio, and the procedure essentially guarantees us that the animal can only be doing one thing at the moment of stimulus presentation. The subsequent response to stimulation is under better control (than if there were no required observing response)—its probability of occurrence is greater and its latency is less. Without an experimenter-defined observing response, the animal will produce some variety of his own depending on what he happens to be doing just prior to stimulus onset. The stimulus has become a conditioned or acquired reinforcer since, in the past, responding in its presence has been followed by food or water; thus whatever response precedes stimulus onset is likely to occur again in similar form. The topography of such an observing response will vary considerably since the animal will probably not be engaging in exactly the same activity before stimulation every time. The consequence (of no explicit observing response) for sensory experiments with animals may well be reflected in more variable baselines and less reliable measures of sensitivity.

Although thus far we have emphasized procedures which utilize nutrient consequences (positive reinforcers like food or water) for behavior, there is a sizeable literature on the application of stimulus events (negative reinforcers) which can be shown to strengthen behavior by a reduction in their intensity or by their complete removal. In the study of pain thresholds, Weiss and Laties (see their chapter) employ a behavioral baseline which is maintained on the basis of reduction in electric shock intensity. Carlisle (see his chapter), reporting on thermoregulation, provides heat reinforcement for his subjects for responding in a cold environment.

While the stimulus conditions being studied may be fundamentally aversive, such as shock, often stimuli such as moderately soft tones or dim lights without strong affect may quickly acquire aversive properties by close temporal pairing with primary aversive events. Thus, if given the opportunity, an animal will soon learn to respond during a signal which, in the past, has invariably preceded shock if in so doing he can terminate the signal and postpone the shock. The procedure is referred to as discriminated avoidance and can serve in the analysis of sensory function in animals since training will produce differential responding along a stimulus dimension in much the same way as the discrimination procedure using positive reinforcement.

It is perhaps unfortunate that the book does not include a discussion of the discriminated avoidance procedure. However, it is not now widely used in animal psychophysics (see Krasnegor and Brady, 1968; Hanson, 1966). It has been the experience in our laboratory that behavioral baselines during threshold testing are less reliable under a shock avoidance regimen as compared to food reinforcement. Administering shock for failure to respond on the part of the animal, presumably to below threshold stimulation, may be partly responsible for the increased variability we have seen in behavior maintained by shock avoidance. The issue is unresolved and badly needs more attention in the laboratory.

Another discrimination procedure using shock has become prevalent in animal psychophysics. Again, stimuli (lights or tones) are paired with shock similar to the avoidance procedure; however, the animal is given no opportunity to avoid the shock. Normal, ongoing behavior is severely attenuated in the presence of these once neutral stimuli, and the procedure has been called conditioned suppression. The ongoing behavior is a specified baseline maintained by a schedule of positive reinforcement designed to produce stable responding over time. Stimuli which have been previously paired with shock disrupt the responding when presented and the effect can be quantified as a change in response rate.

An index is computed comparing the rate during the stimulus to a rate sample taken immediately before it is presented. The suppression index can then be used as a measure of sensory effect. A significant decrease in the animal's response rate would indicate seeing, hearing, etc. That this has proven to be a useful baseline in animal psychophysics is demonstrated by Ray, Rosenberger, and Smith (see their chapters).

This chapter, as an outline of the basic psychophysical methods and operant conditioning procedures, cannot do justice to the wealth of information that exists on human psychophysics and animal conditioning. I have tried simply to preview elements of basic procedures, many of which are in common use in animal psychophysics. My hope is that this material will provide some familiarity with these procedures before they are introduced in the subsequent chapters. Perhaps an obvious common denominator of all the contributors is their knowledgeable use of operant conditioning as a powerful tool to construct their behavioral baselines and as an effective way of creating reliable and precise sensory observers without benefit of language. The key lies with the appropriate use of reinforcement for behavioral acquisition and maintenance. There are risks involved when we consider that the delivery of reinforcement is a stimulus event not likely to be overlooked by the animal and clearly an important source of stimulus control. The sensory experiment places the control in other stimuli which precede the response so that the control exercised by reinforcement delivery is unwanted and a source of trouble if it can be shown to significantly affect our measures of sensory function. Similar to verbal instructions with human subjects, too little is known about the effects of this variable. The bibliographic appendix at the end of the chapter should be examined by those who would use these conditioning procedures. The contributors also share an intense interest in precise laboratory control procedures, and in particular, with accurate specification of the stimuli they use in their experiments. These concerns are a prerequisite if we are ever to obtain complete and exact formulations of the sensory capabilities of lower animals.

The theory of signal detectability raises some interesting possibilities for research in animal psychophysics (see Nevin's chapter). Since so little work has been done, it is impossible to evaluate the utility of the approach as compared with traditional methods. For the most part, signal detection experiments have not been concerned with the basic data of sensitivity to relatively simple stimulus events. In animal psychophysics, many of us are still occupied with the problem of obtaining normative evidence on the more fundamental sensory functions such as audibility, visibility, and so on. Furthermore, the complex nature of the discriminations called for in many signal detection experiments necessitates difficult and very extensive training regimens for animals. Experimental designs often require a very large number of stimulus trials per data point. It is perhaps consideration of issues such as these described above that has delayed the application of signal detection theory to the study of sensory function in animals.

In the chapters that follow, not every sensory system is treated and, in fact, undue attention is perhaps paid to seeing and hearing if only because most of the work has been done on these two systems. The number and variety of animals is not large, but ranges phyletically from goldfish to monkey. We have included most but not all of the procedures in current use. For these reasons, among others, the book precludes simple and orderly arrangement of the chapters on any of these bases, e.g., modality, procedure, animal, etc. The book is not meant to be an exhaustive reference work on animal senses but rather an illustrative survey of what is possible, of behavioral methodology which has been successfully applied to the study of sensory function in animals. In some instances, examples are given of the application of these behavioral techniques to help solve problems in other research areas. Most important, some authors have dealt with one modality and one organism (e.g., Dalland, Nevin, or Yager), but the basic procedures are undoubtedly applicable to other sensory systems and other species. Perhaps the best example of this is Smith's work (see his chapter) which successfully uses a behavioral baseline across many species and modalities. The intent of the book is to promise that such generality is possible and that neither the psychophysical methods nor the conditioning techniques are restricted to a single modality or organism. One major issue which has not received the attention it deserves is the comparative evaluation of the different conditioning and psychophysical testing procedures for animals. There is some evidence that psychophysical measures such as threshold are relatively invariant with different testing procedures. Additional laboratory work of this nature is necessary to confirm that our findings are reliable and are not overly influenced by the methods we use.

There are, of course, a number of considerations which are modality specific or organism specific, but with few exceptions these are not matters which pertain to the general conditioning procedure to be used or to the psychophysical strategy employed. Rather, these specific concerns relate to matters of the mechanics of stimulus presentation and measurement, of care, diet, and housing; and, in the laboratory, to the nature of the reinforcement, to the response and restraint requirements, and to the experimental space itself. Considerable attention is devoted to these critical details in the subsequent chapters. In some instances, break-throughs have been made in that some species whose suitability for laboratory work has long been in doubt are found to make very good psychophysical subjects under the appropriate experimental arrangements (see Berkley's chapter on the cat, and Dalland's on the bat).

Finally, I leave it to the contributors themselves to establish that we now have a solidly based set of procedures for studying sensory function in animals, and that the range of questions that can be asked is only limited by the ingenuity of the investigator. And, these procedures which base their evidence on the behavioral responses of the awake, intact, trained animal preparation can be used effectively with techniques from other areas of biology and biomedicine to provide answers on the relationship of behavior to other processes (e.g., physiologic function) and to anatomic structure.

REFERENCES

Bernard, C. 1949. An Introduction to the Study of Experimental Medicine (H. C. Greene, transl.), New York, Henry Schuman, Inc.

Boring, E. G. 1950. A History of Experimental Psychology, New York, Appleton-Century-Crofts.

Brown, R. H. 1936. The dim visibility curve of the rabbit. J. Gen. Psychol., 14:62–82.

——— 1937. The bright visibility curve of the rabbit. J. Gen. Psychol., 17:325–328.

Cornsweet, T. N. 1962. The staircase method in psychophysics. Amer. J. Psychol., 75:485–491.

Crozier, W. J., and H. Hogland. 1934. The study of living organisms. *In* Murchison, C., ed. Handbook of General Experimental Psychology, Worcester, Clark University Press, pp. 3–108.

Dalton, L. W., Jr. 1967. Summed evoked cortical responses to pure-tone stimuli in the rhesus (*Macaca mulatta*) monkey. U.S. Air Force 6571 Aeromed. Res. Lab. Tech. Rep. No. 67–3.

Fechner, G. T. 1860. Elemente der Psychophysik, Leipzig, Breitkopf and Hartel.

Ferster, C. B., and B. F. Skinner. 1957. Schedules of Reinforcement, New York, Appleton-Century-Crofts.

Fraenkel, G. S., and D. L. Gunn. 1961. The Orientation of Animals, New York, Dover Publications Inc.

Galanter, E. 1962. Contemporary psychophysics. *In* Brown, R., Galanter, E., Hess, E. H., and Mandler, G., eds. New Directions in Psychology, New York, Holt, Rinehart & Winston, Inc., pp. 87–156.

Graham, C. H. 1934. Psychophysics and behavior. J. Gen. Psychol., 10:299–310.

——— 1950. Behavior, perception and the psychophysical methods. Psychol. Rev., 57:108–120.

———1965. Some basic terms and methods. *In* Graham, C. H., ed. Vision and Visual Perception, New York, John Wiley & Sons, Inc., pp. 60–67.

——— and P. Ratoosh. 1962. Notes on some interrelations of sensory psychology, perception, and behavior. *In* Koch, S. ed. Psychology: A Study of a Science, New York, McGraw-Hill Book Company, vol. 4, pp. 483–514.

Green, D. M., and J. A. Swets. 1966. Signal Detection Theory and Psychophysics, New York, John Wiley & Sons Inc.

Guilford, J. P. 1954. Psychometric Methods, 2nd ed., New York, McGraw-Hill Book Company.

Hanson, H. 1966. Psychophysical thresholds and aversive control. Paper read at meetings of Amer. Assn. for the Advancement of Science, Washington, D.C.

Hecht, S., S. Shlaer, and M. H. Pirenne. 1942. Energy, quanta, and vision. J. Gen. Physiol., 25:819–840.

Jamison, J. H. 1951. Measurement of auditory intensity thresholds in the rat by conditioning of an autonomic response. J. Comp. Physiol. Psychol., 44:118–125.

Jennings, H. S. 1923. Behavior of the Lower Organisms, New York, Columbia University Press.

Krasnegor, N. A., and J. V. Brady. 1968. The effect of signal frequency and shock probability on a prolonged vigilance task. Paper read at meetings of Amer. Psychol. Assn., San Francisco.

Loeb, J. 1918. Forced Movements, Tropisms, and Animal Conduct, Philadelphia, J. B. Lippincott Co.

McCleary, R. A., and J. J. Bernstein. 1959. A unique method for control of brightness cues in the study of color vision in fish. Physiol. Zool., 32:284–292.

Pavlov, I. P. 1927. Conditioned Reflexes: An Investigation of the Physiological Activity of the Cerebral Cortex (G. B. Anrep, transl. and ed.), London, Oxford University Press.

Schoenfeld, W. N., and W. W. Cumming. 1963. Behavior and perception. In Koch, S., ed. Psychology: A Study of a Science, New York, McGraw-Hill Book Company, vol. 5, pp. 213–252.

Skinner, B. F. 1938. The Behavior of Organisms, New York, Appleton-Century-Crofts.

Stebbins, W. C., S. Green, and F. L. Miller. 1966. Auditory sensitivity of the monkey Science, 153:1646.

Stevens, S. S. 1951. Mathematics, measurement, and psychophysics. In Stevens, S. S., ed. Handbook of Experimental Psychology, New York, John Wiley & Sons, Inc., pp. 1–49.

――― 1957. On the psychophysical law. Psychol. Rev., 64:153–181.

Struhsaker, T. T. 1967. Auditory communication among vervet monkeys (Cercopithecus aethiops). In Altmann, S. A., ed. Social Communication Among Primates, Chicago, University of Chicago Press, pp. 281–324.

――― 1970. Notes on the behavioral ecology of Galagoides demidovii, in Cameroon, West Africa. Mammalia, in press.

Swets, J. A., ed. 1964. Signal Detection and Recognition by Human Observers: Contemporary Readings, New York, John Wiley & Sons, Inc.

Thorndike, E. L. 1911. Animal Intelligence: Experimental Studies, New York, The Macmillan Company.

Torgerson, W. S. 1958. Theory and Methods of Scaling, New York, John Wiley & Sons, Inc.

Woodworth, R. S., and H. Schlosberg. 1954. Experimental Psychology, New York, Holt, Rinehart & Winston, Inc.

Yerkes, R. M., and J. B. Watson. 1911. Methods of studying vision in animals. Behav. Monogr., vol. 1, #2, iv, 90 pp.

APPENDIX

References: Operant Conditioning

1. Elementary Texts:

Ferster, C. B., and M. C. Perrott. 1968. Behavior Principles, New York, Appleton-Century-Crofts.

Holland, J. G., and B. F. Skinner. 1961. The Analysis of Behavior, New York, McGraw-Hill Book Company.

Keller, F. S., and W. N. Schoenfeld. 1960. Principles of Psychology, New York, Appleton-Century-Crofts.

Millenson, J. R. 1967. Principles of Behavioral Analysis, New York, The Macmillan Company.

2. Brief Introduction to Operant Conditioning:

Ferster, C. B. 1963. Essentials of a science of behavior. In Nurnberger, J. I., Ferster, C. B., and J. P. Brady, eds. An Introduction to the Science of Human Behavior, New York, Appleton-Century-Crofts, pp. 199–345.

Stebbins, W. C. 1966. Behavioral technics. In Rushmer, R. F., ed. Methods in Medical Research, Chicago, Year Book Medical Publishers, Inc., vol. 11, pp. 270–287.

Keller, F. S. 1954. Learning (Reinforcement Theory), New York, Random House, Inc.

Reese, E. P. 1966. The Analysis of Human Operant Behavior, Dubuque, Iowa, William C. Brown Company, Publishers.

3. Reprinted Research Reports, Readings:

Verhave, T. 1966. The Experimental Analysis of Behavior, New York, Appleton-Century-Crofts.

Skinner, B. F. 1961. Cumulative Record, New York, Appleton-Century-Crofts.

Skinner, B. F. 1969. Contingencies of Reinforcement: A Theoretical Analysis, New York, Appleton-Century-Crofts.

Catania, A. C., ed. 1968. Contemporary Research in Operant Behavior, Glenview, Illinois, Scott, Foresman and Company.

4. Research Areas and References:

Honig, W. K., ed. 1966. Operant Behavior: Areas of Research and Application, New York, Appleton-Century-Crofts.

Ferster, C. B., and B. F. Skinner. 1957. Schedules of Reinforcement, New York, Appleton-Century-Crofts.

5. Method and Design:

Sidman, M. 1960. Tactics of Scientific Research, New York, Basic Books, Inc.

JOHN I. DALLAND [1]

2

THE MEASUREMENT OF ULTRASONIC HEARING

INTRODUCTION

Measures of sensory acuity are obtained for varied reasons. For instance, an investigator may wish to know the effects of a drug, or a lesion, on the capacity of an animal to see, hear, or feel stimulation to which it is normally sensitive. More specifically, it is desirable to accurately assess the degree of sensory impairment resulting from some experimental treatment. Depending on the accuracy desired, the experimenter may choose an appropriate measurement technique from among a variety of procedures. No matter which technique is selected, however, the animal is always required to indicate it has detected a stimulus input by responding in some distinctive manner. Typically a cat may learn to move from one end of a box to the other when it hears a tone. Since past experience in the experimental chamber has shown the cat that failure to move during tone presentation resulted in painful electric shock, the cat usually learns to avoid shock by quickly moving across the box. Movement across the box during tone presentation is thus taken to indicate hearing. The tone may then be made progressively weaker until a signal level is reached to which the cat cannot respond, i.e., its threshold of hearing has been reached.

The apparent simplicity of this method, the simplicity and inexpensiveness of the apparatus, and the ease with which most cats learn to avoid "troublesome situations" may account for much of this method's appeal. It is not difficult to see why such "simple" conditioning techniques should be a favorite of many investigators directing sensory research. Very often these researchers are advanced in physiologic competence and less sophisticated in behavior theory.

It may be asked, however, what theory is there to consider in such an uncomplicated situation as a cat in a shuttle box? Why incur the expense and trouble involved with some other method? The answer depends both on the degree of measurement accuracy desired and on the sheer number of measurements to be made. For an approximate, "quick-and-dirty" estimate of a relatively few sensory thresholds, it is obviously pointless to employ complex and/or costly methods.

[1] DIVISION OF SOCIAL SCIENCES, RICHMOND COLLEGE, THE CITY UNIVERSITY OF NEW YORK, STATEN ISLAND, NEW YORK.

CONDITIONING: A LOGICAL PROBLEM

If, however, a large number of relatively precise measurements are needed, the investigator must face a logical problem implicit in all animal psychophysical techniques. The logical confrontation involves the administration of proper rewards and/or punishments to the animal when it is presented with a subthreshold stimulus. From the point of view of the cat in the shuttle box, a subthreshold stimulus is equivalent to no stimulus. Thus if the cat remains where he is (this is what he has been trained to do when he does not hear a tone), he will be shocked for not responding to the (nonaudible) tone which the experimenter has presented. The result is punishment for a "subjectively correct" response; or if the animal incorrectly responds during the presentation of a nonaudible tone, it will be rewarded by the experimenter. This problem has been dealt with in many ways; indeed each author in the present book is concerned with one or another strategy relevant to this issue. The point is that ignoring the issue does not insure a solution.

A fairly typical solution to the aforementioned problem was presented by Miller et al. (1963). They were apparently able to obtain stable estimates of hearing thresholds with minimum time expenditure. On the other hand, in a similar experimental situation which required extensive threshold measurements, Elliott (1967) reported that:

> "the determination of reliable thresholds of discrimination is a time consuming process. . . . as a result of this extensive exposure to the unsettling avoidance procedure, the cats, almost without exception, developed neurotic behavior so severe that further satisfactory testing was impossible" (p. 185).

It must be stressed that a conditioning technique appropriate for one type of psychophysical measurement may fail entirely in another situation. An investigator who wishes to obtain maximum information regarding the sensory acuity of a given animal is well advised to either take time and learn about available techniques or to collaborate with someone who does possess the necessary skills.

ECHOLOCATION IN BATS

Many people today are aware that bats orient in space by means of a "sonar mechanism." That is, they emit brief pulses of high frequency sound during flight, and detect the echoes returned from objects in the environment. This echolocation technique is of sufficient accuracy to detect and apprehend even such an elusive target as a tiny mosquito in flight.

For many years it had been noted that bats could fly expertly in the dark. In fact, Spallanzani in 1794 (see accounts by Galambos, 1942; Dijkgraaf, 1960) had shown that vision played little, if any, role in the bat's nocturnal navigations. This work, however, was subsequently forgotten. A century and a half later, many of

Spallanzani's findings were rediscovered. Griffin, in 1958, described both the historical and then current knowledge of bat echolocation. By this time it was fairly well established that the auditory sense alone was sufficient to guide the bat during flight.

Griffin (1958) cites many instances of the bat's ability to avoid thin piano wires stretched across its flight path. These difficult obstacles were successfully avoided even when loud jamming noise was introduced in an effort to mask the bat's hearing of its returning echoes (Griffin et al., 1963). The accuracy of these navigational performances suggested that perhaps the bat's auditory capacities were of an unusual sort.

HEARING AND PHYSIOLOGIC CORRELATES

This challenging problem was taken up by several electrophysiologic investigators. Wever and Vernon (1961) recorded cochlear microphonic (CM) potentials from the round window of the Little Brown Bat. They showed that the bat's peripheral auditory system (presumably the hair cells) responded to acoustic stimulation over a very broad frequency range. CM responses to frequencies as high as 100 kHz were obtained. In 1963, Grinnell published an extensive electrophysiologic study of the bat's auditory nervous system. He recorded acoustically evoked potentials principally from the inferior collicullus and the cochlear nucleus of two species of bat. Grinnell's data were entirely consistent with the notion that the bat is neurologically well equipped to process the sort of acoustic information required for effective echolocation. So it seemed that from the cochlea to the inferior colliculus, high frequency acoustic information posed no special problem to the bat's auditory system.

It is one thing, however, to show how certain sensory or neural units respond electrically to various ultrasonic frequencies, and quite another thing to specify what the awake bat actually hears. With the exception of Dijkgraaf's (1946) account of having trained a bat to turn and obtain a mealworm in response to a 40 kHz tone of unknown intensity, there existed no direct measurements of hearing in the bat. A systematic investigation of the bat's hearing was, thus, a logical next step. Toward this end a suitable technique was developed by the author to measure ultrasonic hearing in the bat. The technique will be described later, but two points may be mentioned here. First, it was found (Dalland, 1965b) that bats could hear very well up to frequencies as high as 100 kHz, and even beyond. Surprisingly, however, the bats did not detect tones of weaker magnitude than do other mammals with good hearing. However, the bat's hearing appeared to be specialized for detection of those high frequencies potentially useful for echolocation in air.

BEHAVIORAL AND PHYSIOLOGIC DATA

The data shown in Figure 1 are illustrative of the psychophysical information generated by the previously mentioned technique. The subjects were two bats of

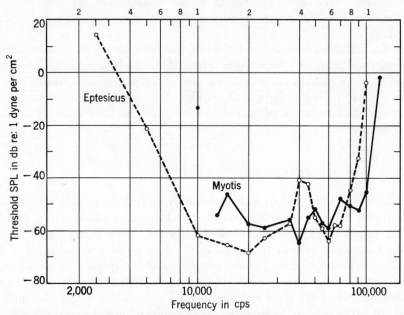

Fig. 1. Pure tone thresholds for two bats. (From Dalland, 1965b. **Science,** 150:1185. Copyright 1965 by The American Association for the Advancement of Science.)

the family Vespertilionidae: an *Eptesicus fuscus* and a *Myotis lucifugus.* Each data point shows the minimum sound pressure level (SPL) required to elicit evidence of hearing. Each bat was conditioned to respond in a specific manner in the presence of a tone and to respond in another manner when the tone was not present. At each frequency, tones of various intensities were presented. That intensity at which the bat could no longer discriminate tone from no-tone was taken as an estimate of threshold SPL. For each successful tone detection, the hungry bat received a food reward—a live mealworm.

It may be seen that the tiny (5 g) *Myotis lucifugus* appeared unable to hear tones lower in frequency than 10 kHz, while the larger (17 g) *Eptesicus fuscus* gave evidence of hearing down to 2.5 kHz. At the higher frequencies, however, *Myotis* responded at 120 kHz while *Eptesicus* failed to detect signals above 100 kHz. In their most sensitive frequency regions, both bats were approximately of equal sensitivity; and indeed, their hearing thresholds (approximately 65 dB below 1 μbar) were not lower than those of man in his most sensitive frequency region.

It should be noted that each bat yielded reliable threshold data for a fairly large number of frequencies. The fact that very extensive data were obtained from a single animal demonstrates that with a properly designed technique an animal below man on the evolutionary scale can be trained to tolerate extensive "questioning." These "fine grain" threshold functions permitted an interesting comparison with subsequently obtained electrophysiologic measures of receptor function.

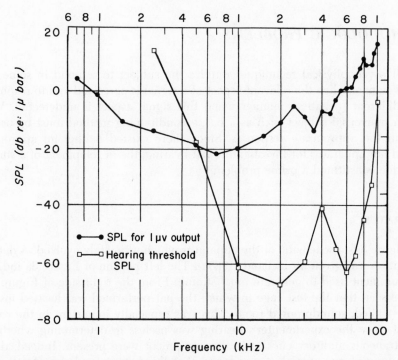

Fig. 2. A comparison of two types of data obtained from a single bat. The top curve is the cochlear microphonic (1 μ volt) sensitivity curve. The lower curve represents hearing thresholds obtained by a conditioning technique. (After Dalland, Vernon, and Peterson, 1967. **J. Neurophysiol.,** 30:703.)

The upper curve of Figure 2 (solid circles) represents the SPL required to produce a constant (1 μv) electrical potential at the round window membrane of this same *Eptesicus*. Since this cochlear microphonic (CM) potential is believed to be generated by the hair cells of the inner ear (Wever, 1966), the SPL required to produce a 1 μv CM may be viewed as a measure of receptor sensitivity. The upper curve, then, shows the way in which receptor sensitivity varied over a frequency range extending to 100 kHz. The lower curve (open squares) is a replot of the *Eptesicus* hearing threshold function from Figure 1, and is a measure of sensitivity of the entire auditory system. A comparison of the two functions shows very clearly that the way in which hearing sensitivity changes with frequency is not at all the same as the way receptor sensitivity changes over the same frequency range. From 20 to 40 kHz the hearing curve (lower) shows a 28 dB increase in SPL. The curve then sharply reverses itself and displays a 22 dB decrease between 40 and 60 kHz. However, the 1 μv sensitivity curve (upper) fails to mirror the gyrations of the hearing curve. Between 20 and 60 kHz the CM sensitivity curve merely increases, in a somewhat irregular manner, by about 10 dB. One may infer from this that hearing sensitivity is not primarily determined at the hair cell level. We see that by combining psychophysical and electrophysiologic measurements from the same animal, it is possible to draw a conclusion not derivable from either method alone.

METHODOLOGIC PROBLEMS

All psychophysical techniques require the subject to respond in some affirmative manner when the relevant aspect of a signal is perceived and to respond in some different (negative) manner when this signal aspect is undetected. When using a nonverbal subject such as a bat, a conditioning method must be used to build in the appropriate responses. Since there existed neither an appropriate method nor apparatus for investigating bat hearing, the development of a suitable technique constituted a prime problem.

APPARATUS

Figure 3 is a schematic of the apparatus which ultimately evolved. A detailed description was given by Dalland (1965a). The left portion of Figure 3a indicates the equipment used to generate tonal stimuli. From the right side of Figure 3a it may be seen that the test cage in which the bat performed was located inside a double-walled, soundproofed room. This was especially important in the case of the bat since the experimenter's hearing was useless in determining whether or not extraneous auditory cues from the equipment were present. Indeed, during the training of one animal, it was found that this bat responded perfectly to all "tones" presented—even when the oscillator was switched off. It appeared that a piece of equipment preceding the amplifier picked up "electrical emissions" from the programming apparatus. Certain high frequency features of these electrical emissions then became ultrasonic cues audible to the bat but undetectable by the experimenter (or by a monitoring oscilloscope).

Sound was produced by a speaker, tightly sealed to one end of a rigid plastic tube (1.8 cm inside diameter). This sound tube extended into the soundproof room and terminated against the back wall of the test cage. Figure 3b shows the end of the sound tube and a floor plan of the test cage. The cage was constructed of 1-cm hardware cloth, and was 46 cm long, 19 cm wide, and 20 cm high.

The bat was trained to place its two front paws upon a small metal platform (LP) 0.9 cm high, and face toward the rear of the cage. It may be seen (Fig. 3b) that while the bat was in this position, it was necessarily facing directly into the open end of the sound tube. The sound tube end was about 8 cm away from the bat's head, and was at the same height as the bat's ears. A picket fence (A, Fig. 3b) ringed the listening platform (LP), and served to keep the bat in a proper position to listen for a tone.

Figure 4 is a photograph of a bat listening for the onset of a tone. The open end of the sound tube (the signal source) may be seen just beyond the rear cage wall. While in this position the bat interrupted a light beam from a photocell light placed on the cage top just above LP. This light beam normally shone through a

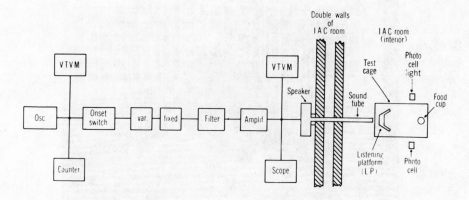

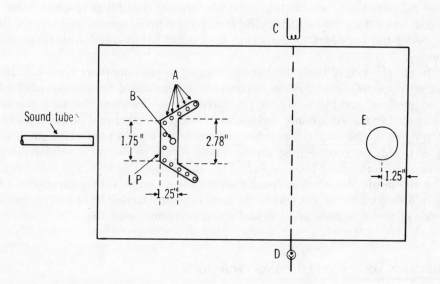

Fig. 3. Block diagram of the signal apparatus and sketch of the conditioning apparatus. (From Dalland, 1965a. **J. Auditory Research,** 5:98.)

Fig. 4. Photograph of the bat's observing response while listening for a tone.

small hole (*B,* Fig. 3b) in the listening platform to a photocell located below *LP*. When the bat's head or body broke this photobeam, two things resulted. First, a test trial was initiated by a silent, solid state programming system, and second, the position of the bat's ears in the sound field could be specified with reasonable accuracy.

In the absence of tone, the bat was trained to place its paws upon *LP*. This listening response (or observing response) was maintained for an unpredictable period until an audible tone was presented. Upon detecting the tone the bat backed off *LP*, turned around, and walked toward the other end of the test cage. Halfway across the cage the bat then interrupted a second photocell light (*C-D,* Fig. 3b). This, in turn, caused an automatic feeder to deliver a reinforcement (a live mealworm) to a food cup (*E,* Fig. 3b) recessed in the cage floor. After eating the mealworm, the bat could then initiate a new trial by returning to *LP*. Figure 5 shows a bat on his way to the food cup after having left *LP*. The dish at the side of the cage contains water and was continuously available.

EVOLUTION OF A CONDITIONING TECHNIQUE

The choice of a conditioning technique for an animal psychophysics experiment depends on more than the whim of the experimenter. At least three considerations impose constraints on the choice of method: the desired degree of

Fig. 5. Photograph of a bat crossing the test cage to obtain reinforcement, following detection of a tone.

measurement accuracy, the biologic features of the animal, and the physics of the stimulus. In the present instance, as much accuracy as possible and a fairly large number of measurements were desired.

THE OBSERVING RESPONSE: ACOUSTIC CONSIDERATIONS. If a constant intensity sound is introduced into an enclosed space, one should not expect the SPL to remain constant throughout that space. Since sound is reflected from walls and other solid objects, and since these reflections interact with each other, a rather inhomogeneous distribution of SPLs could be expected. When high frequency (short wavelength) sounds are employed, the possibility of large sound field variations is considerably enhanced. This is because even small objects will reflect sound of very short wavelength. Since the test cage is located within an enclosed space it is obviously imprecise to speak of *the* sound pressure level within the test situation. An animal inside the test cage listening to an acoustic signal may experience great variation in sound intensity just by moving his head a few centimeters. No accurate measurement of threshold SPL can be made in such a situation.

Earphones are commonly employed to produce a specifiable sound field in human audiometric work. However, the use of earphones was not deemed feasible for the bat. Besides, rather serious measurement problems may arise when high frequency sound is used with earphones. It seemed more appropriate to restrict the bat's movement in the sound field so that it occupied a reasonably homogeneous pressure region.

It was suggested by Dr. Glen Wever of Princeton University that if the bat's position in the sound field were such that the distance from its ears to the sound source (the direct pathway) was appreciably smaller than the indirect pathways from source to reflecting objects to ears, a fairly homogeneous "listening region" could result. This is because sound intensity diminishes according to the square of the distance. The relative contributions of the sound source and the reflections would thus differ as the square of the ratio of their sound path distances.

Figures 3b and 4 show that sound reaches the bat's ears directly from the sound tube end, about 5 cm away. If one visualizes a side view of this listening situation, it will be realized that there are no significant reflecting objects interposed between source and ears. Since tone onset could only occur while the bat remained in the photobeam, the position of its ears in the sound field was more or less fixed.

THE OBSERVING RESPONSE: BIOLOGIC CONSIDERATIONS.   The anatomic structure of the bats used in our experiments is such that they are unable to perform certain commonly employed conditioned responses. For instance, many conditioned responses require an animal to manipulate some physical feature of the test apparatus, such as a lever or a wheel. In this way the experimenter can unambiguously ascertain that the desired response has occurred. The bat, however, does not possess anatomic appendages suitable for these sorts of manipulations. Another form of response was thus necessary.

The bat's natural food-seeking behavior involves flight. When not flying, however, the bat is typically quiescent: it generally hangs in one place on a cage (or cave) wall. But observation revealed that just prior to flight the bat typically moved its head about as though scanning its prospective flight area. This suggested an interesting possibility. Since this natural orienting response involved minimal movement, it would be advantageous to incorporate this into the conditioned listening situation. This was successfully accomplished and the result was an observing response which could be classified as conditioned immobility.

This observing response had several desirable features: (1) it was morphologically feasible; (2) it was similar to an activity in which the bat normally engages; (3) it resembled an "attention-like process" directed toward an acoustic signal source; (4) it (breaking the photobeam) was recognizable by the automatic programming equipment; (5) it was silent and did not mask the signal which the bat was to detect; and most important, (6) it permitted an accurate specification of signal SPL.

OTHER RESPONSES.   Following tone onset the bat had 4 seconds to back out of the photobeam and out of the listening position shown in Figures 3 and 4. This signified (to the programming equipment) that the bat had detected a tone. If the bat remained in the photobeam longer than 4 seconds following tone onset, this was taken as an instance of an undetected tone. There was no time limit on how long it took a bat to cross to the far end of the cage to obtain a reinforcement. When the bat was hungry, it made the trip as rapidly as was possible for an animal whose normal behavioral repertoire does not include walking. The justification for requiring this unnatural (walking) response was that this type of activity permitted unequivocal recording of tone detections. This occurred when the bat walked through the photobeam (C-D, Fig. 3) which swept across the cage floor. If the bat's more normal mode of travel (flying) were permitted, it would simply have been more difficult to detect with a photocell.

A more serious objection to flying (or jumping) is that it is too quick. The automatic feeder required about a half second to operate after the feeder photobeam (*C-D*) had been broken. If the bat arrived during the time the feeder was operating, it was possible to get caught in the mechanism and suffer serious injury (see Dalland, 1965a for a description of the feeder). On the other hand, if the photobeam (*C-D*) were moved close to *LP*, this could make the "reporting response" too easy for the bat and could encourage random responding (guessing) irrespective of the presence or absence of tone. Blough (1966) also notes that when aversive stimulation is not employed, discrimination seems to be improved if the animal is made to work hard. Walking across the cage floor following tone onset was thus a compromise between the nature of the organism and the requirements of the experimenter.

REINFORCEMENT AND MOTIVATION. Live mealworms were used as a reinforcement. Furthermore, when the bat was in capitivity, his diet was restricted to mealworms, plus a multivitamin supplement. Mealworms are not "natural reinforcers" for a bat; the bat normally does not eat when on the ground. In fact, the bat normally does not eat anything but living, flying insects—a commodity not easily adaptable to most commercially available test apparatus. The bat had to be taught first to eat mealworms, and then to eat them from a dish placed upon the cage floor.

It was not possible to control the bat's drive level in the usual manner by maintaining the animal at 70 or 80 percent of normal free-feeding weight, for the bat's "normal" weight changed with the seasons of the year. For instance, the same daily food intake which produced active responding during the months of June and July could result in a weight gain (and hence inactivity) during the winter months in which hibernation was the bat's normal activity. The amount of food deprivation necessary to maintain responding thus varied during the year; accordingly, it was necessary to "play the deprivation procedure by ear."

An attempt to use water as a reinforcer failed because of the small size of the bat. The *Myotis* responded well when on water deprivation, but after 3 days became very ill. This procedure was then abandoned.

DISCRIMINATION TRAINING

The response sequence of listening for a tone in a narrowly defined area and then, upon hearing the tone, walking across the cage for a reinforcement is not normal behavior for the bat. The above response sequence had to be built into the animal's behavioral repertoire by successively reinforcing ever closer approximations to the desired behavior. For the bat, it was a painstaking process. Before this shaping procedure could begin, the bat was starved sufficiently so that it readily approached and explored the food dish from which it had previously been conditioned to eat.

SHAPING THE OBSERVING RESPONSE. It may be instructive to look at the successive training stages in the shaping process. Figure 6 schematically depicts the physical features of the training situation for six stages of training. In all stages (a through f, Fig. 6) the large, outer rectangle represents the training cage walls. The small circle represents the food dish, and the smaller rectangle within the training cage represents the listening platform: a metal plate about 0.9 cm high resting upon the cage floor.

After the bat learned to eat from a small food dish, the dish was placed upon a smooth aluminum plate covering the entire cage floor (Fig. 6a). The bat was then placed in the cage and a 14-kHz tone was turned on. In keeping with its previous training, the hungry bat soon approached and explored the food dish which contained a mealworm. Thus the tone was paired with a reinforced response. In addition, tone onset was paired with the tactual stimulation provided by a smooth metal surface resembling the surface of the listening platform which would ultimately be used in the test situation. The tone was terminated when the bat found the mealworm. After consuming the worm, the bat would eventually move away from the food dish. Then the tone would again be presented and another worm dropped into the food dish. Approaching and exploring the food dish was never reinforced in the absence of tone. During this stage of training, the bat learned to associate tone with a food-approach response and to associate contact with a smooth metal surface with the occurrence of a tone.

After establishing a connection between tone and food availability, a smaller metal plate (Fig. 6b), about 18 cm wide by 10 cm deep, was substituted for the larger plate. The empty food dish was placed adjacent to the plate, but not on it. The experimenter had to wait until the bat was not exploring the food dish, and was instead touching the adjacent plate. At this point the tone was turned on, the bat responded by going to the food dish, a worm was dropped into the dish and the animal was reinforced. As training progressed the metal plate was moved farther away from the food dish and the bat was required to walk longer distances. In the next stage (c), whenever the bat touched the metal plate with its legs, the tone would come on and the bat then walked all the way across the cage to the food dish for a reinforcement. The waiting time during which the bat was required to listen for a tone was gradually increased. Ultimately the required waiting time was of random (unpredictable to the animal) duration with a mean of 16 seconds. That is, on any given trial the bat might be required to wait on *LP* anywhere from 0 to 32 seconds. When the sequence was fairly well learned, it was also observed that the bat left the listening position rather promptly (1- to 3-second latency) following tone onset. The next step was to progressively reduce the size of the plate (Fig. 6d and e) until (f) it ultimately became identical to the *LP* used in the test cage as previously shown in Figure 4.

When the bat was sufficiently trained, it was transferred from the training cage to the test cage, and one additional refinement was added to the listening situation. Upon placing its legs upon *LP* and orienting toward the sound source, the bat interrupted the photocell light shining through the little hole (*B*) shown in Figure 3b. When in this photobeam, the bat was also in the desired listening position. In order to feed back information to the animal that it was indeed in the correct position (in the position that leads to tone and food), the photolight shining from above would begin to flicker at a rate of about one on-off period per second whenever the bat broke the photobeam. Since the animal was often required to

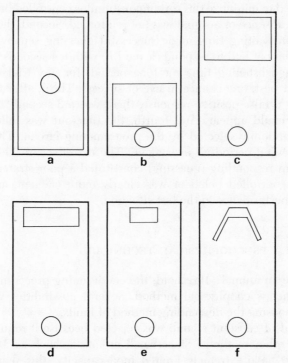

Fig. 6. Sketch of the floor plan of the training cage. Cage arrangements for six stages of training are shown (a) through (f).

wait upon *LP* for fairly long time periods, this position cue was felt to be desirable.

STIMULUS CONTROL.   A well-trained bat would thus place its legs upon *LP* while facing the sound source, wait an average of 16 seconds (0 to 32 seconds) for tone onset, move out of the *LP* photobeam within 4 seconds of tone onset, and walk to the other end of the test cage where food was made available by an automatic feeder. Failure to leave *LP* promptly following tone onset was not observed with a hungry, well-trained animal, since this type of behavior results only in delayed reinforcement. Long latencies were no problem except as the bat became satiated with food. When satiated, however, the bat stopped responding altogether, and this simply terminated the session.

During training, only clearly audible tones were employed and there was little tendency for the well-trained bat to respond prematurely, even when long waiting times were required. During testing, however, tones of various intensities were employed. Some of these tones were at or near the bat's threshold of hearing, and were presumably difficult for the bat to detect. Occasionally the bat responded during one of these subthreshold tone presentations and was reinforced. This was reflected in an increased tendency for the bat to "guess," to leave *LP* prior to tone onset.

The usual technique for controlling false-positive responding (or guessing) involves the introduction of some sort of penalty. In the present case, four contingencies combined to minimize this sort of nonstimulus controlled behavior. First, responding in the absence of a signal was not reinforced. Second, the relatively long, random duration waiting time made successful guessing somewhat difficult. To be reinforced, the bat had to respond (leave *LP*) within 4 seconds after tone onset. Since the average listening time (no-tone period) for any trial was 16 seconds, guessing had, at best, one chance in five of success. Third, after the bat returned to *LP* following a false-positive response, there was a 3-second "time-out" during which no tone could appear. And fourth, the time-out was followed by a new waiting time, randomly selected by the programming circuit. Thus, the bat had to begin its listening period all over again. The net effect of these consequences was that random responding (guessing) constituted a poor strategy for obtaining food. Stimulus controlled behavior was clearly more efficient, and hence dominated the bat's performance in the test situation.

SELECTION OF A PSYCHOPHYSICAL TECHNIQUE

To measure an animal's threshold, the conditioning procedure must be combined with some psychophysical method. Several possibilities were considered before finally choosing the descending method of limits.

The method of constant stimuli was rejected because it required many more test trials than other methods. Since small organisms such as *Myotis* (5 g) and *Eptesicus* (17 g) have extremely limited food capacity, this sharply limited the number of reinforcements (and hence test trials) obtainable during a single session. A less "wasteful" method seemed desirable.

Clack and Herman (1963) successfully used a "tracking procedure" to obtain auditory thresholds from monkeys. The essence of this method is that each time a signal is detected, it is presented on the next trial with reduced intensity. After a certain number of detections, the intensity finally reaches a level at which it is not detected. On the trial following such a "miss" the tone intensity is increased. Throughout a session, detections reduce tone intensity and "misses" increase intensity. The consequence is that tone intensity levels remain just above or just below the animal's threshold throughout the session. The animal is thus subjected to a series of "difficult" discriminations. Perhaps the monkey is capable of performing in such a situation, but when variations of the tracking procedure were employed with various lower organisms, e.g., the rat (Gourevitch et al., 1960), the starling (Adler and Dalland, 1959), and the pigeon (Blough, 1956), very extensive and time consuming training was required. The problem is that when a signal is frequently presented at a value just below threshold, any "chance" response by the animal will be reinforced. Reinforcement in the presence of a subthreshold stimulus has the same predicted effect as reinforcement in the absence of a stimulus: it increases the probability of false-positive responding. The bat was not deemed a good subject for such a demanding procedure.

In seeking to maximize the information obtained per reinforcement, a modified ascending method of limits was derived. In this procedure an approximate estimate of the bat's threshold was first obtained. The logic system was programmed to present stimuli above and below threshold. If a suprathreshold stimulus was presented, the bat detected it and responded and was reinforced. If on another trial, the bat maintained its listening response on *LP* when presented with a subthreshold tone, the tone was switched off after 4 seconds, remained off for 1 second, and was then re-presented at a 10 dB greater SPL. As long as the bat maintained its listening response beyond the initial required waiting time, tone intensity increased in 10 dB steps approximately every 5 seconds until it reached an audible level to which the bat responded and was reinforced. The virtue of this procedure was that subthreshold tone trials did not lead to food consumption. When the tone reached an audible level, only then did the bat respond and hence consume a mealworm. Since in this method a threshold estimate is traditionally defined as the sound level midway between the last undetected tone intensity and the first detected tone intensity, each such ascending series of trials yielded a threshold estimate at a cost of only one reinforcement. The only "wasted" trials were those involving suprathreshold tone presentations.

Four test sessions were run using the ascending method of limits. The signal frequency was 30 kHz. Each session yielded 19 threshold estimates and the median of the 19 estimates was taken as the threshold value for the session. When the four session thresholds were averaged, the resulting mean value appeared very reliable. The average absolute deviation of the four session thresholds around the mean was only ±0.5 dB.

EVALUATION. Although the ascending method of limits yielded very reliable data for the four test sessions, visual observation of the bat in the test situation gave the impression that its performance was deteriorating. The bat seemed to tend increasingly to leave the listening position prematurely in the absence of a tone.

A formula permitting an approximate evaluation of the probability of the bat making a positive response in the absence of a signal was devised by Dalland (1965a). Application of this formula to the data showed that the bat's "false-positive rate" was 0.10. That is, there was a 10 percent chance that the bat would respond when no tone was present. In a sense it could be said that the bat was guessing about 10 percent of the time. This guessing rate was not considered excessive, but the further observation that it was progressively worsening prompted a change in psychophysical method. The program for the next day's session was then changed to a descending method of limits, the principal change being that now the initial tone in a series of trials was always at a clearly audible intensity. It should be pointed out that the change from ascending to descending method of limits was carried out without any intervening retraining of the animal. The signal frequency remained at 30 kHz. Fifteen test sessions were then run.

The change to descending limits seemed to stabilize the bat's performance. The mean threshold for the 15 sessions was 3 dB higher than the previous mean threshold. However, the false-positive rate for this procedure dropped to 0.02. The bat now tended to "guess" as to the presence of the tone on only 2 percent of the available opportunities. Furthermore, the drop in the probability of false-positive responding occurred abruptly on the very first test session of the descending limits procedure. It appeared that the ascending method of limits produced a slightly lower threshold value but a greater tendency to respond in the absence of a signal.

One can see why the ascending limits procedure produced unstable discriminative behavior. First, there were many trials in which the stimulus was presented below threshold intensity. The listening response, prior to tone onset, required the bat to remain on *LP* for an average of 16 seconds. Further, each undetected signal presentation required an additional 5-second wait. On some trials, then, the total required waiting time could be as much as 30 or 40 seconds. Thus, if the bat chanced to respond when a tone was physically on, but below threshold, a false-positive response would be reinforced. If the opportunity for this inappropriate reinforcement contingency is frequently present (as it was in the ascending procedure), an increasing tendency to "guess" would be a logical outcome. The descending method of limits was thus chosen for the experiment.

DESCENDING METHOD OF LIMITS.   In the procedure which finally evolved, all stimulus presentations, reinforcing contingencies, and data recording were automatically controlled by an appropriate programming system. During the first trial in each descending series, the bat's listening response produced a "loud," clearly perceptible tone to which the bat promptly responded. Following a reinforcement, the next listening response initiated a trial in which the tone SPL was 10 dB less than on the previous trial. Each successful tone detection, then, led to reinforcement and a 10 dB signal decrement on the succeeding trial. When a trial was reached in which the signal level fell below the bat's threshold (the bat remained in the photobeam for more than 4 seconds following tone presentation), the tone switched off for 1 second and then reoccurred at a clearly audible level. The undetected tone level was automatically recorded and the entire procedure was then repeated; the next descending series began. Threshold for each series was computed in the traditional way: halfway between the "missed" tone level and the previously "heard" one. Following a "miss," the next trial was always at maximum intensity so that each descending series began at a tone level that was easily detected. A complete session generally consisted of six descending series. Additional series were sometimes included if there was too much variability in performance. It should be noted that the variability pertained to the degree to which the threshold estimates from the six descending series formed a coherent pattern around some central value. It was the magnitude of the within-session variability that determined whether the data were to be even considered.

The median of six (or more) threshold estimates from the descending series was then computed. This median value was accepted as the threshold for that session only if the mean absolute deviation of the six (or more) threshold estimates from the median was no greater than 7 dB. There was nothing magic about the chosen value of 7 dB. But once this value was adopted as a criterion, the experimenter was forced to honor it even if it meant throwing out data which conformed well with some theoretical value, but which was classified by the criterion as "lacking reliability." Final threshold values for each frequency were determined by a minimum of two sessions per frequency.

CRITERIA. It is well known that data are not always consistent from one session to the next. Sooner or later an experimenter must face the decision to either include or exclude some particular session result. Suppose two data points, each differing from some theoretically expected value, were obtained. Suppose a third data point was added. If this third data point was very different from the first two, but much closer to the experimenter's expectations, a decision would have to be made to either average all three data points, exclude the last point, exclude the first two points, gather additional data, and so on. Accordingly a formal set of decision rules was adopted as criteria for the calculation of final threshold values for each frequency.

1. Threshold for a given session is defined as the median threshold value obtained in the session.
2. If two session medians for a given frequency are within 8 dB of each other, then the mean of these two values is sufficient to define the final threshold for that frequency.
3. If the two session medians are greater than 8 dB apart, then an additional threshold estimate from a third session must be obtained. The mean of these three medians shall define the final threshold if all fall within a 12 dB range.
4. If the three medians fail to fall within a 12 dB range, then additional sessions shall be run at that frequency until the required criterion of three values within a 12 dB range is met. If for any set of results there exists uncertainty as to whether data are to be included or rejected, then sufficient additional data are to be obtained until the uncertainty is resolved.

The benefit of these criteria was felt to reside not in the particular values chosen, but in the fact that they minimize the experimenter's bias as a factor in selecting experimental values.

STIMULUS SPECIFICATION AND CALIBRATION

The hearing of many animals extends well beyond the upper frequency limits of humans. The investigation of hearing in these animals necessitates dealing with the problems of ultrasonic measurement. If one wishes to measure the effective SPL present in an area in which a subject is listening, it is advantageous to restrict the subject's head movements. In electrophysiologic work this is frequently done by anesthetizing the subject. In behavioral work, the same immobility could be obtained by using Pavlovian conditioning and observing a conditioned response which does not involve gross movement of the animal. When using high frequency sound, however, immobilization does not completely solve the problem. The ear's position in the sound field may indeed be fixed but how does one *measure* the effective SPL? A typical solution is to mark the spot occupied by the ear, remove the animal, and then place a small microphone at the position formerly occupied by the ear. If one plays around with this situation using ultrasound it becomes apparent that very small changes in the placement of the microphone sometimes lead to rather large changes in the sound field (see

Vernon et al., 1966, for a treatment of this problem with the bat). Since the microphone placement can never be exactly at the ear's previous position, immobilization of the subject may be far from a satisfactory solution. In fact, unless rather sophisticated procedures are adopted, it may create more problems than it answers. When using an awake organism some head movement is inevitable. In restricting the bat's head movement, by means of the photocell-light arrangement (Fig. 3) we were able to specify the maximum (and the average) variation in sound field encountered by the bat during the listening period. A one-quarter-inch Brüel and Kjaer condenser microphone was placed successively at six different positions above *LP*. These positions were felt to represent a likely sample of the locations which the bat's head occupied while listening for a tone. The microphone readings were converted to SPLs (in decibels) and the average SPL was computed. Observation of a bat listening in the test situation indicated that the bat does move his head in the indicated region. Thus the average SPL computed from the six microphone positions was probably a reasonable approximation of the average tone intensity encountered by the bat.

The pressure response curve supplied by the microphone manufacturer was used for calibration. This curve indicates the microphone voltage output produced by an acoustic SPL of 1 μbar. Implicit in the use of a pressure response calibration is the assumption that the "sound pressure disturbance" created by the presence of the bat in the sound field is approximately the same as the pressure disturbance caused by the microphone when it is substituted for the bat. One may question this assumption, but the alternative procedure of using free-field calibration contains the even less plausible assumption that the animal's presence in the sound field produces little or no disturbance.

Calibration was carried out at each session. Since day-to-day calibration values were observed to vary (sometimes considerably), the alternative practice of calibrating only once was not considered feasible, at least not for ultrasonic measurements. For instance, the electrostatic speaker which we used was found to have a drifting output over time. With a constant input to the speaker, the output was found to vary cyclically over an 8-hour period. Variations as large as 6 dB were found. High frequency calibrations should thus be made as close as possible in time to the test sessions.

For low frequencies (20 kHz and below), the SPL variations which a listening bat might encounter over *LP* were found to be quite small. For instance, at 20 kHz the difference between the smallest and greatest pressure measured at the six microphone positions was about 4 dB. At 50 kHz and 100 kHz, the maximum variations were 9.2 dB and 7.4 dB respectively. Note that this refers to maximum variation, the respective mean deviations being only ±2.9 dB and ±2.4 dB. It is felt that the reliability of the threshold measurements which were obtained was closely related to the success achieved in reducing the sound field variations to which the bat was exposed while listening. This accurate specification of the stimulus depended greatly on the form of the observing response required of the animal: a conditioned "holding still" response. In animal psychophysics measurement, precision may be affected considerably by the conditioning method adopted.

SUMMARY AND CONCLUSIONS

Psychophysical measures yield information about sensory acuity. The acuity, however, is not simply that of the sensory receptors; rather it reflects the integrated functioning of the entire sense system from receptor to cortex. Psychophysical measures may be combined with electrophysiologically derived measures of sensory function. When both measurement sets are from the same animal, the use of parallel techniques may yield information not obtainable from either method alone. For instance, in the bat the lack of parallelism between the obtained hearing function and the receptor sensitivity function led to the conclusion that auditory processes central to the sensory receptors are very important in determining hearing thresholds.

To adequately compare electrophysiologic and behavioral measures it is necessary that they be both accurate and fairly numerous. However, the process of obtaining a large number of accurate psychophysical measures may impose a rather demanding requirement on an animal subject.

When more than simple demands are made on an organism (particularly a lower organism), problems of measurement logic come to the fore, and these problems cannot be successfully ignored. As an example, the use of the relatively simple shuttle box technique for obtaining auditory thresholds in cats is quite appropriate for some situations. It was pointed out, though, that this same technique could utterly fail when more difficult discriminations were demanded of the cats. Maximum utility of the psychophysical-electrophysiologic measurement combination very likely requires psychophysical measures which are not of the simplest variety.

It is usually recognized that the proper usage of electrophysiologic techniques demands considerable attention to instrumentation and methodologic problems. It should also be recognized that the proper usage of animal psychophysical techniques makes equally stringent demands; unfortunately, this is not always recognized. The logic underlying a conditioning technique employed in animal psychophysics should be explicitly considered. To maximize the utility of psychophysical measures obtained from animals, the theoretical basis of the conditioning technique should be clearly understood by the experimenter.

The present report dealt with a rather esoteric animal, the bat. In order to use such an unusual experimental animal, it was necessary to develop a special behavioral technique. It is instructive to study the evolution of such a technique because it sharply focuses attention on the basic assumptions and on the basic logic underlying the method by which sensory acuity is measured. Reinforcement logic, apparatus design, psychophysical methodology, and the reliability of obtained results were closely examined in order to demonstrate their dependence on the physics of sound, on the required measurement accuracy, and on the biologic and behavioral features of the animal.

In addition, solutions to problems inherent in the use of ultrasonic signal frequencies were considered. It is hoped that this discussion will be useful to other investigators employing animals whose hearing extends into high frequency regions.

REFERENCES

Adler, H. E., and J. I. Dalland. 1959. Spectral thresholds in the starling (*Sturnus vulgaris*). J. Comp. Physiol. Psychol., 52:438–445.

Blough, D. S. 1956. Dark adaptation in the pigeon. J. Comp. Physiol. Psychol., 49:425–430.

———— 1966. The study of animal sensory processes by operant methods. *In* Honig, W. K., ed. Operant Behavior: Areas of Research and Application, New York, Appleton-Century-Crofts, pp. 345–379.

Clack, T. D., and P. N. Herman. 1963. A single-lever psychophysical adjustment procedure for measuring auditory thresholds in the monkey. J. Aud. Res., 3:175–183.

Dalland, J. I. 1965a. Auditory thresholds in the bat: A behavioral technique. J. Aud. Res., 5:95–108.

———— 1965b. Hearing sensitivity in bats. Science, 150:1185–1186.

———— J. A. Vernon, and E. A. Peterson. 1967. Hearing and cochlear microphonic potentials in the bat *Eptesicus fuscus*. J. Neurophysiol., 30:697–709.

Dijkgraaf, S. 1946. Die Sinneswelt der Fledermäuse. Experientia, 2:438–448.

———— 1960. Spallanzani's unpublished experiments of the sensory basis of object perception in bats. Isis, 51, part 1, 9–20.

Elliott, D. N. 1967. Effect of peripheral lesions on acuity and discrimination in animals. *In* Graham, A. B., ed. Sensorineural Hearing Processes and Disorders, Boston, Little, Brown and Company, pp. 179–189.

Galambos, R. 1942. The avoidance of obstacles by flying bats. Spallanzani's ideas (1794) and later theories. Isis, 34:132–140.

Gourevitch, G., M. H. Hack, and J. E. Hawkins. 1960. Auditory thresholds in the rat measured by an operant technique. Science, 131:1046–1047.

Griffin, D. R. 1958. Listening in the Dark, New Haven, Yale University Press.

———— J. J. G. McCue, and A. D. Grinnell. 1963. The resistance of bats to jamming. J. Exp. Zool., 152:229–250.

Grinnell, A. D. 1963. The neurophysiology of audition in bats. J. Physiol. (London), 167:38–127.

Miller, J. D., C. S. Watson, and W. P. Covell. 1963. Deafening effects of noise on the cat. Acta Otolaryng. (Stockholm), Suppl. 176.

Vernon, J. A., J. I. Dalland, and E. G. Wever. 1966. Further studies of hearing in the bat, *Myotis lucifugus*, by means of cochlear potentials. J. Aud. Res., 6:153–163.

Wever, E. G. 1966. Electrical potentials of the cochlea. Physiol. Rev., 46:102–127.

———— and J. A. Vernon. 1961. Hearing in the bat, *Myotis lucifugus*, as shown by the cochlear potentials. J. Aud. Res., 1:158–175.

WILLIAM C. STEBBINS [1]

3

STUDIES OF HEARING AND HEARING LOSS
IN THE MONKEY *

INTRODUCTION

Detailed information about the sensory function of animals is of concern to sensory physiologist, evolutionary biologist, and comparative psychologist. A basic issue is the procedural one of how information about sensory function in animals can be obtained. Until recently the behavioral evidence has been lacking, probably because reliable experimental techniques have not been available. In keeping with the intent of the book, this chapter will describe in detail a behavioral conditioning procedure and several psychophysical testing procedures which together have enabled us to characterize several aspects of the monkey's auditory acuity. It is worth noting that the methodology for the study of sensory function in animals is based on discriminative behavioral training procedures developed with lower animals (Terrace, 1966; Blough, 1966) and on the psychophysical testing methods which have been so successful in the study of man's sensory acuity (Stevens, 1951).

For many of us involved in the study of sensory function in animals, the procedural problems—particularly those connected with the behavioral training techniques—provide the real challenge and sometimes may become an end in themselves. The behavior of the subject in studies of human sensory function is directed through language, and questions to the subject concerning audibility or visibility, for example, are responded to in kind. In lower animals, ways to ask questions about sensory acuity without the benefit of language must be found, and hopefully the answers will contain some evidence of validity. One has to demonstrate, as unequivocally as possible, that the animal's behavior is indeed under the control of the relevant (i.e., experimenter-intended) dimensions of the stimulus. We should also like to show that our findings are invariant, to a reasonable extent, with method used. While no one would deny that under extreme

[1] KRESGE HEARING RESEARCH INSTITUTE, AND DEPARTMENTS OF OTORHINOLARYNGOLOGY AND PSYCHOLOGY, UNIVERSITY OF MICHIGAN MEDICAL SCHOOL, ANN ARBOR, MICHIGAN.

* The preparation of the chapter was supported in part by grants (NB 05077 and NB 05785) from the National Institute of Neurological Diseases and Stroke. I am indebted to Dr. R. N. Lanson for his incisive comments on the manuscript.

41

conditions we can change an organism's discriminative behavior which may indicate a change in his acuity, this is not our present object of interest.

A brief description of a procedure for determining the auditory sensitivity of the monkey and the basic findings have been reported (Stebbins et al., 1966). The data are reproduced in Figure 1. Monkeys (at least macaques) are able to respond to acoustic frequencies as high as 45 kHz, or at least an octave above man; their absolute sensitivity at lower frequencies (below 8 kHz) is comparable to man's, with the exception of a slight loss shown by a "dip" in the function at about 4 kHz. High frequency hearing in monkeys had not been determined previously; at lower frequencies our results are in agreement with earlier findings (Wendt, 1934; Elder, 1934; Behar et al., 1965; Fujita and Elliott, 1965) and with more recent results by Gourevitch (see Chapter 4).

METHODS

BEHAVIOR FOLLOWING TRAINING

Although conditions vary somewhat from one experiment to another, a generalized terminal procedure for a trained animal under threshold testing conditions can be described. The animal is first restrained in a chair as depicted in Figure 2. For testing, the head is immobilized and earphones are fitted carefully over the ear canals. Food reinforcement in pellet form is delivered by tube directly to the animal's mouth. Two response keys are located directly in front of the chair. Responding on one key is followed intermittently by a 3-second presentation of a pure tone. While the tone is on, a single response on the second key is followed by food. Responses on this second key either prior to or after the tone interval fail to provide food and instead result in a 3 to 10 second time-out from the experiment (all experimental conditions are deferred during this period).

The trained subject responds steadily and continuously (observing response) on one key; at intervals ranging from 3 to 30 seconds, a tone is presented. The animal reports the tone quickly by pressing the second key once, and is reinforced with food. Following a brief warm-up period at the beginning of the session, thresholds are determined by a method which calls for change in the intensity of tonal stimulation as a function of the subject's behavior on the immediately preceding tone trial. If the animal correctly detects the tone, the intensity is lowered by a fixed amount on the subsequent trial; if he fails to report its presence, the intensity is increased by the same amount on the next presentation.

We assume that the animal's threshold lies midway between the intensity which he correctly detects and that which he fails to report. Ten transitions of the stimulus from either a detectable value to one not detected, or in the opposite direction, are averaged in the calculation of the threshold. A new acoustic frequency is then presented and this tracking procedure is repeated. In a single session, monaural pure tone thresholds at nine frequencies for each ear can be determined.

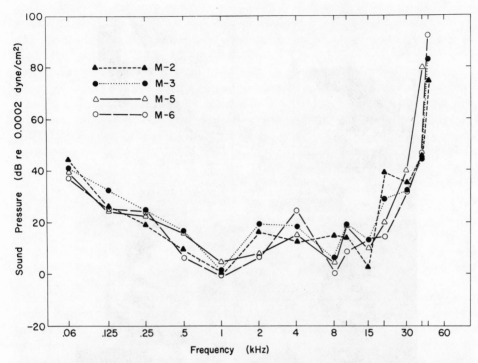

Fig. 1. Normal auditory thresholds for four monkeys. (From Stebbins et al., 1966. **Science,** 153:1646–1647. Copyright 1966 by the American Association for the Advancement of Science.)

SUBJECTS AND THEIR PRETRAINING HISTORY

For the most part, our subjects have been macaques, including *Macaca nemestrina, M. fascicularis, M. arctoides,* and *M. mulatta.* We have had some experience with the tree shrew *Tupaia glis,* and have obtained threshold data from the Carneau pigeon *Columba livia.* With a similar procedure, Gourevitch and Hack (1966) have reported auditory acuity measures for the albino wistar rat *Rattus norvegicus* and for *M. nemestrina* (see Chapter 4).

Our monkeys are imported and spend 6 weeks in quarantine where they are routinely checked and tested for disease prior to experimental use. Following quarantine, they are individually caged in the working monkey colony and fitted with a special Plexiglas collar with an attached chain. The collar inserts into a restraining chair which the monkey occupies during each daily experimental session (Moody et al., 1970) (Fig. 2). Sessions are conducted with the chair-restrained subject in a double-walled, soundproofed chamber (*Industrial Acoustics*). Prior to any systematic behavioral training, each animal is placed in the restraint chair and brought to the experimental room several times in the course of a week for periods of from 1 to 2 hours.

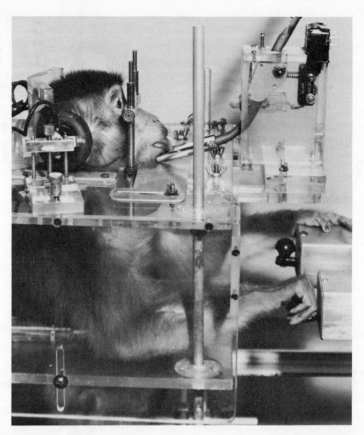

Fig. 2. Photograph of subject restraint during threshold measurement. Earphone, response keys, and feeder tube are shown. The monkey is correctly responding to the tone on the near key and is extending his tongue for the food pellet. (From Stebbins et al., 1969. **Ann. Otol.**, 78:1107–1019.)

During chair adaptation, a food deprivation regimen is begun and the animals are given the experimental food pellets (Ciba, 190 mg or Deitrich and Gambrill, 150 mg) in the chair which is placed in the sound room. When an animal will accept the pellets in the chair, the automatic food dispenser is attached to the chair, and in a few minutes the animal is trained to eat from the dispenser. An audible click is paired with the food presentation and the monkey soon learns to extend his tongue to receive the food when the click occurs.

TRAINING SEQUENCE

After feeder training is complete, one key (A) is made available to the monkey at waist level (see Fig. 2). A moderately intense pure tone (about 80 dB re 2×10^{-4} µbar of a frequency usually between 500 Hz and 5 kHz) is turned on and every depression of key A is followed by delivery of a food pellet. As soon as there is clear evidence of conditioning (usually within a few minutes), the tone is turned off and further responses go unreinforced. When responding has considerably diminished, the tone is turned on; one response is reinforced with food and the tone is again terminated. Discrimination training is continued until responses have decreased in number when the tone is off, and yet occur with short latency to tone onset.

The second key (*B*) is then introduced. Initially, responding on key *B* when the tone is off turns on the tone and the sequence just described above is in effect. A single response on key *A* is then followed by food and the tone is turned off. At this stage, inappropriate responses (on key *A* when the tone is off; on key *B* during the tone) have no experimentally arranged consequences.

The next change in the experiment requires that a programmed variable-interval of time elapse between tone trials. The tone is presented after 3 to 30 seconds have elapsed, and an observing response has occurred on key *B*. The addition of this particular contingency produces a steady rate of observing responses on key *B*. When the tone is presented after a key *B* response, the trained subject switches quickly to key *A* and is reinforced. At this time, the tone duration is gradually decreased to about 2.5 seconds. At relatively high intensity stimulation, the subjects have little difficulty in switching to key *A* within this time requirement. Late reporting responses are without consequence. In the course of training, at the longer intervals between tones, premature switching to key *A* occurs frequently. In some animals, complex patterns of switching between the two keys become established.

The above problem is treated when subjects have had some exposure to the variable-interval schedule of tone presentation, and after the rate on key *B* is fairly stable. We introduce a time-out from the experiment of from 3 to 10 seconds contingent upon key *A* responses which occur when the tone is off. No stimulus change occurs, but all experimental events are delayed for a fixed interval; additional responses during this time-out interval further prolong it. For example, if the interval is 10 seconds, the subject must refrain from making a key *A* response for 10 seconds before the experiment will resume.

The number of earned time-outs usually decreases over time to a comparatively low, but fluctuating, level. To obtain a measure of the key *A* responses under the tone-off condition, "catch trials" are randomly programmed to occur on occasion in place of tone trials throughout the session. A "catch trial" is simply a 2.5-second period of silence following a key *B* response when key *A* responses are separately tabulated. These trials provide a measure of the number of incorrect guesses or false-positive responses and are used as an estimate of discriminative stability during threshold testing.

We have recently found it helpful to introduce one final contingency in the behavioral training paradigm. Some animals will pause between tone trials and then, at an interval close to the maximum programmed interval between tones, will respond once on key *B* and then on key *A* in rapid succession. Reinforcement frequency is sufficient for some animals to maintain this response sequence and the "waiting" behavior which precedes it. The problem lies with the training procedure which times the tone interval from the preceding reinforced response. A

punched tape progam sets the end of the interval, and the next response, regardless of when it occurs, turns on the tone. The trouble is alleviated by the addition
of a limited hold of about 5 seconds on the interval. If the animal has not responded on key B within 5 seconds of the end of the programmed interval, that
opportunity for a tone trial is lost. The effect of this contingency is usually seen
within two or three sessions and is evidenced by a rate increase on key B.

During discrimination training, the animal is exposed to the different pure
tone frequencies which will be used during threshold testing. Intensity of stimulation is also varied and preliminary estimates of threshold are made by decreasing tone intensity until the subject fails to switch to key A.

BASELINES AND DESCRIPTION OF THE PSYCHOPHYSICAL TESTING PROCEDURES

STABILITY CRITERIA

In the course of training and testing, there are many times when the consideration of stability criteria becomes important. During training, there are several
transition points where new conditions are introduced. It has been our experience that the extent of behavioral disruption due to the insertion of a new contingency is inversely related to the degree of behavioral stability at the time of
insertion. In most instances, we have not adopted rigid stability criteria, but
instead have simply observed the subject during a brief probe with the new contingency. If emotional behavior, cessation of responding, or other signs of disruption occur, the new contingency is removed and its introduction attempted after
two or three more training sessions.

There are a few obvious signs of stability that we expect. A fairly restricted
response topography and the absence of long pauses between responses are
usually ample evidence of conditioning. Satisfactory progress in discrimination
training (prior to introduction of the second key) can be said to have occurred
when the response rate in the tone-off condition has decreased substantially and
is no longer changing very much from session to session, and when the response
latency to the tone is clearly less than 3 seconds. Together with these signs of
stability, the probe technique has proved quite successful.

There are two specific stages in the experiment when a more restricted definition of stability might be considered. The first stage occurs when the behavioral
discrimination with the final contingencies in effect is regarded as sufficiently
stable to begin threshold testing; the second, when the thresholds are thought to
be stable enough for the introduction of a new independent variable, i.e., a drug,
sound exposure, and so on. We have treated the first stage much as we have the
earlier transition points in training. If the day-to-day behavior of the subject measured by the number of time-outs, the number of catch trials responded to, the
rate on key B, and the number of reinforcements is relatively invariant, the intensity of the tone at a selected midrange frequency is gradually decreased until the

animal fails to respond to it. In this manner, several initial estimates of threshold are made. If the behavior remains stable by these criteria, the same procedure is attempted at other frequencies. During this period, the intensity of the tone remains low and is seldom raised more than 30 dB above the first threshold estimates.

If the subject's behavior begins to break up during these manipulations, the most recently introduced condition is withdrawn. Thus, threshold testing is introduced gradually. The clearest indication of trouble appears when the subject is responding to a high proportion of catch trials and is producing a large number of time-outs. The discriminative behavior of the animal has deteriorated, and he can be observed to be continually switching back and forth between the two keys. Occasional reinforcement can maintain this erratic behavior for some time. Often, on the other hand, responding will cease and not resume again during a particular session. Aside from returning to an earlier stage of training, the other methods which have been effective in restoring stimulus control are: (1) a temporary increase in the duration of the time-out; and, (2) in the situation where responding has stopped, a moderate increase in deprivation. Disruptions may be transient within a session or may continue for a few weeks. However, we have never had to remove an animal from an experiment for this reason.

The use of a more strictly defined stability criterion becomes necessary in the determination of auditory thresholds. We have adopted arbitrarily a 10 percent criterion for the number of catch trials. Should the number of catch trials responded to exceed 10 percent of the total number presented in a session, the threshold data for that session are rejected as being unreliable. We feel that the rate of "guessing" is too high. Under certain unusual circumstances, i.e., in a drug study where the threshold is changing daily in one direction, threshold data with a catch-trial rate as high as 30 percent may be retained.

Typically, initial estimates of threshold appear high. On successive tests, threshold values decrease. Our criterion for threshold stability, based on experience but nonetheless arbitrary, requires that two of three successive threshold determinations at a single frequency shall be no more than 5 dB apart. This criterion is used before a drug is introduced, for example, and also at the end of the drug regimen before the experiment is terminated.

The use of stability criteria in this work is not altogether satisfactory. The degree of arbitrariness in the selection of these criteria raises a question about their acceptance as standards. We need to know a great deal more about steady state criteria before we can assign and use them properly. Meanwhile, our faith is maintained by the data, their reliability, and their basic agreement with the findings of others obtained often with quite different procedures.

THRESHOLD TESTING PROCEDURES

Since it had such a good reputation for reliability in human psychophysical experiments, the method of constant stimuli was selected and used in much of our early work with monkeys. Following threshold estimates (when intensity of the tone had been decreased to the point at which the subject failed to respond to it), five to six values of stimulus intensity, 10 dB apart, and bracketing this estimate were presented in a mixed order to the animal. At the higher tone intensities, switching to the second key occurred almost every time and with a short, relatively invariant latency. The lowest stimulus intensity was chosen such that the switching frequency was usually well below 50 percent. In the manner of experiments with human subjects, "frequency of hearing" (operationally, frequency of switching to the second key, A) functions were constructed at each acoustic frequency tested. Threshold values were defined as the stimulus intensity which was followed by a switching response 50 percent of the time. The exact values were taken directly from the plotted functions.

The method has proven reliable for work with monkeys, and aside from some preliminary disruptions, discriminative responding remains stable over time. Perhaps the only disadvantage of the method lies in the wasted information it produces. Of the five or six points in a "frequency of hearing" function, only two are useful: the two adjacent values which bracket either side of the 50 percent point. Unless the other points overlap with these two, they can be discarded since they make no contribution to the determination of threshold. Since the subject's daily time in the experiment is limited by the amount of food he will ingest, we have found that two to four frequencies are all that can be tested; thus a complete audiogram (over a wide range of frequencies) has not been possible within a single daily session.

We have had limited experience with the psychophysical method of limits. Stimulus intensity is varied over successive trials in discrete steps (5 and 10 dB)—first a series in descending order (from a value well above estimated threshold), and then one in ascending order (from below). When the subject changes his response from a correct detection on one trial to failure to report the tone on the next, or vice versa, the series is terminated and a new series is begun. The starting point of a series is varied. Average thresholds are calculated from the point in each series where the animal's response changes.

A third procedure which we now commonly use is similar to the technique of Békésy audiometry with human subjects. Each correct switching response to the tone decreases the stimulus intensity by 5 to 10 dB on the subsequent trial, while failure to switch (indicating failure to "hear") raises the intensity 5 to 10 dB on the next trial. The method differs from the others in that the intensity of the stimulus is a function of the subject's behavior on the preceding trial. Thresholds are determined by averaging 10 to 20 transition points (stimulus values at which the response changes). Unlike the method of constant stimuli, there is little information which is not used, so it is often possible to obtain a complete monaural audiogram (nine frequencies) for each ear in a single session. The primary disadvantage of the procedure is the problem of maintaining good stimulus control when the stimulus is always very close to threshold. Disruption indicated by cessation of responding, or by a large number of catch trials responded to, is more frequent under this procedure. The probability of reinforcement for a response to "below threshold" stimulation is higher with this procedure than with the constant stimulus method where a greater proportion of supraliminal stimuli are presented.

We have examined, at least in an exploratory way, the effects in the individual subject of variation in some of the basic parameters of the testing situation such as schedule of tone presentation, tone duration, time-out duration, and step size for stimulus intensity variation. In addition, we have looked at stability of the threshold data over time and have compared the three psychophysical testing methods in individual subjects. The effects of these parameters are discussed in the subsequent section.

We have also adopted the constant stimulus method for determining absolute auditory thresholds in the pigeon. The basic training and testing procedures are similar to those reported for the monkey. The bird is required to insert his head and neck through a hole into a small, padded, sound-deadened chamber. The observing response consists of interrupting a vertical path between a photocell and a light source. Successful interruption of the path turns on a small light in the bird's line of sight. At the moment of the response, the right external auditory canal is close to and aligned with an earphone. The interrupting response is followed on a variable-interval schedule by a pure tone signal. The bird is reinforced with food for removing his head from the chamber in order to peck a small transilluminated disc on the other side of the testing cage. The values of the various temporal parameters are approximately the same as for the monkeys. A slight modification of the same procedure is currently being used to determine the acoustic sensitivity of the tree shrew. Another variation of the same behavioral conditioning method is being used to obtain the monkey's difference threshold for acoustic frequency and intensity.

In the frequency discrimination experiment, the standard or base frequency is presented repetitively (1 pulse per second of 0.35-second duration). Responding on one key is followed on an intermittent schedule by the addition of the second or comparison frequency, which is also presented as a pulse train alternating on successive pulses with the standard for 3 seconds. The animal is reinforced with food for switching to the second key during this frequency alternation period. The constant stimulus method is used for threshold determination; in other respects, the procedure is that described previously. The same basic format is used in the intensity discrimination experiment where standard and comparison intensities are alternated during a trial.

BEHAVIORAL DATA

The basic frequency of hearing data obtained by the constant stimulus method are shown in Figure 3 for one animal. The stimulus intensity corresponding to the 50 percent point is defined as the threshold and is read directly from the functions. Similar data have been used to construct the sensitivity curves shown in Figure 1. The individual functions in Figure 1 meet the stability criterion referred to earlier, and each point represents the mean of the final two sessions for which the thresholds were no more than 5 dB apart.

Since the original data were obtained, we have examined auditory sensitivity functions in at least 12 additional monkeys. For the most part, the variation seen

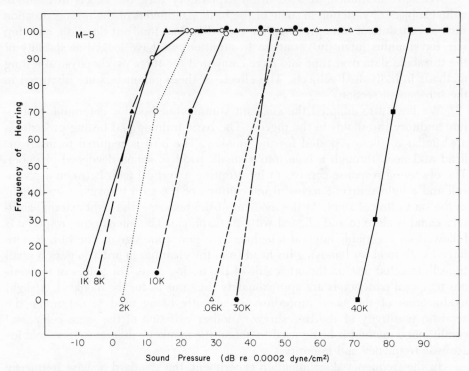

Fig. 3. Frequency of hearing functions for one monkey at different sound pressure levels for seven frequencies.

in Figure 1 encompasses these data. The hearing of all the monkeys we have studied extends at least to 40 kHz. The individual differences appear in the mid-range frequencies. The position of the "dip" or sensitivity loss is usually close to 4 kHz, and most subjects are maximally sensitive at 1 and 8 kHz.

Some data for an animal whose absolute threshold function is slightly atypical in midrange are shown in Figure 4. This animal, unlike most others, shows an extended sensitivity decrement to 8 kHz; otherwise, the data are comparable. Thresholds taken almost 2 years apart by the same method show no significant deviations from the points in this function. We have used three different psychophysical methods, with two methods in a single session in "ABBA" sequence. Thresholds by constant stimuli, limits, and tracking are shown for one animal in Figure 5. In Figure 4, the results of using the tracking method with three different step sizes for increase and decrease in stimulus intensity are presented. Similar results are shown in Figure 6 for the method of constant stimuli. Clearly, these and other data we have obtained suggest that auditory threshold is not overly sensitive to changes in testing method or (within limits) to size of step for stimulus change.

On the other hand, removal of the time-out condition does seem to produce behavioral changes which are probably not a reflection of a change in acoustic

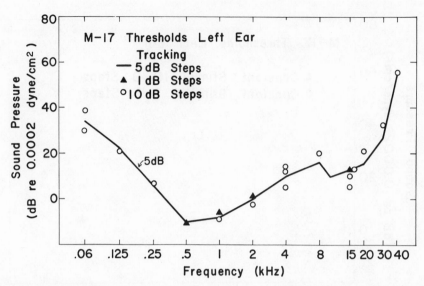

Fig. 4. Auditory threshold function for one monkey for 3 different step sizes of stimulus intensity variation.

sensitivity. Quite predictably, within several sessions following deletion of the time-out contingency, the rate of switching between keys increases to the point where reliable threshold functions by our stability criteria cannot be determined.

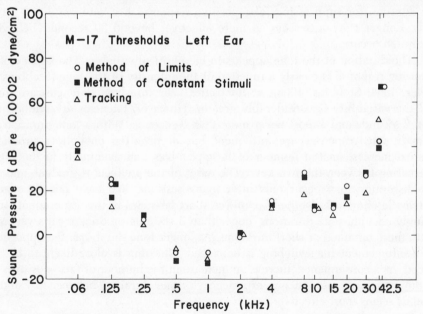

Fig. 5. Auditory threshold function for one monkey tested with 3 different psychophysical methods.

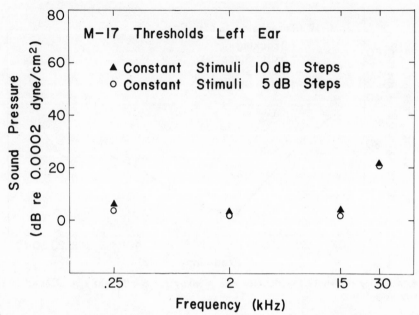

Fig. 6. Auditory thresholds for one monkey at four frequencies obtained for 2 different step sizes of stimulus intensity variation.

In addition, we have some evidence which indicates that the most effective time-out duration for suppressing false positive responses lies between 3 and 10 seconds. Longer time-outs seem no more effective; beyond 30 seconds, behavioral disruption occurs.

The duration of the tone appears to be a critical variable. The latency of the reporting response is clearly a function of the intensity of the tone (Stebbins and Miller, 1964; Stebbins, 1966); at intensities near threshold, latencies are longer and the variability is considerably greater. However, latencies are seldom more than 2 seconds and almost never more than 3 seconds. With a tone duration of 2 seconds, late responses are infrequent but occur often enough to produce a gradual increase in the number of false-positives and eventually in the rate of alternating between the two keys. The onset of these effects is gradual, and serious disruption may occur only after many sessions. We have not yet made a systematic effort to selectively reinforce short latencies in this experiment. Interestingly enough, tone durations longer than 3 seconds produce results very similar those obtained at short durations. At longer tone durations, the opportunity for reinforcement for switching is enhanced. Guessing is more likely to be reinforced. As a consequence, there is an increase in the number of false-positives and in the switching rate. In our experience, a tone duration between 2.5 and 3.5 seconds seems most effective.

Our results on variation of the schedule of tone presentation are not conclusive. We have found that fairly wide variations in the mean length of the variable-interval schedule (5 to about 30 seconds) have little effect on either discriminative

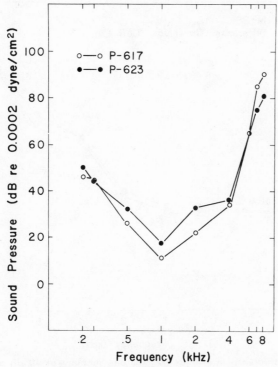

Fig. 7. Normal auditory thresholds for 2 pigeons.

responding or threshold. Limited experience with a variable-ratio schedule (tone onset is contingent upon a varying number of responses rather than on a time requirement) indicates an increased rate of observing responses but no effect on threshold. Gourevitch has used a variable-ratio schedule and his results are relevant for comparison (see Chapter 4).

The same procedure with a different organism brought with it unexpected difficulties. Our results for the pigeon are shown in Figure 7. The threshold data for our two subjects are in good agreement with Heise's findings (1953). We found the pigeon a recalcitrant subject, as others apparently have, for auditory experimentation. It took a relatively long time to reduce the switching rate and the number of false-positives to the 10 percent criterion we had set for the monkeys. The fault, of course, may be in our procedures and selection of parameter values; the question remains unanswered. The conclusion is that the procedure is workable with the birds and reliable data can be obtained. There should be, however, more rapid means of obtaining stimulus control and more effective ways of preventing disruption of the discrimination once acquired.

In addition to using the basic procedure for discrimination training and determination of absolute auditory thresholds in other organisms, we have used a variant of the procedure for assessment of difference thresholds (ΔF) for acoustic frequency in the monkey. Some data at 40 and 60 dB re absolute threshold are

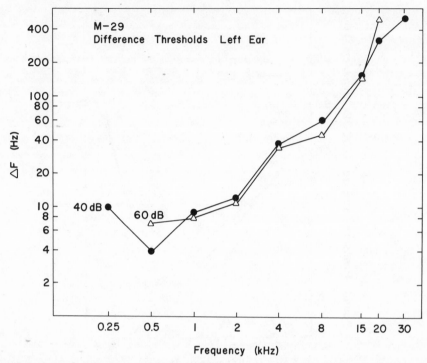

Fig. 8. Frequency difference thresholds (ΔF) for one monkey at 40 dB and 60 dB above absolute threshold.

shown in Figure 8. Findings from a second animal add further support to these data and our results are close to those of Heffner et al. (1969) for the bushbaby (*Galago senegalensis*). Essentially, the monkey (macaque) appears to discriminate small differences in frequency with an acuity only slightly less than that of man. Different frequencies of stimulation were adjusted to equal sound pressure levels above absolute threshold for the individual subject to help ensure that discriminative responding would be under the control of frequency rather than loudness. One of the more interesting findings was the gradual decrease in the initially high frequency difference thresholds to a stable terminal level where the stability criterion was eventually met. The same "learning" effect in studies on absolute threshold was less dramatic.

RELATION OF BEHAVIORAL AND HISTOLOGIC FINDINGS

The hearing of a species can be characterized if the threshold function for audibility is known and if there is adequate information concerning the organism's differential sensitivity to frequency and intensity of the acoustic input. By these criteria, only man's hearing is adequately specified. However, we hope soon to have sufficient normative data to describe the hearing of the nonhuman primates. Certainly, an important purpose of the behavioral training and testing procedures detailed throughout this book is that their use does enable one to fully describe an animal's sensory acuity in behavioral terms.

An issue which many of the contributors of this volume have considered is the integration of these behavioral methods with methods from other areas of experimental inquiry in an attempt to answer questions which could not be answered by one method alone. The purpose of this section will be to describe our findings on the relation between hearing loss and related cellular changes in the cochlea of the inner ear of the monkey. The thresholds already described provide baselines against which to measure the effects of agents which are toxic to the ear. Histologic and microscopic procedures (Johnsson and Hawkins, 1967) allow a detailed description of the state of the receptor cells and supporting cells in the inner ear of normal and treated animals. The use of the two procedures (behavioral and anatomic) together can give us information helpful in the future prevention of hearing loss in man as well as be of value in contributing to a better understanding of the normal functioning of the primate auditory system.

The place principle of hearing requires some form of spatial organization of sound frequency in the neuroanatomic structures subserving hearing. The most compelling evidence thus far comes from Békésy's analysis of the traveling wave in mechanical models of the cochlea and in cadaver specimens (Békésy, 1960) and from electrophysiologic recording from single cells in the cochlear nucleus and higher centers which have been shown to be differently sensitive to the frequency of the acoustic input (Kiang, 1965; Katsuki et al., 1962). Our findings provide further support for a place principle of hearing in attempting to relate behavioral evidence of frequency-specific hearing loss in the monkey to changes in the cellular structure of the organ of Corti and of the cochlear nucleus in the brain stem. Permanent hearing loss and related cochlear and brain stem histopathology can be produced in a predictable and reasonably well-controlled manner with certain antibiotics such as kanamycin and neomycin (Stebbins et al., 1969) and also (but perhaps less predictably) with exposure to intense sound. In addition, we have found that temporary hearing loss can follow as a consequence of sound exposure and also of administration of large doses of salicylates (Stebbins et al., 1968). Temporary structural changes in the inner ear, such as vasoconstriction, can be demonstrated in animals sacrificed shortly after treatment.

Our results for temporary hearing loss are incomplete and as yet uncorrelated with histologic evidence. In one monkey, thresholds determined at 4 kHz were followed immediately by exposure to wide band noise at one of several different sound pressure levels for 10 minutes. Thresholds were completely redetermined within less than one hour following exposure. The constant stimulus method was used in threshold determination and the functions obtained before exposure (solid lines) and after exposure (dashed lines) at different noise levels are shown in Figure 9. Reliability of the daily threshold measurements can be seen in the preexposure data. Thresholds (at the 50 percent point) on different days do not differ by more than 1 dB. Threshold shift following noise exposure was most pronounced at the 127 dB exposure level. While recovery of normal threshold oc-

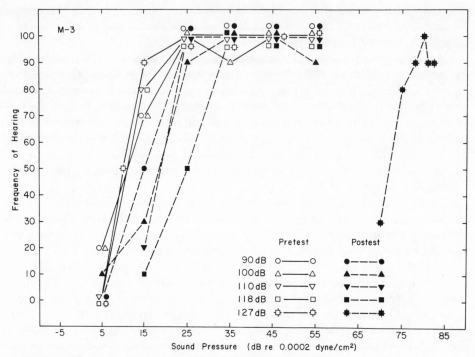

Fig. 9. Frequency of hearing functions for one monkey at 4 kHz immediately prior to and following 10 minutes of exposure to varying sound pressure levels of noise.

curred within 24 hours following exposure to the lower noise levels, the loss following exposure at 127 dB persisted. The threshold recovery function after this most intense exposure is shown in Figure 10. Recovery was not quite complete after 6 days. Additional work on sound-induced temporary hearing loss with a very different behavioral procedure is described by Moody in this volume (Chapter 13).

A large single intramuscular injection of sodium salicylate can also lead to temporary hearing loss. At certain dose levels, the maximum effect may not occur for several hours after drug administration. The results of two dose levels for one monkey are shown in Figure 11. At 500 mg/kg the greatest hearing loss that was measured (about 20 dB) occurred in the hearing test given 6 hours post injection. Hearing was normal when tested 24 hours later. At 250 mg/kg the effect on hearing was small and recovery occurred within 6 hours post injection. The stability of the control series provides further evidence of the sensitivity of the behavioral method in picking up small changes in hearing and also in being relatively insensitive to motivational effects and to the time of the day at which the session occurs. The point to be made about these effects of intense sound and salicylate administration is that, more than anything else, they demonstrate the feasibility of the behavioral method for inquiry into the general nature of temporary hearing loss and recovery in nonhuman primates.

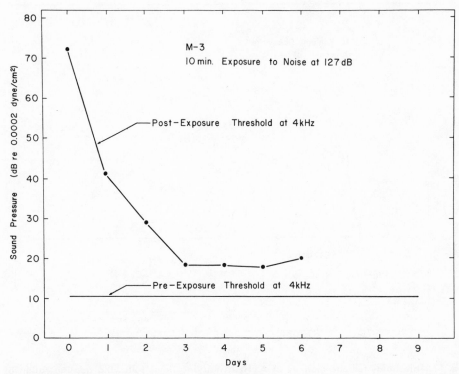

Fig. 10. Thresholds at 4 kHz for one monkey taken at daily intervals during recovery from 10 minutes exposure to noise at 127 dB re 0.0002 dynes/cm².

The evidence for permanent hearing loss in the monkey from chronic daily treatment with antibiotics is more substantial. Here we have the somewhat unique opportunity to correlate, in the same animal, hearing loss with the extent of the cellular destruction in the inner ear produced by these drugs. Results for one animal (M-14) are shown in Figure 12. The hearing loss is progressive beginning at the higher frequencies. Changes in threshold from the predrug baseline (0 dB) occurred first at the highest frequency (15 kHz) tested and subsequently at 11, 8, and 4 kHz. The drug (kanamycin) was discontinued after 180 days; the experiment was terminated shortly after 200 days when no further hearing loss had occurred. The final threshold data at 200 days postdrug are shown in Figure 13. The frequency cut-off is relatively sharp from normal hearing at 2 kHz in each ear to at least a 100 dB loss at 4 kHz. The arrows for the points from 4 kHz to 15 kHz indicate no response at the output limit (with low distortion) of the earphones. A less severe hearing loss but with the same characteristic sharp cut-off between 30 and 40 kHz can be seen for a neomycin-treated animal (M-16) in Figure 14. Thresholds prior to drug administration are shown for each ear on the left panel and after only 5 days of neomycin on the right panel of Figure 14. Treatment was discontinued due to indications of nephrotoxicity to the drug. Finally, results for a third animal (M-13) (kanamycin) are presented in Figure 15.

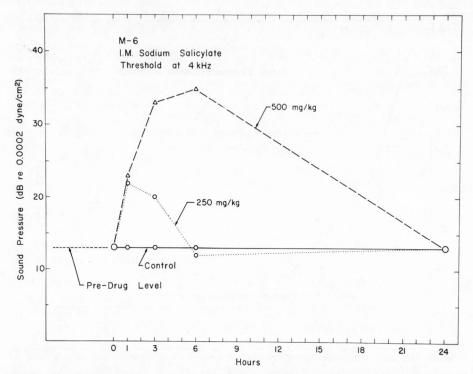

Fig. 11. Thresholds for one monkey at 4 kHz at varying times following administration of sodium salicylate at 2 dosages, compared with undosed control.

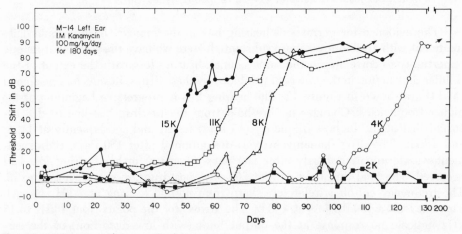

Fig. 12. Progressive changes in threshold for one monkey for different test frequencies during daily kanamycin treatment. (From Stebbins et al., 1969. **Ann. Otol.**, 78:1007–1019.)

The extent of hearing impairment is intermediate between that seen for the first two animals. The sharp frequency cut-off is evident between 8 and 11 kHz.

The histologic findings complement the behavioral results in a very straight-

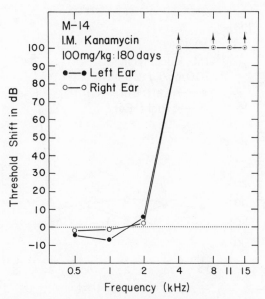

Fig. 13. Threshold shift for the same animal shown in Figure 12 after 180 days of daily kanamycin. (From Stebbins et al., 1969. **Ann Otol.**, 78:1007–1019.)

forward manner. First, high frequency hearing loss is correlated with loss of receptor cells in the lower or basal turn of the cochlea; as hearing loss progresses to the lower frequencies, the cochlear involvement spreads to the upper turns. Secondly, the gradient between presence and complete absence of receptor cells in the cochlea is a very sharp one corresponding to the sharp frequency cut-off for hearing. Consequently we can begin to construct a frequency map of the monkey's cochlea as shown in Figure 16. The data support the place theory at least for frequencies of stimulation above 2 kHz.

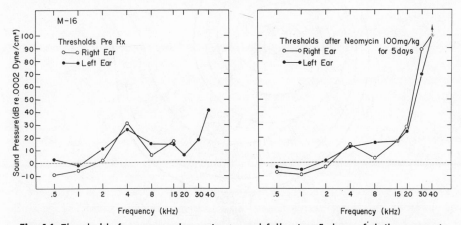

Fig. 14. Thresholds for one monkey prior to and following 5 days of daily neomycin.

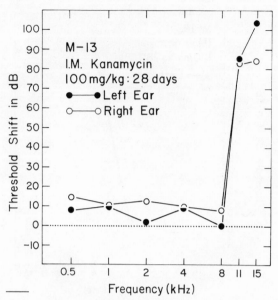

Fig. 15. Threshold shift in one monkey after 28 days of daily kanamycin. (From Stebbins et al., 1969. **Ann. Otol.,** 78:1007–1019.)

The location and extent of the cochlear lesions produced by kanamycin in two animals can be seen in the phase contrast microphotographs in Figures 17 and 18. The entire basal coil of the right cochlea of monkey M-13 was removed

FREQUENCY LOCALIZATION IN THE MONKEY

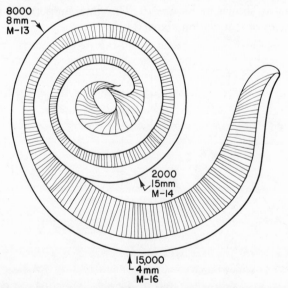

Fig. 16. Cochlear locations of the regions for threshold responses at 15, 8, and 2 kHz in the monkey, as determined in the experiment with kanamycin and neomycin. (From Stebbins et al., 1969. **Ann. Otol.,** 78:1007–1019.)

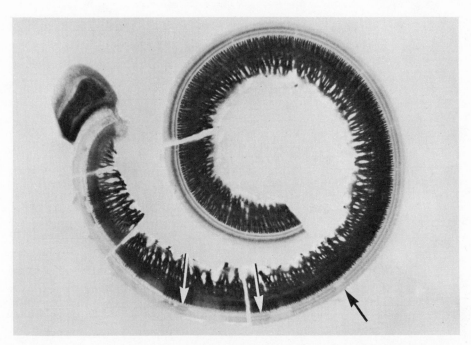

Fig. 17. Dissection of basal coil, right cochlea of kanamycin-treated monkey M-13. No normal organ of Corti remains to the left of the arrow (↘). The darker "islands" (↓) contain no receptor cells. Note partial nerve fiber degeneration at basal end.

from the otic capsule and is shown in Figure 17. In Figure 18, the left cochlea of M-14 is shown in situ within the otic capsule. Nerve fiber bundles from the cochlear branch of the eighth nerve are shown together with the organ of Corti which is evident as a well-defined series of dark bands on the translucent basilar membrane.

For monkey M-13 (Fig. 17), the area most affected is in the lower part of the basal coil where one can see regions of complete loss of Corti's organ together with some degeneration of the nerve fibers. For monkey M-14 (Fig. 18), the damage is more extensive. In the lower basal turn, there is a long stretch of transparent basilar membrane without receptor cells or supporting cells. The remainder of the basal coil contains well-organized supporting structures but almost no receptor cells. Nerve degeneration is also considerably more widespread in M-14's cochlea. In the animals we have examined, the lesions in the two ears have been essentially symmetrical. The cochlear map (Fig. 16) which illustrates the sharp gradient between presence and absence of receptor cells is based on microscopic examination of the basilar membrane at higher levels of magnification.

In an additional animal, we have found minimal residual hearing (almost a 100 dB loss) at frequencies between 500 Hz and 4 kHz following daily neomycin treatment correlated with a massive loss of receptor cells throughout most of the cochlea. A few cells remained in the upper reaches of the third or apical turn and a small patch of cells in the lower turn of one ear. An explanation of the findings from this animal awaits further results on experimentally produced loss intermediate between this subject and the others.

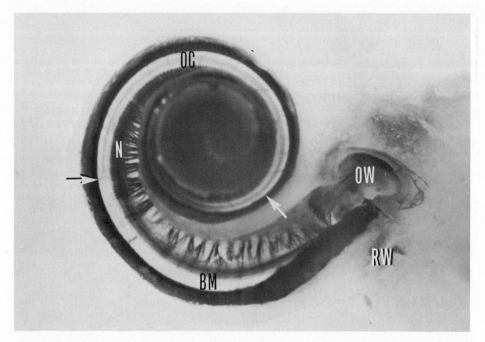

Fig. 18. Left cochlea of kanamycin-treated monkey M-14. Below the arrow (→) Corti's organ has disappeared. Between the arrows well-organized supporting structures remain, but the receptor cells are absent. The abrupt transition to a normal receptor cell pattern occurs near the beginning of the middle turn (↘). OW, RW: oval and round windows; N: nerve fibers; OC: organ of Corti; BM: basilar membrane. (From Stebbins et al., 1969. **Ann. Otol., 78:1007–1019.**)

Further, histologic analysis with Nauta staining procedures in the cochlear nucleus of the brain stem of two monkeys (M-13 and M-14) reveals a pattern and extent of nerve fiber degeneration correlated with the cochlear findings and the behavioral results.

Finally, in addition to obtaining information on the ototoxicity of these drugs, the regularity and orderliness of their action can provide insight into the problem of acoustic-frequency transduction in the normal primate ear.

INSTRUMENTATION

There are three aspects of the research which are heavily instrumented. Logic circuits and more recently, a small, integrated circuit, digital computer control most phases of the behavioral training and testing. Descriptions of these instruments are detailed elsewhere in this book (Moody, Chapter 13, and Reynolds, Chapter 15). The histologic and microscopic procedures have been thoroughly reported (Johnsson and Hawkins, 1967; Engström et al., 1966; Bredberg, 1968).

The particular acoustic instrumentation for experiments with animals is less well known and may appropriately be examined here.

Earphones as the acoustic transducer can be coupled with reasonable precision to the monkey's ear (see Fig. 2). Consequently, monaural stimulation is possible and the well documented problems in free-field stimulation and its measurement are avoided. Sound reflection and the presence of standing waves at certain pure tone frequencies with a subject who is moving relative to the sound source (shock avoidance in a two-compartment shuttle box, for example) produce substantial variability in the stimulus reaching the ear from one moment to the next. The variability is considerably reduced, though not eliminated, when the sound source is coupled in a closed system to the ear. At certain frequencies, there will be standing waves in the ear canals, but a transducer which couples directly to the drum membrane is not available, and there is the cogent argument that any acoustic distortion in the outer ear reflects a given property of the organism and therefore should not be bypassed or extracted from the data.

The earphones (PDR 600, Permoflux) were chosen because they have a frequency response greater than that of the monkey (to 50 kHz). They are sensitive and have relatively low harmonic distortion (at most frequencies the harmonics are 50 dB below the fundamental at greater than 100 dB/spl (2×10^{-4} μbar). Finally, they fit the animals snugly and have proven to be both reliable and rugged. Unquestionably, there are other earphones as good in all respects. The problem is to find and calibrate them. Manufacturer's specifications are seldom useful other than to clearly rule out certain selections. The greatest limitation in any earphone, already the weakest link in the acoustic stimulating system, is the sharp drop-off in the frequency response above 20 kHz. The high frequency problem is compounded because it is also true that our measuring instruments are least sensitive to high frequency stimulation.

In an attempt to measure pure tone stimulation at the entrance to the ear, a small probe tube (6 cm long, 1 mm in diameter) is inserted through the cushion of the earphone in such a way that it rests in front of the opening to the external canal. The probe tube is connected to a condenser microphone (Brüel and Kjaer, model 4134) and cathode follower (Brüel and Kjaer, model 2615). The output of the cathode follower is connected to a wave analyzer (model 302A, Hewlett-Packard). Additional equipment includes a frequency counter as a continuous monitor of the pure tone frequency and a vaccum tube volt meter to record the voltage across the phones. A tone switch permits changes in the rise and decay time of the tone; however, in these experiments, both rise and decay time are kept constant at 50 msec. Short rise times are known to produce an audible click with the pure tone for human subjects. The entire experimental arrangement is shown in schematic form in Figure 19.

In spite of the care and precautions taken for measurement of sound intensity, error at the highest frequencies is almost unavoidable. The problem is easily demonstrated by observing a change in sound pressure with a modest change in the placement of the probe tube or the earphones. I know of no solution to the problem if one wishes to work in the ultrasonic frequency range. The one hopeful feature is the stability of the behavioral thresholds even at high frequencies and the agreement between animals. Possibly the variability in the stimulus over many trials is averaged out.

APPARATUS FOR SOUND PRESENTATION AND MEASUREMENT

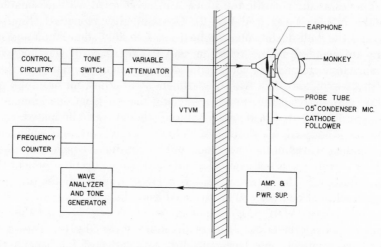

Fig. 19. Diagram of experimental arrangement for stimulus control and measurement. (From Stebbins et al., 1969. **Ann. Otol.**, 78:1007–1019.)

Here, as in any high fidelity system, the acoustic transducer (speaker or earphone) sets most of the limits on the acoustic system. The most important considerations in any system which we have mentioned are sensitivity, amount of distortion, and the nature of the frequency response. The other components in the stimulating system, audio-oscillator, attenuator, tone switch, and amplifier have better performance specifications than earphones. Other qualities not a property of the phones include drift in oscillator settings and noise level; these are less of a problem today with transistors and integrated circuits. One serious difficulty arose in our attempt to automate frequency and intensity change with a programmable oscillator. Those with which we have had experience show too much frequency distortion and drift. Repeat accuracy in the automatic selection of frequency is also poor. Our solution has been to use a series of many preset, transistorized audio-oscillators (model 204C, Hewlett-Packard). Filters which can be programmed remotely might be a means for improving the output characteristics of the programmable oscillators.

In summary, there are some obvious technologic developments which would be a boon to acoustic research with animals. An improvement in some of the specifications of existing equipment would be extremely helpful.

SUMMARY

The chapter has described in detail an operant conditioning procedure together with several psychophysical testing procedures for auditory threshold determination in monkeys. In addition, the threshold has been used as a baseline against which to assess the effects of agents toxic to the ear. Throughout, the purpose has been to demonstrate the utility of the behavioral method per se and to suggest its potential use with other biologic methods in providing basic information about the functioning of the sensory systems. Although the examples have been primarily limited to the study of hearing in the higher nonhuman primates, the method should be applicable for the study of other sensory systems and other lower organisms (e.g., our findings for the pigeon and Gourevitch's for the rat).

Problems with the procedures were discussed in the context in which they arose; the most serious ones deserve additional comment. Probably the greatest methodologic difficulty is unrelated to the behavioral methods but concerns the issue of error in stimulus measurement. The very nature of sound makes its measurement difficult particularly where the wavelength is short relative to the chamber through which the sound must pass (the external ear and the probe tube). At frequencies above 20 kHz where the monkey's threshold is presumably changing most rapidly, we have least confidence in our acoustic measurement. Standing waves and slight movement of objects (probe tube, earphones) in the sound field add considerably to the measurement error. However, the consistency of the threshold data to some extent belie the seriousness of the problem. A solution awaits the development of a small transducer with an excellent frequency response which can be inserted in the ear canal. Although not a complete solution, this step would represent a great improvement over present conditions.

The primary disadvantage of the behavioral procedure is the training time required before stable threshold determinations can be made. Sometimes behavioral disruption will occur after a threshold testing procedure has been introduced for the first time. With some subjects, the disruption with a high rate of false-positive responses may last for many sessions. Increasing the time-out requirement has often been helpful. However, alternative procedures must be tried. The use of electric shock has thus far been avoided since it was felt that it might produce response bias and yield high estimates of threshold. We now have sufficient normative data on hearing in monkeys to answer this question and to determine the effectiveness of shock in suppressing false-positive responses. It seems reasonably clear that the major source of difficulty with the behavioral procedures is the number of these reporting responses in the absence of the tone. Consequently, any decrease in training time must depend upon a more successful method for suppressing these responses and keeping them in check when the discrimination becomes more difficult (i.e., when threshold testing is begun).

We do feel that we have demonstrated the advantages of the behavioral procedure particularly for its use in concert with other biologic precedures as a way of answering basic questions concerning sensory function. Drugs which act in a very lawful manner to destroy the receptor cells in the inner ear produce sharply defined frequency-specific hearing loss, as determined by behavioral techniques. Postmortem microscopic examination of the inner ear indicates a well-defined, place-specific pattern of cellular loss. Together, these two sources of information provide powerful evidence for the way in which the ear resolves acoustic frequency. For the higher frequencies (above 2 kHz), the classic place principle of hearing is supported by these data.

REFERENCES

Behar, I., J. N. Cronholm, and M. Loeb. 1965. Auditory sensitivity of the rhesus monkey. J. Comp. Physiol. Psychol., 59:426–428.

Békésy, G. von. 1960. Experiments in Hearing, New York, McGraw-Hill Book Company.

Blough, D. S. 1966. The study of animal sensory processes by operant methods. In Honig, W. K., ed. Operant Behavior: Areas of Research and Application, New York, Appleton-Century-Crofts, pp. 345–379.

Bredberg, G. 1968. Cellular pattern and nerve supply of the human organ of Corti. Acta Otolaryng. (Stockholm), 236:1–135.

Elder, J. H. 1934. Auditory acuity of the chimpanzee. J. Comp. Psychol., 17:157–183.

Engström, H., H. W. Ades, and A. Andersson. 1966. Structural Pattern of the Organ of Corti, Stockholm, Almquist and Wiksell.

Fujita, S., and D. N. Elliott. 1965. Thresholds of audition for three species of monkey. J. Acoust. Soc. Amer., 37:139–144.

Gourevitch, G., and M. H. Hack. 1966. Audibility in the rat. J. Comp. Physiol. Psychol., 62:289–291.

Heffner, H. E., R. J. Ravizza, and B. Masterton. 1969. Hearing in primitive mammals, IV: bushbaby (Galago senegalensis). J. Aud. Res., 9:19–23.

Heise, G. A. 1953. Auditory thresholds in the pigeon. Amer. J. Psychol., 66:1–19.

Johnsson, L-G., and J. E. Hawkins, Jr. 1967. A direct approach to cochlear anatomy and pathology in man. Arch. Otolaryng., 85:599–613.

Katsuki, Y., N. Suga, and Y. Kanno. 1962. Neural mechanisms of the peripheral and central auditory system in monkey. J. Acoust. Soc. Amer., 34:1396–1410.

Kiang, N. Y-S. 1965. Discharge Patterns of Single Fibers in the Cat's Auditory Nerve, Cambridge, Mass., M.I.T. Press.

Moody, D. B., W. C. Stebbins, and J. M. Miller. 1970. A primate restraint and handling system for auditory research. Behav. Res. Methods and Instrumentation, in press.

Stebbins, W. C. 1966. Auditory reaction time and the derivation of equal loudness contours for the monkey. J. Exp. Anal. Behav., 9:135–142.

―――― and J. M. Miller. 1964. Reaction time as a function of stimulus intensity for the monkey. J. Exp. Anal. Behav., 7:309–312.

―――― S. Green, and F. L. Miller. 1966. Auditory sensitivity of the monkey. Science, 153:1646–1647.

―――― J. M. Miller, L-G. Johnsson, and J. E. Hawkins, Jr. 1968. Behavioral measurement and histopathology of drug-induced hearing loss in subhuman primates. In Vagtborg, H., ed. Use of Nonhuman Primates in Drug Evaluation, Austin, University of Texas Press, pp. 382–399.

―――― J. M. Miller, L-G. Johnsson, and J. E. Hawkins, Jr. 1969. Ototoxic hearing loss and cochlear pathology in the monkey. Ann. Otol., 78:1007–1019.

Stevens, S. S. 1951. Mathematics, measurement, and psychophysics. In Stevens, S. S., ed. Handbook of Experimental Psychology, New York, John Wiley & Sons, Inc., pp. 1–49.

Terrace, H. S. 1966. Stimulus control. In Honig, W. K., ed. Operant Behavior: Areas of Research and Application, New York, Appleton-Century-Crofts, pp. 271–344.

Wendt, G. R. 1934. Auditory acuity of monkeys. Comp. Psychol. Monogr., 10:1–51.

GEORGE GOUREVITCH [1]

4

DETECTABILITY OF TONES
IN QUIET AND IN NOISE
BY RATS AND MONKEYS *

INTRODUCTION

Sensory systems in humans have been investigated by means of psychophysical methods. These methods define the rules for systematic presentation of stimuli to the subject and for the analysis of the subject's responses from which various characteristics of the particular sensory system can be abstracted. Human psychophysical experiments rely heavily on language for instruction of the subject in his task and for his cooperation throughout the study. A crucial difference between human and animal psychophysics is the absence of language in animals. Thus, a systematic investigation of sensory characteristics in animals requires application of techniques which evolved not only from psychophysics, but also from another branch of psychology, namely, conditioning. In order to instruct animals in their task in a psychophysical experiment and maintain their behavior during these experiments, conditioning techniques have been required. Both classical and instrumental conditioning techniques have supplied appropriate precedures, although instrumental conditioning has been the more prevalent source of these techniques.

In this chapter, two psychophysical methods widely used with animals will be described in some detail as well as the instrumental (operant) techniques used to train and maintain appropriate responding in monkeys and rats during auditory psychophysical experiments.

Two fundamental measures of hearing investigated in rats and monkeys will also be presented in this chapter. One is the absolute threshold function; the other, the critical band function. The first reflects the sensitivity of the auditory system; that is, the sound pressure level of just detectable tones as a function of frequency. The second indicates how well "tuned" the ear is, i.e., how successfully

[1] HUNTER COLLEGE, THE CITY UNIVERSITY OF NEW YORK, NEW YORK.

* The experimentation on monkeys was carried out when the author was on a Special Fellowship from the National Institute of Neurological Diseases and Blindness, at the Auditory Research Laboratories, Princeton University.

it can capture a signal buried in noise by filtering out the noise and how this filtering changes with frequency.

CRITICAL BANDS AND ABSOLUTE THRESHOLDS

ABSOLUTE THRESHOLDS IN RATS AND MONKEYS

Absolute auditory threshold measurements in rats prior to the 1940's were hampered by inadequate sound generating and sound measuring equipment. Often, because of this, results were contradictory or erroneous, e.g., Hunter's (1927) results indicating that rats could not hear pure tones below 1 kHz.

In the late 1930's and early 1940's, a number of studies of absolute thresholds in rats were conducted (Henry, 1938; Eccher, 1942; Blackwell and Schlosberg, 1943; Gould and Morgan, 1942; Cowles and Pennington, 1943). Although some of these investigators had adequate sound generating equipment, they did not have, except for Cowles and Pennington, sound calibrating equipment. Instead they used an indirect procedure to calibrate their acoustic stimuli. They placed human subjects at the location where presumably the rat had been during threshold testing and measured the human subjects' thresholds. The rats' thresholds were then given in decibels relative to human thresholds (Gould and Morgan, 1942). Human threshold functions determined under "ideal" conditions and reported in sound pressure levels were available (Stevens and Davis, 1938; Fletcher, 1929). On the assumption that the human subjects tested in the rat studies had the same thresholds as those determined under "ideal" conditions, the rat thresholds which were measured in decibels relative to the human subjects could now be expressed in sound pressure levels. This calibrating procedure was, of course, not very precise since it depended on how well the "ideal" human threshold function represented the subjects tested in the rat studies. Furthermore, there was no way to determine what differences existed in the sound field when human and rat subjects were tested in it. (Studies of hearing in rats conducted prior to the 1950's were thoroughly reviewed by Munn, 1950 and Ash, 1951.)

More recently, rat auditory thresholds were investigated again (Jamison, 1951; Clack and Harris, 1963; Gourevitch, 1965; Gourevitch and Hack, 1966). These investigators were able to calibrate the sound stimuli they used. Their results are shown in Figure 1 with those of Cowles and Pennington (1943) since they had also calibrated the acoustic stimuli.

The lower thresholds around 10 kHz reported by Cowles and Pennington and by Jamison may have been due to upper harmonics in their signals. It is less likely that the difference in behavioral techniques between these authors and the others accounts for the discrepancies since agreement of the results for the other frequencies is good.

Auditory thresholds have been determined on various subhuman primates including chimpanzees, baboons, marmosets, macaques, squirrel and spider mon-

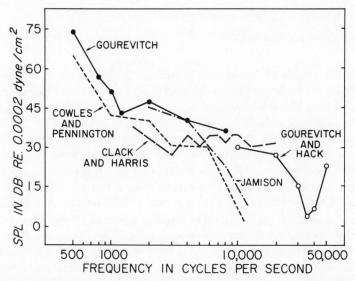

Fig. 1. Auditory thresholds in rats. (From Gourevitch and Hack, 1966. **J. Comp. Physiol. Psychol.**, 62:289–291. Copyright 1966 by the American Psychological Association, Inc.)

keys (Elder, 1934; Wendt, 1934; Harris, 1943; Seiden, 1958; Clack and Herman, 1963; Semenoff and Young, 1964; Fujita and Elliott, 1965; Behar et al., 1965; Stebbins et al., 1966). Agreement among the audiograms of these animals is amazingly good especially if the differences in testing procedures and in the animal species are taken into account (Fig. 2). (For an extensive review of hearing in primates see Stebbins, 1970.)

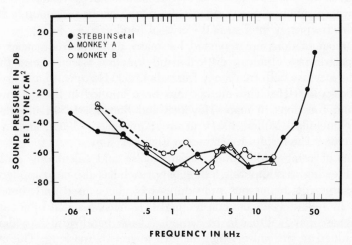

Fig. 2. Auditory thresholds for two **Macaca nemestrina.** The thresholds obtained by Stebbins et al., 1966, on three **M. irus** and one **M. nemestrina** were averaged for inclusion in this figure.

CRITICAL BANDS AND MASKING

When two sounds are generated in unison, they produce a complex wave of sound pressure which impinges on the ear. Under certain conditions the auditory system can resolve this sound into its components. Under other conditions, one of the sound waves may reduce the audibility of the other. Auditory masking refers to the decreased audibility of one sound in the presence of the other.

When a wide band of noise is used to mask a pure tone, it is only a small portion of the total power of the wide band noise which is producing the masking. The effective masking power is concentrated in a narrow band of frequencies surrounding the tone. This observation reported by Fletcher and Munson (1937) was elaborated into the critical band concept by Fletcher (1940). The critical band concept he proposed rested on two assumptions. First, the acoustical power of a band of noise surrounding a particular tone acts upon the same neural endings in the cochlea as does the pure tone, and within a critical band the acoustic power of adjacent frequencies sum. Outside the critical band they do not. The second assumption was that the power of a just audible tone in the presence of a masking noise is equal to the power of a narrow segment of the noise (critical band) surrounding the tone.

The determination of critical bandwidths under Fletcher's assumption requires measurement of masked thresholds in the presence of a wide band of noise. If the masking noise is "white," the spectrum level is uniform; all the frequencies in the noise contribute the same power. To determine the critical bandwidth, the power of the just audible tone is divided by the spectrum level (power in a one cycle band) of the noise. The result of this calculation gives the number of frequencies whose summed power equals the power of the just audible signal. The width of this frequency interval is the critical band.

Similar calculations are repeated for many different frequencies across the audible spectrum to obtain a critical band function which shows that critical bandwidths increase with frequency from about 500 Hz upward and are relatively constant below 500 Hz. This method has been applied in the determination of critical band functions in man (Hawkins and Stevens, 1950), in cats (Watson, 1963), in chinchillas (Miller, 1964), in rats (Gourevitch, 1965), and in porpoises (Johnson, 1968). The results are shown in Figure 3.

Instead of using wide band masking noise and calculating critical bands following Fletcher's assumptions, a direct approach has also been applied to critical band measurement. Numerous procedures have been used and these are mentioned briefly below. One common method is to mask a signal by a narrow band of noise whose bandwidth can be varied. As the bandwidth is widened, more power is added to the noise which in turn augments masking. This increase in masking ceases as the noise bandwidth exceeds a critical width, i.e., the masked threshold remains relatively constant as the width of the noise is made greater. It should be noted that the change from increasing to steady masked thresholds does not occur precisely at some bandwidth of the noise as would occur if the critical

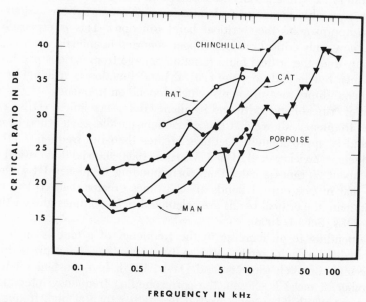

Fig. 3. Critical ratio functions measured in porpoises (Johnson, 1968), in rats (Gourevitch, 1965), in chinchillas (Miller, 1964), in cats (Watson, 1963), and in man (Hawkins and Stevens, 1950). A critical ratio of 20 dB represents 100 cycles per second, one of 30 dB represents 1000 cycles per second, and so on.

band were an ideal band-pass filter, but is more gradual. A number of direct measurements of critical bandwidths by narrow bands of masking noise have been conducted (Schafer et al., 1950; Feldtkeller and Zwicker, 1956; Hamilton, 1957; Greenwood, 1961a; Bos and de Boer, 1966).

Distinction is now made between critical band measurements based on Fletcher's assumptions and those measured directly. The first are appropriately called *critical ratios* since they are given by the ratio of the masked threshold to the spectrum level of the noise. The empirically determined measurements are called *critical bands*. This term not only refers to measurements from narrow band masking, but also to those obtained in a variety of psychophysical experiments in which a sudden change in the reports of the subject occurs as the frequency separation of complex tones or noise bandwidth exceeds a particular width. Such experiments include estimates of loudness of complex sounds with different frequency separations of the components (Zwicker et al., 1957); masking of narrow bands of noise by two tones, one on each side of the noise, separated by different frequency intervals (Greenwood, 1961a); masking of a tone instead of the noise by two side tones (Green, 1965); and ratings of pleasantness of two-tone sounds with different separations of the component tones (Plomp and Levelt, 1965). (Scharf, 1966, has written an extensive review of critical band studies including description of the above mentioned experiments.)

Critical bands and critical ratios are not equal. The former are found to be approximately 4 dB greater (a factor of 2.5) than critical ratios for most of the audible spectrum. The difference between the two functions has been observed in human auditory experiments. On the assumption that a similar difference exists in animals, it is possible to use critical ratio functions reported for various animals (Fig. 3) to approximate their critical band functions. This is especially useful since, until now, only critical ratios had been reported in animals.

Not only does the critical band function emerge from various psychoacoustic measurements, but in addition, the critical band function is strikingly similar in form to other auditory measurements which depend on frequency.

A plot of critical bandwidth and frequency difference limens (DLs), each as a function of frequency, shows that these functions parallel each other. In man, the critical band is approximately 30 times greater than the frequency DL at any given frequency (Zwicker et al., 1957). Watson (1963) showed that critical ratios in cats were about 20 times greater than corresponding frequency DLs. On the assumption that in cats critical bands are 2.5 times greater than critical ratios, as they are in man, the critical bands are calculated to be 50 times greater than their frequency DLs (Scharf, 1966).

Corresponding to an increase in the frequency of a tone is an increase in pitch. The difference in pitch between two tones can be expressed in mels, which are units of pitch (Stevens and Davis, 1938). If a constant pitch interval (fixed number of mels) is chosen, the corresponding frequency interval will not have the same width when measured at low rather than at high frequencies. In other words, a small change in the frequency of low tones will produce the same change in pitch as does a larger change in frequency at higher frequencies. The function which relates the frequency interval for a fixed pitch interval (50 mels wide) to frequency is very similar to the critical band function (Licklider, 1951).

It has also been proposed that critical bands may correspond to equal intervals along the basilar membrane. This hypothesis is based on the similarity of the critical band function and the function relating location along the basilar membrane of maximum vibration to frequency (Békésy and Rosenblith, 1951). (Functions relating critical bandwidths to frequency and location along the basilar membrane were derived by Greenwood, 1961b.)

The numerous ways by which the critical band has been determined, the similarity in the shape of the critical band function and other auditory functions, and the possible correspondence of a critical band to a unit length along the basilar membrane all stress its importance in hearing.

APPLICATION OF THE METHOD OF CONSTANT STIMULI TO THRESHOLD MEASUREMENTS IN MONKEYS AND RATS

The procedures described in this section are used to train an animal (monkey or rat) to respond consistently to a series of sound stimuli and prepare him for threshold measurement. Essentially, this measurement consists in the animal pressing one key until an audible tone is turned on for a few seconds; then, while the tone is on, shifting to another key and pressing it once to receive a reinforcement. From trial to trial the intensity of the tone is changed, i.e., some of the tones are

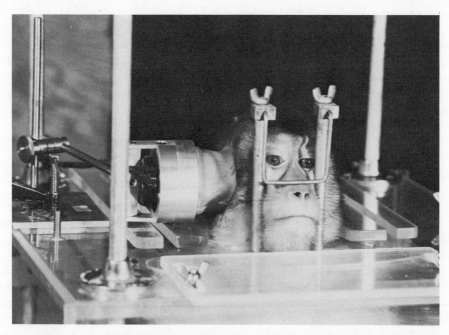

Fig. 7. Earphone and rubber coupler positioned against the monkey ear.

while in the chairs. This is an important procedure since it is used later to train the monkey to chair himself (see below). After a few days of short adaptation periods, the monkey is left in the chair for longer intervals up to a few hours. Four days to a week of daily chairing is required before the animal will remain in the chair without struggling, except for an occasional short outburst.

Two other adaptation procedures are necessary before training of the monkey can begin. Since earphones will eventually be placed against the monkey's ears, his head must be restrained. The head restraint consists of a V- or a U-shaped holder lined with foam rubber which is pushed up against the back of the monkey's head, forcing him to position his snout between two vertical posts (Fig. 5). This arrangement prevents the monkey from rotating his head. The crossbar connecting the two vertical posts restricts the up and down motion of the monkey's head, and yet allows the animal to open his mouth and stick his tongue out to pick up the food pellet (Fig. 6). At first the animal will resist being restricted in this way. To shorten the adaptation process, food is given to the animal only when his head is secured as described above. Again adaptation is gradual and must be observed carefully so that the animal does not hurt himself when struggling. This adaptation is more rapid than the first one, and in two or three days the animal becomes quiet for extended time periods. Finally, the animal is ready to have the earphone placed over his ear. Although the earphone is not an additional restraint, the slight pressure change applied to the ear by the sealed earphone coupler, as well as the sound which is turned on, are, at first, disturbing to the monkey and he will increase his outbursts (Fig. 7). Usually, this adaptation is quite rapid since bar press training is begun at the same time and the monkey receives a large number of food pellets.

Although a number of experimenters, including the author, have maintained monkeys in chairs for durations ranging from a week to many months, it has been found that it is quite a simple task to chair monkeys daily (Barrow et al., 1966). A monkey can be trained in one or two days to enter a transfer cage and exit into the chair by feeding him only in the chair. Since this transfer procedure is easily accomplished by one person and at the same time allows the monkey to live in a cage rather than a chair, it is being adopted in many laboratories.

TRAINING

Once adaptation to the chair, head holder, and earphone has been achieved, preliminary training is started. The first step is to train the monkey to press bar B, which is the last response in the chain of responses the monkey emits during threshold measurements. A tone is turned on. While the tone is on, the animal is reinforced with banana pellets (Ciba, 75 mg) for all movements of his right arm which bring it near the telegraph key. Shaping behavior depends on the quickness of the experimenter in reinforcing those movements of the animal which approximate the desired bar press. Once the animal begins bar pressing, he is reinforced on a CRF schedule, i.e., for every bar press. It is desirable to reinforce not more than 50 responses on B before introducing the second bar; otherwise, the animal will continue pressing bar B after bar A is introduced and thus delay acquisition of bar A pressing.

At the beginning of the next session, bar A is also attached to the chair. The tone is off. The programming equipment is arranged so that a single press on bar A will turn on the tone which will remain on until the animal presses bar B. At first, when bar A is introduced, the monkey ignores it and presses bar B only. At some point during the session the monkey will press bar A and turn the tone on. He will then press bar B and receive his banana pellet. Most monkeys quickly develop the appropriate chain of responses; namely, they press bar A turning on the tone, then switch to bar B, press it once and obtain the reinforcer. Various undesirable behaviors often develop at this stage of training and require special contingencies to insure that they are eliminated.

Some monkeys will continue pressing bar B, the one which produces reinforcers, although no tone is present. And even after occasionally emitting the correct chain, i.e., pressing bar A, turning on the sound and then pressing bar B for a reinforcer, the monkey may continue pressing bar B for very long intervals before switching back to pressing bar A. For these monkeys the bars are switched, i.e., bar A which was on the left is now moved to the previous location of bar B and vice versa. This interchange is very helpful especially when the schedule on bar A is increased (see below).

Once the chain of bar A and bar B presses has been established, it is reinforced on a CRF schedule for one session. The schedule on bar A is then gradually increased over the next 10 to 12 sessions. The first increase on bar A is from a requirement of one to a requirement of two presses to turn on the tone. During the next session, the schedule is increased from a fixed ratio of 3 (FR 3) to a fixed ratio of 8, i.e., the monkey must press bar *A* at first 3, and finally 8 times to turn on the sound. For the next 10 sessions the schedule is increased gradually from FR 8 to a variable ratio of 18 (VR 18). The VR schedule is introduced as early as possible. Under this schedule, the number of presses required to turn on the signal varies from trial to trial. Thus, under a VR 18, an average of 18 presses will turn on the tone. The range of the ratio is usually limited to between 10 and 25. Not all monkeys perform as rapidly as one another and therefore schedules must be adjusted for the particular monkey.

The schedules used during training are not the same as those used during threshold determination when shorter schedules must be introduced. The change is necessary because during threshold determination, many trials consist of inaudible tones; on such trials the monkey continues pressing bar *A* and forgoes the opportunity for reinforcement. Unless the schedule is reduced, the monkey receives fewer reinforcements during threshold testing than during training for the same amount of bar pressing.

The extent of schedule reduction depends on the relative intensities of the tones that are presented to the animal. If the intensities of the tones are so chosen that he will detect the occurrence of only the two most intense tones and detect less and less accurately the three lower intensities, then a large reduction of the schedule is necessary. On the other hand, if only two of the five tones result in low detection, a smaller decrease in the schedule requirement is sufficient.

The duration of the tone trial is also changed during training. In the first stages of training, when the monkey presses bar *A* the tone is turned on and remains on until he presses bar *B*. Soon the monkey develops the correct chain of responses, i.e., he presses bar *A* until the tone comes on and then switches to bar *B*. He may, however, linger a while on bar *A* and not switch immediately at the onset of the tone. During these earlier stages of training, the duration of the tone trial is reduced gradually to 15 seconds, and later on to 5 seconds. When the chain of responses is well established, the tone trial is usually maintained at 2.5 seconds. This interval allows the animal sufficient time to switch to bar *B* after the tone comes on. By the same token the short interval reduces the likelihood that a "guess" by the monkey will occur during the time when he can be reinforced.

When the monkey has been trained to criterion (see below), his performance is quite stereotyped. He proceeds through the chain of responses without much deviation; he presses bar *A* continuously until the tone comes on, and then quickly shifts to bar *B*, presses it once, and receives his reinforcement. The tone is turned off and he repeats this sequence.

During the early stages of training, the monkey will often switch to bar *A* prematurely, when the tone is off. These intertrial errors are recorded during training and during threshold testing. It should be noted that when the monkey is reporting consistent thresholds and showing no perturbations in his behavior, i.e., performing at criterion, the intertrial bar *B* presses can often be as high as 30 percent of the total bar *B* presses.

Intertrial errors include all bar *B* presses except those emitted when the tone is on and those emitted during a 1.5-second interval after the tone is turned off by the monkey's press of bar *B*. Monkeys often will press this bar more than once for reinforcement. To avoid counting these extra presses as errors and to avoid initiating error contingencies, the small delay is included.

The most appropriate indicator of the animal's guessing behavior is obtained by introducing blank trials. These trials are interspersed randomly with signal trials. The blank trials are presented as frequently as is each intensity; if each intensity is presented 50 times during one session, 50 blank trials would occur. The apparatus selects randomly which of six attenuators is introduced into the circuit for the next trial; one of these attenuators has infinite attenuation across it. Thus, the blank trial is identical to other trials except for the extreme attenuation of the signal and the lack of reinforcement for a press of bar *B*. The rate of presses during blank trials is not simply related to the intertrial errors, i.e., bar *B* presses between trials. If, as is often the case in the early stages of training, the monkey emits many intertrial errors, he will usually also make a number of blank trial errors. This simply reflects a high rate of bar *B* presses. At more advanced stages of training the animal makes relatively few intertrial errors. Yet, he may commit many blank trial errors. Two obvious sources for such errors must be checked. First, some cue (usually auditory) other than the signal informs the animal that a "trial" has appeared. Such cues are occasionally induced at the transducer by the programming equipment. Second, the schedule controlling trial presentations may be too short and have little variability so that the animal develops a "time discrimination" and often shifts to bar *B* after a short time successfully guessing the occurrence of a trial.

BEHAVIORAL PERFORMANCE

Before the monkey's thresholds can be determined, his performance under nonthreshold conditions must be evaluated. This is done when he is in the last stage of training, i.e., when different intensity tones (all audible) are presented from trial to trial. The intertrial errors and the blank trial errors are observed. In a given session, the monkey's performance is not considered acceptable if the blank trial errors are greater than 10 percent. This criterion is made more stringent for some monkeys whose daily performance is erratic. When incorrect responding exceeds the criterion, it is necessary to introduce contingencies which decrease the rate of errors. Two common procedures used are time-out and shock. They are administered to the monkey only for intertrial errors, not for blank trial errors.

TIME-OUT

If the monkey presses bar *B* between trials, a time-out results during which the testing chamber light is turned off and the keys are electrically disconnected from the circuit. The consequence of a time-out is the postponement of any opportunity for reinforcement; bar *A* presses during this interval are not counted toward the number of responses required to turn on the tone. Moreover, any partial fulfillment of this number attained before the error is erased, and only after the time-out period is ended are the animal's responses tallied again. Bar *B* presses during this period are also without consequence. Usually one time-out duration is used in a given session, but it may be changed for another session or for another monkey. Time-outs range from 5 to 40 seconds. Eventually, after many long time-outs (15 seconds or more) have occurred, the monkey ceases to press either bar during the time-out.

Extended time-outs (15 seconds or more) are introduced at the advanced training stage if the animal's errors have not decreased sufficiently before then. Some monkeys require maintenance of long time-outs even during threshold testing; otherwise, their intertrial and blank trial errors gradually increase. Time-outs are often effective by themselves in decreasing incorrect responding. The particular duration of the time-out will depend on the stage of training and the individual monkey.

SHOCK

In some instances the time-out contingency alone has not been successful in reducing the intertrial errors, especially in the early stages of threshold testing. The use of shocks in conjunction with the time-outs have often produced the best results. The shock is administered only for intertrial bar *B* presses. Its strength and duration are adjustable. When shock is first administered the monkey's response is observed. Since the shock is delivered through the rods of the chair on which the monkey perches, a "mild" shock is taken as one for which the monkey raises his feet from the rods, usually pivoting on his heels. The duration of the shock is set for half a second or less.

"Intense shock" produces the raising of both feet from the chair seat and general excitement with vocalization. The duration of this shock is 250 msec or less. Intense shocks are used rarely, and never during threshold testing since the excited behavior which accompanies these shocks can hinder some monkeys' performance and stop them from responding altogether.

Shock is never administered by itself, but is combined with time-outs; an intertrial error produces simultaneously a shock and a time-out. At first, when shock is used during training, its intensity is moderately high and the associated time-out is long. Shortly thereafter (two or three sessions), the shock strength is reduced while the time-out duration remains long. From time to time, especially if the animal's errors increase, the shock intensity is raised for one session. This occasional exposure to more intense shocks reduces the error rate and increases the effectiveness of time-outs in maintaining low error rates. Some animals require continuance of the shock and time-out contingencies throughout the experiment to maintain low errors; in others, shock can be removed and only time-out used. The contingency used, time-out or shock plus time-out, and the shock intensity and time duration selected depends on the particular animal. (See Chapter 3 by Stebbins for other training procedures.)

THRESHOLD MEASUREMENT

The psychophysical method of constant stimuli provides a set of procedures for the determination of thresholds, including absolute and masked thresholds. The method consists in the presentation of different intensities of the signal in random order, some above and some below the threshold. For each intensity level of the signal, the number of correct identifications is recorded as is the number of presentations of the particular intensity. The percentage of detections of each intensity is then calculated and the threshold is taken as the intensity corresponding to 50 percent correct detection.

To measure absolute thresholds in the monkeys, five signal intensities are chosen. The choice of five sound levels is a compromise between using a large number of intensities which would define more precisely the psychophysical function and the practical requirement of limited time during a testing session. The intensity levels are 5 dB apart; the range of tonal intensities is then 20 dB. This range is usually sufficient for obtaining 90 percent or above correct detection for the more intense signals and less than 10 percent correct detection for the low signals.

During a session, each signal intensity is presented no less than 20 times, and most often 30 times or more. Typically, threshold measurement for a given tone consists in the presentation of 150 trials of varying signal intensities and 30 blank trials.

The method of constant stimuli requires a preliminary estimate of the threshold value so that the signal intensities used in determining the threshold can bracket the threshold intensity. Before this estimate is taken, the monkey is run under identical conditions as those in threshold testing except that all five signal intensities are above threshold. This training stage exposes the monkey to the presentation of varying tone intensities from quite loud to just audible. Four or five sessions under these conditions eliminate the temporary disruption in performance which would occur if the monkey were switched abruptly from discrimination training with a fixed, loud tone to threshold conditions of varying tone intensities.

After the few sessions when all intensities are audible, two or three sessions are used to estimate the threshold. During the first session, 10 dB of attenuation is added to all the signal intensities and the monkey's performance observed. If detection is still 90 percent or better at all intensities, attenuation is increased another 10 dB. This procedure is continued until correct detection of the two least intense signals is 25 percent or less. The threshold is above these intensities and below the most intense signals, since these are detected 90 percent or better.

The performance of the monkeys is such that the percentage of his correct detections usually shifts from 70 percent or so to 25 percent or so within a 5 dB step. The steep change in performance allows a reasonably accurate estimation of the threshold.

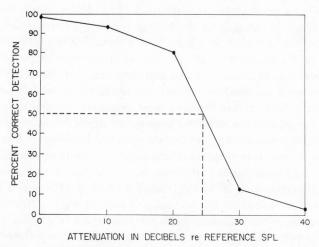

Fig. 8. Psychophysical function determined on one rat. (From Gourevitch and Hack, 1966. **J. Comp. Physiol. Psychol.,** 62:289–291. Copyright 1966 by the American Psychological Association, Inc.) Similar functions are obtained from monkeys.

The psychophysical function for each monkey's daily session is plotted and the threshold intensity is visually estimated from the figure. A similar plot for rats is shown in Figure 8.

Threshold variability from day to day remains within ±6 dB. Most thresholds, however, cluster within ±4 dB. Stability is observed also over long time intervals when the same thresholds are measured weeks or months apart.

The performance of the monkey during threshold testing must occasionally be examined to verify whether he is "paying attention" to the signal. This can be accomplished quickly by decreasing (or increasing) all intensities by a fixed amount. If, for example, the signal is made 10 dB more intense, the monkey should shift his percentage of correct identifications correspondingly.

ABSOLUTE THRESHOLD MEASUREMENT IN RATS

The procedures described above were first developed for the determination of absolute thresholds in rats (Gourevitch and Hack, 1966). Although certain details in procedures differed between threshold measurements in monkeys and rats, e.g., monkeys were restrained and sound delivered in a closed system while rats were not restrained and were tested in a free field, the principal training steps and the contingencies to control poor performance were essentially the same.

MASKED THRESHOLDS AND CRITICAL BAND MEASUREMENT IN MONKEYS

Critical bands were determined on monkeys whose absolute thresholds had already been ascertained. Measurement of critical bands was made in two ways:

at some frequencies, the maskers were narrow bands of noise; at others, the maskers were two pure tones, one on each side of the signal frequency. The maskers remained on throughout the testing sessions. (It would be preferable to turn on the maskers just prior to a trial, thus minimizing any fatiguing effects due to the maskers. Early attempts by the author to use this approach resulted in extremely variable performance by the monkeys and was abandoned.)

Introduction of the maskers, at first, disrupted the monkey's performance in detecting signals. Two to five sessions were required for adaptation to the new experimental conditions. During these sessions all signal intensities were increased so that at least 90 percent correct detection occurred at all signal levels. Gradually the signal intensities were decreased and masked threshold measurements were started in the same manner as had previously been done for absolute thresholds.

For the determination of critical bandwidth at 1 kHz and 5 kHz, masked thresholds were measured in the presence of four or more different bandwidths of noise. Selection of the widest noise bands that could be applied about a given frequency depended on the frequency response of the transducer around that frequency. In some instances, the response of the transducer was not flat beyond certain frequencies and, therefore, noise bands including these frequencies could not be used.

Typically, masked thresholds for two to five noise bands were obtained during a testing session. For most sessions measurements progressed from narrow to wide noise bands.

At 600 Hz, 8,000 Hz, and 17,000 Hz, critical bands were measured by varying the separation of a two-tone masker. The procedure in this instance was similar to the one used with the noise; during a testing session masked thresholds were determined under several two-tone separations. Each component of the masker was set at a sound pressure level (SPL) of 50 dB during masked threshold mea-

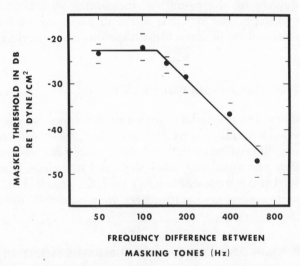

Fig. 9. Masked thresholds of a 600 Hz tone measured in one monkey in the presence of two side tones at 50 dB sound pressure level.

surements. In addition, masked thresholds were also determined, in one monkey, with the masker components set at 60 dB SPL.

Masked thresholds of a 600 Hz tone were measured over five or more sessions at different frequency separations between the components of the masker. The mean and range of the masked thresholds for one monkey are shown in Figure 9.

The critical band was estimated from the bandwidth at which a marked change in the behavior of the masked thresholds occurred. To facilitate this estimation, two lines were drawn through the data, one through the unvarying thresholds and the other through the decreasing thresholds. The frequency interval at which the lines intersected was taken as the critical band (Fig. 9).

Masked thresholds for 1 kHz and 5 kHz tones were determined in the presence of narrow bands of noise (Figs. 10 and 11). As in the case of the two-tone masker, critical bandwidths were estimated from the intersection of two straight lines drawn through the data.

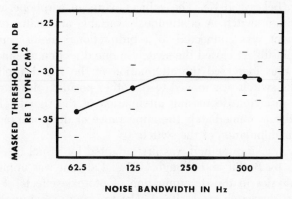

Fig. 10. Mean and range of masked thresholds of a 1 kHz tone measured in one monkey under different bandwidths of noise. Spectrum level 25 dB/cycle SPL.

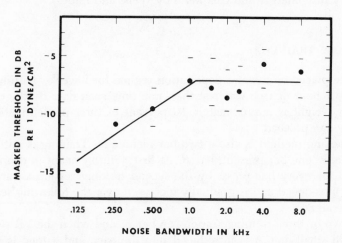

Fig. 11. Mean and range of masked thresholds of a 5 kHz tone measured in one monkey under different bandwidths of noise. Spectrum level 37 dB/cycle SPL.

The difficulty in generating flat noise over wide bands of noise seems to be reflected in the behavior of the masked thresholds of the 5 kHz tone at the wider noise bandwidths. The spectrum level of the noise was 37 dB per cycle ±2.5 dB. However, for noise bandwidths greater than 2 kHz, the spectrum level was 37 dB ±5.5 dB, which may have contributed to the instability of the masked thresholds at wider noise bandwidths.

The critical band function measured in the monkeys with two-tone maskers and bands of noise appears in Figure 15.

THRESHOLD MEASUREMENT IN RATS BY THE TRACKING METHOD

The Békésy tracking method was developed for measurement of human auditory thresholds (Békésy, 1947). The subject wore an earphone and held in his hand a two-position switch. A continuously variable attenuator coupled to a recording instrument was connected to a bidirectional motor controlled by the switch. When the subject closed the switch in one direction, the motor turned the attenuator and thus increased the attenuation of the signal applied to the earphone. When the switch was moved to the other position, the attenuator rotated in the opposite direction decreasing attenuation of the signal. The subject was instructed to indicate immediately the appearance or disappearance of the signal by appropriate manipulation of the switch.

The Békésy tracking method was first adapted for visual threshold measurement in animals by Ratliff and Blough (1954). Later, it was applied to auditory animal psychophysics in the determination of ototoxic effects of kanamycin on hearing in rats (Gourevitch et al., 1960). The tracking technique has been incorporated in numerous studies investigating vision, audition, pain, and so forth (see Chapter 7 by Rosenberger and Chapter 8 by Weiss and Laties).

PRELIMINARY TRAINING

Rats are placed on a water deprivation regime for 2 weeks. During this time they receive 1 hour of free water at the same time each day. By the end of this period their weight is approximately 80 percent of their predeprivation weight and training can proceed.

The tracking method is also a two-bar technique. Training is initiated in silence with only one bar present, bar B. At first, reinforcement (a drop of water) is delivered for every bar press; by the second training session a variable ratio schedule is introduced and is gradually increased over the following sessions to a VR 16 or greater.

After two or three training sessions on bar B, and when the VR schedule on bar B is still small, bar A is introduced into the cage and a tone is turned on. Typically, during the same session the rat, after much pressing of bar B, wanders over to bar *A* and presses it once; this is sufficient, at this time, to turn the tone off. The rat then shifts to bar *B*, presses it the required number of times and receives a reinforcement. As training proceeds, variable ratio schedules are in effect on both bars and are gradually increased.

At this stage in training the tone is not turned back on every time reinforcement is delivered. Approximately 20 percent of the time the tone remains off after reinforcement, so that the rat must "listen" after receiving the water before selecting the appropriate bar to press. Many weeks of daily training sessions are required to obtain steady performance from the rat, i.e., so that the rat will routinely approach bar *A* when the sound is on and continue pressing it until reinforcement occurs.

The sound stimuli used during training are all above threshold. Within a session, the tone remains at fixed intensity; between sessions, the intensities are changed preparatory to threshold testing. They range from quite loud to quite soft; for most training sessions, however, soft sounds are used because during threshold testing the tonal stimuli remain near threshold.

THRESHOLD TESTING

For threshold determinations, a recording attenuator is introduced into the circuit. This instrument increases or decreases the intensity of the signal and at the same time records the intensity level of the signal.

The programming is now arranged so that as the rat presses bar *A* he activates (under a special program) the recording attenuator which decreases the intensity of the signal by 5 dB steps. The decrease of the tone intensity does not occur with every bar press, but is controlled by a separate variable ratio program. It should be remembered that there exists at the same time a different variable ratio program controlling the number of bar *A* presses required to turn off the tone. This ratio is greater than the ratio controlling the attenuator. Usually, then, as the rat presses bar *A* the tone intensity may decrease one, two, or three steps before it is turned off. When the tone is off, the rat's bar *B* presses eventually result in a reinforcement. If, however, the rat switches to bar *B* when the tone is still on, and presses it three times, the intensity of the tone is increased 5 dB. An additional three presses increases the tone another 5 dB, and so on.

The following describes the sequence of events during a typical threshold testing session with a well-trained rat. The session is started in silence. Consequently, the rat presses bar *B*, receives a reinforcement and a tone comes on. The tone is about 30 dB above the rat's assumed threshold. As the rat presses bar *A*, the tone intensity is decreased by 5 dB. He continues pressing the bar, and another 5 dB decrease results. He presses on. At some point the tone is turned off, i.e., the rat emitted the required number of presses on bar *A* determined by the VR schedule controlling the offset of the signal. The rat quickly switches to bar *B* and presses it until reinforcement appears. The tone now comes back on at the same intensity level as when it had been turned off. The rat goes back to bar *A* and begins this sequence again. Eventually, while the rat is pressing bar *A*, a 5 dB decrease in the tone intensity brings it below his threshold. Since tone off and tone below threshold are similar events for the rat, he switches to bar B. Three bar presses increase the tone by 5 dB. If the tone has now become audible the rat returns to bar A and begins the sequence once again. The consequence of this behavior is oscillation of the tone intensity from just above to just below the rat's threshold. It must be noted that the rat can obtain reinforcement throughout the testing session because under these schedules, from time to time, a few bar A presses turn an audible tone off; the rat can then switch to bar B and secure reinforcement.

To verify that the rat is under control of the sound stimulus, the reference intensity is occasionally changed. In other words, if the rat is tracking his threshold around 40 dB of attenuation below the reference intensity and it is increased by 10 dB, he must attenuate the signal to 50 dB to remain at the same level. Indeed, immediately after the reference level change, the rat changes to the appropriate attenuation level.

CONTINGENCIES FOR INCORRECT BAR PRESSING

In the course of threshold testing, certain inappropriate behaviors can appear. Most common are continued pressing of bar A after the tone is off and premature switching to bar B.

Overpressing bar A usually results from long response bursts during which the tone is sometimes turned off. A time-out contingency of 20 seconds is introduced. During this time-out, the bars are disconnected from the circuit and a light is turned on in the testing box (the rat works normally in the dark). After a few testing sessions with time-out, the rat rarely overpresses bar A.

To control premature switching to bar B, i.e., when the tone is still on, two contingencies are used. First, a one-half–second delay is required between the last bar A press which turned the tone off and the first bar B press. If the rat presses sooner, the tone is turned on again. This contingency demands more deliberate "listening" before switching to bar B. Second, if the tone is still on and the rat presses bar B once, he erases the count of bar A presses he has accumulated to that moment toward the number required by the VR schedule to turn the tone off. He is forced to start from zero, thus delaying opportunity for reinforcement.

ABSOLUTE THRESHOLDS AND MASKED THRESHOLDS

The threshold for a session is given by the mean of the reversal points, i.e., by the mean of the SPL values at which the rat changes from decreasing to increasing the tone intensity and vice versa. These values (peaks and troughs) can be read directly from a record as shown in Figure 12. (The record in this figure was obtained under three levels of noise. If the noises were removed instead of a

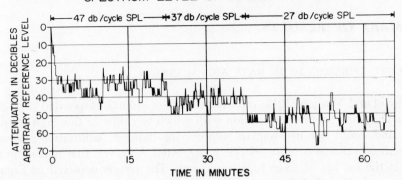

Fig. 12. Record produced by one rat during a testing session under 3 levels of noise. (From Gourevitch, 1965. **J. Acoust. Soc. Amer.**, 37:439–443. Copyright 1965 by the Acoustical Society of America.)

pattern of three levels of oscillations, a single steady oscillatory pattern would result centering about some smaller SPL value.)

The stability of the thresholds from session to session is good; typically, over 85 percent of the daily thresholds will fall within a ±5 dB range. The thresholds for the first month, depicted in Figure 13, were obtained on a normal rat prior to drug administration.

Masked thresholds were determined in the same manner as the absolute thresholds except that a wide band noise of uniform spectrum level was present during the testing. Once the masked threshold for a given frequency is measured, a simple calculation gives the critical ratio for that frequency (see the section on critical bands). To obtain the critical ratio function for the rat, masked thresholds were determined at four different frequencies and corresponding critical ratios were calculated (Fig. 3).

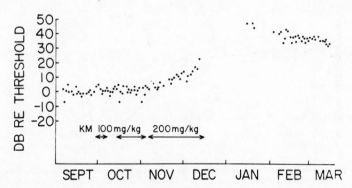

Fig. 13. Daily thresholds from one rat before, during, and after kanamycin administration. (From Gourevitch et al., 1960. **Science**, 131:1046–1047. Copyright 1960 by the American Association for the Advancement of Science.)

SUMMARY OF RESULTS

ABSOLUTE THRESHOLDS IN RATS AND MONKEYS

Gould and Morgan (1942) reported that their animals responded to a 40 kHz signal. They had no instrumentation with which to calibrate this high frequency signal and could not use human subjects for indirect "calibration"; therefore, no threshold value was reported. They suggested, however, that maximum sensitivity in the rat lies at some high frequency. The results depicted in Figure 14 and Figure 1 show that the region of maximum sensitivity is in the neighborhood of 30 to 40 kHz. (Cochlear microphonic measurements in rats have also shown maximum sensitivity to be around 40 kHz; Crowley et al., 1965.)

The frequency interval of greatest sensitivity in the rat audiogram is narrow (approximately one octave wide). A similar interval, centered more than an octave below the corresponding region for the rat, has been reported for the mouse (Berlin, 1963; see Chapter 5 by Ray).

Recent determinations of absolute thresholds in macaques are shown in Figure 2 (Stebbins et al., 1966; Gourevitch, unpublished data). Macaques have a broad interval of high sensitivity extending over approximately five octaves except for a "notch" in the vicinity of 4 kHz where the sensitivity decreases by 10 or more decibels. In the interval between 15 and 30 kHz, depending on the type of monkey, the sensitivity to tonal stimuli begins to decrease very rapidly (Seiden, 1958; Stebbins et al., 1966).

The audiogram of macaques extends about one octave above the upper frequency limit of the human audiogram and exhibits a "notch" in the frequency

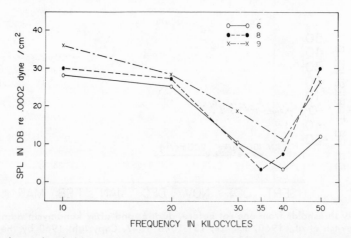

Fig. 14. Auditory thresholds in 3 rats defining the region of greatest acuity. (From Gourevitch and Hack, 1966. **J. Comp. Physiol. Psychol.**, 62:289–291. Copyright 1966 by the American Psychological Association, Inc.)

region of maximum human sensitivity. Except for these differences, the threshold functions of the human and macaque ears are similar.

CRITICAL BANDS AND CRITICAL RATIOS IN ANIMALS

Critical bandwidths determined in monkeys (*M. nemestrina*) and shown in Figure 15 agree quite closely with those reported for man. It is, therefore, reasonable to expect that auditory functions which are correlated with the critical band function, e.g., frequency difference limens, would be similar in man and in monkey. Indeed, the frequency DLs for the monkey reported by Stebbins (Chapter 3) are, for the most part, quite similar to human frequency DLs. Since in man the critical band is approximately 50 times greater than the DL at a given frequency, the same should be true in monkeys. Apparently, the frequency DLs for the monkey are about 50 times smaller than the critical bands shown in Figure 15, except at 15 kHz.

Only critical ratios have been measured in animals other than the monkey. Estimation of critical bands, however, is made possible by the observation that critical bands in humans are approximately 2.5 times greater than critical ratios. On the assumption that this relationship holds for animals it is a simple matter to calculate critical bandwidths from critical ratio measurements. Over a comparable frequency range, the cat's critical ratio function is the one closest to man's (Fig. 3). Estimation of the cat's critical band at 1 kHz under the above mentioned assumption is 360 Hz (Scharf, 1966). For the same frequency, critical bandwidth in the monkey is approximately 160 Hz. Similarly, at the other frequencies the monkey's critical bands are narrower than those of cats and all other animals tested with airborne sound.

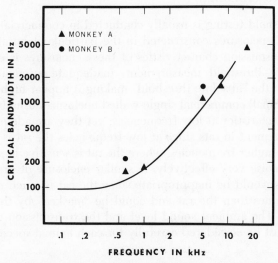

Fig. 15. Critical band function for the monkey. At 1000 and 5000 Hz narrow band noise was the masker; at 600, 8000 and 17000 Hz two side tones comprised the masker. The solid line represents averaged critical band measurements in humans and was adapted from Scharf, 1966.

The prominent features of the critical ratio functions depicted in Figure 3 (the monkey critical ratio function would almost coincide with man's) are the similarity in the shapes of these functions and the displacement along the ordinate of these functions. The larger critical ratios in all land animals relative to man may be due in part to the wider frequency ranges audible to them and their correspondingly shorter basilar membranes. At the same time, the similarity in different animals of the shape of the critical band and critical ratio functions suggests that they reflect a common auditory mechanism (Scharf, 1966). The extension of critical band determination to various animal species has further supported the suggestion that the critical band is a fundamental measure of hearing.

INSTRUMENTATION

The most common procedure used for delivery of sound to an animal whose threshold is being tested is to place the animal in a cage, located in a sound-attenuating enclosure, and place a speaker above or in front of the cage. The sound field generated in this arrangement is never uniform throughout the volume in which the animal moves. All objects, such as the cage walls, stands, and walls of the room, reflect the sound and so distort the sound field. A most desirable enclosure would have anechoic inner walls and massive, sound-attenuating outer walls. At its center, the animal would stand still listening to the sound from a speaker as far removed from him as possible. The animal could then be exposed to a uniform sound field. Such conditions, although highly desirable, are rarely encountered.

ANIMAL TESTING CHAMBER

Animal threshold testing is usually conducted in commercial sound attenuating booths or in enclosures constructed in the particular laboratory. Knowledge of the sound transmission characteristics of these enclosures is especially important for absolute threshold measurement; inadequate attenuation of ambient noise can elevate the "absolute threshold" making it appear higher than it would be in the quiet. Small commercial single-walled enclosures usually have very poor attenuation characteristics at low frequencies; yet they are adequate for absolute threshold measurement in rats since at low frequencies the rat is quite insensitive to sound. At the higher frequencies, where the rat is sensitive to sound, the enclosure attenuates noise very effectively. A similar enclosure of greater dimensions for use with cats would be inappropriate since the cat is much more sensitive to low frequency tones than the rat and could be "masked" by the penetration of ambient sounds. The ambient sound level and the transmission characteristics of the enclosure must be considered carefully for each animal species which is to be tested.

RESTRAINING ARRANGEMENTS FOR RATS

Since ideal acoustic conditions are not usually available, it is important to devise restrictions upon the animal which will limit him to some confined volume when he is being tested. The sound field in such a volume can be measured and is, hopefully, reasonably uniform.

A variety of restraining devices have been used on rats to maintain them immobile during auditory testing. These have ranged from small harnesses (Cowles and Pennington, 1943) to taping the rat to a stand (Jamison, 1951). Most often, however, the behavior demanded from the animal requires a free-moving animal. Instead of using a cage to restrain the rat, an open platform constructed of steel rods one-eighth of an inch in diameter and spaced one-half inch apart with an electrified wire circumscribing the platform was used successfully for threshold measurement (Gourevitch and Hack, 1966). This arrangement eliminated interference with the sound produced by walls and ceilings of standard cages.

There still remain many sources of distortion of the sound field. It is, therefore, most desirable to confine the rat's behavior to a relatively small volume of space. The platform described above does not restrict the rat sufficiently. To insure that the rat is within a small volume when detecting signals, instead of requiring a bar press of the rat, a nose target (steel disc, three-eighths of an inch in diameter) was designed which required the rat to maintain his head and ears in a restricted volume when nosing it.

Another approach used to locate the animal in a specified volume when tone signals are presented requires the rat to place his head through a metal ring. As the rat's head penetrates through the hoop it breaks a beam of light directed at a photocell. If the rat remains in this position for the required time (it is changed from trial to trial), a tone appears during which he can withdraw from the ring and receive reinforcement. If the rat withdraws before the onset of the tone, the timer is reset and the rat has to hold his head in position that much longer (Hack, 1966).

MONKEY CHAIR

In some studies, monkeys were not restrained but tested in a free-field situation (Harris, 1943; Seiden, 1958; Fujita and Elliott, 1965); in others, the monkey was restrained and the sound delivered through earphones (Stebbins et al., 1966). The advantage of this latter procedure is that the sound field does not change during a session as it does for an unrestrained monkey tested in a free-field situation. Great care must be taken, however, in attaching the earphones to the animal at each session since a small change in location of the earphone relative to the ear can change the sound drastically.

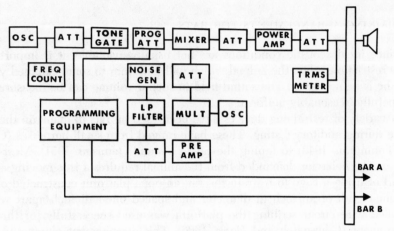

Fig. 16. Block diagram of auditory and programming equipment.

Restraint of the monkey in a chair and delivery of acoustic signals through an earphone was described earlier and is shown in Figures 4 through 7.

SOUND GENERATING EQUIPMENT

The production of pure tones and noise is achieved by standard electronic equipment and transducers. The various components are depicted in Figure 16. When the tracking method is used, the "prog att" block represents a recording attenuator which changes attenuation levels in fixed decibel steps under the command of the programming equipment. Similarly, when the method of constant stimuli is used, the "prog att" block represents five or six attenuators set with different attenuations which are introduced at random into the signal circuit by the programming equipment. The transducer shown in Figure 16 represents either an earphone (PDR-10) and coupler used with the monkeys or a speaker used with the rats.

NARROW BAND NOISE

For the investigation of critical ratios in rats, wide band noise was necessary and was supplied by a standard commercial noise generator. The noise was sent through a band-pass filter to limit it to that portion of the spectrum over which the response of the transducer was reasonably uniform.

Critical band measurement in monkeys required the use of narrow bands of noise. A system was developed for the generation of narrow bands of noise which could be centered about any frequency up to 35,000 Hz (Palin and Gourevitch, 1970). In this system, a solid state analog multiplier was used instead of the ring modulator which had been used previously in a similar arrangement (Greenwood,

1961a). The multiplier functioned as a suppressed carrier modulator and was used in conjunction with a low-pass filter, a noise generator, and a sine wave oscillator (Fig. 16). To produce narrow bands of noise centered about the carrier frequency, broad band noise was sent through a low-pass filter which served to control the width of the noise applied to one input of the multiplier. The other input to the multiplier came from the sine wave generator (carrier frequency). The product of these two inputs appeared at the multiplier output as two adjacent bands of noise each equal in width to the noise applied to the multiplier and extending from 5 Hz above and 5 Hz below the carrier frequency. Any change in carrier frequency shifted the noise correspondingly. The 10 Hz "hole" around the carrier was due to the characteristic of the noise generator whose output decreased rapidly below 5 Hz. The low-pass filter attenuated the noise above the cutoff frequency at a rate of 84 dB per octave. When this low-pass noise was shifted to higher frequencies it preserved the roll-off imposed by the low-pass filter; since an octave at low frequencies represents only a small portion of an octave at high frequencies, the skirts of the translated noise were very sharp indeed. As the noise was shifted to higher frequencies, the slope of the skirts became sharper still. Finally, the suppressed carrier function of the multiplier was measured with a wave analyzer. The carrier signal was found to be 40 to 45 dB below the sideband amplitude for all frequencies up to 35 kHz.

CALIBRATION PROCEDURES

Measurement of sound is a delicate procedure and is especially difficult at high frequencies. Yet, the hearing of most mammals which have been investigated until now exceed the upper frequency limits of man. It is, therefore, necessary to develop careful calibrating procedures for these measurements.

Calibrated microphones include two sets of calibrations: free-field and pressure responses over the frequency range of the microphone. The pressure response indicates the sound pressure that impinges on the microphone. The free-field response is a measure which takes into account the disturbance in the sound field produced by the presence of the microphone and indicates the sound pressure which would exist at the location of the microphone if it were not there. At low frequencies the two responses are essentially identical. However, at frequencies whose wavelengths approximate the dimensions of the microphone, the two measures are quite different. The sound field is seriously disturbed by the microphone. This diffraction effect depends upon the angle of incidence of the sound upon the microphone. At 90° (grazing) incidence, the free-field response remains more nearly constant than at other angles.

Although the preferred measure would be the sound pressure impinging at the eardrum of the subject, this is almost never achieved, especially in intact animals. When animals are free to move in a sound field, pressure response measurements are usually made at various locations in the sound field and the average of these measurements used to represent the sound pressure of the field. However, this measurement does not indicate how the sound field will be disturbed by the animal and what the sound pressure will be at the eardrum when he enters the sound field. In experiments in which the animal's position is fixed with regard to the sound source, sound pressure measurements are usually made at the entrance to the external meatus.

PROGRAMMING AND RECORDING EQUIPMENT

More and more investigations in animal auditory psychophysics are conducted automatically. The use of relays or solid state logic modules to construct programming circuits that control the presentation of stimuli, record the animal's responses, and change experimental conditions when necessary is widespread. Since the manufacture of these components is constantly changing and diversifying, it is impossible to select any one configuration of these modules as most appropriate.

SOME SOURCES OF ERROR

Measurement of the harmonic content of the signal is important. A tone that is not audible at its fundamental frequency can have harmonics which can be audible especially if they fall in the more sensitive portion of the threshold function of the animal. If possible, it is advisable to place a band-pass filter after the oscillator. By selecting the pass band appropriately, the harmonic content of the signal is eliminated.

For threshold measurement, it is important to have gradual onset and offset of the tone to prevent transients which would be audible. The animal could respond to the audible transient whereas if the tone had been turned on gradually, the transient would have been inaudible.

Great care must be taken to be sure that no transient is generated by the programming equipment, e.g., stepping motors, solenoids. Such transients often induce a click at the speaker, and if they are time-locked with the onset of the tone they will serve as a cue to the animal that a trial is starting. These transients are often very soft and hard to detect.

Often the particular behavior required of the animal may produce excessive noise which distorts measurement of the absolute threshold. For example, the microswitch attached to a bar will produce a loud click when it is tripped by the rat's bar press. A rat pressing at high rates will generate in this way a masking noise. Thus, the transducer for the animal's response must be designed to be very quiet even when handled roughly by the animal, e.g., nose target (Gourevitch and Cole, 1963).

SUMMARY

The methods described above have been quite effective in measuring absolute and masked thresholds in normal animals. These procedures have also been used successfully in the measurement of hearing loss induced in rats by ototoxic agents. Thus, the broad applicability of these methods appears to be supported.

Which procedure is preferable, the method of constant stimuli or the tracking method, depends to a large extent on the time available for training. The method of constant stimuli is much more quickly trained. After one month of training, rats will report thresholds consistently from day to day and often can be tested twice a day. The tracking method, on the other hand, requires many months of training before reliable thresholds can be obtained. If, however, investigation of an auditory phenomenon with rapid changes in time, such as temporary threshold shifts, is desired, then the tracking method is better suited.

In the future these methods may be used in the determination of auditory functions in other species, thus contributing to "comparative audition." These techniques will also probably be very useful in the investigations of neurophysiologic activity underlying sensory detection, especially in those studies concerned with simultaneous neural and behavioral measurement of sensory detection.

REFERENCES

Ash, P. 1951. The sensory capacities of infrahuman mammals: vision, audition, gustation. Psychol. Bull., 48:289–326.

Barrow, S., E. Luschei, M. Nathan, and C. Saslow. 1966. A training technique for the daily chairing of monkeys. J. Exp. Anal. Behav., 9:680.

Behar, I., J. N. Cronholm, and M. Loeb. 1965. Auditory sensitivity of the rhesus monkey. J. Comp. Physiol. Psychol., 59:426–428.

Békésy, G. von. 1947. A new audiometer. Acta Otolaryng. (Stockholm), 35:411–422.

——— and W. A. Rosenblith. 1951. The mechanical properties of the ear. *In* S. S. Stevens, ed. Handbook of Experimental Psychology, New York, John Wiley & Sons, Inc., pp. 1075–1115.

Berlin, C. I. 1963. Hearing in mice via GSR audiometry. J. Speech Hearing Res., 6:359–368.

Blackwell, H. R., and H. Schlosberg. 1943. Octave generalization, pitch discrimination, and loudness thresholds in the white rat. J. Exp. Psychol., 33:407–419.

Bos, C. E., and E. de Boer. 1966. Masking and discrimination. J. Acoust. Soc. Amer., 39:708–715.

Clack, T. D., and J. D. Harris. 1963. Auditory thresholds in the rat by a two-lever technique. J. Aud. Res., 3:53–63.

——— and P. N. Herman. 1963. A single-lever psychophysical adjustment procedure for measuring auditory thresholds in the monkey. J. Aud. Res., 3:175–183.

Cowles, J. T., and L. A. Pennington. 1943. An improved technique for determining auditory acuity of the rat. J. Psychol., 15: 41–47.

Crowley, D. E., M. C. Hepp-Reymond, D. Tabowitz, and J. Palin. 1965. Cochlear potentials in the albino rat. J. Aud. Res., 5:307–316.

Eccher, W. 1942. Comparative thresholds of pitch and intensity in rat, dog and man. Paper delivered at the meetings of the Eastern Psychological Association.

Elder, J. H. 1934. Auditory acuity of the chimpanzee. J. Comp. Psychol., 17:157–183.

Feldtkeller, R., and E. Zwicker. 1956. Das Ohr als Nachrichtenempfänger, Stuttgart, Hirzel.

Fletcher, H. 1929. Speech and Hearing, New York, D. Van Nostrand Co., Inc.

——— 1940. Auditory patterns. Rev. Mod. Physics, 12:47–65.

——— and W. A. Munson. 1937. Relation between loudness and masking. J. Acoust. Soc. Amer., 9:1–10.

Fujita, S., and D. N. Elliott. 1965. Thresholds of audition for three species of monkey. J. Acoust. Soc. Amer., 37:139–144.

Gould, J., and C. T. Morgan. 1942. Auditory sensitivity in the rat. J. Comp. Psychol., 34:321–329.

Gourevitch, G. 1965. Auditory masking in the rat. J. Acoust. Soc. Amer., 37:439–443.

——— and B. Cole. 1963. A manipulandum for use with rats responding to auditory stimuli. J. Exp. Anal. Behav., 6:413–414.

——— and M. H. Hack. 1966. Audibility in the rat. J. Comp. Physiol. Psychol., 62:289–291.

——— M. H. Hack, and J. E. Hawkins. 1960. Auditory thresholds in the rat measured by an operant technique. Science, 131:1046–1047.

Green, D. M. 1965. Masking with two tones. J. Acoust. Soc. Amer., 37:802–813.

Greenwood, D. N. 1961a. Auditory masking and the critical band. J. Acoust. Soc Amer., 33:484–502.

——— 1961b. Critical bandwidth and the frequency coordinates of the basilar membrane. J. Acoust. Soc. Amer., 33:1344–1356.

Hack, M. 1966. Receiver operating characteristics in the rat. J. Aud. Res., 6:229–234.

Hamilton, P. M. 1957. Noise masked thresholds as a function of tonal duration and masking noise bandwidth. J. Acoust. Soc. Amer., 29:506–511.

Harris, J. D. 1943. The auditory acuity of preadolescent monkeys. J. Comp. Psychol., 35:255–265.

Hawkins, J. E., and S. S. Stevens. 1950. The masking of pure tones and of speech by white noise. J. Acoust. Soc. Amer., 22:6–13.

Henry, F. M. 1938. Audition in the white rat. III. Absolute and relative thresholds. J. Comp. Psychol., 26:45–62.

Hunter, W. S. 1927. Further data on the auditory sensitivity of the white rat. Pedag. Sem., 34:177–187.

Jamison, J. H. 1951. Measurement of auditory intensity thresholds in the rat by conditioning of an autonomic response. J. Comp. Physiol. Psychol., 44:118–125.

Johnson, C. S. 1968. Masked tonal thresholds in the bottlenosed porpoise. J. Acoust. Soc. Amer., 44:965–967.

Licklider, J. C. R. 1951. Basic correlates of the auditory stimulus. In S. S. Stevens, ed. Handbook of Experimental Psychology, New York, John Wiley & Sons, Inc., pp. 985–1039.

Miller, J. D. 1964. Auditory sensitivity of the chinchilla in quiet and in noise. J. Acoust. Soc. Amer., 36:2010. (Abstr.)

Munn, N. L. 1950. Handbook of Psychological Research on the Rat, Boston, Houghton Mifflin Company.

Palin, J., and G. Gourevitch. 1970. An improved narrowband noise source. Electroenceph. Clin. Neurophysiol. (In press.)

Plomp, R., and W. J. M. Levelt. 1965. Tonal consonance and critical bandwidth. J. Acoust. Soc. Amer., 38:548–560.

Ratliff, F., and D. S. Blough. 1954. Behavioral studies of visual processes in the pigeon. USN, ONR, Tech. Rep., Contract N5 ori-07663, Proj. NR 140–072.

Schafer, T. H., R. S. Gales, C. A. Shewmaker, and P. O. Thompson. 1950. The frequency selectivity of the ear as determined by masking experiments. J. Acoust. Soc. Amer., 22:490–496.

Scharf, B. 1966. Critical bands: Special Report, LSC-S-3. Laboratory of Sensory Communication, Syracuse University.

Seiden, H. R. 1958. Auditory acuity of the marmoset monkey (Hapale jacchus). Ph.D. dissertation, Princeton University, Univ. Microfilms, Inc., Ann Arbor, Mich.

Semenoff, W. A., and F. A. Young. 1964. Comparison of the auditory acuity of man and monkey. J. Comp. Physiol. Psychol., 57:89–93.

Stebbins, W. C. 1970. Hearing. *In* Schrier, A. M. and F. Stollnitz, eds. Behavior of Nonhuman Primates, New York, Academic Press, Inc., vol. 3.

———— S. Green, and F. L. Miller. 1966. Auditory sensitivity of the monkey. Science, 153:1646–1647.

Stevens, S. S., and H. Davis. 1938. Hearing, New York, John Wiley & Sons, Inc.

Watson, C. S. 1963. Masking of tones by noise for the cat. J. Acoust. Soc. Amer., 35:167–172.

Wendt, G. R. 1934. Auditory acuity of monkeys. Comp. Psychol. Monogr., 10:1–51.

Zwicker, E., G. Flottorp, and S. S. Stevens. 1957. Critical band width in loudness summation. J. Acoust. Soc. Amer., 29:548–557.

BARBARA A. RAY [1]

5

PSYCHOPHYSICAL TESTING OF NEUROLOGIC MUTANT MICE *

INTRODUCTION

In taking psychophysical measurements of animals, the tester cannot simply tell his subjects what behavior he requires. Nothing is accomplished by saying to a mouse: "Tell me whenever you hear the tone." The tester must use nonverbal methods to teach the animal to respond to the test stimuli, and only the test stimuli. The experimenter's choice of indicator response and teaching method will, to some degree, influence the psychophysical measurements obtained. For example, one response may have a higher "false alarm" rate than another. A high false alarm rate will lower threshold measures. It may be more difficult to train one response than another. The complexity of the training procedure will restrict the number of animals that can be tested in a given time. These variables can be manipulated over a wide range by the experimenter, who will choose his method to suit his particular purpose.

The methods described in this chapter were developed for the neurologically diseased mouse. These mice have suffered single-gene mutations which affect the form and function of the nervous system. The mutation can be viewed as an experimental manipulation that deranges the normal nervous system in a specific and repeatable way. The available mice (Jackson Memorial Laboratories, Bar Harbor, Maine) rival the fruitfly in their range and purity of genotypes. The neurologic mutant is a natural subject for behavioral study since behavior is an expression of nervous function.

Since many of the neurologic mutant mice suffer from muscular weakness and incoordination, a response was selected to be effortless and available to any mouse that had survived weaning, i.e., a licking response.

[1] Neurology Research, Massachusetts General Hospital, Boston, Massachusetts.

* This research was supported by U.S.P.H.S. research grant MH-05408 from the National Institute of Mental Health.

BASELINE BEHAVIORS

CONTROLLING BODY WEIGHT

When a mouse arrived in the laboratory, it was weighed on a regular schedule, usually daily, and fed a varied diet to be sure that it was not deprived of food. Some of the neurologic mutants have sufficiently poor coordination to interfere with their eating certain foods properly. For example, a hyperactive, circling mutant, called Kreisler, lived in a cage with a food-filled trough suspended from the wall of its cage. The food was formed into rectangular blocks that the mouse could reach through the coarse wire mesh of the trough. When one of the food blocks was accidentally dropped on the floor of its cage, the Kreisler mouse immediately began to eat it. From then on, the mouse was fed by putting food blocks on the floor of its cage and the mouse began to gain weight. The weight stabilized at a higher value that showed the animal had previously been sustained at only 80 percent of its free-feeding body weight. Establishing what constitutes free feeding for these neurologic mutants requires some experimentation with variables such as type of food (solid, powder, or liquid); placement of food (on the wall or on the floor); and cage-mate competition, which is easily eliminated by placing mice in individual cages.

Weight control, which is a fairly trivial problem in animals the size of monkeys or rats, can be exceedingly difficult in an animal the size of a mouse. A fat mouse is likely to weigh no more than 25 to 30 g. A half a gram is upwards of 2 percent of the total body weight of most of the mice run in these experiments. The situation is further complicated since mice do not have an immediate weight reaction to changes in their daily food intake. If a mouse's daily ration is reduced by 25 percent, it may take 2 or 3 days for the mouse to show any drop in weight. If, during the 2 days, further decreases are made in the daily ration, the mouse will later lose weight at an alarming rate. A precipitous drop in weight can lead to overfeeding during the next 2 days before the weight trend reverses. Until this phenomenon was discovered, the weights of the mice tended to oscillate over an unacceptably wide range.

When a mouse seems as well-fed and healthy as proper feeding and fairly constant room temperature can accomplish, it is fed a measured quantity of food each day to determine the quantity necessary to maintain free-feeding body weight. With this quantity established, the mouse is put into an anechoic chamber containing the test cubicle (Fig. 1) just before its usual feeding time. The anechoic chamber, model 444–250–2 Eckel Corporation, tended to absorb, not reflect, sound waves incident upon its walls. An anechoic chamber was used in anticipation of testing the mouse for sensitivity to high frequency tones that can reflect sharply off small surfaces and make it difficult to specify sound intensity at a given point in the chamber. An ancillary benefit of using the anechoic chamber was a 60 to 65 dB drop in noise through the walls of the chamber. This all but

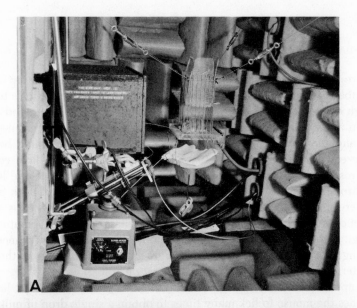

Fig. 1A. Anechoic chamber containing test cubicle, center, electrostatic speaker, left, and milk-filled infusion pump, below speaker.
Fig. 1B. Enlargement of test cubicle and mouse in 1A. Note the position of the mouse's ears while licking at the tube.

eliminated the possibility of a mouse responding to signals that emanated from the automatic programming equipment.

The time between a mouse's arrival and its first day in the test cubicle can vary between a week and several months, depending upon the animal's robustness when it arrives.

LICKING BASELINE

Figure 1 shows a mouse, enlarged in Figure 1A, licking the tip of a long slender tube that terminates just outside the testing cubicle. The tube terminates far enough outside the cubicle that a mouse licking it has its head, and therefore its ears, in a restricted position. The tube position automatically ensures a fairly constant alignment of the mouse's ears with a sound source located behind the tube. The end of the tube is ball-shaped and contains a small hole continuous with the rest of the tube. The tube may be traced in Figure 1 to the left of the cubicle through a downward bend, obscured in the picture, and back to the left again where it attaches to a hypodermic syringe. The syringe contains a mixture of sweetened condensed milk, water, and multivitamins. The apparatus holding the syringe is a motor-operated infusion pump (Harvard Apparatus model 1100) for pushing a small amount of milk through the tube. The size of the drop of milk is determined by the length of motor operation.

This apparatus for delivering milk into the mouth of a mouse that licks at the tube teaches the mouse to lick many times to obtain a single drop of milk. At first, the mouse is attracted by a drop of the milk mixture hanging from the end of the tube. When the mouse licks the tube, more drops of milk are delivered. Almost immediately, the apparatus is set to deliver a drop on the average of every sixteenth lick. The mouse continues to lick on this schedule until it lets 15 or more minutes go by without responding, when it is removed and fed. Following this session, the mouse's weight is gradually reduced and the average number of licks required per drop is increased. Weights and response ratios are selected that produce steady licking for 1 hour. There is no way to predict exactly what these values will be for a given mouse. Some mice run beautifully at 90 percent of their free-feeding weights, while others must be brought down to 75 percent. Some mice will respond continuously when the average number of licks required is 48; others may be most reliable at 96 or even 200. Here, and at every other phase of investigating these mutant mice, the parameters of each procedure must be tailored to individual mice.

Figure 2 is a record obtained from a Reeler mutant after its baseline parameters had been determined. The name Reeler, as with the names of many mutant strains, derives from the motor disturbance apparent in the animal's gait. The mouse in Figure 2 had difficulty walking for more than an inch in the same direction, frequently fell down, made writhing and shaking movements in all four limbs, and displayed general muscular weakness. Histologic examination of Reeler cerebral and cerebellar cortex have revealed severe cell disorganization, apparently the result of incomplete granule and Purkinje cell cross-migration during early cortical development (Sidman, 1968). It is thought that the locus of the Reeler allele may normally control the cross-migration of granule and Purkinje cells. Falconer (1951) observed that Reeler mice failed to fight with strange adult mice and suggested that Reeler might be a "retarded" mouse. Nevertheless, this

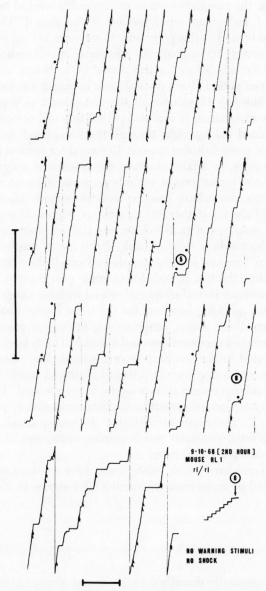

9·10·68 [2ND HOUR]
MOUSE RL 1
rl/rl

⑤   ①   ⑧

NO WARNING STIMULI
NO SHOCK

Fig. 2. Cumulative curve of stable licking. The height of each full excursion is 371 licks and the time interval marked below the curve is 3 min. The auxilliary recorder, lower right, indicates stable responding during test periods by making an upward step. Test period 8 yielded no stability decision, since the mouse stopped licking before the test period began.

mouse was able to maintain a steady licking rate with little difficulty. In Figure 2, each lick at the tube moved a pen up the paper by a very small amount until 371 licks had been made when the pen reset to the bottom of the paper. Time moved the paper to the left 1 cm every minute. Thus, the slope of this cumulative curve represents the rate at which the mouse licked: the steeper, the faster.

Every so often, the cumulative curve in Figure 2 is marked by a pair of dots at the beginning and end of an offset section of the record. These offsets mark 1-minute test periods used at this point only to measure licking stability, but to be used later for presenting test signals. An automatic circuit compared the mouse's licking rate for 30 seconds before the test period to the licking rate during the last 15 seconds of the test period. Since the indicator response was going to be a pause in licking during the last 15 seconds of the test period, it was imperative that licking be steadily maintained in any test period that did not contain a signal. If the mouse maintained licking right through the test period, licking was judged stable. If the mouse paused during the last 15 seconds of the test period, the pause was judged a detection, or a false alarm in the absence of a signal. If the mouse paused before the test period began, no judgment was made about licking during the test period, since the licking baseline was temporarily missing. An auxiliary recorder, its record shown at the bottom right of Figure 2, registered each stability decision by making a step. If licking was stable before and during the test period, the recorder made a step upward. If the mouse paused during the test period, the auxiliary recorder made a step downward. If the mouse paused during the 30 seconds before the test period, for example period eight, this prevented a decision and the auxiliary record simply advanced without a step.

Figure 3 shows a licking baseline, for the same Reeler, that was not stable. During this session, there was a programming error that prevented milk from being delivered between the points marked *a* and *b*. The licking became irregular and this was reflected in the auxiliary record, periods four, five, and six. Period five is another case of no-decision. This record illustrates nicely the rapidity with which licking restabilizes once a disrupting factor is removed. The irregular licking baseline in Figure 3 was obtained in the hour immediately prior to the stable baseline in Figure 2. The drops of milk that the mouse drank in the first hour contributed to the satiation effects just beginning at the end of the second hour, Figure 2, that produced a no-decision.

Licking was considered stable when there were no signs of satiation at the end of a session and no more than one or two false alarms in a session.

CONDITIONED SUPPRESSION

A procedure, originally described by Estes and Skinner (1941) and reviewed by Sidman (1960) and Lyon (1968), was used to suppress licking during 1-minute signal presentations that ended in unavoidable shock. The cessation of licking during a signal indicated the mouse had detected the signal, and thus suppression of licking was the indicator response. Similar techniques have been used extensively at Florida State University at Tallahassee to measure detection of x-irradiation (Morris, 1966), changes in temperature, odors, tones, light flicker, and changes in brightness. An unusual variety of animals has been tested at the Florida State Laboratories, including the slow loris, opossum, hedgehog, and bush-baby (see Chapter 6 by Smith, Table 1). Rosenberger (Chapter 7) has adapted the suppression procedure for measuring visual brightness thresholds in white rats.

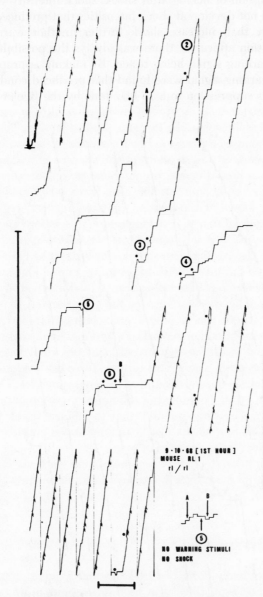

9·10·68 [1ST HOUR]
MOUSE RL 1
rl / rl

NO WARNING STIMULI
NO SHOCK

Fig. 3. Cumulative curve of licking temporarily disrupted between points marked "a" and "b." This record was obtained in the hour immediately preceding the one represented in Figure 2. Test period 4 is an example of a false-alarm "suppression" decision. Response and time scales are the same as in Figure 2.

To establish conditioned suppression, a mouse was run in the usual way and aperiodically an intense signal, for example white noise, was turned on for 1 minute and terminated in brief (100 msec) unavoidable shock. Shock was delivered to the grid floor of the test cubicle by a BRS, model SGS 001, generator-scrambler. If, after several signals, there was no suppression during the warning period and no disruption of licking after shock, shock intensity was increased. If suppression still did not develop at shock intensities that produced suppression in normal mice, rather than increase shock further another warning signal was tried. Until suppression appeared, there was always the possibility a mouse was insensitive to the warning signal being tested. By making appropriate changes, a shock level and a warning signal were found that produced conditioned suppression. Figure 4 shows suppression to a 15 kHz tone by the Reeler mouse, RL 1.

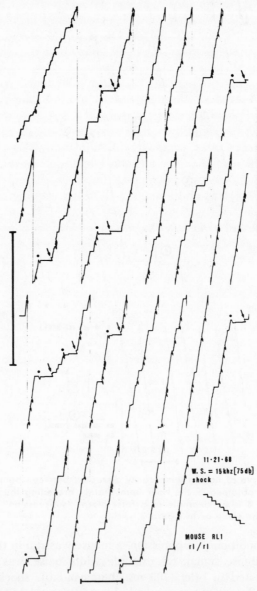

11·21·68
W. S. = 15 khz [75 db]
shock

MOUSE RL1
rl / rl

Fig. 4. Cumulative curve of licking interrupted by conditioned suppression. Each 1 min test period presented a 75 dB tone terminated by unavoidable shock. Shocks are indicated by arrows. The auxilliary recorder indicates "suppression" by making a downward step. All test periods produced suppression. Response and time scales are the same as in Figure 2.

In Figure 4, RL 1 suppressed during almost the entire 1-minute warning period of tone, except for one or two responses at the very beginning of some of the test periods. After several sessions of suppressing, a mouse is likely to learn that the beginning of the 1-minute warning period is "safe." This is indicated when a mouse suppresses only toward the end of the warning period. An example of a well-formed temporal discrimination in a normal mouse is shown in Figure 5. The 1-minute warning periods have been extracted from the cumulative licking curve, and the duration of each pause is indicated in seconds.

To recognize suppression by a mouse with a temporal discrimination, its rate of licking before the warning signal was compared to its rate at the end of the signal, the last 15 seconds. This comparison would also identify suppression lasting the entire warning period. Originally (Sidman et al., 1966), a drop to 12.5 percent of the preperiod rate defined suppression. This value has since been raised, for convenience, to 16 percent. The exact value of the rate criterion makes little or no difference at above-threshold values of a test signal. When signals are presented at near-threshold intensities, a more or less stringent criterion can raise or lower the absolute threshold by a small amount, 2 to 4 dB in the case of auditory signals. In general, other parameters of the suppression procedure, for example, number of signals per session and shock intensity, exert a greater influence on the decisions made for each test period than the decision criterion itself. By either criterion, 12.5 percent or 16 percent, all of the warning signals in Figure 5 produced suppression.

Should a mouse fail to lick during the preperiod, there was no baseline for

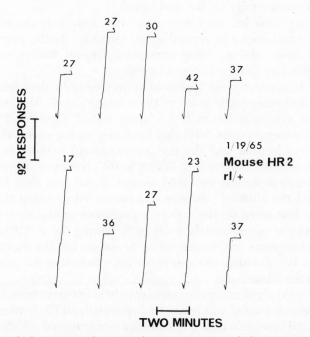

Fig. 5. Test periods for a normal mouse showing a temporal discrimination of the 1 min warning period for unavoidable shock. The shortest suppression interval was 17 sec, the time between the animal's last response and the end of the warning signal. (From Sidman et al., 1966.)

measuring suppression and a no-decision was recorded. Currently, a minimum of nine responses is required in the preperiod to make a decision.

THRESHOLD DETERMINATION

BASIC PROCEDURE

To measure threshold, it was necessary that the mouse lick steadily in the absence of the test signal and suppress during each test signal. When these baseline conditions were met, signal intensity was gradually reduced until suppression to the signal disappeared. The technique of intensity adjustment is similar to that described by Békésy (1947) as a method for obtaining auditory thresholds in humans, and later adapted by Blough (1955) for pigeons. The procedures described by Békésy and Blough provided for continuous tracking of signal intensity. In the conditioned suppression procedure, tracking is done during trials that are scheduled by the experimenter.

The mouse's response to each test signal determined the intensity of the next signal. Three decisions were possible: suppression, no-suppression, and no-decision. If the mouse suppressed, the next signal was attenuated by a predetermined amount. If the mouse did not suppress, the next signal was increased by the same predetermined amount. If the mouse was not licking during the period before the test signal came on, suppression could not be evaluated and no change was made in signal intensity for the next signal.

The auxiliary recorder, used until now to indicate only decisions, was connected to the signal source to control signal intensity. As the pen stepped (i.e., moved) up or down, the recording attenuator, Grason Stadler model E3262A, made a corresponding change in signal intensity.

Figure 6 demonstrates the threshold technique with data from the Reeler mouse, RL 1, and using white noise as the warning signal. The auxiliary record from a baseline session is shown at the upper left of Figure 6. The first seven decisions were no-suppression, indicated by a step up the chart. The eighth test period was a no-decision and the pen moved ahead without stepping up or down. This record, indicating steady licking in the absence of warning signal and shock, is the baseline for the threshold records in the next row. The signal was white noise and the auxiliary recorder was connected to adjust the intensity of the signal. The first seven decisions were suppression, producing seven decreases in noise intensity of approximately 2 dB each. During the eighth and ninth test periods, the white noise was turned off at its source but the shock was left on. The result was two decisions of no-suppression, confirming the mouse had been suppressing to the white noise.

The test period segments of the cumulative licking curves from each threshold session have been extracted and arranged sequentially at the bottom of Figure 6. Periods eight and nine, in which the white noise was turned off, show the mouse responded through the test period, pausing briefly after the unsignalled shock.

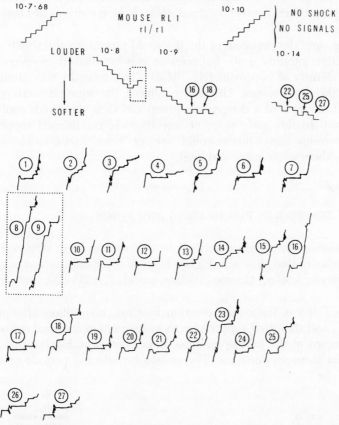

Fig. 6. Procedure for determining threshold intensity. Top row shows nonsuppression baseline without warning signals and without shock. Next row shows threshold obtained by decreasing signal intensity each time the mouse suppressed (and increasing it when the mouse did not suppress). The portions of the cumulative licking curve that include the test periods have been extracted and are shown at the bottom of the figure. The warning signal was turned off and shock left on during test periods 8 and 9.

These probes control for the possibility that the mouse is anticipating the shock by some means other than the intended warning signal. Such probes must be used sparingly because they destroy the exclusive association of warning signal and impending shock.

The second threshold session contains two failures to obtain suppression, periods 16 and 18, and indicates entry into a threshold range of intensities. The licking baseline was reexamined in the next session before continuing with the threshold measurement. The next threshold session contained eight decisions but covered a range of only four steps, indicating a threshold range. The licking during periods 22 and 25 followed a pattern, frequently observed to near threshold intensities, of suppression at the beginning of the warning signal and responding toward the end. This pattern may reflect a real threshold phenomenon of adaptation to weak signals. At some future point, it may be useful to distinguish between this adaptation pattern and uninterrupted licking throughout the warning period. As the decision criteria currently stand, these licking patterns are both called no-suppression.

During early development of the threshold procedure, thresholds were specified in relative intensity units. Suppression was established in several mice to a reference intensity of approximately 104 dB. This intensity was attenuated non-linearly to threshold values. Although nonlinear, the same attenuation series was used for all the mice of a comparison group and their thresholds could therefore be compared. In this early stage of investigation, conditioned suppression was used to determine that a mouse could "see" or "hear," and then to measure relative thresholds to white noise and light.

RELATIVE THRESHOLDS FOR HEARING AND VISION

The relative thresholds described in this section were obtained in an apparatus similar to that shown in Figure 1, but the test cubicle was contained in a modified picnic cooler, Grason Stadler model E3125A-300, not an anechoic chamber.

Figure 7 shows the nonsuppression baseline, acquisition of suppression to white noise, and stabilized suppression to white noise in a normal mouse, 008. The auxiliary record of the licking baseline, upper left, is stable except for one suppression and three no-decisions. The session introducing periods of white noise

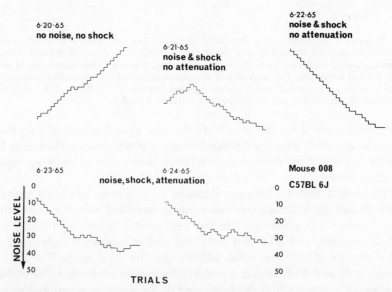

Fig. 7. Nonsuppression baseline, acquisition of conditioned suppression, suppression baseline, and threshold for white noise in a normal mouse. (From Sidman et al., 1966.)

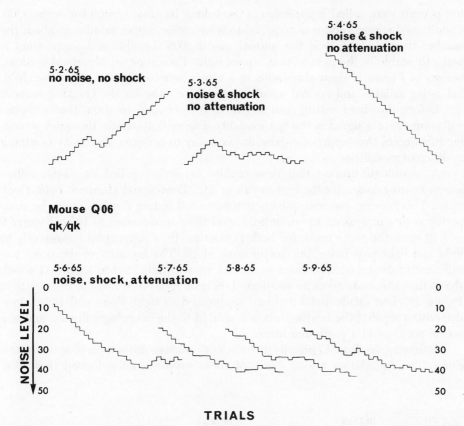

Fig. 8. Same as Figure 7, but subject was a neurologic mutant, quaking, and threshold for white noise was replicated four times instead of two. (From Sidman et al., 1966.)

terminated by shock, upper middle, shows the acquisition of conditioned suppression as the change in direction of the auxiliary record. These records established that the mouse could "hear" and was able to learn the conditioned suppression.

The next session, upper right, shows stabilized suppression to white noise except for a few no-decisions at the end of the record, and is the necessary baseline for threshold testing. Threshold was tested in two sessions, using the auxiliary recorder to attenuate the white noise, which gave comparable results. Threshold lay between the numbers 30 and 40 as they were marked on the chart. These numbers do not refer to absolute sound pressure level in decibels, but rather to the series of nonlinear steps of attenuation from a fixed intensity. Thus, each position on the chart represented a constant, but unknown, sound pressure level.

Figure 8 shows the results of the same procedures for a neurologic mutant called Quaking. The outstanding clinical feature of the Quaking strain is pronounced body tremor that can be stopped by body contact with stable environmental objects. Quaking mice have frequent seizures lasting a few seconds. Perhaps because of these seizures, the licking baseline, upper left of Figure 8, is not quite as stable in Quaking as in the normal mouse, Figure 7. Five out of 28 test periods were called suppression in the licking baseline session for mouse Q06. Conditioned suppression was acquired to white noise, upper middle, in about the number of periods it took the normal mouse, 008. Conditioned suppression is perfectly stable in the next session, upper right. Four separate threshold sessions, bottom of Figure 8, show thresholds in a range between 30 and 40 on the chart, indicating reliable and normal sensitivity to white noise for the Quaking mutant.

Before threshold testing can begin, it is necessary to show that a mouse will suppress to a signal in the test modality. Figure 9 illustrates the quick screening function of the suppression baseline as a way to compare sensitivity to stimuli in different modalities.

A neurologic mutant that runs rapidly in circles, called Pirouette, suffers severe hearing loss after the first month of life (Davies and Harmon, 1948; Deol, 1956). This hearing loss was quickly demonstrated in two Pirouette mice by comparing their suppression to white noise and their suppression to light. Figures 9 and 10 show the same result for both Pirouettes: they suppressed consistently to light and light plus noise, but not to noise alone. The intensity of the noise was sufficient to produce suppression in normal mice as indicated in Figure 11 which shows the same tests given an unaffected, heterozygous littermate of the mouse in Figure 10. The unaffected littermate suppressed to light alone and noise alone demonstrating that the hearing loss was related to the neurologic disease and was not an accident of a particular litter.

Referring back to Figure 9, this Pirouette mouse did suppress to noise five times. The cumulative licking curve of these suppressions indicated they were

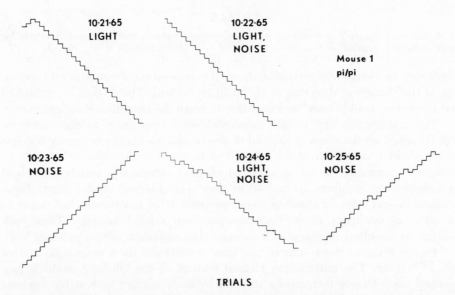

Fig. 9. In the pirouette mutant mouse, acquisition of conditioned suppression is shown for light and light-plus-noise, but not for noise alone. Suppression to light demonstrates the mouse is capable of making the association between a warning signal and impending shock. (From Sidman et al., 1966.)

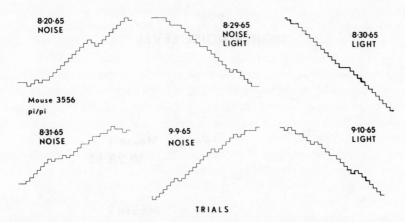

Fig. 10. Same as Figure 9, but a different pirouette mouse. (From Sidman et al., 1966.)

genuine since they were not accompanied by a deteriorating baseline. This feeble indication of hearing prompted a test of three Pirouette mice using a white noise signal of higher intensity. The results were positive and are shown in Figure 12. Using this higher noise level as the reference intensity, thresholds were compared from four Pirouette mice and one normal mouse, a littermate to the Pirouette animals. In Figure 13, the Pirouettes all had thresholds just above the intensity that had been used in the original suppression tests. The unaffected mouse had a much lower threshold which is probably comparable to the thresholds for the normal and the Quaking mice treated earlier. The change in reference intensity, however, makes a direct comparison impossible.

Since the intensity of white noise required to produce suppression in the Pirouette mice was so high, it was possible that the mice had detected the signals as vibration in the tactile modality. A histologic examination of the cochleas of two Pirouettes and the unaffected littermate helped to confirm that the Pirouettes had heard, rather than felt, the white noise. Dr. R. J. Ruben (see Sidman et al., 1966, for illustrations and procedure) examined the cochleas in detail and his findings are summarized in Table 1. Compared to the unaffected

Fig. 11. A normal mouse, heterozygous for the pirouette gene. Suppression is learned to light, noise-plus-light, and noise alone warning signals. (From Sidman et al., 1966.)

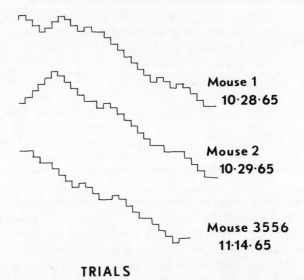

Fig. 12. Acquisition, by pirouette mice, of conditioned suppression to white noise of a higher intensity than that used in Figures 9, 10, and 11. (From Sidman et al., 1966.)

TABLE 1

Number of Cells [a] *in Each Quarter of the Cochlea*

MOUSE	AGE (DAYS)	COCHLEAR REGION	INNER HAIR CELLS	OUTER HAIR CELLS	GANGLION CELLS
3 (*pi*/+)	160	Base–¼	13	5	513
		¼–½	46	136	884
		½–¾	35	119	850
		¾–apex	40	122	377
1 (*pi*/*pi*)	160	Base–¼	0	0	101
		¼–½	3	0	234
		½–¾	18	4	455
		¾–apex	18	11	277
3556 (*pi*/*pi*)	239	Base–¼	0	0	101
		¼–½	0	0	144
		½–¾	8	0	302
		¾–apex	15	11	259

a *The cochleas were cut at 10μ and every fourth section was examined.*

littermate, mouse 3, the two Pirouettes show degeneration of all three cell types, the inner and outer hair cells, and ganglion cells. The degeneration is concentrated at the basal end of the cochlea, which should correlate with a hearing loss of middle and high frequencies. This histologic evidence may eventually be corroborated by audiograms for individual Pirouette mice.

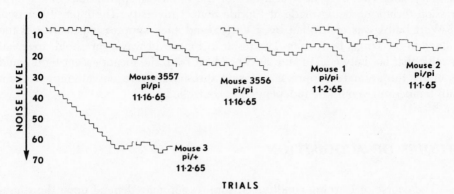

Fig. 13. Relative threshold for white noise in four pirouette mice, and one normal control. (From Sidman et al., 1966.)

Evidence for hearing has been obtained in the following strains: the normal, *C57BL/6J*; the Quaking mutant, *qk/qk*; the unaffected carrier of Pirouette, *pi/+*; the Pirouette mutant, *pi/pi*; the unaffected carrier of Reeler, *rl/+*; the Reeler mutant, *rl/rl*; the normal Himalayan, c^h/c^h; and a Baggs Albino, *BALB/cGn*. No evidence of hearing has been found in the Kreisler mutant, *kr/kr*, using white noise of 95 dB. This mutant suffers malformation of the inner ear starting in embryonic life and is missing the cochlear branch of the auditory nerve.

Evidence for vision has been obtained in the following strains: the normal *C57BL/6J*; the unaffected carrier of Pirouette, *pi/+*; the mutant Pirouette, *pi/pi*; the Kreisler mutant, *kr/kr*; the normal Himalayan, c^h/c^h; and the Reeler mutant, *rl/rl*.

Before the preliminary apparatus was superceded by a more complex system to deliver pure tones, a visual brightness threshold was taken for the unaffected, heterozygous Pirouette, mouse 3. The procedure was intended merely to demon-

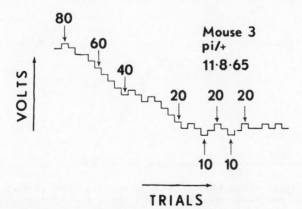

Fig. 14. Relative brightness threshold in a normal mouse, heterozygous for the pirouette gene. Numbers on the record indicate the voltages supplied to the warning-signal lamp. (From Sidman et al., 1966.)

strate that conditioned suppression could be used to test thresholds in another modality, since we were not yet aware of the extensive applications of the suppression technique being made at Florida State University. The intensity of two, 7.5-Watt bulbs was controlled by a Variac, and each suppression decreased the voltage to the lamps by 5 volts. The result in Figure 14 was a threshold, specified in volts, that lay between 10 and 20. Since heat from the incandescent light could be cuing the animal's suppression, visual thresholds were not attempted again until temperature could be independently controlled.

STUDIES OF ACQUISITION

The course of learning conditioned suppression may depend upon the stimulus and the mouse being tested. Mice may acquire conditioned suppression more or less rapidly depending on their threshold sensitivity to the test stimulus, their unconditioned reaction to the stimulus, or their ability to associate the stimulus with impending shock. Any of these might be related to an inbred neurologic abnormality.

Figure 15 shows the different reactions to white noise of three strains of mice:

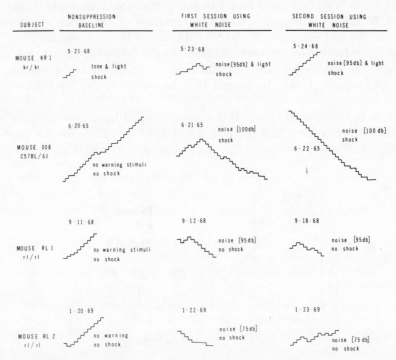

Fig. 15. Three different reactions to a white noise warning signal in the Kreisler mouse, a normal mouse, and two Reeler mice. The Kreisler mouse does not suppress to white noise that signals impending shock, the normal mouse does, and the Reeler mice suppress to white noise without benefit of shock.

Kreisler, *C57BL/6J*, and Reeler. The left column shows the nonsuppression base-lines of the mice. Note the difference in conditions during the nonsuppression session for the Kreisler mouse and the other two strains. The Kreisler mouse, KR 1, although not suppressing, was warned of impending shock by a tone-plus-light combination. Only a small number of test periods were scheduled for KR 1 to limit the number of apparently "unsignalled" shocks and preserve the licking baseline. The number of warning signals and shocks was increased slightly in its following sessions, causing a temporary disruption of licking. The second mouse, 008, was a normal animal and it was expected to lick steadily despite frequent interruptions by warning signals and shocks, so a large number of test periods were scheduled during the nonsuppression session. The bottom two mice in Figure 15 were Reelers. A conservative number of test periods was planned for these animals, since the effect of shock, either signalled or unsignalled, on their licking was not known.

The three strains of mice represent three different reactions to the white noise signal. The first and second sessions of white noise are shown for each mouse in the second and third columns of Figure 15. Note that the normal mouse, 008, quickly learned to suppress to the white noise signal. By the second session, the normal mouse suppressed from the start of the session to the end, which contained an occasional no-decision. This is the most familiar course of acquisition of conditioned suppression.

NONSUPPRESSION: FAILURE TO DETECT OR TO ASSOCIATE SIGNAL WITH SHOCK

The Kreisler mouse still did not suppress when white noise was substituted for tone in its warning signal complex. The no-decisions and suppressions during the first session of white noise reflect a general disruption of the licking baseline produced by an increased number of test periods and, therefore, shocks. This disruption of the licking baseline was gone in the second session of white noise and KR 1 licked steadily through all of the white-noise-plus-light signals. The Kreisler mouse was either insensitive to these stimuli, or was unable to learn the conditioned suppression. Until suppression was demonstrated in Kreisler, there would be no way to decide whether the mouse was insensitive to stimuli in several modalities, or simply unable to make the association between a warning signal and impending shock. The top left record, in Figure 16, shows that KR 1 did not suppress when shock was signalled by tone-plus-light. The next two sessions established that KR 1 also did not suppress to noise-plus-light. The left record in the second row demonstrates that KR 1 did not suppress to cage-tremble without shock (cf. HIM 1 below), and the next two records show suppression developing to cage-tremble when it was terminated by shock. This was the first indication that Kreisler could make the association between a signal and impending shock. The change from nonsuppression to suppression when cage-tremble was associated with shock indicates KR 1 "learned" something.

It is evident from Figure 16 that Kreisler's conditioned suppression to cage-

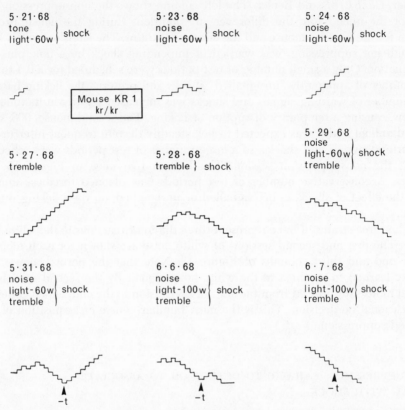

Fig. 16. Establishing that the Kreisler mouse can learn to associate a warning signal with impending shock. Kreisler failed to suppress to tone, light (60 W), and white noise when these signalled shock. Kreisler did not suppress to cage-tremble until it signalled impending shock. Using cage-tremble to maintain suppression, the reaction was transferred to light (100 W).

tremble tended to disappear at the beginning of consecutive sessions. This may be a gross indication of a learning or retention deficit associated with the Kreisler neurologic syndrome. Since suppression was difficult to maintain in KR 1, any combination of signals that maintained suppression was used to start a session and the critical component was identified through a process of elimination. The bottom left record in Figure 16 shows what happened when cage-tremble was removed from a complex warning signal of noise, light, and cage-tremble. Suppression stopped immediately when cage-tremble was removed, identifying it as the controlling stimulus.

The intensity of light was increased by replacing the 60-watt houselight with a 100-watt houselight. With a higher intensity light included in the warning signal complex, removing cage-tremble abolished suppression for only two periods and then suppression reappeared (bottom middle of Fig. 16). When the same procedure was repeated in the next session, the removal of cage-tremble did not disrupt suppression. Presumably, suppression had transferred to the 100-watt light.

The general procedure of pairing a sufficient with an insufficient stimulus may be viewed as either a testing or teaching procedure. Viewed as a teaching procedure, it seems important to ask whether teaching KR 1 to suppress to the 100-watt light might not also have taught it to suppress to the lower intensity of 60-watts. Unfortunately, KR 1 died after the last record shown in Figure 16. Had the animal lived, each signal that produced suppression would have been removed, in its turn, from the signal complex to test for possible transfer to the stimuli that remained.

SUPPRESSION: DETECTION WITHOUT ASSOCIATING SIGNAL AND SHOCK

The Reeler mice, RL 1 and RL 2, suppressed to white noise without benefit of shock, indicating an unconditioned reaction to noise. RL 1 suppressed to a 95 dB noise and RL 2 to a 75 dB noise. The unconditioned reaction to noise apparently did not depend on extremely high intensity. A similar response to sound has been reported in the guinea pig by Miller and Murray (1966). In the Reeler mice, the first white noise signal produced suppression in both Reelers, and then some no-suppressions and no-decisions followed. Both of these mice were able to detect the white noise, as indicated by their unconditioned reaction, but had not demonstrated that they could learn to associate the signal and shock: conditioned suppression. In the second white noise session without shock, both Reelers showed an increasing tendency to lick through the white noise periods. One of these mice, RL 1, was run for several sessions of white noise without shock to see if the unconditioned suppression might eventually disappear. The suppression occurred less often with continued exposure, and this is shown in Figure 17.

The top row of Figure 17 shows RL 1's nonsuppression baseline with no signals and no shocks. The second row shows successive sessions of testing with white noise alone. The unconditioned reaction occurred fewer times as testing progressed, especially during the first half of each session. The Reeler reliably licked through at least the first four test signals of each session. Using this as the nonsuppression baseline, suppression was reestablished by adding shock. The auxiliary recorder was connected to attenuate the 95 dB level whenever suppression occurred. The first session using shock is at the bottom left of Figure 17 and the first two signals look like no-decisions, but this is because the recorder was at its limit and could not make steps up the chart. Actually, these first two signals were nonsuppression, providing a local baseline for the subsequent series of consecutive suppression decisions. The change from no-suppression to suppression was due, presumably, to the mouse's learning to associate white noise with impending shock. The attenuation of the noise was continued until threshold was reached at about 20 dB.

Another mouse, of the normal Himalayan strain, showed an unconditioned reaction to cage-tremble. Cage-tremble was produced by the eccentrically turning shaft of a test tube mixer, Cole Parmer model 4722 Super Mixer, attached by a wire to the test cubicle. The mixer can be seen in the lower left corner of Figure 1. The Himalayan mouse, HIM 1, suppressed during periods of cage-tremble as shown in the top two records in Figure 18. The suppression was allowed to con-

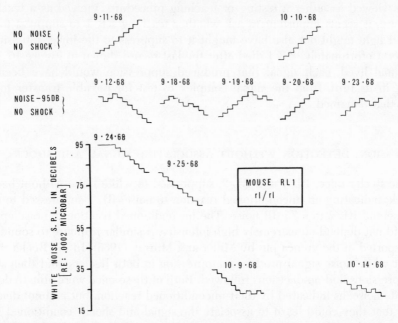

Fig. 17. Nonsuppression baseline; gradual dissipation of unconditioned suppression to white noise without shock; reinstatement of suppression by shock; and white noise threshold for a Reeler mouse.

tinue with the expectation that it would adapt out. The next three records show a decreasing tendency to suppress until HIM 1 licked through all of the test periods in one session. After the first five signals in the next session, suppression was reinstated by adding shock. The decisions immediately following the introduction of shock were no-suppression, suppression, and no-decision. The last session shows suppression was reliable and that HIM 1 had learned to associate cage-tremble with impending shock.

These data make it clear that not all suppressions are conditioned by shock. By carefully establishing a mouse's baseline reaction to a signal before it is associated with shock, the suppression procedure can be used to study acquisition of an association between stimuli, or "learning."

PURE TONE AUDIOMETRY

The successful measurement of relative thresholds using suppression as the indicator response recommended the suppression technique for more sophisticated threshold measurements. An apparatus was designed to present pure tones of known absolute intensity.

Pure tone signals were generated by a Hewlett-Packard model 200 CD oscillator and attenuated in 2 dB steps by a Grason Stadler model E3262A recording

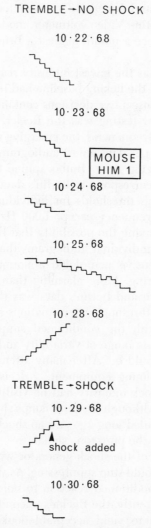

TREMBLE → NO SHOCK

10 · 22 · 68

10 · 23 · 68

MOUSE
HIM 1

10 · 24 · 68

10 · 25 · 68

10 · 28 · 68

TREMBLE → SHOCK

10 · 29 · 68

shock added

10 · 30 · 68

Fig. 18. Unconditioned suppression to cage-tremble, gradual dissipation of suppression, and reinstatement of suppression by shock in a normal, Himalayan mouse.

attenuator. To avoid "clicks" when the tone was turned on or off, the oscillator output was fed through an electronic switch, Grason Stadler model 829C, set at 50 msec rise or decay time. As an extra precaution, the tone was fed through an adjustable band-pass filter, Spencer-Kennedy model 302, with the low-pass filter set at the test frequency and the high-pass filter set at one half the test frequency. From the filter, the signal was fed into the recording attenuator and then to a MacIntosh Power Amplifier, MC-40. The output of the power amplifier was continuously monitored by a voltmeter, Brüel and Kjaer 2409, and fed into a Janszen model 65 electrostatic speaker.

Before each session, the sound pressure level was calibrated at the position in the test cubicle occupied by a mouse's ears when it licked at the tube. Maximum intensity was measured in decibels re 0.0002 µbar with a one-quarter–inch condenser microphone, Brüel and Kjaer 4135, associated power supply, Brüel and Kjaer 2801, read on a Ballantine Video voltmeter, model 310B. The measuring system was checked at least once a month against a Brüel and Kjaer 124-dB pistonphone calibrator, type 4220.

Threshold was defined as the lowest intensity reached during a session meeting two basic requirements: the licking baseline had to be steady between signals, and there had to be nine consecutive decisions contained in a five step range.

The animal selected for testing was the Reeler, RL 1. After threshold had been determined at several frequencies, the emerging audiogram was compared to an averaged (31 to 44 mice per data point) audiogram for a normal strain of mice injected with the immobilizing drug, Bulbocapnine (Berlin, 1963). The Reeler's audiogram did not seem to correspond to Berlin's data, but this was not surprising considering that: (1) Berlin's thresholds for individual mice covered a range of 40 to 50 dB at every test frequency except 1,000 Hz, (2) Berlin did not present data for individual mice, leaving the possibility that the averaged audiogram was a different shape from the individual audiograms that it was supposed to represent, and (3) Reeler's extensive neurologic abnormalities might influence any behavioral measure of hearing. More alarming than the lack of agreement between the Reeler audiogram and Berlin's data was the range of variation, up to 20 dB, between successive threshold determinations at a given frequency. Previous thresholds obtained with the conditioned suppression technique had not shown anything like this wide range of variability and suspicion was aroused that things were not as they should be. After many attempts to locate failures in the sound system and programming equipment, a decision was made to raise the shock level. Increases in shock intensity had no visible effect upon the Reeler. It was finally discovered that although the pilot lamps showed the shock generator to be working, in fact it had failed long ago and no shock was being delivered to the mouse at the termination of the pure tone signals.

Ordinarily, this failure of the shock generator would have been immediately apparent since the mouse would stop suppressing. As shown earlier, Figures 15 and 17, the Reeler had an unconditioned reaction to noise that tended to adapt out after several sessions. Apparently, the Reeler's unconditioned reaction to the pure tones was durable enough to yield acceptable-looking threshold measures. In Figure 19, the thresholds obtained without shock are shown as black dots. It is impossible to say what these points signify about the Reeler's hearing. In the same figure, the open circles are thresholds obtained after shock was reinstated. The recording attenuator delimited threshold sharply during sessions with shock compared to the broadly ranging oscillations obtained without shock. This suggests that the with-shock thresholds will be reliable when replications are obtained.

The curve described, in Figure 19, by the with-shock data points cannot yet be interpreted as an audiogram for the Reeler. The flat portion of the curve between 8 and 40 kHz may reflect the presence of a constant signal artifact present in this frequency range. In addition to replicating some of the data points

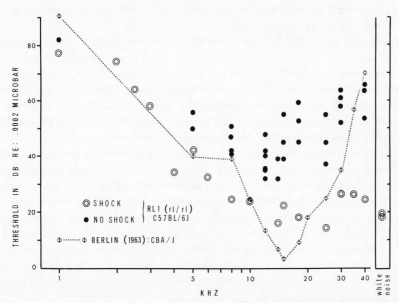

Fig. 19. Threshold determinations at several pure-tone frequencies with and without shock in the Reeler mouse, RL 1. These data cannot be interpreted as an audiogram until the shock data points are replicated and normal control animals are run. Averaged data for the normal (CBA/J) mouse is offered for comparison (Berlin, 1963).

a second and third time, normal animals must be tested. If the normal controls show the same flat range between 8 and 40 kHz, we may be dealing with an artifactual audiogram. If the normal-control audiograms are a distinctly different shape from the Reeler audiogram, the difference must be attributed to the hearing of the mice and not to an artifact of the sound generating equipment. Until the validity of the pure tone audiogram is assured, there is no point to seeking its histologic correlates, or comparing these data to those of Berlin or to those of Gourevitch and Hack (1966) for the rat.

SUMMARY

The conditioned suppression technique is admirably suited to psychophysical testing of neurologic mutant mice provided several sources of variability are adequately controlled: motivational, attentional, and physiologic.

Motivation is a function of body weight, time since feeding, length of session, size of the drops of milk, and the intensity and duration of shock. Motivation refers, generally, to the probability that a mouse will emit learned behavior; for example, licking the tube. If a session is too long, or the drops of milk are too large, or the mouse is too fat, then the probability of licking will decline during a session and invalidate measures taken late in the session. There is no set of magic values for these variables that will guarantee a steady licking rate for a specified amount of time. The only meaningful safeguard against fluctuating motivation is the experimenter's demonstration that his subject will produce steady and sustained licking from one session to the next.

Attention is primarily influenced by the exclusivity of the association between the warning signal and shock. Unsignalled shocks are presented because the signal is sometimes below threshold. By purposely scheduling unsignalled shocks, the experimenter demonstrates that a certain number of unsignalled shocks can be delivered without destroying either the licking baseline or suppression to above-threshold signals. As long as the number of unsignalled shocks at threshold is kept within this safe number, the threshold is measured accurately.

Finally, a variable that has only been touched upon is progressive physiologic change in the neurologic mutant. The elevated white noise threshold for the Pirouette mutant might never have been discovered had the mice been a month or so older and their cochlear degeneration complete. Many of the single-gene neurologic mutations create a disease process that progresses through various stages as the animal ages. Neurologic mutant mice of the same strain, but of different ages, cannot be treated as exact duplicates. As the procedures for testing these mice are further refined, information can be gathered more quickly. It may then be possible to trace the course of a progressive neurologic disease over several months or perhaps a mouse's lifetime.

REFERENCES

Békésy, G. von. 1947. A new audiometer. Acta Otolaryng (Stockholm), 31:411–422.

Berlin, C. I. 1963. Hearing in mice via GSR audiometry. J. Speech Hearing Res., 6(4):359–368.

Blough, D. S. 1955. Method for tracing dark adaptation in the pigeon. Science, 121:703.

Davies, H., and P. J. Harmon. 1948. Relative volume of the cochlear nuclei in pirouette and normal mice. Anat. Rec., 100:736–737.

Deol, M. S. 1956. The anatomy and development of the mutants pirouette, shaker–1 and waltzer in the mouse. Proc. Roy. Soc. (Biol.), 145:206–213.

Estes, W. K., and B. F. Skinner. 1941. Some quantitative properties of anxiety. J. Exp. Psychol., 29:390–400.

Falconer, D. S. 1951. Two new mutants "trembler" and "reeler" with neurological actions in the house mouse (Mus musculus). J. Genet., 50:192–201.

Gourevitch, G., and M. H. Hack. 1966. Audibility in the rat. J. Comp. Physiol. Psychol., 62:289–291.

Lyon, D. O. 1968. Conditioned suppression: operant variables and aversive control. Psychol. Rec., 18:317–338.

Miller, J. D., and F. S. Murray. 1966. Guinea pig's immobility response to sound: threshold and habituation. J. Comp. Physiol. Psychol., 61:227–233.

Morris, D. D. 1966. Threshold for conditioned suppression using X-rays as the pre-aversive stimulus. J. Exp. Anal. Behav., 9:29–34.

Sidman, M. 1960. Normal sources of pathological behavior. Science, 132:61–68.

——— B. A. Ray, R. L. Sidman, and J. Klinger. 1966. Hearing and vision in neurological mutant mice. Exp. Neurol., 16:377–402.

Sidman, R. L. 1968. Development of interneuronal connections in brains of mutant mice. In Carlson, F. D., ed. Physiological and Biochemical Aspects of Nervous Integration, Englewood Cliffs, New Jersey, Prentice-Hall, Inc., pp. 163–193.

JAMES SMITH [1]

6

CONDITIONED SUPPRESSION AS AN ANIMAL PSYCHOPHYSICAL TECHNIQUE *

INTRODUCTION

The purpose of this chapter is to describe and evaluate the conditioned suppression technique for the measurement of sensory thresholds in animals. Conditioned suppression was described by Estes and Skinner in 1941, but the technique was not used in animal psychophysics until recently. In a conditioned suppression experiment, a warning stimulus, which is terminated with a brief unavoidable electric shock, is superimposed on a baseline of ongoing lever pressing or key pecking independent of any responding by the animal. Conditioned suppression has, then, the advantages of aversive control while the ongoing behavior of the animal is being maintained on a positive reinforcement schedule.

It seemed to us that some of the problems of stimulus control in behavioral measurements of animals' sensory thresholds could be minimized with some adaptation of this technique. In many conditioning designs, the animal is trained to respond at the onset of a stimulus and therefore remain silent at all other times. Quite often the animal makes bursts of responses which are not correlated with stimulus presentation. These responses have been called "anticipatory" or "interval" responding. In the conditioned suppression design, on the other hand, the animal continually responds except for the suppression of responding during the presentation of the warning stimulus. The analogy to "interval responding" in the conditioned suppression design would be pauses in the ongoing responding which were not correlated with stimulus presentation. We thought that a conditioned suppression design would allow more stimulus control than other techniques because the technology for maintaining a steady baseline of responding is better developed than a technology for withholding responses. A reduction in interval responding would immediately lead to more precise behavioral threshold measurements. As we began to use the technique we found further advantages. The technique was efficient since differential responding in the presence of the condi-

[1] PSYCHOLOGY DEPARTMENT, FLORIDA STATE UNIVERSITY, TALLAHASSEE, FLORIDA.

* Work described in this chapter was supported by the United States Air Force contract number F 29600-67-C-0012, project 6893, 6571st Aeromedical Research Laboratory, Holloman Air Force Base, New Mexico, and by the Atomic Energy Commission contracts At-(40-1)-2903 and AT-(40-1)-2690 with the Florida State University.

tioned stimulus was quickly established. The only limiting factor has been in the development and maintenance of a smooth rate of responding in the operant situation. Another advantage has been the maintenance of stimulus control at near-threshold values of the stimulus. In general, no long periods of retraining have been necessary, and reliable threshold measures have been taken in some subjects over a 3-year period.

In the Florida State University psychology laboratories, the conditioned suppression technique has been used to measure thresholds in vision, audition, olfaction, and somesthesis in a wide variety of animals. References for these studies are summarized in Table 1 and more thoroughly discussed in later sections of this chapter. In other laboratories, conditioned suppression techniques have been used to measure x-ray sensitivity in rats (Garcia et al., 1962), to measure auditory thresholds in mice (Sidman et al., 1966), and taste thresholds in rats (Shaber et al., 1967).

Before discussing the results of the above investigations, a general overview of some of the methodologic considerations of the conditioned suppression technique may be helpful.

TABLE 1

A Summary of Research Done in the Florida State University Laboratories Using the Conditioned Suppression Technique for Sensory Threshold Measurements

SENSORY MODALITY	SPECIES	REFERENCES
Vision		
Critical flicker fusion	pigeons	Hendricks, 1966; Powell, 1967; Powell & Smith, 1968; George, 1968; Shumake, 1968; Shumake et al., 1968; Shumake et al., 1966
Critical flicker fusion	rhesus monkeys	
Brightness difference thresholds	pigeons	
Color vision and acuity	opossum and tree shrew	Masterton et al., 1969b
Audition		
Audiograms	opossum, hedgehog, tree shrew, bushbaby	Masterton et al., 1969a
Audiograms	potto, slow loris, rabbit	Masterton et al., 1969b
Audiograms	pigeon	Dalton, 1967
Frequency difference thresholds	pigeon	Price et al., 1967
Olfaction		
Absolute intensity thresholds, quality discriminations	pigeon	Henton, 1966, 1969; Henton et al., 1966, 1969
Somesthesis		
Temperature sensitivity	rhesus monkey	Duncan, 1968
X-ray Discrimination		
Exposure rate thresholds and role of olfaction in x-ray detection	rats, pigeons, rhesus monkeys	Dinc & Smith, 1966; Morris, 1966; Smith et al., 1964; Smith, 1967; Smith & Tucker, 1969; Taylor et al., 1967, 1968

DESCRIPTION OF THE GENERAL TECHNIQUE

In this section a more thorough consideration will be given to the type of baselines used, the modifications made in the original Estes and Skinner design (1941), and finally, the techniques for quantification of the data.

BASELINES. The ultimate goal of the operant training is to achieve a very steady baseline with a relatively high rate of responding. The baseline response rate also had to be reliably alterable throughout short-term discrete changes in the local environment. We chose a VI 2 (variable interval between reinforcements averaging 2 minutes) as optimal because steady response rates can be maintained over many sessions and it is maximally sensitive to subtle manipulations, including stimulus changes associated with electric shock. Most of our subjects have been trained on this schedule. It is possible to maintain the operant behavior on a richer VI schedule (more frequent reinforcements) and several of the studies referred to in this chapter have conditioned the suppression on a variable ratio baseline (Masterton et al., 1969a). Several approaches have been used to achieve smooth responding on the VI 2, but we have made no systematic observations as to the best procedure. Generally, the body weight of the animal was reduced to approximately 85 to 90 percent of free-feeding and the appropriate response was shaped by successive approximations. After approximately 150 continuous reinforcements, the schedule was changed to VI 30 seconds for several sessions, VI 1 minute for several sessions and to VI 2. Variations have been made in this training procedure; however, VI 1- or VI 2-minute schedules have been used most frequently as baselines for conditioned suppression.

MODIFICATION OF CONDITIONED SUPPRESSION DESIGN. The conditioned suppression technique used in our experiments differs in two significant ways from the original design by Estes and Skinner (1941). First, the duration of the conditioned stimulus (CS) is much shorter in our studies. In most of our studies, the CS has been 20 seconds or less in comparison with the earlier studies where CS durations were typically over 1 minute. Originally these short durations were introduced because we were using x-rays as the warning stimulus and, because of the destructive nature of the stimulus, we wanted to minimize the deleterious effects. The shorter durations also allowed for more conditioning trials per session.

Secondly, in our experiments the CS and shock were presented between reinforcements and never allowed to coincide with eating. Hence, the conditioned stimulus became an S^Δ (stimulus in the presence of which no reinforcement is presented) as well as the signal for subsequent shock. The power of the stimulus as an S^Δ may not be significant however, since the stimulus durations were so short and occurred between widely separated reinforcements, seldom causing a missed or delayed reinforcement. Sidman et al. (1966) and Masterton et al. (1969a) programmed the CS presentations independently of the schedule of reinforcement so that the reinforcement could occur during a trial and the CS was not an S^Δ.

They report no difficulty with stimulus control at near-threshold intensities. The shorter duration of the CS does apparently eliminate the temporal discrimination problem described by Sidman et al. (1966). In their experiment, the stimulus duration was 1 minute and the animals did not suppress until the latter part of the CS period.

THE SUPPRESSION RATIO (SR).   This modified conditioned suppression technique lends itself to rigorous data analysis for determination of the magnitude of the suppression. The responding of the animal during the CS can be compared with responding in a comparable period of time in the absence of the CS. This quantification has been accomplished in a variety of ways (Kamin, 1961; Dinc and Smith, 1966; Sidman et al., 1966; Hoffman et al., 1963). We have used the ratio described by Hoffman et al. (1963). Their formula is:

$$SR = \frac{(\text{Prestimulus Responses}) - (\text{CS Responses})}{\text{Prestimulus Responses}}$$

where SR is the suppression ratio, and the prestimulus period precedes the CS period and is identical in duration. When suppression is complete, i.e., no responding during the CS, the suppression ratio is one. When there is no suppression, the ratio is zero. In a typical experiment, three kinds of trials are presented: (1) CS trials are presented and terminated with shock. If the stimulus is above threshold and discriminated by the animal, suppression ratios approaching a value of one should be achieved after the appropriate number of pairings of the CS with shock; (2) If there is the possibility of extraneous cues occurring at the onset of the CS, control trials must be run. A typical example would occur in x-ray discriminations. The onset of the x-ray machine is accompanied by auditory signals and other electrical transients to which the animal could learn to suppress. For the control trial, the x-ray would be turned on, but directed away from the subject. These trials would never be terminated with shock. A suppression ratio near zero would be expected if the x-ray stimulus can be discriminated from the transients; (3) Baseline trials are run to check the smoothness of the responding and to note any possible transients resulting from timers or programming relays. For these trials, neither the CS nor the shock are presented, but the responses are merely sampled for two equal periods of time. If the responding is steady, these trials result in SRs of near zero.

In the studies reviewed in this chapter, the SR becomes the dependent variable as a function of trials when studying acquisition of conditioned suppression; the SR is the dependent variable as a function of stimulus intensity when measuring a threshold and checking threshold reliability. And finally, the SR can serve as a dependent variable in conditioning a discrimination between two above-threshold stimuli. One stimulus is followed by electric shock, but the other is not. The SR for the former should approach unity and the SR for the latter approach zero after the appropriate number of trials if the subject is making the discrimination.

A typical example of suppression ratios used to illustrate the acquisition of conditioned suppression can be seen in Figure 1, where the ratios are plotted as

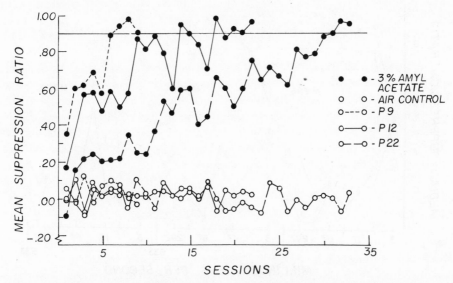

Fig. 1. Mean suppression ratios are plotted as a function of sessions during acquisition to 3 percent of vapor saturation of amyl acetate for three birds (filled circles). Air control trials for the three birds are plotted with open circles. Each session is based on 10 amyl acetate and 10 air control trials. (From Henton, 1966. Doctoral Dissertation, Florida State University.)

a function of trials in training pigeons to suppress to amyl acetate odor stimulations. Each session consisted of 10 trials and a criterion of three successive mean daily suppression ratios above 0.90 was reached in 9, 23, and 28 sessions respectively, for the three birds shown. The birds were trained to work in a flow of clean air and the warning stimulus was presented by switching a flow director so that amyl acetate (3 percent of vapor saturation) flowed through the bird's chamber. In order to show that the response was correlated with odor and not a transient resulting from a change in air flow rate, trials were run where the flow switch was manipulated but the concentration of the odor was reduced to zero. It can be seen in Figure 1 that these air control trials resulted in suppression ratios which remained about zero throughout the training.

Typical threshold functions can be seen in Figure 2 where SR is plotted as a function of exposure rate of irradiation. This figure presents data collected on three rhesus monkeys where the warning stimulus was a 15-second exposure to x-rays at the exposure rates reported on the *x*-axis. Since these curves drop so rapidly for the low intensity values of the stimulus, the selection of a SR as the threshold point is not critical. We have arbitrarily selected the point 0.50. It can be seen that exposure rate thresholds in this case would vary from 8 to 17 mR/ second. The curves labeled as *B* in this figure represent baseline data and the S curves represent sham exposures. It can be seen that the SRs for baseline and sham trials fluctuate around zero. The curves labeled *R* represent a replication of the x-ray presentation for M 283 and M 391. The *R* curves allow for a reliability check of the threshold value.

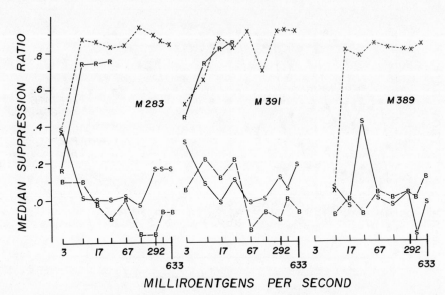

Fig. 2. Median suppression ratios are presented as a function of x-ray exposure rate for each of the three subjects. The x-curves represent suppression ratios for x-ray exposure trials; the S-curves, suppression ratios for sham exposure trials; and the B-curves, suppression ratios for baseline trials. The R-curves represent a replication of the x-ray trials for subjects M283 and M391. The exposure rates are plotted on a log scale and represent rates of 3, 8, 17, 33, 67, 133, 292, 425, and 633 mR/sec.

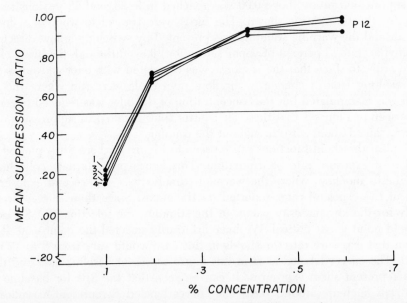

Fig. 3. Suppression performance of one subject at each of four amyl acetate concentrations over four consecutive desending method of limits threshold training sessions. Concentration is in terms of vapor saturation at 25° C. Each data point represents the mean of three suppression trials. (From Henton, 1966. Doctoral Dissertation, Florida State University.)

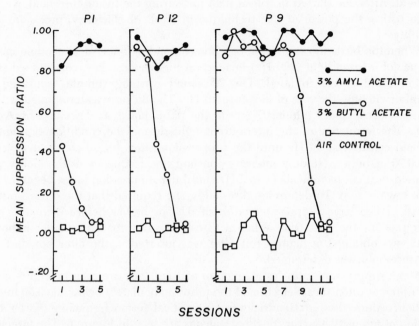

Fig. 4. Performance of three subjects during discrimination training with amyl acetate and butyl acetate concentrations of 3 percent of vapor saturation at 25° C. All subjects were trained with 10 amyl acetate suppression trials, 5 butyl acetate trials, and 10 air control trials per session. Butyl acetate trials and air control trials were never terminated with electric shock. (From Henton, 1969. **J. Exp. Anal. Behav.,** 12:175.)

A further example of reliability of threshold measurement can be seen in Figure 3 taken from Henton (1966). The mean suppression ratios as a function of odor intensity for 4 consecutive days are plotted. Again, if the SR of 0.50 is taken as threshold value, the reliability is rather remarkable.

An example of discrimination learning between two above-threshold stimuli can be seen in Figure 4 where the suppression ratio is plotted as a function of training trials. A discrimination between amyl acetate and butyl acetate was learned. Trials with amyl acetate were terminated with electric shock, whereas trials with butyl acetate were not. No differentiation occurred in early sessions, but discrimination between the two stimuli was clearly evident after a few sessions. Further examples of these uses of the SR for quantification will be reported later in this chapter.

VISION

When Hendricks (1966) began her study of the modified conditioned suppression technique as a threshold procedure, the conditioned stimulus was intermittent light. After she started to collect data measuring the fusion threshold, we began to realize the power of this technique in terms of efficiency, precision, and reliability.

When the birds showed stable baseline responding on a VI 2 schedule in the presence of a fused light (220 Hz) imaged on the response key, conditioned suppression training was initiated. The 20-second warning stimulus consisted of abruptly switching the rate of flicker to 10 Hz. The flicker was terminated with a 45 msec electric shock administered via the pubis bones as described by Azrin (1959). The frequency of the intermittent light during the conditioned stimulus was held constant at 10 Hz until the suppression ratios for 10 consecutive trials were 0.90 or better. Holding intensity constant, the frequency of the flicker was increased in small increments (1 to 2 Hz) until the suppression ratios began to decrease toward zero. To determine thresholds, she required that three trials out of a block of five have suppression ratios of 0.50 or higher before increasing the flicker rate for the next trial. When a threshold value for a particular light intensity was obtained, a neutral tint filter was inserted in the filter box and another threshold was determined.

Mean suppression ratios as a function of frequency are seen in Figure 5 for eight different intensities. Selection of the ratios immediately below the 0.50 line as threshold values allowed Hendricks to plot critical fusion frequency (CFF) as a function of intensity. Curves for three pigeons are seen in Figure 6. The intersubject variability averaged less than 4 Hz across sessions.

It can be seen that in the upper portion of the curves in Figure 6, CFF seems to be a linear function of log I. The low output of the glow modulator tube used to generate the visual stimulus was not intense enough to allow for the study of

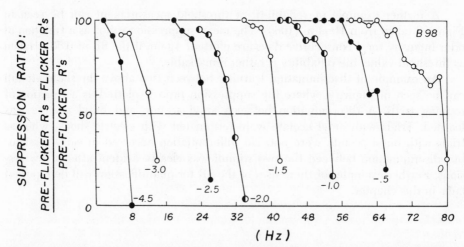

Fig. 5. Mean suppression ratios obtained for eight intensities of the stimulus during threshold sessions. Each point represents the mean suppression ratio for all trials at the frequency and intensity indicated. Intensity = 0 (41.86 ml) represents Day 1 of threshold investigation while intensity = −4.5 log units represents Day 17. Suppression ratios of 0.50 or above indicate pre-fusion flicker frequencies. Ratios immediately below the 0.50 line indicate the determined value of the critical fusion frequency. (From Hendricks, 1966. **J. Exp. Anal. Behav.**, 9:501.)

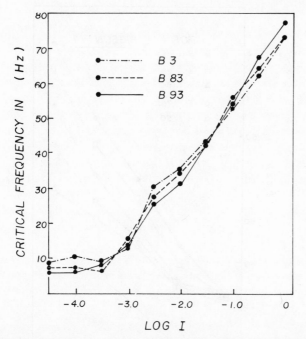

Fig. 6. Critical flicker fusion frequencies for each of three subjects plotted as a function of stimulus intensity. 0 intensity = 41.86 ml. (From Hendricks, 1966. **J. Exp. Anal. Behav.,** 9:501.)

the upper end of the curve. A new apparatus was constructed to yield an increase in intensity and to allow for variations in duty cycle and wavelength. The optical system has undergone various modifications to incorporate a 650-watt iodine lamp, heat filters, neutral tint wedges, an interference filter, interchangeable sector discs, and other optics, as described by Powell (1966, 1967) and Shumake et al. (1968). By precisely constructing the sector discs, presentation of pulse-to-cycle fractions ranging from 0.025 to 0.90 were possible.

Powell (1967) and Powell and Smith (1968) trained birds in a similar fashion to Hendricks and measured CFF as a function of not only intensity but also of pulse-to-cycle fraction. The reliability in these studies was slightly better than that reported by Hendricks, since the mean range of frequency variability within subjects for fusion was only three Hz. Figure 7 illustrates the family of curves obtained for pigeon #74 for pulse-to-cycle fractions from 0.10 to 0.90. It can be seen that the bird's CFF threshold is almost 150 Hz with the pulse-to-cycle fraction of 0.10. In a subsequent experiment, the pulse-to-cycle fraction was lowered to 0.050 and 0.025, and the fusion point dropped to 112 Hz and 76 Hz, respectively.

Using the same apparatus and technique described above, George (1968) showed that the technique for measuring CFF could be simplified considerably. The purpose of this experiment can be seen graphically in Figure 8. Hendricks (1966) and Powell (1967) held the light intensity constant and increased the rate

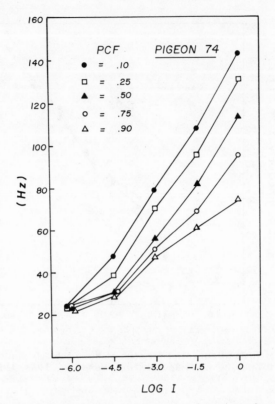

Fig. 7. The median critical flicker fusion as a function of intensity for each pulse-to-cycle fraction for one bird. Intensity ranged from 30,300 to 0.0303 millilamberts. (From Powell, 1966. Doctoral Dissertation, Florida State University.)

of repetition of the light until fusion threshold was obtained (method I). In the study by George (1968), she showed that the same CFF threshold values could be obtained by holding frequency constant and gradually lowering the intensity of the light (method II). Figure 9 shows that the thresholds are the same using method I and method II in each of three different birds for each of three different intensities. This modification of method I has two distinct advantages: (1) It is much easier to manipulate the intensity of the light (with a calibrated neutral tint wedge) than it is to manipulate and monitor the frequency of a rotating disc, and (2) more important, the method lends itself to the study of spectral sensitivity via the CFF.

Interference filters were calibrated for equal energy in the present optical system. By placing one of these filters in the filter box, the CFF could be obtained for 10 different filters and the intensity required for fusion was plotted as a function of the fixed frequency for each of the wavelengths as seen in Figure 10. These data, when replotted with relative sensitivity as a function of wavelength, illustrate a spectral sensitivity curve in the pigeon as seen in Figure 11.

All of the above studies, except the one involving manipulation of the pulse-

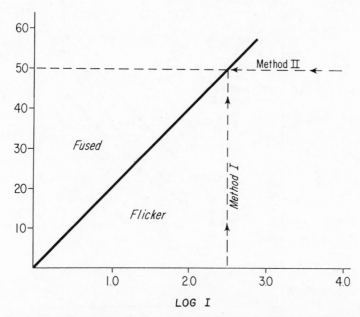

Fig. 8. A graphical presentation of two methods used to determine CFF in the pigeon. In Method I, given a fixed intensity, the repetition rate of a rotating disc was increased until fusion was obtained. In Method II, given a fixed repetition rate, the intensity of the stimulus was decreased until fusion was obtained. Any stimulus value to the right of the curve would appear as flickering light, and any value to the left would appear as fused. (From George, 1968. Unpublished Master's Thesis, Tulane University.)

to-cycle fraction, have been replicated with the rhesus monkey. Shumake et al. (1968), using the same optical system as described above, reported CFF as a function of luminance of the stimulus light.

The apparatus was a Foringer Primate Chair housed in a black soundproofed box. The stimulus light was transmitted from the fiber optics to a ground glass approximately 7½ inches in front of the monkey's face. The monkeys were reinforced with 0.7 g D & G whole diet pellets and were run on VI 2-minute schedules. The shock was presented by a foot electrode described by Weiss and Laties (1962). The monkeys were handled by the chain and collar procedure (Hurst and Lucero, 1966), seated daily in the chair, and run for approximately 1 hour.

The procedure for threshold determinations was similar to that described by Hendricks (1966). Suppression ratio as a function of flicker frequency for 16 different light intensities can be seen in Figure 12 for monkey 285. The same abrupt drop in the suppression ratio that Hendricks described in pigeons can be seen in monkeys. The plot of CFF as a function of luminance for this and two other monkeys can be seen in Figure 13. The obvious break in the curve at about −0.09 log foot lamberts is presumed to be a rod-cone separation. Shumake (1968) replicated the work of George (1968) with the rhesus monkey showing that CFF as a function of frequency with intensity held constant yielded the same curves. This is illustrated for monkeys 285 and 392 in Figure 14.

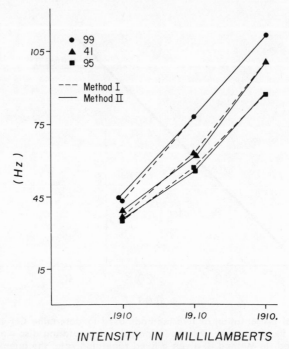

Fig. 9. The data from three pigeons, #99, #41, and #95, are presented. The solid lines represent CFF values obtained by Method I (i.e., fusion as a function of repetition rate for a fixed intensity) and the dashed lines CFF values obtained by Method II (fusion as a function of intensity for a fixed repetition rate). (From George, 1968. Unpublished Master's Thesis, Tulane University.)

By measuring CFF as a function of intensity with frequency held constant, Shumake (1968) was able to replicate in the rhesus monkey spectral sensitivity measurements previously described for the pigeon. Figure 15 shows log relative sensitivity as a function of wavelength for the photopic region. The frequency was held constant at 50 Hz for those measures. Similar measures, taken at 10 Hz, yielded a scotopic curve seen in Figure 16. The photopic curve shows maximum sensitivity at 535 mμ and the scotopic curve peaks at approximately 500 mμ. The peak sensitivity in the photopic curve is about midway between those described by DeValois (1965) and Schrier and Blough (1966). Schrier and Blough, using a tracking technique, plotted a spectral sensitivity curve which peaked at about 520 mμ. In DeValois' experiment, he required the monkey to select the flickering light out of four choices and obtained a curve which peaked at about 570 mμ. Shumake's data agree quite well with those of Schrier and Blough at wavelength below 583 mμ, but show less spectral sensitivity for the longer wavelengths.

Shumake et al. (1966) have reported using the conditioned suppression technique for brightness discrimination in pigeons, and Masterton and co-workers

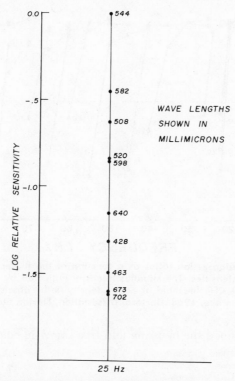

Fig. 10. At 25 cps and with one of the above 10 filters in the optical system, the intensity of the spot was lowered until fusion occurred. The relative sensitivity of the 10 wave lengths are plotted.

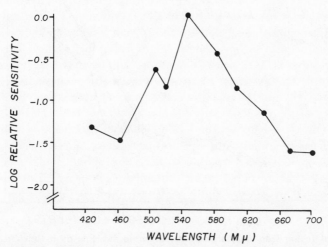

Fig. 11. The photopic spectral sensitivity curve for bird #71. The points are the obtained mean threshold values.

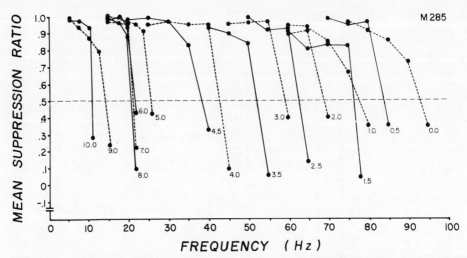

Fig. 12. Mean of four suppression ratios as a function of the flicker frequency for subject M285 at 16 stimulus intensities. The stimulus intensity indicated by the curve labeled 0.0 equals 4.1 log ft. L. The CFF threshold at each intensity is the abscissa of the point below the 0.50 line. (From Shumake, 1968. Doctoral Dissertation, Florida State University.)

(1969b) have conditioned the opossum and tree shrew in color, acuity, and luminus flux discriminations.

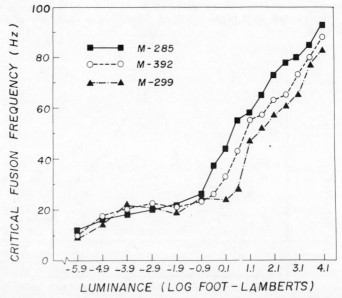

Fig. 13. Critical fusion frequency thresholds for three subjects as a function of the luminance of the stimulus light. (From Shumake, Smith, and Taylor, 1968. **Psychol., Rec.,** 8:537.)

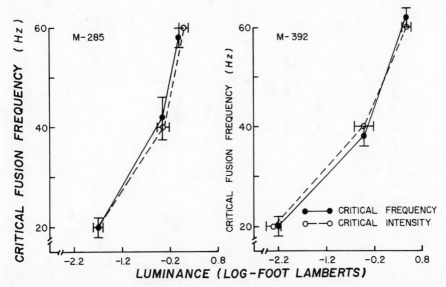

Fig. 14. Critical fusion frequency thresholds of subject M285 as a function of the luminance of the stimulus light for the method of critical frequency versus the method of critical intensity. (From Shumake, 1968. Doctoral Dissertation, Florida State University.)

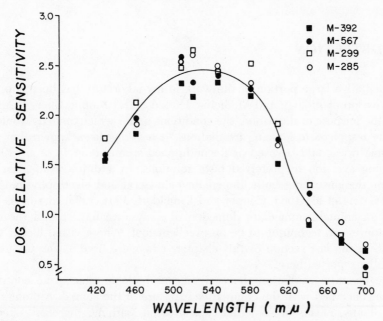

Fig. 15. Intersubject variability of photopic spectral sensitivity for four rhesus monkeys. The solid curve represents the smoothed mean curve. (From Shumake, 1968. Doctoral Dissertation, Florida State University.)

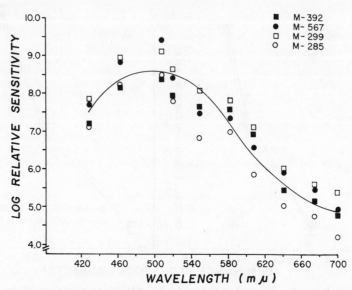

Fig. 16. Intersubject variability of scotopic spectral sensitivity for four rhesus monkeys. The solid curve represents the smoothed mean curve. (From Shumake, 1968. Doctoral Dissertation, Florida State University.)

X-RAY DETECTION

Since 1961 a large portion of the work in my laboratory has been supported by the Division of Biology and Medicine, United States Atomic Energy Commission, for the purpose of describing the conditions under which animals would give immediate responses to ionizing irradiations. It has long been known that x-rays and gamma rays could be used as unconditioned stimuli (Garcia et al., 1961) in conditioning aversion to preferred taste solutions. In addition, some work had been done demonstrating both immediate behavioral and electrophysiologic responses (Garcia et al., 1963; Cooper and Kimeldorf, 1964, 1965) to x-rays. In the study of an animal's immediate detection of x-rays, we have found the conditioned suppression technique to be an excellent tool. Where visual flicker served as the CS in the last section of this chapter, x-rays are used as the CS in these studies to be reported here.

Since ionizing irradiations have significant biologic effects, we continually had to be concerned with the cumulative exposure of the animal. Although there are few, if any, effects of sublethal exposures on learning, there are effects on sensory mechanisms, the general health of the animal, and longevity. In the conditioned suppression design where an x-ray exposure is the CS, the cumulative effective x-ray dose could be minimized by: (1) partial body exposures, (2) lower dose rates, (3) shorter stimulus duration, and (4) fewer x-ray trials. Although we now know a great deal about these four factors, we have not studied their interactions in enough detail to state the most efficient (i.e., least cumulative dose) method of training a suppression to ionizing irradiations.

PARTIAL BODY EXPOSURES

Garcia et al. (1964) did show that for immediate x-ray detection, the head of the rat was most sensitive. Since the LD 50/30 (lethal dose for 50 percent of the population within 30 days) for head-only exposure exceeds that for whole-body exposure by a large factor, an immediate advantage in x-ray training is attained by shielding the body. In the rat, this is accomplished by using a lick tube as the manipulandum, so that the position of the rat's head is relatively stable. The animal places his head through an opening in a "head size" tunnel and licks at a tube at the back of this compartment. The top of the box is covered with lead except for this small tunnel, allowing for x-ray exposure from the vertical position. In our arrangement, reinforcement was sucrose solution, presented by a Foringer dipper through a small hole in the floor of the head tunnel. The animal was shaped to lick on the tube for the sucrose reinforcements and was maintained on a VI 2-minute schedule. Photocells were also arranged in the head compartment to detect the presence of the animal's head during suppression of licking.

A word is in order about the presentation of the x-rays. Most of our work was initiated with a GE Maxitron operating at 250 kVp. Presentation of the x-rays could be accomplished by turning on the high voltage to the x-ray tube or by manipulating a hydraulically operated lead shutter with voltage constantly on the x-ray tube. Masking noise was always present in the animal's chamber and we took the added precaution of doing sham x-ray trials where the x-rays were presented but were attenuated by the addition of extra lead. Manipulation of a focal plane shutter generates clicks and low frequency auditory signals. Turning the x-ray machine on and off presented clicks and high frequency noise. In most cases, the latter method of presentation has been easier to attenuate with sound-proofing and has been used exclusively with the primate studies. The rise time of the x-rays with this latter method was faster and became an important consideration in subsequent studies where we gave only a short pulse of x-rays.

With the rhesus monkey, the head-only exposure is easy to accomplish. The sides and top of the Foringer cockpit were lined with lead. In addition, the exterior of the soundproofed box was also coated with lead except for a port 8 inches in diameter aligned with the monkey's head. A schematic of this apparatus is seen in Figure 17. The monkeys were handled with the chain and collar technique and seated daily in the chair for approximately 1 hour.

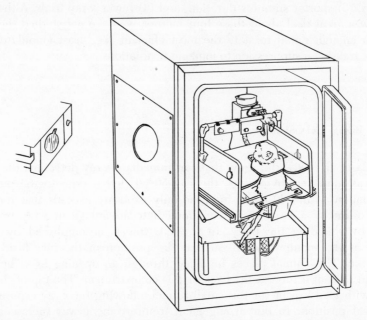

Fig. 17. Schematic of the apparatus for conditioning the rhesus monkey to x-ray stimulations. Lead is attached to the side of the chair and the side of the box shielding all but the animal's head. (From Taylor, Smith, and Hatfield. 1967. 6571st Aeromedical Research Laboratory, Technical Report Number ARL-TR-67-20.)

EXPOSURE RATE THRESHOLDS

The exposure rate thresholds for rats and monkeys have been thoroughly explored. Morris (1966) trained rats to bar press for a 16 percent sucrose solution on a VI 1-minute schedule. He initially trained 12 rats to suppress responding with a 15-second x-ray exposure of 500 mR/second by terminating the exposure with a 30 msec electric shock to the feet. After 15 such exposures (and 112.5 r accumulated), all animals were suppressing to the x-ray warning stimulus and no suppression was evident on sham trials. On subsequent days the rats received five trials each at lower exposure rates and the magnitude of the suppression was noted. Figure 18 shows the suppression ratio as a function of exposure rate for four rats. An abrupt drop in the curve can be seen as the exposure rate decreases. The point of 4 mR/second was significantly different from the sham exposures for all four of the rats. These animals had accumulated only 236 R by the end of the experiment. The whole-body LD 50/30 for the rat is between 550 and 600 R for a single dose. No evidence of radiation sickness was noted in the behavior of these animals.

These results were replicated with the rhesus monkey (Taylor et al., 1967) and the threshold values here have already been presented in Figure 2. It can be noted that the exposure rate threshold for rats and monkeys is quite similar.

It is not clear how low the exposure rate can be in the initial training. Chad-

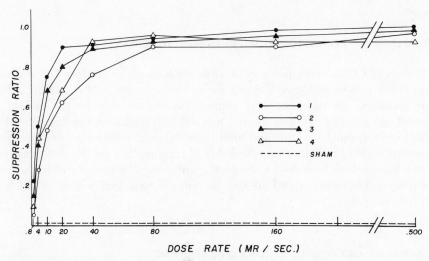

Fig. 18. Mean suppression ratio to x-ray stimulatiòns as a function of dose rate for four rats. Each data point is the average of five trials. (Adapted from Morris, 1966. **J. Exp. Anal. Behav.,** 9:29.)

dock et al. (1969) trained a rat at 165 mR/second and completed the training with a cumulative dose of less than 20 R. Other rhesus monkeys in the laboratory have been trained at exposure rates of 450 and 367 mR/second.

CONDITIONED STIMULUS DURATION

The duration of each x-ray exposure can be drastically reduced in training both rats and monkeys to detect x-rays. It is necessary in the conditioned suppression design for the CS to be of sufficient length so that suppression to the stimulus can be discriminated from other pauses in the baseline. In order to avoid the problem of warning stimuli being too short in duration, we kept the temporal relation between onset of the x-ray and the shock constant at 15 seconds. The duration of the x-ray was gradually reduced from 15 to 12, to 9, to 6, and finally to 3 seconds (Chaddock et al., 1969). By use of the photocell in the head tunnel, it was noticed that the rat withdrew his head into the shielded compartment at the onset of the irradiation and remained in the shielded compartment until after the shock. Hence, the rat was responding only to the onset of the x-ray. Chaddock et al. (1969) then shaped a rat with x-rays of 3 seconds duration where onset and shock were 15 seconds apart. They were able to train the animal in less than 40 trials with a cumulative dose of only 19.8 R. Data on a rhesus monkey in the same study show that the rhesus can be trained with pulses of x-rays 200 msec (500 mR/second) separated from the shock by 15 seconds. This animal acquired a mean suppression ratio of 0.93 on the ninth day after 54 trials and a cumulative x-ray dose of only 5.4 R.

ACQUISITION OF CONDITIONED SUPPRESSION TO X-RAYS

It does not take many pairings of x-ray with shock to produce the suppression in either rats or monkeys. Table 2 shows the acquisition of detection in four rhesus monkeys. All monkeys were suppressing significantly by the end of 20 trials and one monkey (M 390) showed marked suppression in the first five trials. Of the 14 rats trained by Dinc and Smith (1966), eight reached a criterion mean suppression ratio of 0.90 on the second day of training, five on the third day, and only one animal took four days to reach the criterion. The number of trials given per day varied between 5 and 10 and no animals took longer than 20 trials to reach the criterion.

THE ROLE OF OLFACTION IN X-RAY DETECTION

Garcia et al. (1964) noted that the olfactory region of the head seemed to mediate the x-ray detection. Cooper and Kimeldorf (1965) found that rats which previously responded by a desynchronization in the EEG pattern to x-ray stimulation lost this change in EEG after ablation of the olfactory bulbs. We used the conditioned suppression technique to test the effects of olfactory bulb ablation on x-ray detection (Dinc and Smith, 1966). Ten rats were trained to suppress to x-rays. Six subsequently had their olfactory bulbs removed, two had the prefrontal lobes removed, and two had sham operations. Table 3 shows the effects of this surgery on the mean suppression ratios. Where removal of the bulbs was incomplete, in cases where prefrontal tissue was removed and in sham operated animals

TABLE 2 [a]
Median Suppression Ratios of Monkeys to X-Rays
(In Blocks of Five Trials)

| | | SUPPRESSION RATIO | | |
SUBJECT	BLOCK	X-RAY	BASELINE	CONTROL
M 391	1	0.29	0.14	0.12
	2	0.60	0.09	−0.05
	3	0.60	−0.03	0.26
	4	1.00	−0.07	0.02
M 283	1	0.08	0.12	0.11
	2	0.26	−0.05	0.19
	3	0.56	0.59	0.05
	4	0.81	0.06	−0.11
M 389	1	0.45	0.00	0.03
	2	0.12	0.00	0.03
	3	0.45	0.12	0.03
	4	0.78	−0.06	0.00
M 390	1	0.74	0.08	0.33

a From Smith and Tucker, 1969. In *Olfaction and Taste*, Vol. III. Courtesy of Rockefeller University Press.

TABLE 3 [a]
Effects of Surgical Procedures on Mean Suppression Ratios of Rats to X-Rays

| | SUPPRESSION RATIO | | |
| | PRE- | POST- | |
SUBECT	OPERATION	OPERATION	POSTMORTEM EXAMINATION
4B	0.92	0.24	Complete bulb removal
11B	1.00	0.02	Complete bulb removal
8A	1.00	0.06	Complete bulb removal
3B	1.00	0.97	Incomplete bulb removal
6B	1.00	1.00	Incomplete bulb removal
10B	1.00	0.94	Incomplete bulb removal
3A	1.00	1.00	Frontal lobe removal
9A	0.95	1.00	Frontal lobe removal
10A	0.96	0.86	Sham operation
11A	0.93	0.96	Sham operation

a From Smith and Tucker, 1969. In *Olfaction and Taste*, Vol. III. Courtesy of Rockefeller University Press.

there was no change in the high mean suppression ratios after surgery. In the three cases where the bulbs were completely removed, however, the suppression ratio was drastically reduced.

A similar finding was observed with the rhesus monkey as the subject (Taylor et al., 1968). After the x-ray detection was obtained, the olfactory tracts of five subjects were lesioned with two subjects serving as experimental controls. Table 4 illustrates the dramatic effect of the surgery on the x-ray detection capability of the rhesus. In the one animal where the tract was only partly cut on the left side, x-ray detection remained. The exposure rate threshold increased, however, almost one log unit. Pathologic verification of the surgery is illustrated in Figure 19 for M 391 (tracts sectioned) and M 390 (sham operated).

These above data indicate the necessity of an intact olfactory system for x-ray detection, but they do not specify that x-rays directly excite the olfactory receptors. It is not clear if an odorant produced at the receptor site at the onset of the

TABLE 4 [a]
Effects of Surgical Procedures on Mean Suppression Ratios of Monkeys to X-Rays

| | SUPPRESSION RATIO | | OLFACTORY TRACTS AFTER SURGERY | |
| | PRE- | POST- | | |
SUBJECT	OPERATION	OPERATION	LEFT	RIGHT
M 283	0.88	0.07	opened	opened
M 391	0.86	0.14	opened	opened
M 595	0.85	0.03	opened	opened
M 46G	0.89	0.03	opened	opened
M 390	0.75	0.72	partially interrupted	opened
M 389	0.80	0.89	intact	intact
M 600	0.81	0.82	intact	intact

a From Smith and Tucker, 1969. In *Olfaction and Taste,* Vol. III. Courtesy of Rockefeller University Press.

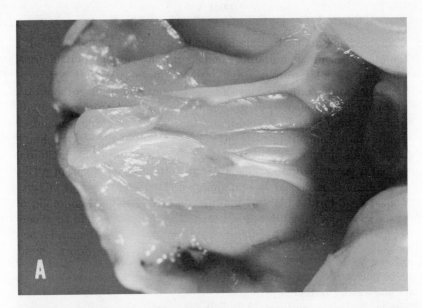

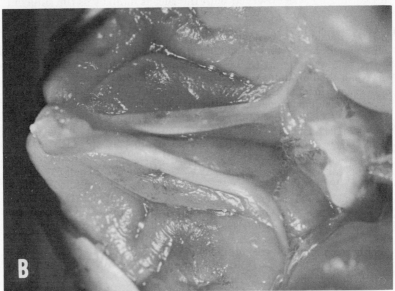

Fig. 19. A shows the ventral surface of the brain of subject M391 where the olfactory tracts were sectioned bilaterally. B shows the ventral surface of the brain of subject M390, a sham operated animal, with the olfactory tracts left intact. (From Taylor, Smith, Wall, and Chaddock. 1968. **Physiol. Behavior.**, 3:929.)

x-ray is the manner in which x-rays are detected or if there is some direct effect of x-rays on elements in the peripheral or central nervous system.

Because of the olfactory anatomy of rats and monkeys, separation of the receptor from the bulbs by sectioning the primary olfactory nerves is extremely difficult. The anatomy does not have this form in birds, since the olfactory organ and bulbs are several millimeters apart, permitting sectioning of the primary olfactory nerves without damage to the other olfactory structures.

For several years we have attempted to train pigeons to detect x-rays, to section the primary olfactory nerves, and to note the effects on x-ray detection. Training pigeons to make the x-ray detection has been much more difficult than with mammals and has required much higher exposure rates. At an exposure rate of 2,000 mR/second we have been successful in training only about half the birds attempted (Smith et al., 1964; Smith, 1967; Smith and Tucker, 1969). Birds that did learn to detect x-rays lost this detection after sectioning of the olfactory nerves. This loss of detection presumes that mediation of the x-ray effect is at the peripheral level, but it is possible that the olfactory bulb is altered considerably because of the loss of normal afferent inflow. Since the behavioral evidence for olfactory sensitivity in birds was mostly negative, we faced an even more severe criticism in interpreting bird x-ray detection as resulting from an odorant detected in the olfactory receptor. It will be shown in the next section how the conditioned suppression technique can be applied to the study of olfactory sensitivity in pigeons.

OLFACTION

The results of our x-ray studies made it strongly desirable that we demonstrate a functional behavioral response to olfactory stimuli using the conditioned suppression technique.

Since the early part of the 19th century there has been much discussion on olfactory sensitivity in birds. A review of the literature from Audubon (1826) to Stager (1967) yields a host of studies indicating that birds have no sense of smell. An honors thesis at Harvard by Wolfgang J. Michelsen (1959) contradicted these early results with a well-controlled experiment in pigeon olfaction. Using an operant technique, a discrimination based on olfactory stimuli was conditioned in two pigeons.

Most recent studies give credit to the idea that pigeons could make olfactory discriminations on the basis of their anatomy and physiology. The elegant analysis of Bang and Cobb (1968) gives morphologic evidence that the pigeon is about halfway between the kiwi (highest ratio) and the sparrow (lowest ratio) in the ratio of olfactory bulbs to cerebral hemispheres. Tucker (1965) showed that the olfactory system of the pigeon, and 13 other birds, was functional. He recorded integrated neural activity from a twig of the olfactory nerve to amyl acetate breathed in air at various concentrations.

Our olfactory system was designed by Dr. Don Tucker, and Dr. Wendon Henton developed the training technique for the birds (Henton et al., 1966). A pigeon key and grain hopper were mounted behind a glass breathing chamber as shown in Figure 20. The birds placed their heads through the open port to peck on the key and to eat grain. The feathers seemed to "seal" the port so that little odor escaped from the chamber. The floor of the box was covered with activated charcoal in an effort to trap any escaping odor. The odorant delivery

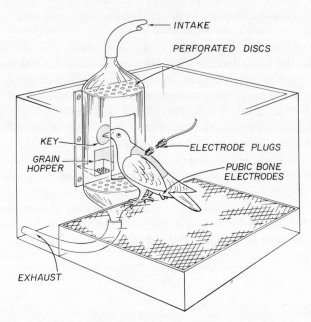

Fig. 20. A breathing chamber for pigeon olfactory studies. The chamber is made of glass and has perforated discs at both the intake and exhaust ports to facilitate an even flow of air through the chamber. The key and hopper are located on the backside of the chamber and the bird places his head through the large part in the front.

system was similar to that reported by Tucker (1963). The air was diverted into separate channels, and flowed through a system of gas-washing bottles where it was cleaned and subsequently saturated with water or odorant. It was then regulated by Teflon needle valve stopcocks, measured by Fischer-Porter Tri-flat flowmeters, and finally directed either to the bird chamber or to an exhaust port by a Teflon flow switch. Since all parts of the system were either glass or Teflon, the problem with residual odor retention was reduced. The animal worked in a known flow rate of clean air, and by manipulating only the Teflon flow switch, odor of a known concentration could be diverted into the bird's chamber.

The bird was outfitted with pubis bone electrodes, shaped to peck the key, and stabilized on a VI 2 schedule of reinforcement. The CS for shock was an 18-second presentation of odor. "Air control" trials were run to show that the animal was not responding to some artifact in the air delivery system. In these control trials, the concentration of odor was reduced to zero and therefore the flow switch merely changed from clean air to clean air. These trials were never followed by shock. Typical learning curves have already been presented in Figure 1 for three birds to amyl acetate stimulation. It can be seen from this figure that no suppression was ever observed in the air control trials.

Figure 3 demonstrates the reliability Henton (1966) found in measuring an olfactory threshold. The characteristic abrupt drop in the suppression ratios seen previously in the flicker and x-ray data is evident also in olfactory thresholds. Thresholds to amyl acetate for four different pigeons are presented in Figure 21.

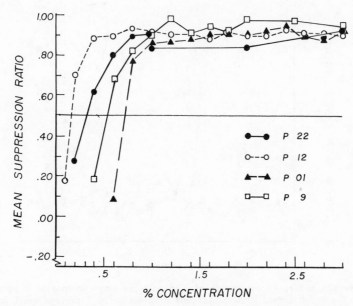

Fig. 21. Initial descending method of limits amyl acetate suppression thresholds of four Ss. Concentration is in terms of vapor saturation at 25° C. Each data point represents the mean of three suppression trials. (From Henton, 1966. Doctoral Dissertation, Florida State University.)

Henton (1966) also found that if the olfactory nerves were sectioned, the suppression ratios to odor dropped abruptly to zero. Henton et al. (1969) noted that animals with sectioned olfactory nerves could, however, learn to suppress to an odor stimulus if the concentration was quite high. Thresholds obtained from these animals were higher than those obtained from animals with intact nerves. The role of trigeminal mediation for these higher concentrations is discussed in these papers (Henton, 1966; Henton et al., 1969).

The conditioned suppression procedure had not been used with any psychophysical method other than the descending method of limits in our laboratory (e.g., Hendricks, 1966; Morris, 1966) and a tracking method described by Ray, Chapter 5. Henton (1966) further demonstrated the usefulness of the conditioned suppression technique by comparing threshold values to amyl acetate obtained by the ascending and descending series of stimulus intensities with the method of constant stimuli. Henton compared the mean ascending and mean descending method of limits thresholds in terms of vapor saturation for four birds. He found values of 0.37 percent and 0.33 percent for bird #22, 0.16 percent and 0.16 percent for bird #12, 0.73 percent and 0.73 percent for bird #1, and 0.50 percent and 0.50 percent for bird #9. This remarkable precision also was found in his use of the method of constant stimuli in bird #9. Four stimulus concentrations of amyl acetate in 0.2 percent increments were randomly presented three times each during a training session. The stimulus concentration was reduced over days until a mean suppression ratio of 0.50 was obtained. This procedure was replicated three times and Henton reported values of 0.48 percent, 0.46 percent, 0.47 percent, and 0.47 percent of vapor saturation as threshold values of amyl acetate. These compared

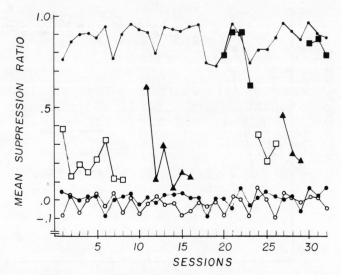

Fig. 22. Intensity difference thresholds of bird #91 for amyl acetate of 2 percent vapor saturation. The small closed circles represent suppression to 7 percent amyl acetate. The rectangles represent 3 percent of vapor saturation. The triangles 2 percent, and the open squares 1 percent. The larger closed circles and open circles fluctuating around zero represent baseline and air control trials respectively. It can be seen this bird discriminates 7 percent from 1 percent and 2 percent but not 7 percent and 3 percent. (Adapted from Shumake, Smith, and Tucker. 1969. **J. Comp. Physiol. Psychol.**, 67:64.)

with a threshold of 0.50 percent obtained by either ascending or descending series with the same bird. Thus it was demonstrated that equivalent thresholds could be obtained with the conditioned suppression technique and the reliability of the threshold measurements was independent of the stimulus presentation procedure.

Shumake et al. (1969), using the same bird olfactory apparatus, showed that the pigeon could make intensity discriminations. Amyl acetate stimuli at 7 percent of vapor saturation were paired with shock, and intensities of 3 percent, 2 percent, and 1 percent were presented without shock. It can be seen from Figure 22 that mean suppression ratios for 1 percent and 2 percent were clearly distinct from the 7 percent stimuli, but that the pigeon in six sessions could not discriminate 7 percent from 3 percent. Out of six birds trained, four were able to discriminate at least 2 percent from 7 percent and the other two could discriminate only 1 percent from 7 percent.

An apparatus has been developed to test olfactory discrimination in the rhesus monkey. The odorant delivery system is similar to that described by Shumake et al. (1969) except that the air handling capacity is greater. The animal chamber consists of a glass "helmet" placed over the monkey's head after he has been seated in the cockpit (Fig. 23). The port in the side of the glass allows the monkey to feed himself the 0.7 g pellets. The exhaust system is set to draw at a slightly greater flow rate than the intake system so that a minimum amount of odor leaks through the food port. If any error is involved it would be a slight dilution of the concentration of the odor in the chamber.

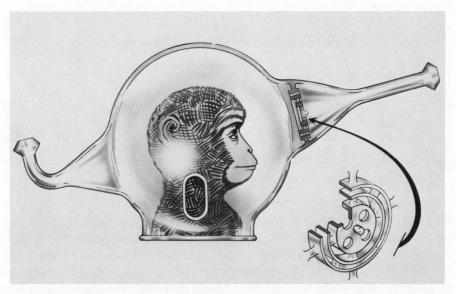

Fig. 23. An olfactory chamber for the rhesus monkey. The collar is constructed of sheet teflon and the chamber is placed over the monkey's head after he is seated in the cockpit. The glass chamber has a perforated disc at the intake port to facilitate a linear flow.

Two monkeys have been trained thus far to suppress to odors. Attempts have been made to obtain threshold values to amyl acetate and discrimination between amyl and butyl has been demonstrated. Replications of those preliminary investigations are now in progress. All indications are that the system works and significant olfactory information can be obtained with the rhesus using this technique.

AUDITION

Sidman et al. (1966) first used the conditioned suppression technique to determine auditory thresholds to white noise in mice. Their procedure differed slightly from the procedure described earlier in this chapter and is discussed in detail in Chapter 5 in this book.

Dalton (1967) conditioned suppression in pigeons to pure tone frequencies of 1, 2, and 4 kHz delivered through an 8-inch GE 16-ohm extended range speaker. The birds were trained on a VI 2 schedule and the suppression was conditioned with 20-second auditory stimulations. After suppression was established, the auditory stimuli were attenuated until threshold was reached. Threshold was defined as that intensity of the pure tone frequency resulting in three trials out of five with suppression ratios of 0.50 or less. SRs were plotted as a function of intensity in dB re 0.0002 dynes/cm^2.

Price et al. (1967) used the conditioned suppression technique to measure frequency DLs in the pigeon. The birds were shaped to key peck in the presence

TABLE 5 [a]
Absolute and Relative Frequency DLs in Pigeons

FREQUENCY IN KHZ

BIRD NO.	0.5		1		2		4	
	ΔF	ΔF/F	ΔF	ΔF/F	ΔF	ΔF/F	ΔF	ΔF/F
29	20	0.040	25	0.025	40	0.020	120	0.030
31	20	0.040	25	0.025	45	0.023	100	0.025
46	25	0.050	30	0.030	50	0.025	90	0.023
Mean	21.7	0.043	26.7	0.027	45	0.023	103.3	0.026

[a] From Price et al., 1967. J. Aud. Res., 7:229–239.

of a 2 kHz tone pulsing at a duration of 200 msec on a 50 percent duty cycle. They were maintained on a VI 2-minute schedule of reinforcement. The warning stimulus was given by alternating a tone of higher frequency with the 2 kHz tone. After the bird learned to suppress to this change in stimulus, the frequency of the higher tone was lowered gradually until threshold was reached. Threshold in this study was defined as the smallest difference in frequency at which suppression could be obtained. The SR criterion of 0.50 or higher on three of five consecutive presentations was used.

The results of these thresholds for three birds are presented in Table 5. The technique proved to be quite satisfactory to collect differential threshold data on pigeons. Good stimulus control was maintained at the near-threshold values.

Masterton et al. (1969a) have found the conditioned suppression technique quite helpful in testing the hearing of primitive mammals. In their efforts to understand the evolution of human hearing, they selected the opossum, hedgehog, tree shrew, and bushbaby because of their common ancestry with man. The subjects were trained to lick a waterspout for dry food reinforcements and maintained on a variable ratio schedule. The warning stimulus was a tone presented for 10 seconds, terminated by a shock to the feet. During the hour-long sessions, they introduced approximately 30 randomly spaced test trials where the intensity of the tone varied from trial to trial. Figure 24 shows the SR plotted as a function of sound pressure level for an opossum. This procedure was repeated at different frequencies. Audiograms for the four animals are shown in Figure 25. These audiograms allowed for detailed study of best frequencies, high frequency cut-offs, and the overall size of the audible field. Masterton and co-workers (1969b) have recently plotted audiograms on the potto, slow loris, rabbit, and rat, using their adaptation of conditioned suppression to obtain the threshold values.

It is apparent from the above studies that the conditioned suppression technique can be a valuable tool in animal auditory work.

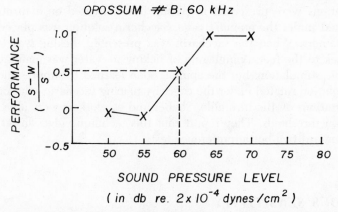

Fig. 24. Lick suppression as a psychophysical function of sound intensity. Dashed line indicates method of choosing a sound pressure level for construction of audiogram. (From Masterton, Heffner, and Ravizza. 1969a. **J. Acoust. Soc. Amer.**, 45:966.)

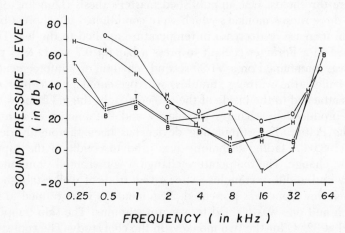

Fig. 25. Audiograms of four primitive mammals. O, opossum (Didelphis virginiana); H, hedgehog (Hemiechinus auritus); T, tree shrew (Tupaia glis); B, bushbaby (Galage senegalensis). Sound pressure level is scaled in dB re 2×10^{-4} dynes/cm^2. (From Masterson, Heffner, and Ravizza. 1969a. **J. Acoust. Soc. Amer.**, 45:966.)

TASTE

The use of the conditioned suppression technique in studying taste thresholds has been quite limited. Shaber et al. (1967) reported measuring saccharin taste thresholds by conditioning a suppression to licking. Rats were shaped to lick through an aperture in the bottom of the cage for hypothalamic stimulation. The licking solutions were presented in plastic bowls located on a turntable which slowly rotated under the animal's cage. Saccharin solution was placed in certain of the containers. When the saccharin was presented, licking was followed by electric shock to the feet. A high rate of licking to water was maintained by the hypothalamic stimulation, but the animals soon learned to suppress licking when the sweet solution rotated under the cage. By placing saccharin solutions of differing concentrations on the turntable, Shaber and co-workers were able to measure concentration thresholds. They report that this technique gives lower thresholds than the standard two-bottle preference tests.

CUTANEOUS SENSITIVITY

Work is now being conducted in Dr. Daniel R. Kenshalo's laboratory at Florida State University using the conditioned suppression technique to measure temperature thresholds. One unpublished master's thesis (Duncan, 1968) reports data from three rhesus monkeys which were conditioned to suppress bar pressing to either an increase or decrease in temperature applied to the leg. The subjects were trained in a Foringer cockpit to press a bar for 0.7 mg D & G pellets. The behavior was maintained on a VI 90-second schedule of reinforcement. The temperature change (the warning stimulus) was presented by a Peltier refrigerator which was attached to the inside of the subjects' right thigh. Changes in temperature were produced by changes in polarity and the amount of current flowing through the Peltier. The stimulating device has been thoroughly described by Kenshalo (1963). A fading technique was used to condition the suppression to temperature change. The temperature change was presented simultaneously with a vibratory and auditory stimulus. After a few trials of well-established suppression, temperature alone was presented. Two monkeys were trained to suppress to cold stimuli and one was trained to a warm stimulus. The skin temperature was maintained at 32° C for the two monkeys in the cool study. The cool stimulus was 27° C. The warm stimulus was a 10° C change from a skin temperature of 34° C. No thresholds were attempted in this thesis, but work toward that end is currently in progress.

SOME METHODOLOGIC CONSIDERATIONS

In conclusion, there are several methodologic considerations which should be noted regarding use of the conditioned suppression technique in animal psychophysics.

BASELINES

Since the key to good signal-to-noise ratio in the conditioned suppression design is a steady baseline, considerable attention must be given to its development and maintenance. It is useless to run conditioned suppression trials as described in this chapter on a baseline that has many pauses. Both variable interval and variable ratio schedules have been reported to provide a steady baseline for the suppression trials. In using the modified conditioned suppression technique described by Hendricks (1966) (i.e., where reinforcements are not available during the trials and the CS may become an $S^{\triangle}$), the variable interval schedule is more suitable. Conditioning trials can be administered between widely separated reinforcements in the VI program resulting in a minimum of interference with the VI schedule. When generating a VR schedule with a probability randomizer, it would be impossible to administer CS shock trials without occasionally overlapping a reinforcement. Masterton and co-workers (1969b) used the VR schedule and scheduled the trials completely independent of the schedule of reinforcement with no loss of stimulus control. They also report good stimulus control on a fixed ratio schedule.

The amount of instability that can be tolerated in the baseline is somewhat dependent on the duration of the CS. If frequent pauses occur which are as long as the duration of the CS, testing is impossible. Short pauses in the baseline are considerably less of a problem, and testing can continue.

Quite often the rate of responding decreases after the animal has been shocked for a period of time. A lowering of the rate does not in itself inhibit testing as long as the baseline remains steady. If the frequency of pauses increases after shocking the animal and the baseline becomes erratic, we often eliminate all trials for a few sessions and merely run the animal on the VI schedule for food reinforcement.

THE CONDITIONED STIMULUS DURATION

The work reported by Kamin (1961, 1965) indicates that the acquisition of conditioned suppression is dependent upon the time elapsing between the onset of the CS and the shock. He noted that rapid acquisition would occur if the time between CS onset and shock was less than 60 seconds. The duration of the CS was not important within this short time range. In all of the studies reported from our laboratory, the CS durations were 30 seconds or less, indicating that the conditioned stimulus duration was always within the limits described by Kamin. Therefore, it is not surprising that Chaddock et al. (1969) were able to train both rats and monkeys with short pulses of x-rays separated from the shock by 15 to 20 seconds. The trace conditioning of these rats and monkeys (CS duration equal to 0.2 to 3.0 seconds) required a few more trials for acquisition than did training when the CS was longer (15 to 20 seconds) and was terminated with shock. In the x-ray work, however, the short duration of the CS cuts the total exposure by a large factor, resulting in a marked decrease in cumulative x-ray dose in spite of the increase in number of training trials.

We have found in the radiation studies that after a large number of trace conditioning trials, stimulus control is more variable. Further research is in progress in order to determine the usefulness of the trace conditioning technique for psychophysical measurements.

THE UNCONDITIONED STIMULUS: ELECTRIC SHOCK

Shock intensities are very important in the conditioned suppression design. The intensity must be high enough to cause some suppression, but not high enough to cause long suppression periods. Usually we start at a lower intensity and gradually increase the shock level until stimulus control is attained. The implanted electrode technique (Azrin, 1959) for birds allows for excellent shock control. The resistance across the electrodes usually measures 700 to 1,200 ohms and remains very stable throughout the duration of the experiment. Control over the shock to the monkey has been about as good. The sides of the cockpit seat are perforated so that a restraining bar can be placed across the monkey's lap, inhibiting movement from the metal seat. A small amount of electrode paste is applied to the monkey's foot before it is strapped to a brass footplate with Velcro tape, and the shock electrodes are connected to the footplate and the metal seat. Rats require no special apparatus and are simply shocked through the feet from a grid floor.

In some of the experiments reported here (Henton, 1966), the unavoidable shock was presented on all of the trials. In other experiments (Hendricks, 1966), the shock was unavoidable but presented on only 60 percent of the trials. If the animal was on a 100-percent shock schedule, when the threshold value was approached and the animal could no longer see the CS, it would receive an "unwarranted" shock. These shocks would soon be associated with the artifacts at CS onset and result in loss of control on the control trials. To avoid this problem Hendricks (1966) suggested the 60-percent shock schedule. In experiments where there was no CS onset artifact (such as the bird olfaction work of Henton, 1966), the 100-percent shock schedule worked quite well with no loss of control on the control trials where the stimulus was merely changed from air to air. In summary, once it is established that there are no other cues available to the animal other than the CS, the schedule of the unavoidable shock can be 100 percent.

PSYCHOPHYSICAL TECHNIQUE

It has been shown in these studies that classical psychophysical methods can be used with the conditioned suppression procedure. For example, Hendricks (1966) used the method of limits with an ascending series of frequencies. George (1968) and Shumake (1968) also used the method of limits but with a descending series of intensities until fusion was reached. Henton (1966) used both an ascending and descending series with the method of limits and compared these thresholds with those obtained by the method of constant stimuli. Masterton and co-workers (1969a, 1969b) have also used the constant stimulus technique in measuring auditory thresholds. Sidman et al. (1966) used the conditioned suppression method wherein the animal tracked the threshold. As long as suppression occurred, the stimulus intensity would decrease on the next trial, but when no suppression occurred, the CS intensity would increase on the subsequent trial.

The suppression ratio allows quantification of the magnitude of the conditioned aversion as a function of change in stimulus intensity. This gives more information than a simple yes-no response to a stimulus, as can be readily seen in Figures 2, 3, 5, 12, 18, 22, and 25.

CONCLUSION

Conditioned suppression has been shown to be an excellent technique for determining sensory thresholds. Extensive research in the area of conditioned suppression has lead to considerable information concerning the parameters which control the behavior. Because of this information, good stimulus control can be attained allowing for precise threshold measurements. Examples of this precision have been given in vision, olfaction, and x-ray detection studies in this chapter. Stability in the threshold measurements have been shown across several weeks in the olfactory studies and several years in the CFF studies with rhesus monkeys.

The variety of animals tested has been quite impressive. The use of the lick response and the fact that it can be maintained on a VI schedule has further broadened the number of animals that can be used with the technique (Chaddock et al., 1969; Masterton et al., 1969a). Of all the species attempted, the only reported failure of the conditioned suppression technique (Dalton, 1968) was not really a failure of the method. It was a failure to establish an operant baseline in cebus monkeys upon which conditioning of suppression could be imposed. It is concluded that as long as a smooth rate of responding can be shaped, a suppression of the responding can be conditioned and used for animal psychophysical measures.

REFERENCES

Audubon, J. J. 1826. Account of the habits of the turkey buzzard, *Vultur aura*, particularly with the view of exploding the opinion generally entertained of its extraordinary power of smelling. Edinburg New Philadelphia J., 2:172–184.

Azrin, N. H. 1959. A technique for delivering shock to pigeons. J. Exp. Anal. Behav., 2:161–163.

Bang, B. G., and S. Cobb. 1968. The size of the olfactory bulb in 108 species of birds. The Auk, 85:55–61.

Chaddock, T. E., D. L. Roll, B. Chaddock, and J. C. Smith. 1969. Immediate detection of brief X-ray exposure. Radiat. Res. Soc., 39:548.

Cooper, G. P., and D. J. Kimeldorf. 1964. Electroencephalographic desynchronization of irradiated rats with transected spinal cords. Science, 143:1040–1041.

———— and D. J. Kimeldorf. 1965. Effects of brain lesions on electroencephalographic activation by 35 kVp and 100 kVp X-rays. Int. J. Radiat. Biol., 9:101–105.

Dalton, L. W. Jr. 1967. Conditioned suppression as a technique for determination of auditory sensitivity in pigeons. J. Aud. Res., 7:25–29.

———— 1968. Auditory sensitivity in the rhesus (*Macaca mulatta*) and the white throated capuchin (*Cebus Capuchinus*) monkey: a comparison of three techniques. 6571st Aeromedical Research Laboratory, Holloman Air Force Base, New Mexico, Technical Report Number ARL-TR-68-14.

DeValois, R. L. 1965. Behavioral and electrophysiological studies of primate vision. *In* Neff, W. D., ed. Contributions to Sensory Physiology, New York, Academic Press, Inc., pp. 137–178.

Dinc, H. I., and J. C. Smith. 1966. Role of the olfactory bulbs in the detection of ionizing radiation by the rat. Physiol. Behav., 1:139–144.

Duncan, D. G. 1968. The establishment of conditioned suppression to temperature increases and decreases in rhesus monkeys. Unpublished Master's Thesis, Florida State University.

Estes, W. K., and B. F. Skinner. 1941. Some quantitative properties of anxiety. J. Exp. Psychol., 29:390–400.

Garcia, J., D. J. Kimeldorf, and E. L. Hunt. 1961. The use of ionizing radiation as a motivating stimulus. Psychol. Rev., 68:383–395.

———— N. A. Buchwald, B. H. Feder, and R. A. Koelling. 1962. Immediate detection of X-rays by the rat. Nature, 196:1014–1015.

———— N. A. Buchwald, G. Back-y-Rita, B. H. Feder, and R. A. Koelling. 1963. Electroencephalographic responses to ionizing radiation. Science, 140:289–290.

———— N. A. Buchwald, B. H. Feder, R. A. Koelling, and L. Tedrow. 1964. Sensitivity of the head to X-ray. Science, 144:1470–1472.

George, H. W. 1968. A comparison of two methods for determination of flicker fusion thresholds. Unpublished Master's Thesis, Tulane University.

Hendricks, J. 1966. Flicker thresholds as determined by a modified conditioned suppression procedure. J. Exp. Anal. Behav., 9:501–506.

Henton, W. W. 1966. Suppression behavior to odorous stimuli in the pigeon. Doctoral Dissertation, Florida State University.

———— 1969. Conditioned suppression to odorous stimuli in pigeons. J. Exp. Anal. Behav., 12:175–185.

———— J. C. Smith, and D. Tucker. 1966. Odor discrimination in pigeons. Science, 153:1138–1139.

———— J. C. Smith, and D. Tucker. 1969. Odor discrimination in pigeons following section of the olfactory nerves. J. Comp. Physiol. Psychol., 69:317–323.

Hoffman, H. S., M. Fleshler, and P. Jensen. 1963. Stimulus aspects of aversive controls: The retention of conditioned suppression. J. Exp. Anal. Behav., 6:575–583.

Hurst, C. M., and J. F. Lucero. 1966. A collar and chain procedure for handling and seating *Macaca mulatta*. 6571st Aeromedical Research Laboratory, Holloman Air Force Base, Technical Report Number ARL-TR-66-14.

Kamin, L. J. 1961. Trace conditioning of the conditioned emotional response. J. Comp. Physiol. Psychol., 54:149–153.

———— 1965. Temporal and intensity characteristics of the conditioned stimulus. *In* Prokasy, W. F., ed., Classical Conditioning: A Symposium, New York, Appleton-Century-Crofts, ch. 7, pp. 118–147.

Kenshalo, D. R. 1963. Improved method for the psychophysical study of the temperature sense. Rev. Sci. Instrum., 34:883–886.

Masterton, B., H. Heffner, and R. Ravizza. 1969a. The evolution of human hearing. J. Acoust. Soc. Amer., 45:966–985.

———— H. Heffner, and R. Ravizza. 1969b. Personal communication.

Michelsen, W. J. 1959. Procedure for studying olfactory discrimination in pigeons. Science, 130:630–631.

Morris, D. D. 1966. Threshold for conditioned suppression using X-rays as the pre-aversive stimulus. J. Exp. Anal. Behav., 9:29–34.

Powell, R. W. 1966. The pulse-to-cycle fraction as a determinant of critical fusion in the pigeon. Doctoral Dissertation, Florida State University.

———— 1967. The pulse-to-cycle fraction as a determinant of critical flicker fusion in the pigeon. Psychol. Rec., 17:151–160.

———— and J. C. Smith. 1968. Critical flicker fusion thresholds as a function of very small pulse-to-cycle fractions. Psychol. Rec., 18:35–40.

Price, L. L., L. W. Dalton Jr., and J. C. Smith. 1967. Frequency DL in the pigeon as determined by conditioned suppression. J. Aud. Res., 7:229–239.

Schrier, A. M., and D. S. Blough. 1966. Photopic spectral sensitivity of Macaque monkeys. J. Comp. Physiol. Psychol., 62:457–458.

Shaber, G. S., J. A. Rumsey III, B. C. Dorn, and R. L. Brent. 1967. Saccharin behavior taste thresholds in the rat. Fed. Proc., 26:543.

Shumake, S. A. 1968. Critical fusion frequency as a method of determining photopic and scotopic spectral sensitivity in rhesus monkeys. Unpublished Doctoral Dissertation, Florida State University.

———— C. A. Hatfield, and J. C. Smith. 1966. Brightness difference thresholds in the pigeon using the conditioned suppression technique. Psychon. Sci., 6:313–314.

———— J. C. Smith, and H. L. Taylor. 1968. Critical fusion frequency in rhesus monkeys. Psychol. Rec., 8:537–542.

———— J. C. Smith, and D. Tucker. 1969. Olfactory intensity difference thresholds in the pigeon. J. Comp. Physiol. Psychol., 67:64–69.

Sidman, M., B. A. Ray, R. L. Sidman, and J. M. Klinger. 1966. Hearing and vision in neurological mutant mice: A method for their evaluation. Exp. Neurol., 16:377–402.

Smith, J. C. 1967. The effect of sectioning the primary olfactory nerves on the immediate response of the pigeon to X-ray exposure. Paper read at meetings of the Eastern Psychological Association, Boston.

———— and D. Tucker. 1969. Olfactory mediation of immediate X-ray detection. *In* Pfaffman, C., ed., Olfaction and Taste, New York, Rockefeller University Press, vol. III, pp. 288–298.

———— J. Hendricks, D. D. Morris, and R. Powell. 1964. Immediate response in the pigeon to brief X-ray exposure (abstract). Radiat. Res., 22:237.

Stager, K. E. 1967. Avian olfaction. Amer. Zool., 7:415–419.

Taylor, H. L., J. C. Smith, and C. A. Hatfield. 1967. Immediate behavioral detection of X-rays by the rhesus monkey. 6571st Aeromedical Research Laboratory, Holloman Air Force Base, Technical Report Number ARL-TR-67-20.

———— J. C. Smith, A. H. Wall, and B. Chaddock. 1968. Role of the olfactory sensory system in the detection of X-rays by the rhesus monkey. Physiol. Behav., 3:929–933.

Tucker, D. 1963. Physical variables in the olfactory stimulation process. J. Gen. Physiol., 46:453–489.

———— 1965. Electrophysiological evidence for olfactory function in birds. Nature, 207:34–36.

Weiss, B., and V. G. Laties. 1962. A foot electrode for monkeys. J. Exp. Anal. Behav., 5:535–536.

PETER B. ROSENBERGER [1]

7

RESPONSE-ADJUSTING STIMULUS INTENSITY

INTRODUCTION

The problem of how to deal with response behavior in the "indifference range" of stimulus intensity is one of the oldest in psychophysics; it has long been recognized that such behavior is not necessarily under the control of intensity alone. Indeed, to some extent, the history of the science is the story of various theoretical approaches to this problem.

Classical human psychophysics, for example, contented itself for the most part with giving a "trustworthy" observer extensive preliminary training "to stability." In fact, ever since the studies of Fechner (1860), many of the classical data of psychophysics have been obtained by experimenters from themselves and each other. As the stabilizing power of statistical analysis came to be appreciated, the smoothness of the ogival curve of the psychometric function provided assurance of stimulus control. Even so, Cattell (1893) was able to make a distinction between "mathematical" and "psychologic" sources of error, the former occurring by "chance," the latter being of a "different sort." Recent theorists have gone further to suggest that the sensory threshold must be viewed as an "operating characteristic" rather than a physical barrier (Tanner and Swets, 1954), or even to question the validity of the concept of sensory threshold (Corso, 1963).

These significant recent contributions may or may not have provided the adequate definition of those skills which characterize the "sophisticated" or "practiced" observer. In any event, it is clear that these skills are infinitely more difficult to achieve with certainty in the experimental animal. It might thus be predicted that expansion of psychophysics to animal studies would demand the development of threshold techniques which promise greater efficiency, if efficiency is defined as amount of available data per unit testing time. This probably accounts for the recent popularity of numerous *response-adjusting* stimulus presentation schedules, variously described as the "staircase" method (Anderson et al., 1946), the "up-and-down" method (Dixon and Mood, 1948), the "titration schedule" (Weiss and Laties, 1958), or the "adjusting" method (Sidman, 1962). The uses,

[1] Division of Neuropsychiatry, Walter Reed Army Institute of Research, Walter Reed Army Medical Center, Washington, D.C. Now at the Pediatric Neurology Unit, Massachusetts General Hospital, Boston, Massachusetts.

advantages, and limitations of the method in human psychophysics have been well reviewed by Cornsweet (1962) and others. The time seems appropriate for a similar treatment in regard to animal studies.

RESPONSE-*DEPENDENT* STIMULUS INTENSITY

The concept of some degree of response-dependence of stimulus presentation is implicit in two of the three psychophysical methods described by Fechner (1860)—the method of "just noticeable differences" and the method of "average error." This dependency is a function of experimenter behavior in the first case, of observer behavior in the second. The methods are described only in their application to difference or comparison thresholds, of course, since at the time Fechner was sceptical of the possibility of measurement of absolute thresholds. Concerning the method of just noticeable differences, Fechner makes passing reference to the convenience of presenting stimuli in *descending order* until a limit of sensitivity is reached—a technique which according to Boring (1942, p. 38) was in use by others as early as 1700. It is with the incorporation of the technique of descending order—usually applied from both sides of the threshold limen—that the method of "just noticeable differences" has been inherited by modern psychophysics as the method of limits.

RESPONSE-*ADJUSTING* STIMULUS INTENSITY—THE TITRATION SCHEDULE

It is difficult to imagine that the same "practical considerations" of which Fechner spoke did not at some time in the past prompt an investigator to reverse the descending order of stimulus intensity upon the *first* "no" response of the observer, to reverse it again on the next "yes" response, and so forth, thus making *each* change in stimulus intensity dependent upon the response to the previous stimulus presentation. In fact, however, the first application of this technique to be recorded in the literature did not occur until World War II, in nonpsychophysical surroundings. It was developed by members of the Explosives Research Team at Bruceton, Pennsylvania, for sensitivity testing of explosives. The data of their experiments consisted of whether or not a given packet of explosives would explode when a weight was dropped on it from a given height. Since a given sample once tested was useless for further testing whether it exploded or not, it occurred to the experimenters that a considerable saving in time and materials could be achieved if the height of a given test were directly regulated by whether or not the previous sample exploded—being decreased if it did and increased if it did not.

This immediate adjustment of stimulus intensity by previous response defines what we shall hereafter refer to as the *titration schedule*. According to Weiss (1969), the name was suggested by Dr. Louis Lasagna, a pharmacologist who recognized its similarities to the chemical technique of titration. Its wider applications to psychophysical studies were quickly recognized (Anderson et al., 1946), and problems of its statistical validity were worked out at an early stage (Dixon and Mood, 1948).

Although Guilford (1954) classifies the titration schedule as a special case of the method of limits, it might also be considered as incorporating an important feature of the method of adjustment; namely, the regulation of stimulus presentation directly by the observer. Although classically the method of adjustment is used only for difference thresholds (since comparison with a standard is required), the behavior of the observer under control of the titration schedule might easily be interpreted as constant "comparison" of sensory input with some internal criterion which distinguishes "stimulus present" from "stimulus not present."

PSYCHOPHYSICAL APPLICATIONS OF TITRATION SCHEDULES

HUMAN PROTOTYPES

The titration schedule was first introduced to psychophysics as a method of audiometry by Békésy (1947), in the best known and most widely quoted report on the subject. The Békésy audiometer, familiar to veterans of Selective Service physical examinations, requires the subject to respond continuously (i.e., keep a button depressed) so long as he hears a tone, and to cease responding (release the button) when the tone disappears. Pressure on the button automatically produces attenuation of the tone at a constant rate, and attenuation is automatically reversed when the button is released.

A typical tracing from the Békésy procedure is shown in Figure 1. A moment's attention to this prototype record should help the reader to interpret any titration threshold more easily. At the beginning of the record, stimulus intensity is set arbitrarily at 50 dB. The subject obeys the instruction, "Press on the button as long as you hear the tone," and stimulus intensity decreases steadily. At point b, the observer is no longer aware of the tone, and releases the button, thus driving stimulus intensity back upward to a level (point c) at which he again presses the button, and so forth.

It should be noted at this point that the Békésy procedure differs in one important respect from that employed earlier at the Bruceton Laboratories. Whereas in the former technique the titration is accomplished in discrete steps by programming stimulus intensity for the next trial, the Békésy method varies the intensity of a continuous stimulus as an *immediate* consequence of *each* response. The effect of this arrangement is that the stimulus intensity record provides a continuous "track" of observer behavior. It has thus become conventional to refer to the Békésy procedure as the "tracking" method, as opposed to the "discrete trial" titration schedule.

Some procedural peculiarities of the tracking method are apparent from inspection of Figure 1. First, since attenuation of the tone is continuous, the amplitude of the individual excursion (distance b to c) is a function not only of the observer's indifference range but of his reaction time as well. When we are

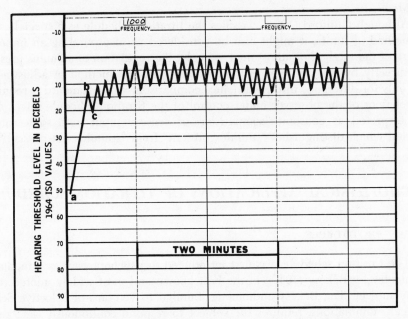

Fig. 1. Tracing of a typical audiogram obtained by the Békésy method. Taken from the right ear of a normal subject, at fixed frequency 1000 Hz. (Courtesy of Josephine Walker, M.A., U.S. Army Audiology and Speech Center, Walter Reed Army Medical Center.)

dealing with normal human auditory reaction time and an attenuation rate of only 2.5 dB per second, this is not a significant variable. It should simply be kept in mind, especially when dealing with experimental animals, that variables affecting the reaction time will increase the apparent indifference range when this technique is used.

Secondly, a momentary deviation of the mean threshold, of the order of 5 dB, is seen at point *d*, about 1.5 minutes after the beginning of the record. It is followed quickly by recovery to the original threshold level. It serves to illustrate that although Békésy's rationale for the new technique was to combat the "slackening of attention" frequently encountered with more laborious audiometry methods, the procedure itself does not eliminate this variable, but merely provides assurance of its temporal nature. This point will be developed more fully below.

Apparently independently of Békésy, Oldfield (1949) applied the same "tracking" method to the study of absolute brightness thresholds for human central vision. This report was purely methodologic, and made no reference to quantitation of the threshold or limina.

Oldfield suggested that a continuous "mean" of individual excursions could be provided by introducing an amount of "backlash" into the recording system approximately equal to the observer's indifference range. That is, from each individual excursion of the stimulus intensity control, the recording system was to subtract an amount equal to the predicted indifference range, thus giving a smooth curve. It is of some interest to note that no subsequent "tracking" experiment recorded in the literature has included this refinement.

Several years later, Lindsley (1957) reported on a technique for monitoring sleep in human subjects involving a tone delivered to the subject's ear, whose decibel level increased steadily with time but could be decreased by the subject through continual presses on a hand switch. He used the slope of a cumulative record of switch responses as an indicator of the depth of sleep, and was able to demonstrate specific effects of increased sleep deprivation and Seconal ingestion on response rate. His control procedure consisted of a session run with verbal instructions and no tone. He was able to conclude that the aversive contingency provided by the tone made the operant response (button-pressing) a more reliable indicator of depth of sleep than was possible when only verbal instructions were provided.

Kappauf (1963) and his co-workers, including McDiarmid (1962), revived the discrete trial application of the titration schedule in a large series of studies with human subjects. Only difference thresholds were studied, and included judgments of loudness and duration of auditory stimuli, heaviness of weights, and stereopsis. Kappauf's reports include an exhaustive methodologic and statistical discussion of the technique as applied to human psychophysics, aspects of which will be considered in the discussion below.

APPLICATIONS TO ANIMAL STUDIES

Titration schedules have been applied to animal psychophysics in two classes of studies: sensory thresholds, where the sensory input acts as a conditioned stimulus (usually discriminative) to control responding; and aversive thresholds, where the input acts as an aversive stimulus to be escaped or avoided. Since the two differ with respect to some of the issues involved, they will be considered separately, although chronology overlaps. Following a brief historical review, more recent data from the author's laboratory will be presented in detail.

SENSORY THRESHOLDS.   The earliest and best-known reports of application of the titration schedule to animal sensory thresholds are those of Blough (1955, 1958), who applied the Békésy tracking method to the study of vision in the pigeon. The experience of this investigator is crucial to our review, for he was also among the first to make use of the stimulus control afforded by operant conditioning techniques for psychophysical studies in nonverbal subjects.

Blough was aware of a basic assumption necessary to animal psychophysics; namely, that for purposes of stimulus control, there is no *operational* distinction between "stimulus absent" and "stimulus below threshold." Thus if an animal is trained to make one response in the presence of a stimulus, and another response in its absence, he can be trusted to make the second response when the stimulus is below his sensory threshold. After differentially reinforcing pecks on one key in the presence of a visual stimulus and pecks on a second key in its absence, Blough then arranged for each peck on the first key to darken the stimulus by a small amount, and likewise for each peck on the second key to lighten it. In this manner, he was able to track dark-adaptation, effects of drugs on visual responding, and differential thresholds to various wavelengths of the light stimulus.

Blough's methodologic report of the technique (1958) provides us with valuable considerations and practical suggestions for its application elsewhere. First, he recognized, as had Békésy, that with this method, a subject not actually under stimulus control can nevertheless generate what appears to be a threshold record (Fig. 2). His simple test for this was to introduce a sudden large-amplitude change in stimulus intensity. As is shown in Figure 2, the animal under stimulus control shows a corresponding disruption in the threshold record.

Secondly, Blough was aware of a point which has general application to psychophysical situations where reinforcement of observer responses plays a prominent role: if positive reinforcement of "stimulus present" responses is anything short of continuous (i.e., delivered on some intermittent schedule), adventitious differential reinforcement of responses to given stimulus intensities is likely to occur. This in turn will affect the probability of response to stimuli of different intensities, all of which are well above threshold. Blough's solution to this problem was to establish a chain of responses during discrimination training in which responses on the "stimulus present" key would turn the stimulus completely off, following which responses on the "stimulus absent" key would deliver the reinforcement and turn the stimulus back on. Then for purposes of threshold testing, the apparatus was adjusted so that responses on the two keys would attenuate the stimulus rather than turn it off or on.

The problem of adventitious differential reinforcement of responses to various stimulus intensities is not peculiar to the Blough two-key paradigm, but will complicate any design in which reinforcement of "stimulus on" responses is intermittent. Also, it is worth noting that by placing attenuation of the stimulus on an intermittent reinforcement schedule, Blough has avoided a problem which con-

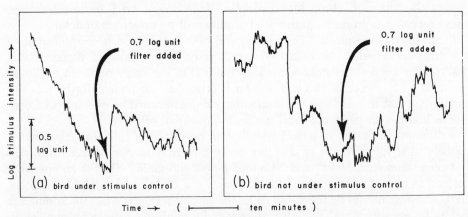

Fig. 2. Threshold records of a bird under stimulus control, and of a bird not under stimulus control. (From Blough, 1958. **J. Exp. Anal. Behav.**, 1:31–43. Copyright 1958 by the Society for the Experimental Analysis of Behavior, Inc.)

tinues to plague Békésy audiometry; namely, the control of observer behavior by time or number of responses rather than by stimulus intensity.

Gourevitch et al. (1960) applied the Blough procedure to the study of auditory thresholds in rats. After achieving satisfactory stability and intersubject agreement of "absolute" thresholds, they demonstrated a change in threshold level as a result of administration of kanamycin, an ototoxic drug. Gourevitch (1965) then applied the technique to the study of masked and quiet thresholds. For reasons which will be detailed below, Gourevitch has since abandoned this technique in favor of the method of constant stimuli for more recent studies described in Chapter 4 of this volume.

Sidman et al. (1966) made the first application of the discrete trial titration schedule to sensory thresholds. They combined the technique with the conditioned suppression paradigm of Estes and Skinner to study hearing thresholds in neurologic mutant mice, correlating elevated thresholds with degeneration of the organ of Corti. Their techniques and findings are described by Ray in Chapter 5, and only a few points relevant to the present discussion will be mentioned here.

The conditioned suppression baseline seems a particularly fortunate choice for psychophysical studies in potentially uncooperative subjects. First, because it involves an *interruption* of ongoing behavior (i.e., suppression of behavior in response to the "warning stimulus"), it tends to provide greater assurance that the subject is "attending to" the stimulus. Secondly, although suppression results in lower reinforcement density, the contingencies maintaining the animal's behavior on baseline probably are not mitigated by the occurrence of the warning stimulus per se—or if they are, at least the effect does not vary from trial to trial. This eliminates the problem of adventitious differential reinforcement of responses to stimuli of given intensities, about which we spoke earlier in the discussion of the Blough experiments.

Since the experimental variable causing elevated thresholds in the mutant mice (i.e., disease of the inner ear) was relatively invariant for a given subject within the context of the experiment, Sidman et al. (1966) found it necessary to introduce another control for the failure of the mice to respond to the stimulus. They suggested that it would suffice in this case to demonstrate that the animal was capable of efficient suppression to a stimulus received through another sensory modality.

AVERSIVE THRESHOLDS.   In a series of studies which pioneered in the development of the titration schedule in psychologic studies, Weiss and Laties (1958, 1959, 1963) showed that rats, monkeys, and human subjects would work to reduce the current level of continuous or intermittently administered electric shock. They termed this behavior "fractional escape" or "fractional avoidance," according to whether the reduction occurred in a currently administered or anticipated shock. Their fractional escape programs employed the Békésy tracking procedure basically, although increment in shock level was discontinuous. They found that all three types of subjects tolerated more shock when the shock level rose more rapidly, that rats and monkeys tolerated more shock when more responses were required to attenuate it, that monkeys tolerated more shock when the incremental step size was reduced, and that humans tolerated more shock when instructed to describe their "pain thresholds" than when asked to "keep the shock comfortable." Their findings were all compatible with their general conclusion that the level of shock tolerated was a function of the response cost of reducing that level. Methodologic considerations arising from the experience of these authors are dealt with by them in detail in Chapter 8 of this volume, and will not be reviewed here.

A number of other investigators followed the lead of these early studies. Weitzman et al. (1960) allowed monkeys to maintain constant regulation of the current level of a pulse train to the Gasserian ganglion by pressing a lever, and tracked this level by the Békésy technique. Boren and Malis (1961) taught monkeys to press a lever to reduce the current level of a pulse train of aversive brain stimulation. An interesting methodologic observation made by these latter authors was that current levels which the animal would tolerate continuously when the peak current was limited were levels which would evoke responding when the peak current was not limited. Their conclusion was that under the latter condition, the animals must be using the lower levels as discriminative stimuli for *avoidance* of shock at higher levels. Fields and Glusman (1967) studied this phenomenon further and showed that when the discrete trial titration schedule is used, the effect is a function of the intertrial interval. Thus Kelly and Glusman (1968), when they used the titration schedule to evaluate the effects of various midbrain lesions on pain sensation in monkeys, selected an intertrial interval of sufficient length to obviate this effect.

BRIGHTNESS DISCRIMINATION IN THE ALBINO RAT. The author has followed the lead of Sidman et al. (1966) in combining the titration schedule with the conditioned suppression baseline to evaluate absolute brightness thresholds in the dark-adapted albino rat. This report will dwell upon the methodologic aspects of these studies; fuller discussion of quantitative results will appear elsewhere (Rosenberger and Ernest, 1969).

Subjects for these studies were adolescent male albino rats, maintained at 70 percent of their free-feeding weight, and trained to press a lever for delivery of 45 mg Noyes pellets on a random ratio schedule with a probability of reinforcement of 2 or 3 percent, whichever maintained an optimal baseline in a given rat. They were then trained to suppress lever pressing during the 60-second presentation of a warning stimulus (a flashing light), which was followed immediately by a brief electric shock to the floor grid of the cage, usually 0.5 ma for 300 msec.

Figure 3 shows a cumulative record of the seventh session of training to conditioned suppression in a single rat. We have followed the usual convention of leaving the reinforcement pen depressed during the warning stimulus (CS) period. It can be seen that suppression was constant and nearly complete by this point. Training was continued until reliable suppression was achieved to a stimulus presented at an average interval of three minutes.

Figure 4 diagrams the threshold procedure. The warning stimulus (CS) emanated from a 500-watt tungsten ribbon filament projection bulb, was interrupted by a sector disc twice per second, passed through neutral density filters which determined stimulus intensity, and appeared as a circular spot about 1 inch in diameter on a translucent Plexiglas screen immediately above the response lever. The stimulus thus subtended about 90 degrees of the rat's visual angle.

R8   24 JUN 68
7th CER Session

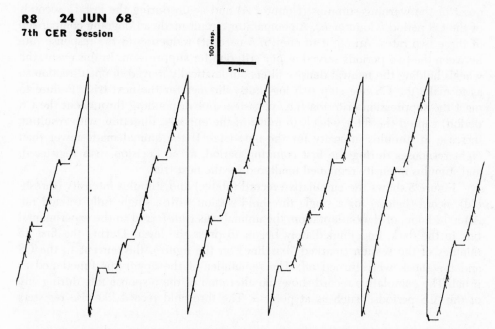

Fig. 3. Cumulative record of the responses of a single rat during the seventh session of training to the conditioned suppression (CER) paradigm. Single blips in the record indicate reinforcements. The reinforcement pen remains down during the "CS period" (presentation of the warning stimulus).

Radiant energy of the stimulus at the point of visibility was checked before each session with a silicon solar battery implanted in the translucent screen. In addition, occasional measurements of absolute luminosity were made with the Macbeth illuminometer.

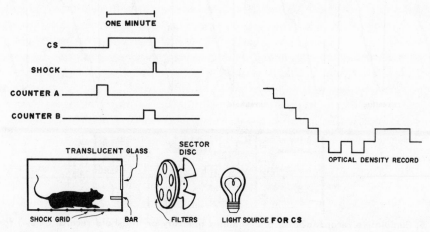

Fig. 4. Diagram of the apparatus for assessment of visual brightness thresholds in the albino rat.

Responses were counted during the 15-second period immediately preceding onset of the warning stimulus (Counter A) and again during the last 15 seconds of the CS period (Counter B). A comparator circuit made an ongoing comparison of these two rates. An eight to one (87.5 percent) reduction in the response rate between the two periods served as our criterion for suppression. In this event, the wheels holding the neutral density filters automatically moved in one direction so as to make the CS one step (0.5 log units) dimmer for the next trial. Failure to meet the suppression criterion (i.e., persistence of responding throughout the CS period) caused the filter wheels to move in the opposite direction, with resulting increase in stimulus intensity for the next trial. If the animal made fewer than eight responses during the first counting period, a "no decision" was registered, and stimulus intensity remained unaltered for the next trial.

Figure 5 shows the cumulative record (above) and stimulus intensity (threshold) record (below) for a single threshold session with a single fully trained rat. After 12 hours of dark-adaptation, the animal was transferred to the experimental box in the dark, and immediately began to press the lever. During the first 15 minutes of the session (marked "baseline" on the figure), the current to the CS and the shock were turned off. The remainder of the apparatus functioned as usual. The cumulative record shows no alteration of the response rate during any of the "CS periods," such as at point a. The threshold record likewise registers

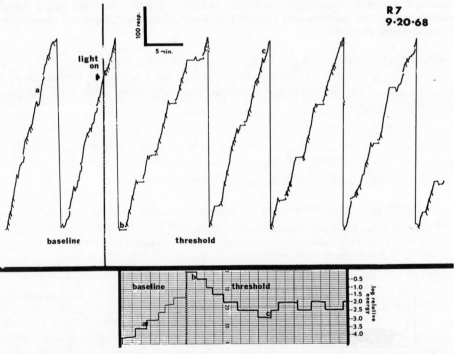

Fig. 5. Cumulative record (above) and stimulus intensity or threshold record (below) for a single threshold session with a single rat.

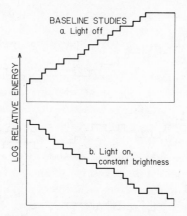

Fig. 6. Two types of baseline studies required to assure stimulus control.

consistent "increase" of stimulus intensity, although the stimulus was actually turned off.

At the dotted vertical line, current for the light stimulus and shock was turned on. The next stimulus presentation (at point *b*) caused immediate and complete suppression, with resulting attenuation of stimulus intensity as recorded by the threshold record. Suppression to succeeding stimuli of ever decreasing intensity occurred until point *c*, at which point the animal failed to suppress, with resulting increase in stimulus intensity for the next trial, and so forth. Thus a threshold was drawn.

The cumulative record at the two CS periods immediately before and after point *c* shows two interesting changes frequently seen within the "indifference range" of stimulus intensity. The first shows persistence of responding until about halfway through the 1-minute period. This change, when it occurs consistently at stimulus intensities above threshold, is sometimes described by other workers as a "temporal discrimination" on the animal's part. The second of the two periods shows initial suppression, with resumption of responding shortly before the shock occurs. We are unable to draw from our data any further conclusions about the relative significance of the two types of change.

Figure 6 shows, again following the lead of Sidman et al. (1966), the two types of baseline studies required for assurance that the animal is under specific stimulus control. First, the response rate should be free enough from spontaneous pauses that if an entire session is run with all the apparatus intact except the power source for the CS (light), the titration record will show consistent reversal. This is shown in baseline *a*. Unfortunately, repeated exposure to this procedure (in which the shocks are completely "out of the blue," so far as the animal is concerned) causes disruption of the original operant baseline in some animals. We have contented ourselves with running such a session only once for each animal. It should also be mentioned that constant failure of suppression on this schedule is not equivalent to a zero false alarm rate; the latter would be assured only by *no* pauses of 15 seconds duration anywhere in the session.

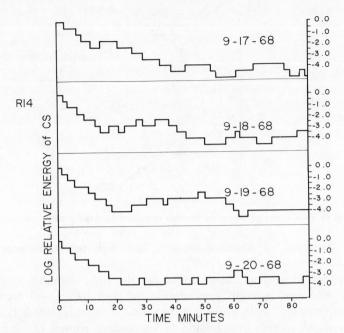

Fig. 7. Repeated thresholds from a single rat on consecutive days.

The second baseline procedure is performed with the CS at constant intensity. Suppression to every stimulus assures that the animal does not tend to "tire" of suppression before the session is over, or otherwise adapt to the contingency. One problem with interpretation of this baseline is that satiation toward the end of the session tends to lead to spontaneous pauses, which favor continued attenuation of stimulus intensity below the "true" threshold.

Repeated thresholds obtained from a single normal dark-adapted rat on four consecutive days are shown in Figure 7. Real time is graphed along the abscissa, in order that the time relationships of the various stimulus intensity reversals may be seen. Statistical calculation of mean thresholds and standard deviations will be described below. For the moment, visual inspection will reveal only minor variations among the different sessions.

Similar consecutive thresholds from a second normal rat are shown in Figure 8. The second of the four graphs in this figure (session of 9/18/68) shows a phenomenon which demonstrates one of the strengths of the titration schedule. The several reversals of stimulus intensity at the beginning of the session are clearly unrelated to the final threshold. We suspect that insufficient dark-adaptation was the cause in this case. In any event, this finding would have been concealed in a threshold obtained by the method of constant stimuli.

We further tested the specificity of the threshold technique by introducing an experimental variable, in the form of damage to the rat's retinal receptor cells by prolonged exposure to visible light, as suggested by Noell et al. (1966). We ac-

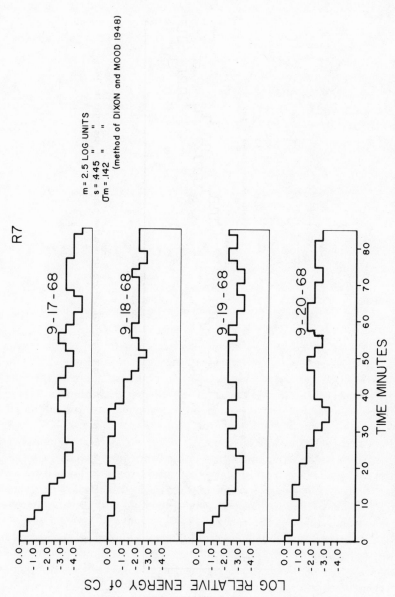

Fig. 8. Repeated thresholds from a second rat on consecutive days. Note the several stimulus intensity reversals at the beginning of the second session.

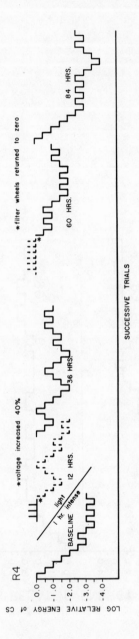

Fig. 9. Brightness thresholds in a single rat before and after exposure of the eyes to intense light.

174

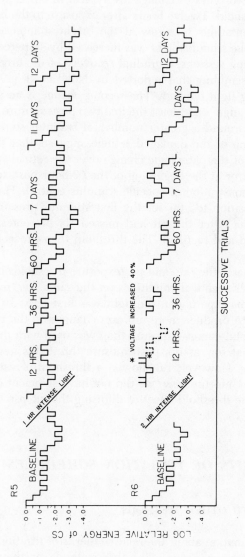

Fig. 10. Brightness thresholds in two rats before and after light exposure. Comparison of one-hour and two-hour exposure.

175

complished this by first anesthetizing the rat with Fluothane, then exposing the proptosed eyes directly to high intensity white light from two 500-watt projector bulbs, passed through a 1-inch water filter to dissipate heat energy.

Figure 9 shows serial thresholds from a single rat before and after exposure to this procedure. Two types of change are typical in our experience. The first is elevation of the threshold. Twelve hours after exposure to the light, the rat missed three stimulus presentations in a row at the brightest intensity available. Only after the voltage of the stimulus light was increased by 40 percent did he begin to respond. In succeeding sessions, a gradual recovery of the original threshold was noted, somewhat resembling that reported by Noell et al. (1966) in the electroretinogram following light damage. The second change is an apparent widening of the "indifference range" on at least the first two postexposure thresholds; that is, the threshold turns around a greater number of stimulus steps. Our preliminary histologic examination of the damaged retinae suggests that this may be due to uneven distribution of the pathologic change over the retinal surface.

An apparatus error at the beginning of the 60-hour postexposure session provided a further demonstration of specific stimulus control. The filter wheels had been moved one position too far for the first stimulus presentation, making the light totally invisible. After the rat had missed six presentations in a row, the error was discovered and rectified. The threshold then proceeded normally from that point.

Figure 10 compares the pre- and postexposure thresholds of two rats exposed to intense light under identical conditions on the same day, for two different exposure times. For this experiment, the light was first passed through a diffusing filter in an attempt to produce more uniform changes on the retinal surface. The result was a lower total energy exposure than was used with the animal of Figure 9. It can be seen that for rat R5, postexposure thresholds never differed significantly from baseline. However, R6 showed a threshold elevation similar to that seen in R4 (Fig. 9). Unfortunately, we did not have sufficient data to permit firm conclusions about the threshold effect of diffusing the intense light.

RELATIVE MERITS OF TITRATION SCHEDULES

COMPARISONS WITH OTHER METHODS

Definitive information about the relative merits of titration schedules is likely to come from direct comparisons with other methods, on the same task with the same subjects. Unfortunately, such comparisons are rare in both the human and animal literature.

Kappauf's studies (1963) included a direct comparison of the titration schedule with the constant stimulus method in two experiments with human subjects. The first concerned the discrimination of time duration. The findings of this study confirmed the author's hypothesis that a previously noted bias in the normal subject (tendency to overestimate short durations and underestimate long ones) would be enhanced if duration was regulated by the titration method.

The second comparison involved discriminations of relative distance (stereopsis). Here again the constant stimulus method gave means which were less variable and closer to the point of objective equality than the titration method, although estimates of standard deviation for the two methods were roughly equivalent.

Corso (1956) compared the Békésy audiometer with the ADC audiometer (method of limits) in the assessment of human auditory thresholds. One purpose of his study was to determine which of two possible interpretations of the Békésy curve—peaks of absolute response or midpoints of oscillations—most closely correlated with thresholds from the ADC apparatus. He found in this regard that the method of limits produced lower thresholds than those derived from reading the midpoints of the Békésy curve oscillations. (Corso adds, however, that instructions to the subjects on the Békésy procedure were to "keep the sound barely audible.") In addition, the method of limits produced less variability among subjects at lower frequencies. This could be interpreted, he adds, to mean that the Békésy method is more sensitive to individual physiologic differences.

Stebbins (Chapter 3, this volume) has made the first definitive comparison of techniques recorded in the animal literature to date. Figure 5 of his chapter shows the results of this comparison. Stebbins uses as his mean titration threshold the simple average of a number of "transition points" (stimulus intensity values at which intensity reverses), and has shown that thresholds obtained by this method are not significantly different from those obtained by the constant stimulus or limits methods.

The "limits comparison" method of Riggs et al. (1957) is not, strictly speaking, a titration schedule. However, their comparison of it with the constant stimulus method provides interesting considerations at this point. In the assessment of visual response to electrical excitation of the human eye, these authors delivered the stimulus in descending current levels until a definite "no" response was elicited. Then at descending current levels *below* this threshold, the stimulus was presented as one of a pair, the other of which was "blank," and the subject was required to judge which "stimulus" contained the current.

The first interesting finding of this study was that below the threshold of the "yes" response, subjects did make consistent and statistically significant correct comparisons. Secondly, a direct comparison with the constant stimulus method showed that the limits comparison method did not enhance reliability, and in fact produced more trial-to-trial variability. The chief advantage again was one of efficiency.

ADVANTAGES

The titration schedule was originally devised to conserve time and materials in the testing of explosives. Greater *efficiency* seems to be an almost uniform conclusion of every comparative study since then. "Efficiency" may be defined for these purposes as "amount of useful data per unit time expended," and is to be distinguished from "stability," "replicability," "validity," and so forth. It has been pointed out earlier that efficiency so defined can be a crucial consideration for psychophysical studies in noncommunicative subjects. This group clearly includes not only experimental animals but mentally defective and brain-damaged human subjects as well. One might thus expect a considerable expansion of such studies in the near future.

A second major advantage of the titration schedule lies in its power to *teach* the discrimination skills required for threshold assessment. That learning improves thresholds is rather implicit in the "practice to stability" tradition of classical psychophysics, but has been demonstrated specifically by Corso and Cohen (1958). The prethreshold trials of the titration series constitute essentially a *fading program,* as described by Moore and Goldiamond (1964) and others. That is, they may be thought of as analogous to the "successive approximations" in the *shaping* procedure of Skinner (1953), in that at first an easy discrimination will suffice, then a slightly more difficult discrimination is called for, and so on. The power of fading to facilitate learning has been repeatedly demonstrated in controlled studies with both animal and human subjects (Terrace, 1963; Moore and Goldiamond, 1964; Sidman and Stoddard, 1967; Sidman and Rosenberger, 1967; Touchette, 1968). While the depression of a threshold by fading has yet to be demonstrated in a standard psychophysical situation, the effectiveness of fading in sharpening the generalization gradient of a line-tilt discrimination has been shown in monkeys by Ray (1967), and Sidman and Stoddard (1966) have lowered the "threshold" of a circle-ellipse discrimination in children by changing the fading program used to teach the task.

Another class of advantages of the titration schedule derives from the fact that time and stimulus intensity are covariant. First, this allows continuous assessment of the effect of temporal variables on thresholds. Thus Blough (1955) was able to plot the course of dark-adaptation in the pigeon, and Kappauf (1963) traced the temporal development of context effects on judgment bias in human subjects. Secondly, in the calculation of limina, the titration schedule allows one to separate out temporal variables unrelated to stimulus intensity which nevertheless affect responding. An example of this has been mentioned above in the discussion of Figure 8.

DISADVANTAGES

Of the disadvantages of the titration schedule as a psychophysical method, greater variance and relative instability have already been mentioned. A "wavering threshold" is a relatively common clinical observation with the Békésy audiogram, as was demonstrated in Figure 1. This problem has been conceived in experimental terms by Stebbins (Chapter 3, this volume) and others as difficulty maintaining stimulus control with repeated stimuli very near threshold. The quantitative comparisons of Corso (1956) and Kappauf (1963) leave little doubt that when number of trials and subject cooperativeness are no problem, traditional methods are preferable for threshold stability.

Another major source of difficulty with titration schedules lies in their susceptibility to *context effects*. These may be defined as any bias introduced into psychophysical judgments by the context of presentation of stimuli. They are long-recognized drawbacks of limits methods (Titchener, 1905; Urban, 1907), but are seen with constant stimulus methods as well under some circumstances (Long, 1937).

Békésy (1947) recognized the possibility that with a constant rate of increase and decrease of the stimulus, the subject's response might come under the control of time of oscillation rather than of stimulus intensity. Kappauf (1963) further observed in this connection that when the titration schedule is used, a "seesaw" record of stimulus intensity is no definite assurance per se of stimulus control at the threshold, since the same result might occur with repeated presentations of a stimulus whose response probability was 0.5 (the "random walk" experiment).

Another important context effect stems from the subject's conscious awareness of stimulus context, and hence ability to predict future stimulus intensity.

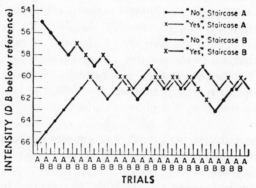

DATA FROM A THRESHOLD-DETERMINATION IN WHICH TWO
STAIRCASE-SERIES ARE ALTERNATED

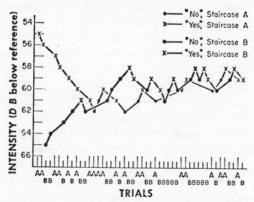

DATA FROM A THRESHOLD-DETERMINATION IN WHICH TWO
STAIRCASE-SERIES ARE MIXED RANDOMLY

Fig. 11. Two different techniques of alternating concurrent titration schedules to discourage context effects. (From Cornsweet, 1962. **Amer. J. Psychol.**, 75:485.)

Thus Békésy (1947) observed that a malingerer might describe an apparently stable record at a stimulus level well above his actual threshold. Cornsweet (1962) suggested that the best remedy for this problem was to run two series of "staircased" or titrated stimuli concurrently, proceeding from two different starting points. Figure 11, taken from his article, shows that this alternation can be either regular or random, and demonstrates slightly different but nonetheless stable data from both conditions.

One might think that awareness of stimulus context would not be a particularly difficult problem in animal psychophysics. We are reminded, however, of the finding of Boren and Malis (1961) that arbitrary limitation of maximum obtainable shock level can itself affect the level of tolerable shock in the titration of aversive thresholds.

STATISTICAL CONSIDERATIONS

Sidman (1960) has made a powerful argument in favor of incorporating primarily nonstatistical controls in psychologic experiments. One of his assumptions is that "chance" is a synonym for uncontrolled variables; the weight of his argument is not so much against the validity of statistics as in favor of devoting one's experimental energies to the mastery of uncontrolled variables rather than to enlarging the N. We suggest that this is a basically physiologic approach, and that its increasing popularity in experimental psychology of late may be taken as a hallmark of the entry of that discipline into the front rank of physiologic sciences.

On the other hand, it may be argued that "consent by inspection" to the validity of a finding is not so much a rejection of the validity of statistics as an affirmation of overwhelming statistical significance. If this is true, it behooves the investigator, when the techniques are available, to reinforce his argument with statistical calculations in any case in which inspection leaves the slightest doubt.

A threshold obtained by the tracking method frequently includes enough reversals of stimulus intensity to leave no question in any reader's mind about where the threshold lies. When a discrete trial titration is used, however, practical considerations frequently limit the number of reversals available in a given session, and the question is then raised, "How many is enough?" Fortunately, the titration schedule was originally developed by statisticians, who took the trouble to work through the statistical considerations involved. It may be of some use to investigators interested in titration schedules to review these briefly.

Two questions usually present themselves to the experimenter using the titration schedule where a limited number of trials are available. The first is, "How many times does the curve have to reverse itself to provide assurance that no wider excursions are likely?" This question involves the stability of estimates of the mean of the population from small samples. The original equations for the estimates of mean and standard deviation of the titration curve (Dixon and Mood, 1948) are as follows:

$$m = A + d\left(\frac{\Sigma f x'}{N}\right) \pm \frac{1}{2}d$$

$$s = 1.620\, d\left(\frac{N\Sigma f(x')^2 - (\Sigma f x')^2}{N^2} + 0.029\right)$$

where A is the stimulus level at which "down" responses or reversals occur most frequently, x' represents deviations from A in step units, fx' is the frequency weighting of these deviations, d is the step size in stimulus units, and N is the total number of "down" responses or reversals in the threshold. On the assumption of asymptotic variance, and because the titration schedule tends to "throw away the tails" of the normal curve, these calculations were estimated by Dixon and Mood to require 40 percent fewer trials for stability than those with data obtained by other methods.

The second question is, "How far apart do two threshold curves have to be in order to be significantly different?" This question involves the reliability of estimates of the standard error of the population mean. Again the formula given by Dixon and Mood is:

$$s_m = \frac{sG}{N}$$

where s is the standard deviation of the sample, N is the total number of "down" responses in the threshold, and G is a function of step size which amounts to 1.0 when the step size is equal to one standard deviation. This equation has been shown by Brownlee et al. (1953) to provide a reasonably stable estimate of the standard error with samples including *as few as five* reversals of the threshold curve.

Kappauf (1963) has facilitated the computation of confidence intervals for evaluating differences between curves by providing a table of calculations of the standard error of the mean as a function of step size. An adaptation of this table is reproduced below (Table 1). In more recent studies, Kappauf (1967) has performed the valuable service of testing the calculations of Dixon and Mood (1948) and of Brownlee et al. (1953) empirically by use of computer-generated up-and-down sequences. His findings largely confirm the predictions of the earlier calculations. By way of new findings, the computer studies have shown that when the step size is greater than twice the standard deviation of the sample, both the mean and the standard deviation are subject to serious bias as estimators of similar properties of the total population. This is another way of saying that they are poor predictors of what the next session will show. The practical lesson of this finding is that when a threshold is obtained which consistently turns around a single

TABLE 1 [a]

*Calculation of the Standard Error of the Mean of a Titration Threshold as a
Function of Step Size and Number of "Down" Responses*

STEP SIZE:	STANDARD ERROR WHEN NUMBER OF "DOWN" RESPONSES IS:		
	10	20	30
2.5σ	0.53σ (0.21 steps)	0.38σ (0.15 steps)	0.31σ (0.12 steps)
2.0σ	0.52σ (0.26 steps)	0.37σ (0.18 steps)	0.30σ (0.15 steps)
1.5σ	0.48σ (0.32 steps)	0.34σ (0.23 steps)	0.28σ (0.18 steps)
1.0σ	0.45σ (0.45 steps)	0.32σ (0.32 steps)	0.26σ (0.26 steps)
0.5σ	0.42σ (0.84 steps)	0.30σ (0.59 steps)	0.25σ (0.49 steps)

[a] Adapted from Kappauf, 1963.

stimulus increment, the indication is for decreasing the step size for the next experiment.

Of course, the foregoing considerations apply only when the values with which we are dealing are normally distributed; often they are not. One such example, to which we have already alluded, is illustrated in Figure 8. Whatever might be the cause of the several reversals at the beginning of the session, it makes little sense to include them in the calculation of a mean threshold either for that session or for the four sessions as a whole.

SUMMARY AND CONCLUSIONS

Because of its greater efficiency (defined as amount of useful data per unit time expended), and because of its ability to teach the discrimination skills involved, the titration schedule is a powerful tool for psychophysical studies with potentially uncooperative and nonverbal subjects, including both experimental animals and subnormal humans. It appears at least at present that the statistical problem of interpretation of sensory behaviors within the "indifference range" is handled in more stable fashion by the psychometric function derived from the constant stimulus method. The titration schedule does lend itself to statistical calculation, however, and it is to be expected that its use in combination with the precise control of sensory behaviors afforded by operant techniques will contribute to a better understanding of the sensory threshold as a behavioral phenomenon.

REFERENCES

Anderson, T. W., P. J. McCarthy, and J. W. Tukey. 1946. "Staircase" methods of sensitivity testing. NAVORD Report, 65-46.

Békésy, G. von. 1947. A new audiometer. Acta Otolaryng. (Stockholm), 35:411–422.

Blough, D. S. 1955. Method for tracing dark-adaptation in the pigeon. Science, 121:703–704.

———— 1958. A method for obtaining psychophysical thresholds from the pigeon. J. Exp. Anal. Behav., 1:31–43.

Boren, J. J., and J. L. Malis. 1961. Determining thresholds of aversive brain stimulation. Amer. J. Physiol., 201:429–433.

Boring, E. G. 1942. Sensation and Perception in the History of Experimental Psychology, New York, Appleton-Century-Crofts.

Brownlee, K. A., J. L. Hodges, and M. Rosenblatt. 1953. The up-and-down method with small samples. J. Amer. Statist. Assoc., 48:262–277.

Cattell, J. M. 1893. On errors of observation. Amer. J. Psychol., 5:285–290.

Cornsweet, T. N. 1962. The staircase method in psychophysics. Amer. J. Psychol., 75:485–491.

Corso, J. F. 1956. Effects of testing methods on hearing thresholds. Arch. Otolaryng., 63:78–91.

———— 1963. A theoretico-historical review of the threshold concept. Psychol. Bull., 60:356–370.

———— and A. Cohen. 1958. Methodological aspects of auditory threshold measurements. J. Exp. Psychol., 55:8–20.

Dixon, W. J., and A. M. Mood. 1948. A method for obtaining and analyzing sensitivity data. J. Amer. Statist. Assoc., 43:109–126.

Fechner, G. T. 1860. Elements of Psychophysics (transl. by Helmut E. Adler) 1966, New York, Holt, Rinehart, & Winston, Inc.

Fields, L., and M. Glusman. 1967. ITI effects upon conditional aversiveness in titration schedules. Read at meetings of the Eastern Psychological Assoc., Boston.

Gourevitch, G. 1965. Auditory masking in the rat. J. Acoust. Soc. Amer., 37:439–443.

———— M. H. Hack, and J. E. Hawkins. 1960. Auditory thresholds in the rat measured by an operant technique. Science, 131:1046–1047.

Guilford, J. P. 1954. Psychometric Methods, New York, McGraw-Hill Book Company.

Kappauf, W. E. 1963. Final report on context effects in psychophysical judgements. Contract No. DA-49-007-MD-877, Office of the Surgeon General, Department of the Army.

———— 1967. An empirical sampling of the up-and-down method using computer-generated series. Report No. 1 on Grant No. NB-05576-01, National Institute of Neurological Diseases and Blindness.

Kelly, D. D., and M. Glusman. 1968. Aversive thresholds following midbrain lesions. J. Comp. Physiol. Psychol., 66:25–34.

Lindsley, O. R. 1957. Operant behavior during sleep. Science, 126:1290–1291.

Long, L. 1937. A study of the effect of preceding stimuli upon the judgement of auditory intensities. Arch. Psychol. N.Y., No. 209.

McDiarmid, C. G. 1962. Context effects in differential loudness judgements. Report under Contract No. DA-49-007-MD-877, Office of the Surgeon General, Department of the Army.

Moore, R., and I. Goldiamond. 1964. Errorless establishment of visual discrimination using fading procedures. J. Exp. Anal. Behav., 7:269–272.

Noell, W. K., V. S. Walker, B. S. Kang, and S. Berman. 1966. Retinal damage by light in rats. Invest. Ophthal., 5:450–473.

Oldfield, R. C. 1949. Continuous recording of sensory thresholds and other psychophysical variables. Nature, 164:581.

Ray, B. A. 1967. The course of acquisition of a line-tilt discrimination by rhesus monkeys. J. Exp. Anal. Behav., 10:17–33.

Riggs, L. A., J. C. Cornsweet, and W. G. Lewis. 1957. Effects of light on electrical excitation of the human eye. Psychol. Monogr., 71:1–45.

Rosenberger, P. B., and J. T. Ernest. 1969. Behavioral assessment of absolute brightness thresholds in the albino rat. Vision Res., in press.

Sidman, M. 1960. Tactics of Scientific Research, New York, Basic Books, Inc.

———— 1962. An adjusting avoidance schedule. J. Exp. Anal. Behav., 5:271–277.

———— and L. T. Stoddard. 1966. Programming perception and learning for retarded children. *In* Ellis, N.S., ed., International Review of Research in Mental Retardation. New York, Academic Press, Inc., vol. 2, pp. 151–208.

———— and P. B. Rosenberger. 1967. Several methods for teaching serial position sequences to monkeys. J. Exp. Anal. Behav., 10:467–468.

———— and L. T. Stoddard. 1967. The effectiveness of fading in programming a simultaneous form discrimination for retarded children. J. Exp. Anal. Behav., 10:3–15.

———— B. A. Ray, R. L. Sidman, and J. Klinger. 1966. Hearing and vision in neurological mutant mice. Exp. Neurol., 16:377–402.

Skinner, B. F. 1953. Science and Human Behavior. New York, The Macmillan Company.

Tanner, W. P., and J. A. Swets. 1954. A decision-making theory of visual detection. Psychol. Rev., 61:401–409.

Terrace, H. S. 1963. Discrimination learning with and without "errors." J. Exp. Anal. Behav., 6:1–27.

Titchener, E. B. 1905. Experimental Psychology, New York, The Macmillan Company.

Touchette, P. E. 1968. The effects of a graduated stimulus change on the acquisition of a simple discrimination in severely retarded boys. J. Exp. Anal. Behav., 11:39–48.

Urban, F. M. 1907. On the method of just perceptible differences. Psychol. Rev., 14:244.

Weiss, B. 1969. Personal communication.

———— and V. G. Laties. 1958. Fractional escape and avoidance on a titration schedule. Science, 128:1575–1576.

———— and V. G. Laties. 1959. Titration behavior on various fractional escape programs. J. Exp. Anal. Behav., 2:227–248.

———— and V. G. Laties. 1963. Characteristics of aversive thresholds measured by a titration schedule. J. Exp. Anal. Behav., 6:563–572.

Weitzman, E., G. S. Ross, W. Hodos, and R. Galambos. 1960. Behavioral method for study of pain in the monkey. Science, 133:37–38.

BERNARD WEISS [1]
VICTOR G. LATIES [1]

THE PSYCHOPHYSICS OF PAIN AND ANALGESIA IN ANIMALS *

INTRODUCTION

The technique that we called the "titration schedule" (Weiss and Laties, 1958) grew out of a problem in pharmacology. At the time, we were located in a laboratory (the Division of Clinical Pharmacology at Johns Hopkins) devoted to studies of the effects of drugs in humans. One focus of this laboratory was the study of analgesia.

Over the years, pharmacologists have developed numerous methods for assessing analgesia in animals (Beecher, 1957). One such method is to paint a black spot on the tail of a restrained rat, focus a bright light on the tail, and measure the latency of the tail flick. Another technique is to place a mouse or rat on a hot plate, and measure how long it takes before the animal jumps off. Some experimenters inject an inflammatory agent into a joint, then measure the latency to withdrawal of the inflamed paw when it is touched. A currently popular technique is to inject mice intraperitoneally with an agent such as phenylquinone, bradykinin, or acetylcholine, and measure the "writhing" response. Some of these methods respond to the narcotic analgesics, but are rather insensitive to nonnarcotic analgesics such as aspirin, and to narcotic antagonist analgesics, such as cyclazocine. Methods that seem sensitive to the milder analgesics also tend to be rather unspecific.

Clinical pain entails a much more complex response than a tail flick. As Lasagna (1962) pointed out, the clinical pharmacologist who studies analgesia is basically a psychophysicist. In one variation of the current methods, for example, subjects recovering from surgical operations are asked to rate their pain as absent, mild, moderate, or severe. The rationale for the psychophysical approach to clinical analgesia is discussed in Beecher's book (Beecher, 1959).

[1] Department of Radiation Biology and Biophysics, The University of Rochester School of Medicine and Dentistry, Rochester, New York.

* The preparation of this paper was supported in part by Grant MH-11752 from the National Institute of Mental Health, Grant NB-08048-01 from the National Institute of Neurological Diseases and Blindness, and by a contract with the United States Atomic Energy Commission at the University of Rochester Atomic Energy Project and has been assigned Report No. UR-49-1116.

By viewing analgesic research in animals within this context, the shock titration schedule evolved naturally out of the earlier work by Békésy (1947) on auditory thresholds, by Oldfield (1949) and by Blough (1958) on visual thresholds, and by Lindsley (1957) on sleep. Our basic premise was that by exposing a subject to a gradually rising shock that he could reduce by making a specified response, we could trace out an aversive threshold. We also reasoned that continuous monitoring of the aversiveness of a stimulus might be useful, not simply for studies of pain and analgesia, but for studying aversive control. As we pointed out earlier (Weiss and Laties, 1959), being able to specify the parameters of a stimulus (which one can't do in an avoidance situation, where they remain covert) confers a number of advantages on the experimenter. The most notable is the ability to relate the behavior of the subject to the properties of the stimulus by a much shorter chain of inferences. Avoidance performance gives the experimenter no direct measure of the stimulus events that prevail at the instant of the response. Hypothetical processes and states such as "fear" are posited to account for the behavior. The escape situation at least allows him to state the parameters of the aversive stimulus when a response occurs.

A second aspect of the titration schedule with implications for behavior was the fact that we knew little at the time about how behavior under aversive control is affected by fractional changes in the intensity of the aversive stimulus (cf., Campbell, 1955). When food is used as a reinforcer, an animal's reduced body weight is not suddenly brought to normal, nor a complete meal made available after a period of food deprivation. But in the typical study with aversive stimuli, which uses electric shock, the shock is turned on or turned off completely. The parametric variations inherent in the titration situation, such as variations in the size of the increments in shock intensity, also appealed to us from these behavioral standpoints, and provided the second motive for undertaking this research.

EXPERIMENTAL METHODS

RATS

Our first studies were done with rats, for which we developed the following arrangement. The shock stimulus was provided by a constant current stimulator. The grids of the chamber were connected to the output of the stimulator so that the rat was in the plate circuit of a pentode vacuum tube. The current flowing through the animal was controlled by the grid voltage which, in turn, was controlled by a two-way stepping switch connected to a bank of resistors. We decided to use a constant current stimulator because of the complex interactions between a rat's impedance and the value of a shock current, which are further complicated by the shifting patterns of contact produced by a scrambler and the rat's movement within the chamber. The Foringer shock scrambler worked successfully when slowed to avoid constant replacement of the microswitches activated by motor-driven cams. A standard Foringer chamber was the experimental space. A precaution we found necessary, in order to reduce the possibility of successful escape without lever-pressing, was to electrify not only the grid floor but also the walls of the chamber and the two levers. In our first experiment, we used 30 steps from the minimum to the maximum shock current. For our later parametric studies, we used 25 equal steps, with currents ranging from a minimum of 0.07 ma to a maximum of 0.65 ma (based on average value of the wave = 0.636 of the maximum amplitude). Thus, each increment equalled 0.023 ma.

The titration schedule seems extremely aversive to animals, even more so than Sidman avoidance. The continuous shock, and the necessity to keep responding in order to maintain the intensity at a reasonable level, induced a lot of competing behavior. We modified the chamber in various ways to reduce such responses. For example, we lowered the roof so that the rats could not stand up. We also shaved their backs so that they could not escape the shock by lying on their backs on the grid floor, letting the fur act as an insulator. The Wistar and Holtzman rats used in these studies proved more difficult to handle than rats in any other kind of experiment we have ever performed.

We measured the amount of time spent at each of the 25 steps from the lowest current to the highest. One counter was assigned to each level. These counters were pulsed by a clock connected to the second bank of the two-way stepper. The output of the stimulator was also traced on a recording voltmeter.

MONKEYS

We turned to studies on monkeys for two reasons. One was pharmacologic: because of their biologic similarity to man, primates can be more useful than rats as predictors of therapeutic effects. The second reason was methodologic. We have already mentioned the difficulties of insuring a situation which does not allow the rat an opportunity to escape or reduce the shock except by lever pressing. Although we also studied small primates in experimental chambers of the kind used with rats, the techniques worked out for larger monkeys, maintained in primate restraining chairs, were more useful. At the same time, we developed another method of varying shock and recording performance.

Figure 1 is a block diagram of the later arrangement. The central instrument was a Grason-Stadler recording attenuator which can be used in two modes. In one, the device operates in the same way as Békésy's audiometer (Békésy, 1947). It moves an attenuator arm continuously in one direction until the subject closes a switch; it then moves the arm continuously in the other direction as long as the switch is closed. It can also be used in a stepped mode, so that switch closures produce a predetermined amount of movement. In order to be able to vary the size of both the shock increment and shock decrement, we used the continuous mode, and governed the size of the step by setting electronic timers. The timers determined the duration of shaft motion and, since the rate of rotation was constant, the amount of change in stimulator output. As the shaft of the recording

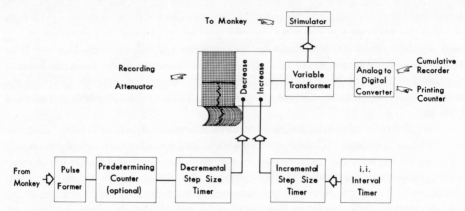

Fig. 1. Block diagram of the programming and recording equipment used in the primate experiments. Responses by the monkey drove the shock level down, with a step size governed by the decremental step size timer. Increments occurred periodically with a frequency determined by the i-i interval timer. The incremental step sizes were governed by the incremental step size timer. (From Weiss and Laties, 1963. **J. Exp. Anal. Behav.**, 6:563–572. Copyright 1963 by the Society for the Experimental Analysis of Behavior, Inc.)

attenuator turned, it rotated the shaft of a rigidly attached autotransformer connected to the primary of a transformer in the shock power supply. The secondary of this transformer was connected in series with a high resistance and the

Fig. 2. Side view of the electrode shoe used with the monkeys. The feet are held in with Velcro strips, and electrode cream (EKG-Sol) is used to assist in maintaining adequate electrical contact.

monkey. This conventional type of shock power supply proved adequate and reliable with monkeys restrained in primate chairs. To maintain a uniform contact surface and impedance, the animal's feet were strapped into shoes of bent strips of aluminum by Velcro strips, as illustrated in Figure 2 (Weiss and Laties, 1962). During an experiment, we continuously monitored the voltage drop across the subject or across a 1,000-ohm resistor in series with it. For a given stimulator output, the voltage drop across the subject remained constant for many hours. Instead of recording the amount of time spent at discrete steps, we used an analog-to-digital converter so constructed that it emitted a pulse rate directly related to the amplitude of the shock. The higher the shock, the higher the rate. By recording the number of pulses within a specified time period, we obtained a measure analogous to the area under the aversive threshold tracing. We labeled this measure the "integrated shock." The incremental step-size timer was pulsed by a timer set to the increment-increment (i-i) interval. The decremental step-size timer was activated by responses from the monkey. These could be arranged on continuous reinforcement or according to a fixed ratio.

PARAMETRIC VARIATIONS

The most cogent lesson behavioral pharmacology has taught is that one must explore behavioral parameters in the same way that one explores drug dose as a parameter. The behavioral action of a drug depends as much on the baseline behavior as on the pharmacologic properties of the agent. For this reason, before undertaking any experiments with drugs, we performed a number of studies aimed at understanding how some of the possible parametric variations might influence aversive thresholds (Weiss and Laties, 1959).

VARIATION IN INTERVAL BETWEEN INCREMENTS

The i-i interval was an obvious parameter to manipulate. In our preliminary work, it was quickly apparent that one of the problems we might have to deal with, a problem outlined for a predecessor of this schedule by Mowrer (1940), would be the confounding of aversive threshold with avoidance behavior. That is, low levels of stimulation can become discriminative stimuli for the later occurrence of high levels, serving the same function as a warning buzzer. Such a development might introduce variables other than painfulness of the shock in determining aversive threshold. One possible way to avert such a problem was to increase the rate of shock elevation to a value that made avoidance behavior increasingly difficult.

Figure 3, from the rat experiments, shows the proportion of time spent on each of the 25 shock levels from minimum to maximum shock as a function of the i-i interval. The shorter the i-i interval, the greater the proportion of time spent at the higher shock levels. Another way of expressing this finding is to look at the

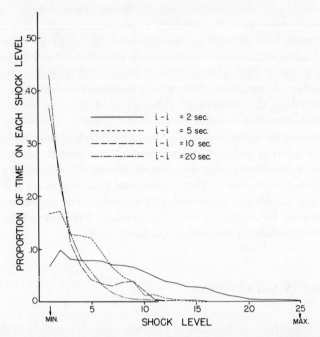

Fig. 3. Proportion of session time spent at each of the 25 equally-spaced steps from minimum (0.07 ma) to maximum (0.65 ma) shock intensity for four different i-i intervals. N = 6. (From Weiss and Laties, 1959. **J. Exp. Anal. Behav.**, 2:227–248. Copyright 1959 by the Society for the Experimental Analysis of Behavior, Inc.)

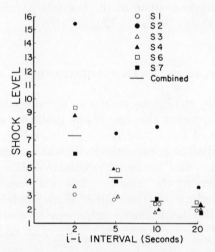

Fig. 4. Median shock levels for each of four i-i intervals. N = 6. The medians are the points below which the shock was kept 50 percent of the session. (From Weiss and Laties, 1959. **J. Exp. Anal. Behav.**, 2:227–248. Copyright 1959 by the Society for the Experimental Analysis of Behavior, Inc.)

median shock level for each of the i-i intervals; that is, the point below which the shock was kept 50 percent of the session. The means for six rats, and the individual points, are shown in Figure 4. A sample of individual performance appears in Figure 5. Two features should be noted. One is the greater amount of shock taken at the two shorter i-i intervals than at the two longer ones. The other is that even at the long i-i intervals, a pattern is apparent, with the shock level allowed to rise only to be brought down with a rapid train of responses. The fact that levels are allowed to rise so high indicates either the presence of avoidance behavior at the long i-i intervals, or the occurrence of competing behavior.

The differences noted with rats are also present in humans (Weiss and Laties, 1963). We used three male subjects, all of whom were paid for their services. The stimulus was delivered through EKG electrodes used for telemetry, so that contact of the electrode with the skin was made through a layer of electrode paste. The subjects responded by pulling a Lindsley manipulandum and were studied under two different sets of instructions. In one, they were told to maintain the electrical stimulus within the "comfort zone"—well below the threshold of pain. In the other, they were told to maintain the stimulus ". . . just below the point at which it hurts." The same stimulator used in the monkey experiments was used here, and as we can see in Figures 6 and 7, the human subjects tended to tolerate more shock under both sets of instructions with a shorter i-i interval. Sample records for the pain threshold condition are shown in Figure 6 and the "comfort zone" condition in Figure 7.

FIXED-RATIO

Shortening the i-i interval is one way to increase the response rate needed to maintain the shock at a constant level. The other way is to put shock reduction on a fixed-ratio (FR) reinforcement schedule, so that n responses must be emitted in order to produce a decrement. In the rat studies, we compared i-i 5 seconds, FR 1, to i-i 20 seconds, FR 4. Thus, in both cases, an average of 1 response every 5 seconds was needed to maintain the shock at a constant level. In a similar way, i-i 2 seconds, FR 1, was compared to i-i 20 seconds, FR 10.

The results for four rats are shown in Figure 8. As might have been predicted from the work on i-i interval variation, the greater the response rate needed to match the i-i rate, the higher the tolerated shock level. Within each rate, however, there is an interesting difference. More shock is taken when the higher fixed ratio requirement is imposed, even though the response rate requirement remains the same. This is particularly striking for i-i 2, FR 1, versus i-i 20, FR 10. Part of the reason is seen in the top half of Figure 9. Under FR 1, the cumulative record tends to be fairly smooth. Under FR 10, the cumulative record displays high rates alternating with low rates, which provides a clue to the threshold differences. Once the shock reaches aversive levels with a long i-i interval,

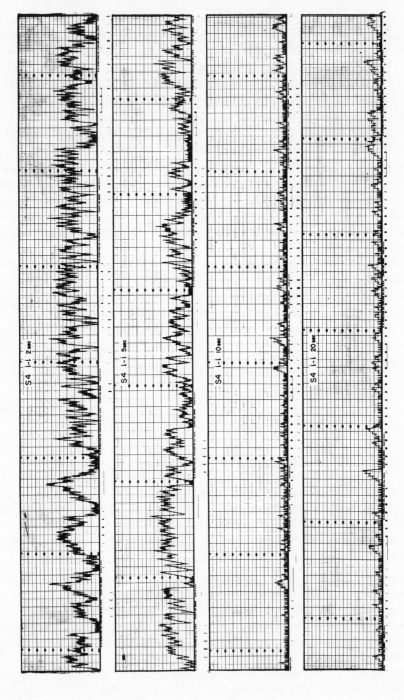

Fig. 5. Tracings of stimulator output for rat S-4 at four different i-i intervals. Programmed rises in shock intensity drive the recording pen upwards. Responses by the rat carry it downwards. Time is left to right. (From Weiss and Laties, 1959. **J. Exp. Anal. Behav.,** 2:227–248. Copyright 1959 by the Society for the Experimental Analysis of Behavior, Inc.)

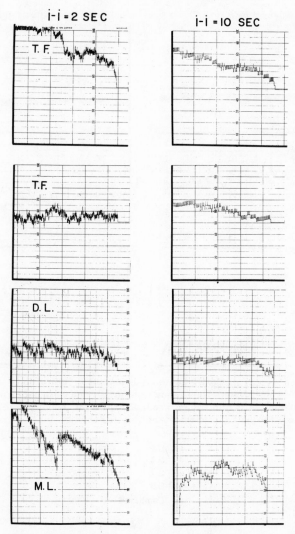

Fig. 6. Attenuator records made by human subjects under instructions to maintain the shock level just below the point at which the shock produces pain. Time reads right to left and each segment represents the last 30 minutes of a 40 minute session. (From Weiss and Laties, 1963. **J. Exp. Anal. Behav.**, 6:563–572. Copyright 1963 by the Society for the Experimental Analysis of Behavior, Inc.)

high FR combination, many responses must be emitted to decrease the level by several steps. Only if lower levels served as warning stimuli would this pattern not appear. The higher shock levels taken under the fixed-ratio condition indicate that avoidance behavior is weak in the titration schedule. In later experiments, we used i-i intervals as high as 300 seconds, with an FR of 99.

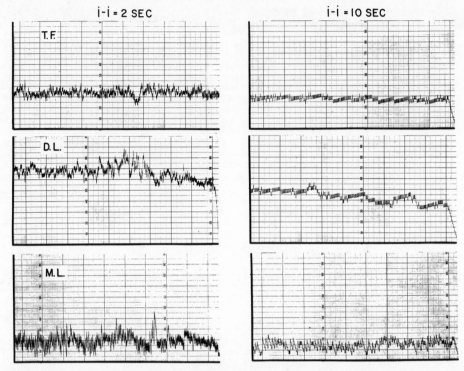

Fig. 7. Attenuator records made by human subjects under instructions to maintain shock level within the "comfort zone." Time reads right to left and each segment represents a 40 minute session. (From Weiss and Laties, 1963. **J. Exp. Anal. Behav.**, 6:563–572. Copyright 1963 by the Society for the Experimental Analysis of Behavior, Inc.)

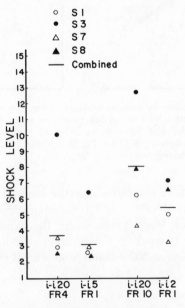

Fig. 8. (Legend on page 195.)

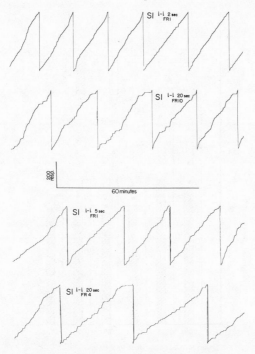

Fig. 9. Cumulative records for rat S-1 under four different conditions. Contrast especially i-i 2 sec, FR 1 versus i-i 20 sec. FR 10. (From Weiss and Laties, 1959. **J. Exp. Anal. Behav.,** 2:227–248. Copyright 1959 by the Society for the Experimental Analysis of Behavior, Inc.)

VARIATIONS IN STEP SIZE

In the parametric studies discussed so far, each change in current was 0.04 of the total range. The ability to vary step size (see Fig. 1) allowed us to explore this dimension in a fashion parallel to our exploration of i-i interval (Weiss and Laties, 1963). In the first set of experiments we used two cebus (*Cebus capucinus*) and one squirrel (*Saimiri sciurea*) monkey. They were studied in a modified rat box of the type used in the earlier studies. The maximum shock was 1.1 milliampere rms and the incremental and decremental steps were set to be equal. The total range was divided into as many as 500 and as few as 14 steps. Figure 10 shows that the influence of step size was great with an i-i interval of 2 seconds, but small with an i-i interval of 10 seconds. With the two smaller step sizes, even though the rate requirements to keep shock level constant were the same, a 30 percent rise in the integrated shock was produced.

Fig. 8. Median shock levels for four rats under the four conditions noted. (From Weiss and Laties, 1959. **J. Exp. Anal. Behav,** 2:227–248. Copyright 1959 by the Society for the Experimental Analysis of Behavior, Inc.)

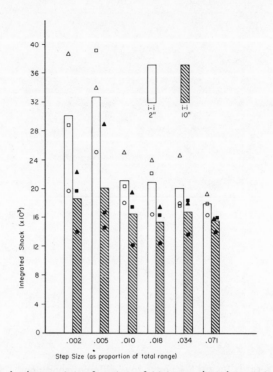

Fig. 10. Integrated shock as a joint function of i-i interval and step size. Incremental step equals decremental step. The height of the bar designates the mean of three monkeys. Each symbol represents an individual monkey. The point for a single monkey represents the mean of 3 one-hour sessions. (From Weiss and Laties, 1963. **J. Exp. Anal. Behav.**, 6:563–572. Copyright 1963 by the Society for the Experimental Analysis of Behavior, Inc.)

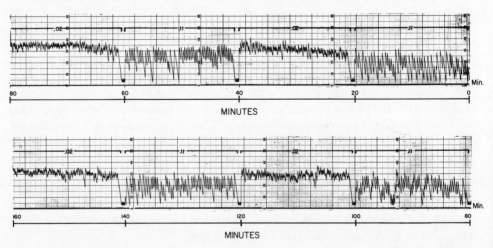

Fig. 11. Sample attenuator record comparing step sizes of .02 and .11. The incremental step size remained at .02. The size of the decremental step alternated every 20 minutes. Time reads right to left. (From Weiss and Laties, 1963. **J. Exp. Anal. Behav.**, 6:563–572. Copyright 1963 by the Society for the Experimental Analysis of Behavior, Inc.)

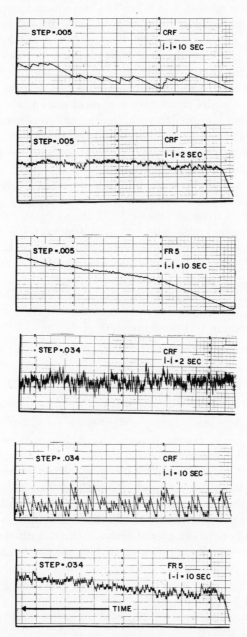

Fig. 12. Sample attenuator records with the step sizes and i-i intervals noted. Each segment covers 1 hour. Time reads right to left. (From Weiss and Laties, 1963. **J. Exp. Anal. Behav.,** 6:563–572. Copyright 1963 by the Society for the Experimental Analysis of Behavior, Inc.)

Another feature of step size is apparent in Figure 11. This record was obtained with one of the animals restrained in the primate chairs and exposed to shock via electrode shoes. The record shows alternating 20-minute segments of decremental step sizes of 0.02 and 0.11. The incremental step size was constant at 0.02 and the i-i interval remained at 2 seconds throughout. As might be expected on the basis of the other data, the integrated shock was higher with a smaller step size; but note from the records something even more interesting. During those periods when the larger step size was in effect, the monkey began responding at a lower level than when the smaller step size was programmed, suggesting that the monkey was discriminating increment size. A rate of 30 responses per minute is not excessive for a monkey; there are numerous examples on the record in which a long train of responses sharply reduced shock level, even with the 0.02 step size in effect. Yet it was permitted to climb back to the previous high level without very many intervening responses.

The effects of step size can be amplified by adding a ratio contingency. A sampling of the possible interactions is given in Figure 12, which compares a number of different conditions; sizes of 0.005 versus 0.034, i-i intervals of 10 seconds versus 2 seconds, and fixed-ratio versus continuous reinforcement. First, compare the effect of step size. Under all conditions (i-i 2 seconds, i-i 10 seconds, and i-i 10 seconds FR 5), the monkey tolerated more shock with the smaller step size. The main features of the tracing persisted, however. It was most stable at i-i 2 seconds, displayed a marked increase in variability and lower tolerated level at i-i 10 seconds, and gradually drifted upward under the FR contingency, although the response rate requirement was the equivalent of that at i-i 2 seconds.

FACTORS MAINTAINING TITRATION SCHEDULE BEHAVIOR

These kinds of data raise some puzzling questions about the aversive control of behavior in fractional escape procedures. Although a variety of conditions maintain the behavior, the variations in threshold demonstrate that the amount of shock tolerated is a function of the situational parameters. Why should the tolerated shock level increase with a shortening of the i-i interval or a decrease in the step size? One possible hypothesis is that the physical ability of the animal to match the programmed rate of rise of shock level simply becomes inadequate. Such an hypothesis is not very cogent because the records show many occasions on which trains of responses in quick succession are emitted that drive the shock level far below the modal value. Once this occurs, all the animal has to do to maintain it at that low level is to emit responses at a rate equal to the programmed rate of rise. In no instance, given this criterion, has the programmed rate of rise in our experiments exceeded the physical capacities of the subject.

For the rat, another possible explanation is that behavior which competes with lever-pressing is reinforced from time to time and, therefore, increases in frequency. Rats develop numerous techniques to make life difficult for the experimenter. They attempt to escape from the chamber, they minimize the effects of the shock by lying on their backs (one reason that we have often shaved animals), they sprawl on the bars, and so on. Competing behavior introduces a lag into the system which is amplified with the shorter i-i intervals. Such an explanation is less cogent for monkeys, restrained in primate chairs, whose feet are strapped into electrode shoes. They can engage in minimal competing behavior, yet the same effect is seen. It is seen, in fact, with humans. The monkeys showed another point of similarity with rats. Especially at the shorter i-i intervals, they tolerated overtly noxious levels of shock. The shock level was often maintained at a point that induced twitches of the feet and vocalizations, even though a few responses in succession could drive the stimulus below this point, and steady responding could keep it there. As we mentioned earlier, the schedule seems to be rather aversive. It is conceivable that this very property reduces the likelihood of responding at shock levels below those noxious enough to overcome the aversive features of the schedule itself.

Whatever the reasons for this phenomenon, our parametric studies provided valuable information for our pharmacologic experiments (Weiss and Laties, 1961; 1964). We saw that it was possible to remove virtually all of the avoidance component from the behavior by using a sufficiently short i-i interval. Such conditions provided a stimulus within a range clearly aversive to the animal and uncontaminated by pharmacologic side effects which might impair performance. This is an important consideration. In order to maintain a constant aversive threshold, the subject must emit a relatively steady response rate. If the threshold is raised by a drug, and remains steady at that higher value, we can attribute it to a change in the aversive threshold and not simply to a generalized motor impairment, since response rate remains the same.

PHARMACOLOGIC STUDIES

RAT EXPERIMENTS

To test our assumptions about the effects of parametric variation, we compared i-i intervals of 2 and 10 seconds after the injection of saline, 2.5 mg/kg of morphine sulfate, or 250 mg/kg of sodium salicylate (Weiss and Laties, 1961). The drugs were given intraperitoneally immediately before placing the rat in the chamber. Sessions lasted 100 minutes, only the last 90 of which were used to obtain the distributions of time over shock levels. The drug effect, described by Figures 13 and 14, was considerably greater with the shorter i-i interval. Note that at i-i 2 seconds, the mode for sodium salicylate appears at shock level 8, while for saline the mode is level 2. For i-i 10 seconds, the mode is level 1 for all treatments.

For a series of later experiments on aspirin, we settled on an i-i interval of 2 seconds. The aspirin was given orally in doses of 62.5, 125, and 250 mg/kg, and the experiment began 60 minutes after administration. Figure 15 shows the distribution of time over shock level for 10 rats. Although, after 250 mg/kg, the rats spent about 10 percent of the session at maximum shock, this dose did not affect

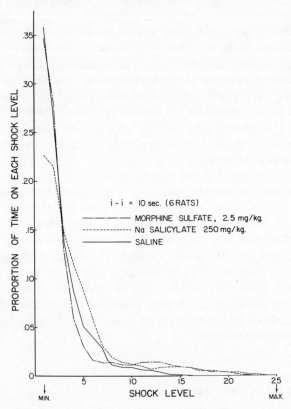

Fig. 13. Proportion of session time spent at each of the 25 shock levels from minimum to maximum shock for 3 different drug treatments at i-i 10 sec. N = 6.

conventional escape performance, in which a response terminates a stimulus, with a shock intensity equal to the maximum level (Weiss and Laties, 1961). This is an important point to remember, because so many of the other techniques used to screen for analgesic drugs rely basically on an escape response. The clinical situations in which aspirin is employed more often involve a relatively steady or slowly changing pain level.

MONKEY EXPERIMENTS

For the drug studies with monkeys, we used an i-i interval of 2 seconds, and 50 steps to span the total range, which was 0 to 5 ma for three monkeys and 0 to 4 ma for two (Weiss and Laties, 1964). One aim of these studies, as we pointed out in the introduction, was to obtain data on the analgesic properties of narcotic antagonists. In this study we looked at two, contrasting their effects with morphine.

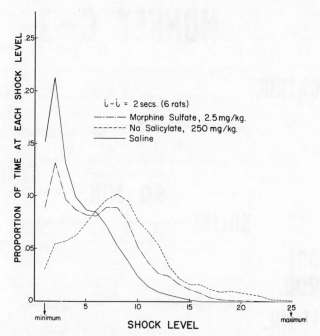

Fig. 14. Proportion of session time spent at each of the 25 steps from minimum to maximum shock for 3 different drug treatments at i-i 2 sec. N = 6.

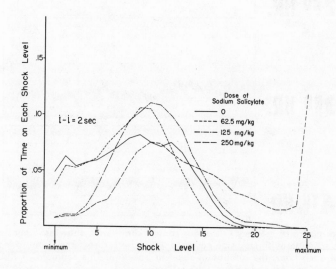

Fig. 15. Proportion of session time spent at each of the 25 shock levels from minimum to maximum shock for different dose levels of sodium salicylate. N = 6.

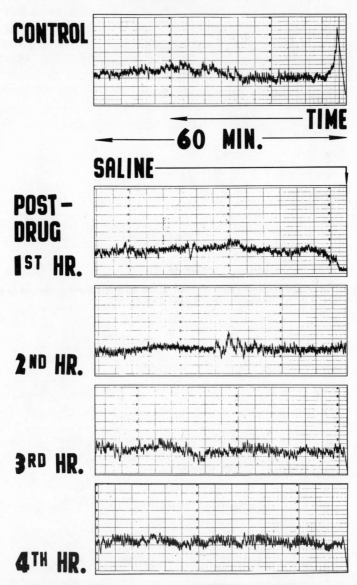

Fig. 16. Performance of monkey C-2 under control conditions, showing 5 consecutive hours on a titration schedule with step size equal to .02 in both directions. Time runs right to left. At the end of each hour, the attenuator reset to baseline. This segment of the record was inadvertently omitted for the second post-saline hour.

One was nalorphine (N-allylnormorphine), the antagonist originally shown by La-sagna and Beecher (1954) to be an analgesic. The other was the drug now called cyclazocine, a benzomorphan shown by Lasagna et al. (1964) to be analgesic in man. This drug was inactive when studied by the D'Amour-Smith tail flick technique (Harris and Pierson, 1964). It was active in the hot plate test, but with an ED 50 (effective dose for 50 percent of the population) in mice of 19 mg/kg, a dose which produces considerable muscular relaxation. We found that both morphine and cyclazocine raised titration schedule aversive thresholds in monkeys, and the potency ratio of the two seemed to be approximately the same as Lasagna et al. had determined for man. Nalorphine had no effect, a finding we believe reflects a species difference.

Figure 16 shows a saline control session extending for 4 hours from the time of injection. Time runs from right to left. The aversive threshold remains at a fairly stable level throughout. Its reliability is also supported by the fact that it

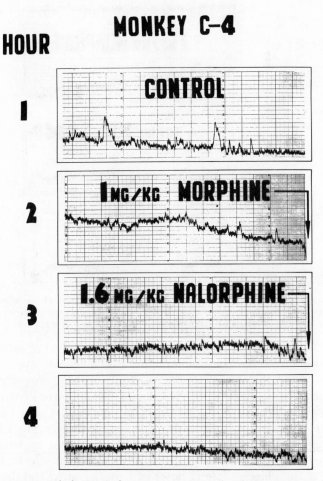

Fig. 17. Attenuator record showing change in aversive threshold produced by morphine, and the antagonism produced by nalorphine. Each segment represents 1 hour. Time reads right to left. The attenuator reset to baseline at the end of each hour.

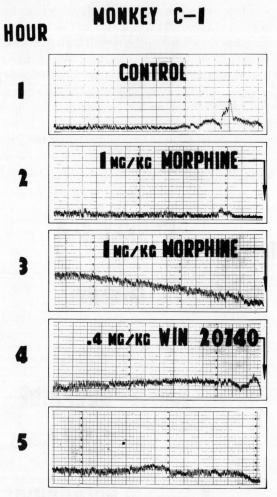

Fig. 18. Attenuator record demonstrating the antagonism of morphine effects on aversive threshold by cyclazocine (here noted as WIN 20740). Each segment represents 1 hour. Time reads right to left. The attenuator reset to baseline at the end of each hour.

rises to the same level after the return to baseline at the end of each hour, a technique used throughout the drug studies to test threshold stability.

Figures 17 and 18 demonstrate the sensitivity of the aversive threshold to the effects of the narcotic antagonists. Note again that time runs from right to left. Figure 17 shows a rise in aversive threshold for monkey C-4 after 1 mg/kg of morphine sulfate. A dose of 1.6 mg/kg of nalorphine hydrochloride, administered at the beginning of the third hour, rather quickly reduced the aversive threshold to the level prevailing before morphine. Figure 18 shows the effects in monkey C-1 of 2 mg/kg of morphine sulfate (2 doses of 1 mg/kg each) and the ability of cyclazocine (noted in the figure as WIN 20,740) to attenuate the action of morphine. This is an interesting effect because cyclazocine itself, at even lower doses, raises the aversive threshold (Weiss and Laties, 1964). It seems clear, therefore, that the

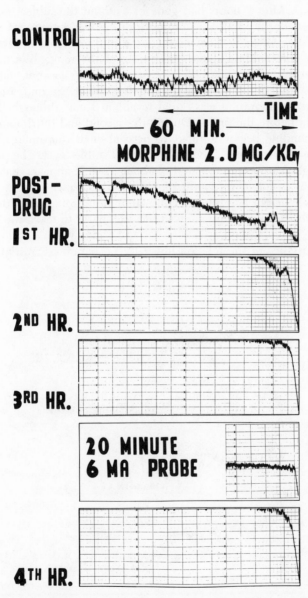

Fig. 19. Attenuator record showing the rise in aversive threshold produced by morphine and the resumption of titration performance after changing the range from 0-4 to 0-6 ma. All segments represent 1 hour except for the 20 minute probe. The attenuator reset to baseline at the end of each hour. The attenuator record encompasses the range from zero to maximum shock, independent of the actual value of the maximum, which is determined by a series resistor.

titration situation is sensitive to this antagonism, as well as to the individual analgesic actions of narcotics and benzomorphan narcotic antagonists.

Perhaps of more interest in the present context is a further exploration of the
relationship between drug action and behavioral parameters. Figure 19, for example, shows a rise in aversive threshold, after 2 mg/kg of morphine sulfate, to
the highest level. After 2 hours had gone by without the subject making any attempts to lower the threshold, a 20-minute probe was introduced during which
the maximum shock level was changed from 4 to 6 ma. Note in Figure 19 a very
stable aversive threshold at about the middle of the range. We may draw two
inferences from this probe. First, the lack of responding was not due to motor impairment or to any other irrelevant disrupting factor. Second, the shock level
maintained during the probe was equal to about 3 ma, although the top of the
range was 4 ma before the probe. During the second and third hours, a high frequency of responding began at about 75 percent of the maximum shock, but the
responding was not frequent enough to insure a stable level. The point at which
responding began can be extrapolated to about 3 ma. It appears that this is a level
great enough to maintain responding only if an increment represents an easily
discriminable change in current; after the 20-minute probe, when the 4-ma range
was restored, the monkey again allowed the attenuator to reach the highest shock
level.

Another instance of the relationship between parametric variation and drug

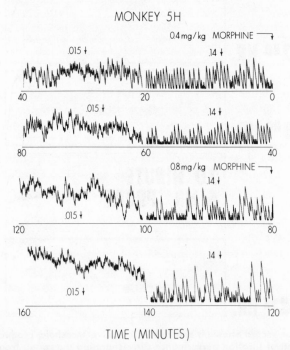

Fig. 20. Attenuator records showing changes in aversive threshold after morphine with
step sizes of .14 and .015. Step sizes alternated every 20 minutes. Time runs right to left.
The attenuator reset to baseline at the end of each 20-minute segment.

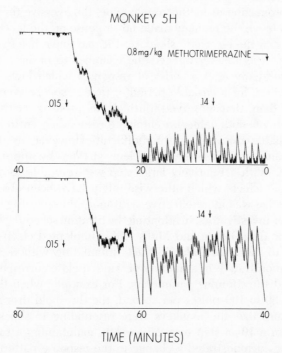

MONKEY 5H

0.8mg/kg METHOTRIMEPRAZINE

.015 ↓   .14 ↓

40   20   0

.14 ↓

.015 ↓

80   60   40

TIME (MINUTES)

Fig. 21. Attenuator records showing the effects of methotrimeprazine with two different step sizes, .14 and .015. In this case, in contrast to morphine, the larger step size was a more sensitive indicator of analgesic effect than the smaller one. Step sizes alternated every 20 minutes and reset to the baseline at the end of each segment.

effect appears in Figure 20. This shows the effect not of changing the range of shock, but of changing the step size. Recall that lower shock levels tend to be maintained with higher step sizes. In this experiment, incremental doses of morphine sulphate were employed, doubling each time, and beginning with a dose of 0.2 mg/kg. The data shown are those obtained after the second and third doses, so that at the beginning of the record in the figure, the cumulative dose is 0.6 mg/kg. After enough morphine had been given to produce a considerable rise in aversive threshold, the decremental step size was changed every 20 minutes with the results seen in the figure. An aversive threshold well below the level achieved with the smaller step size was maintained with the larger step size.

A second indication of the importance of parametric variation in drug action is shown in Figure 21. Methotrimeprazine is a phenothiazine that, like chlorpromazine, has been used successfully with institutionalized psychotics. It was later discovered that methotrimeprazine also possesses analgesic effects (Lasagna and DeKornfeld, 1961). Although it can produce orthostatic hypotension as a rather undesirable side effect, this is not a crucial objection when employed in patients confined to bed. When we tested monkeys to parallel Lasagna and DeKornfeld's human data, we again emphasized parametric variation. Figure 21 demonstrates a frequent effect of phenothiazines in this situation—what might be called a lack of stimulus control (cf., Laties and Weiss, 1969). After the administration of chlorpromazine or methotrimeprazine, the aversive threshold often rose to the maximum level; the monkey made no response on the lever even though its feet were jerking in the electrode shoes, and it may have been vocalizing. Sometimes, when the experimenter opened the chamber to observe the monkey, the subject would suddenly emit a series of responses which lowered the shock. It might then maintain, for a variable period of time, a steady aversive threshold at a level higher than that observed during the predrug control observations. The tendency for phenothiazines to eliminate responding entirely made the procurement of reliable thresholds rather difficult. However, as demonstrated by Figure 21, we could overcome these problems at times by appropriate manipulation of step size. With a relatively large step we were able to demonstrate presumably analgesic effects which otherwise might have been obscured. Note that the smaller step size was more effective with morphine (see Fig. 20).

Several other investigators, in adopting the titration schedule, have contributed useful parametric data. Boren and Malis (1961) implanted electrodes in the midbrain, adjacent to the spinothalamic tract, stimulating with rectangular bipolar pulses. They demonstrated, in a number of ways, a close correspondence between the behavior and the stimulus parameters. For example, when they changed the pulse rate from 50 to 100 pulses per second, the threshold dropped immediately by half, indicating that the monkeys were responding to shock density. When they shifted from a 10-μa step to a 2.5-μa step, maintaining a total range of 100 steps, the tracings demonstrated a change in the response pattern which resulted in approximately the same shock level. Similar results have been reported by Weitzman and Ross (1962) and Ross (1966).

Boren and Malis were also concerned with whether low shock levels might serve as discriminative stimuli for the occurrence of higher ones, a problem we alluded to above in discussing a possible role for avoidance contingencies. To test this notion, they limited the peak current. Their aim here was to determine whether or not the normally tolerated aversive thresholds functioned as primary aversive stimuli (controlling escape behavior) or as warning stimuli (controlling avoidance behavior). They began with a shock level approximately two-thirds of the monkey's threshold, maintaining it there until conventional escape responding extinguished. They then raised it by their standard titration schedule increment, and again waited for extinction to take place. Finally, they reached a level at which escape responding did not extinguish. The data from this experiment demonstrated that the stimulating current levels which these animals tolerated on the titration schedule were levels which normally produce escape responding. They concluded that the monkeys tended to keep the stimulus within an inherently aversive range most of the time. And, as they point out, "The conditioned aversive stimuli are so close to the inherently aversive ones, that it should be possible, by changing the experimental conditions, to force the threshold up to the inherently aversive levels" (Boren and Malis, 1961, p. 433). Kelly and Glusman (1964) stimulated cats with subcutaneous electrodes and demonstrated extremely stable thresholds. They used an i-i interval of 4 seconds, and by requiring at least 0.75 seconds to elapse between successive responses, markedly reduced the number of response bursts. They also introduced a modification of the procedure to make it more like the one originally introduced by Mowrer (1940). Instead of using a fractional escape procedure, each response reduced the shock to zero. Thresholds obtained by this procedure were not markedly different from those obtained by the titration schedule. They also demonstrated that by selectively elevating pain threshold, with an injection of the local anesthetic procaine to one side of the cat's body, they could produce a rise in the aversive threshold not attributable to a generalized behavioral deficit.

CONCLUDING REMARKS

Looking back on the history of our research on titration schedules, we are struck by how much of it was forged by an interplay of behavioral and pharmacologic questions. The development of the technique was spurred by the lack of a satisfactory behavioral approach to questions of pain and analgesia. It rather quickly became clear, however, that our ability to use the titration technique as a pharmacologic tool depended on a thorough understanding of its behavioral properties. In exploring these properties, we encountered a number of interesting behavioral questions. Given what we already knew about the complexity of drug-behavior interactions, it was a natural step to seek out the dimensions of the interaction.

A similar kind of history, substituting physiologic or anatomic for pharmacologic questions, underlies many of the other techniques described in this book. The perspective imposed by having to understand and control behavior, in order to ask intelligent questions about other variables, forces us to speak explicitly about behavioral variables. By driving investigators away from speculation and toward concrete manipulations, research in animal psychophysics should continue to make valuable contributions to a science of behavior.

REFERENCES

Beecher, H. K. 1957. The measurement of pain. Prototype for the quantitative study of subjective responses. Pharmacol. Rev., 9:59–209.
——— 1959. The Measurement of Subjective Responses: Quantitative Effects of Drugs, New York, Oxford University Press.
Békésy, G. von. 1947. A new audiometer. Acta Otolaryng. (Stockholm), 35:411–422.
Blough, D. S. 1958. A method for obtaining psychophysical thresholds from the pigeon. J. Exp. Anal. Behav., 1:31–43.
Boren, J. J., and J. L. Malis. 1961. Determining thresholds of aversive brain stimulation. Amer. J. Physiol., 201:429–433.
Campbell, B. A. 1955. The fractional reduction in noxious stimulation required to produce "just noticeable" learning. J. Comp. Physiol. Psychol., 48:141–148.
Harris, L. S., and A. K. Pierson. 1964. Some narcotic antagonists in the benzomorphan series. J. Pharmacol. Exp. Ther., 143:141–148.

Kelly, D. D., and M. Glusman. 1964. Aversive thresholds for subcutaneous electrical stimulation in the cat. Psychon. Sci., 1:207–208.

Lasagna, L. 1962. The psychophysics of clinical pain. Lancet, 2:572–575.

—— and H. K. Beecher. 1954. The analgesic effectiveness of nalorphine and nalorphine-morphine combinations in man. J. Pharmacol. Exp. Ther., 112:356–363.

—— and T. J. DeKornfeld. 1961. Methotrimeprazine. A new phenothiazine derivative with analgesic properties. J.A.M.A., 178:887–890.

——T. J. DeKornfeld, and J. W. Pearson. 1964. The analgesic efficacy and respiratory effects in man of a benzomorphan "narcotic antagonist." J. Pharmacol. Exp. Ther., 144:12–16.

Laties, V. G., and B. Weiss. 1969. Behavioral mechanisms of drug action. In Black, P., ed. Drugs and the Brain, Baltimore, Johns Hopkins Press, pp. 115–133.

Lindsley, O. R. 1957. Operant behavior during sleep: A measure of depth of sleep. Science, 126:1290–1291.

Mowrer, O. H. 1940. An experimental analogue of "regression" with incidental observations on "reaction formation." J. Abnorm. Soc. Psychol., 35:56–87.

Oldfield, R. C. 1949. Continuous recording of sensory thresholds and other psychophysical variables. Nature, 164:581.

Ross, G. A. 1966. A technique to study pain in monkeys: Effects of drugs and anatomic lesions. In Knighton, R. S., and Dumke, P. R., eds. Pain, Boston, Little, Brown and Company, pp. 91–110.

Weiss, B., and V. G. Laties. 1958. Fractional escape and avoidance on a titration schedule. Science, 128:1575–1576.

—— and V. G. Laties. 1959. Titration behavior on various fractional escape programs. J. Exp. Anal. Behav., 2:227–248.

—— and V. G. Laties. 1961. Changes in pain tolerance and other behavior produced by salicylates. J. Pharmacol. Exp. Ther., 131:120–129.

—— and V. G. Laties. 1962. A foot electrode for monkeys. J. Exp. Anal. Behav., 5:535–536.

—— and V. G. Laties. 1963. Characteristics of aversive thresholds measured by a titration schedule. J. Exp. Anal. Behav., 6:563–572.

—— and V. G. Laties. 1964. Analgesic effects in monkeys of morphine, nalorphine, and a benzomorphan narcotic antagonist. J. Pharmacol. Exp. Ther., 143:169–173.

Weitzman, E. D., and G. S. Ross. 1962. A behavioral method for the study of pain perception in the monkey. Neurology, 12:264–272.

HARRY J. CARLISLE [1]

9

THERMAL REINFORCEMENT AND
TEMPERATURE REGULATION *

INTRODUCTION

Studies of operant conditioning typically have used food as a reinforcer for hungry animals and water for thirsty ones, and similarly, physiologic studies of behavioral regulation have dealt almost exclusively with the control of food and water intake. This emphasis on ingestive reinforcers attests to the fundamental importance of food and water. Temperature, on the other hand, is a variable that has received very little attention in behavioral studies although it is no less basic to life processes than food or water. Nonhibernating mammals maintain an internal body temperature within the very narrow range of a few degrees Celsius in spite of the variation of environmental temperature over a one hundred degree range. Numerous physiologic responses that contribute to thermal equilibrium have been described, including vasomotor, respiratory, and metabolic adjustments, as well as sweating, shivering, and piloerection. A second major class of variables contributes also to thermal balance: the behavioral responses of the animal. These responses are especially important in avoiding the extremes of a hostile thermal environment. This chapter summarizes some attempts to examine behavioral and physiological interactions in temperature regulation.

The general method in this work can be illustrated by Figure 1. An animal is placed in a cold chamber and given access to a lever, the depression of which activates one or more infrared heat lamps. A continuous reinforcement (CRF) schedule is generally used, the reinforcement being a fixed-duration burst of radiant heat of some specified intensity. Each lever press on a CRF schedule turns the lamps on if they are off, but responses during a reinforcement interval have no effect. An additional response contingency allows the subject unlimited access to heat by arranging for the lamps to stay on as long as the lever is depressed. For lack of a better term, this contingency will be called "ad libitum reinforcement."

Temperature information is derived from two sets of receptors, one set lo-

[1] Department of Psychology, University of California at Santa Barbara, Santa Barbara, California.

* Much of the work reported in this chapter was supported by Grants MH-12253 and MH-12414 from the National Institute of Mental Health.

211

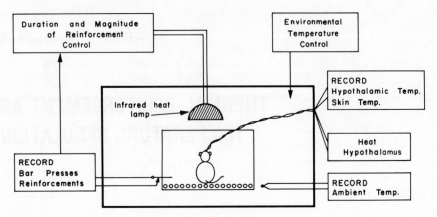

Fig. 1. The experimental situation.

cated peripherally (cutaneous receptors) and the other centrally (hypothalamic temperature-sensitive neurons) (Nakayama et al., 1963). The appropriate sites for measuring temperature are therefore the skin and hypothalamus, as seen in Figure 1. Temperature regulation can best be understood as a dual-control system involving central and cutaneous modulation of a hypothalamic controller. The nature of the control system will not be dealt with here, and the reader is referred to the very excellent reviews by Hardy (1961), Bligh (1966), Hammel (1968), and Corbit (1970) for more information. For now, it is appropriate to note that cutaneous temperature can be influenced by changing ambient temperature, while a number of treatments can be used to get at the central control mechanism. Local hypothalamic heating (Carlisle, 1966b), as noted in Figure 1, is such a treatment. Others include hypothalamic cooling (Satinoff, 1964), chemical stimulation (Beckman and Carlisle, 1969), and electrical stimulation.

An animal with a body temperature of about 38° C is faced with a clear regulatory problem when placed in a cold ambient temperature since a flow of heat is committed to the environment by the body-ambient temperature difference. This transfer of heat can be mitigated to various extents by vasoconstriction, piloerection, or huddling (a reduction of the effective radiating surface exposed to the environment). Piloerection appears to be the most effective of these responses for rats since normal internal temperatures can be maintained for many hours if the fur is intact. Removal of fur, however, results in a decreasing body temperature within 30 minutes (Carlisle, 1968b).

The rate of change of internal temperature is determined by the balance or imbalance between rates of heat production and heat loss. The rate of fall of internal temperature of a shaven rat in an ambient temperature of −5° C is 0.03 to 0.05° C per minute initially, although this rate increases as metabolic resources decline. The survival time for a rat in this situation, without an exogenous source of heat, is about 4 to 6 hours. This can be illustrated by Figure 2, which shows the rate of fall of internal (hypothalamic) temperature of a rat exposed to 0° C.

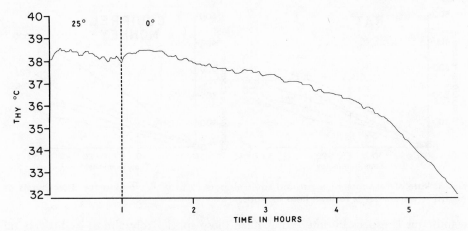

Fig. 2. The change in hypothalamic temperature **(Thy)** of a rat without access to radiant heat. Ambient temperature was lowered from 25° C to 0° C within 10 min at the end of the first hr.

The animal was removed when hypothalamic temperature fell to 32° C. Rats become ataxic at a body temperature of about 25° C, while temperatures of 14° to 16° C are fatal. Clearly, it is incumbent upon an animal to obtain or produce heat if it is to survive. Rats and other mammals will learn an operant response to obtain exogenous heat, and will regulate their body temperature after doing so. The behavioral regulation of body temperature can be very accurate under some conditions. Stable operant performance can be illustrated by Figure 3 which shows cumulative records for a trained rat and squirrel monkey working for different intensities of heat on a CRF schedule. Ambient temperature and the duration of reinforcement are the same for each animal, but a much higher intensity of heat is necessary to sustain a rate of response of the monkey that is comparable to that of the rat.

The first reports of the use of operant techniques for the study of behavioral temperature regulation date from 1957 (Carlton and Marks, 1957a, 1957b, 1958; Weiss, 1957a, 1957b). Carlton and Marks used convective heat as a reward for rats in an ambient temperature of 2° C, while Weiss used radiant heat. Weiss and Laties have subsequently added a number of studies to the small but growing literature on behavioral thermoregulation (Laties and Weiss, 1959, 1960; Weiss and Laties, 1960, 1961). The subjects in these studies typically have been rats, although squirrel monkeys (Carlisle, 1966a), pigs (Baldwin and Ingram, 1967a, 1968a, 1968c), cats (Weiss et al., 1967), and mice (Baldwin and Ingram, 1968b; Revusky 1966) also have been used. One submammalian species, the goldfish, learned to press a lever for a 1-second flow of cold water which lowered the temperature of its warm aquarium water (Rozin and Mayer, 1961). An avoidance response has been used successfully with lizards; this work demonstrated that the behavioral avoidance of thermal extremes was a joint function of hypothalamic and peripheral temperatures (Hammel et al., 1967). The use of lizards and other

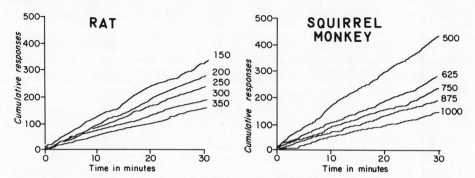

Fig. 3. Rate of response of a rat and squirrel monkey at 0° C working for 2-sec bursts of heat. The parameter is radiant heat in watts.

ectotherms is especially interesting since these species rely almost exclusively on behavior for temperature regulation (Cowles and Bogert, 1944).

Instrumental responses that lead to a reduction in heat stress can be acquired as readily as those that alleviate cold stress. Corbit (1970) has shown that convective cooling is an effective reinforcer for rats in a warm environment, and that regulation can be accurate under these conditions. Lipton (1968) found that rats responded at a high rate in a heat-escape situation, but this did not prevent hyperthermia in animals with preoptic lesions. A natural response of rats when heat-stressed is to groom saliva onto the ventral body surface, thereby increasing evaporative heat loss (Hainsworth, 1967). Similarly, rats will learn an operant response reinforced by a water shower when in a warm environment (Epstein and Milestone, 1968). This chapter will concentrate on behavioral responses to cold stress, and the reader is referred to the paper by Corbit (1970) for more information on responses to heat stress.

The reinforcement for animals in a cold environment is usually a short-duration burst of radiant heat. An interesting variant of this procedure is to provide the subject with ad libitum access to thermal reinforcement. This is easily accomplished by allowing the heat lamps to remain on as long as the lever is depressed. A free-access procedure is particularly suitable with thermal reinforcement, as opposed to the usual nutritive reinforcers, because radiant energy cannot be stored and satiation therefore does not occur. The duration of reinforcement is precisely adjusted by the subject under these conditions, and temperature regulation is quite exact (Carlisle, 1968a). These experiments will be described in more detail below. For the present, it is sufficient to note that heat is an effective reinforcer for animals in a cold environment, as is a draft of cold air or a shower for those in a warm environment. An operant response can be acquired, and the rate of emission of that response reliably related to parameters of reinforcement and to environmental temperature.

Although radiant heat is an effective reinforcer for rats and other mammals on CRF schedules, it is not effective with some intermittent schedules. Rats typically show sporadic responding on fixed-ratio (FR) schedules as low FR 5 or FR 10, while squirrel monkeys work consistently at ratios up to FR 20 (Carlisle, 1969a). Variable-interval (VI) schedules will sustain stable behavior if a high density of reinforcement can be obtained. A VI 12-second schedule, for example, makes reinforcement available at about the same rate that it is received on CRF, and stable responding can be observed (Weiss and Laties, 1960). Part of the explanation for weak schedule control may involve the relation between the lever response and the occurrence of reinforcement. Heat reinforcement is immediate, and the subject need not leave the lever in order to make a consummatory response. Poor schedule control has also been reported with electrical self-stimulation of the brain (Olds, 1962), a situation similar to the present one in that a consummatory response is absent and reinforcement is immediate. Pliskoff et al., (1965) have reported that schedule control can be obtained with electrical self-stimulation by making the response situation more analogous to that occurring with nutritive reinforcement, and by providing for the occurrence of a secondary reinforcer. It should be noted that considerations of the response, immediacy of reinforcement, and secondary reinforcement would not explain the observed differences between rats and squirrel monkeys since these factors are comparable in the test situation for both species. It is, therefore, unclear at this time whether thermal reinforcement has the same properties with respect to schedule control that have been attributed to nutritive and other reinforcers.

ACQUISITION

No specific shaping or training procedures are necessary for acquisition of the lever response with the rat. The shaven animal is simply placed in the cage with the ambient temperature set to 0 or $-5°$ C, and left to discover the lever and its significance. The initial responses of the rat are huddling and shivering, but these do not preclude the fall of body temperature for very long. Bursts of activity are interspersed between periods of huddling, and the lever is thereby accidentally depressed. After a highly variable period of time, ranging from 27 to 230 minutes for rats (Carlisle, 1968b), and 5 minutes to 10 hours for pigs (Baldwin and Ingram, 1967a), the animals begin to work at a steady rate. A large number of factors undoubtedly influenced speed of acquisition, such as the size and shape of the cage, position of the lever, ambient temperature, the response contingency, magnitude of reinforcement, and so on. These variables have not been systematically investigated, although we have found that acquisition is rapid with an ad libitum reinforcement schedule.

The only difficulty that can be noted in the early stages of acquisition on a CRF schedule involves the response topography. Many animals depress the lever, are reinforced with a burst of heat, and then attempt to depress the lever still further rather than releasing and redepressing for the subsequent reinforcement. This difficulty appears to be due to the absence of an active consummatory response in the behavioral chain; the animal need not leave the lever in order to obtain a reinforcement as in the case of ingestive reinforcers, but passively absorb the heat (usually while still holding the lever down). Response acquisition can be hastened by placing the lever microswitch in series with the heat lamps; the lamps will then be activated as long as the lever is depressed. The animals rapidly learn to obtain short bursts of heat at regular intervals under this condition, and the subsequent transfer to a CRF schedule is uneventful.

The squirrel monkey cannot be conditioned as readily as the rat. A cold ambient temperature decreases overt activity in the monkey and lowers the operant level of responding to zero. The animals typically assume a huddled, ball-like posture, and *visually* explore the cage and its surroundings. Shaping procedures must start by reinforcing any activity, and then successive approximations to the lever. This procedure can be long and arduous unless the monkey is first trained to work for food reinforcement. Subsequent transfer to heat reinforcement is then rapid.

During the initial exposure to the cold, naive rats typically wait several hours before suddenly commencing to respond for heat at some rate. The latency to onset of responding is highly variable, but attempts have been made to identify some of the contributing factors. Weiss and Laties (1961) suggested that a fall in body temperature is the critical variable in the initiation of working for heat. Some observations in favor of this view are that precooled rats wait less time before commencing to work (Panuska and Popovic, 1963; Weiss and Laties, 1961), acclimatized animals wait a longer time (Laties and Weiss, 1960), and subcutaneous temperature falls 8.2° C, on the average, prior to the initiation of responding (Weiss and Laties, 1961). This evidence does not, however, distinguish between central and peripheral temperatures, for it is conceivable that peripheral temperature might fall in the cold while deep internal temperature would be constant. Measurements of both hypothalamic and subcutaneous temperature show that the initial thermal response of a shaven rat to a low ambient temperature is a rise in central but a fall in peripheral temperature (Carlisle, 1968b). Hypothalamic temperature remains elevated for about 30 minutes before it begins to fall, and some animals learn to respond for heat during this 30-minute period. A decrease in deep internal temperature, therefore, cannot be a necessary condition for learning in this situation, even though hypothalamic temperature does fall to an average value of 35.6° C prior to commencement of responding. The normal range of hypothalamic temperature of rats in a neutral ambient temperature is 37 to 39° C (Carlisle, 1968b).

One of the curious observations regarding response acquisition is that rats do not appear to have "learned" the lever response after the first session, even though they may respond at a high and consistent rate during the test (Carlisle, 1968b; Weiss and Laties, 1961). On the subsequent test they do not respond immediately for heat, but wait for a period of time typically less than that observed on the first test. This pattern continues for four to six tests, at which time the animals finally begin to respond immediately after being exposed to the cold. It is not clear why rats wait less and less time on each subsequent test before commencing to work for heat, although it has been suggested that they must learn to use peripheral temperature changes as a discriminative stimulus for responding on the lever (Carlisle, 1968b). This inference would not apply to thyroidectomized rats, which respond for heat soon after cold exposure on the first and all subsequent tests (Laties and Weiss, 1959).

BASELINES

Baseline response rates can be obtained with CRF schedules, and related to the parameters of reinforcement and to ambient temperature. Deviations from an operant baseline have been used to assay the effects of drugs (Weiss and Laties, 1963), metabolic imbalance (Laties and Weiss, 1959; Weiss, 1957a, 1957b; Yeh and Weiss, 1963), and food deprivation (Baldwin and Ingram, 1968a; Barofsky, 1968; Corbit, 1970; Hamilton, 1959; Hamilton and Sheriff, 1959). A somewhat different approach to the notion of a baseline can be used with behavioral temperature regulation. Since the problem for an animal working for heat in a cold environment is to maintain body temperature, measures of this temperature can provide an excellent source of information about the consequences of behavior. A stable baseline, in this sense, means a relatively constant temperature. For example, rats reduce their rate of response as the magnitude of reinforcement increases (Weiss and Laties, 1960). Rate of response at each reinforcement condition may be stable, but this does not necessarily mean that the consequences of the behavior are stable in regard to regulation. Measurement of the changes in body heat content, an index of net gains or losses of heat over a specified period of time, show that more heat is obtained at high than at low magnitudes of reinforcement (Carlisle, 1966a). Therefore, rate of response is inversely related to magnitude of reinforcement, heat intake is related directly, and a disproportion exists such that the decrease in response rate as a function of the intensity or duration of reinforcement is not proportional to the heating effect of reinforcement. That is, a behavioral baseline (rate of response at any specific magnitude of reinforcement) may be stable, while a physiologic measure may vary.

Hypothalamic temperature varies over a 2.5° C range, on the average, when rats are tested at 0° C with a variety of reinforcement parameters on CRF (Carlisle, 1966a). A more stable temperature baseline can be obtained if the subject is given free access to radiant heat, in which case hypothalamic temperature varies within the narrow range of 1° C, and this variation is independent of changes in the intensity of reinforcement (Carlisle, 1968a). Thus the stability of a temperature baseline depends very much on the nature of the response contingency.

Deviations from both behavioral and temperature baselines have been used in some studies to assess the effects of hypothalamic chemical or thermal stimulation. Heating the hypothalamus of rats working for radiant heat in the cold produces a decrease in rate of response and an increased rate of loss of heat. The loss of body heat during hypothalamic heating is far greater than can be attributed to the cessation of peripheral heat input from the decreased behavioral response rate, and must therefore represent an activation of heat-loss mechanisms (Carlisle, 1966b). Similar results, but in the opposite direction, have been noted following hypothalamic cooling (Satinoff, 1964). Behavioral and physiologic effects can be obtained by thermal stimulation of the same point in the rostral hypothalamus, as shown by heating or cooling an implanted thermode in the same subject (Baldwin and Ingram, 1967b; 1968d; Corbit, 1970).

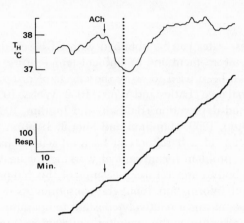

Fig. 4. Decrease in hypothalamic temperature (Th) of 1° C and cessation of responding for 7.5 min after bilateral infusion of 1μl of acetylcholine chloride (50μg/μl) into the preoptic area. The dotted line shows the resumption of responding occurring prior to the base of the temperature decrease. (From Beckman and Carlisle, 1969. **Nature,** 221:561–562.)

Cholinergic stimulation by injection of acetylcholine chloride directly into the preoptic or anterior hypothalamic region produces an activation of heat-loss mechanisms of rats in a neutral ambient temperature. If the injection is made while the subject is working for radiant heat in the cold, the result is a decrease in both response rate and temperature. The decrease in temperature, again, is greater than can be accounted for by the cessation of peripheral heat input (Beckman and Carlisle, 1969). Figure 4 shows an example of the decrease in response rate and temperature following intrahypothalamic injection of acetylcholine. The opposite effects are obtained by hypothalamic adrenergic stimulation, in which case norepinephrine produces an increased rate of response for radiant heat and an increase in hypothalamic temperature (Beckman, 1968).

The results above show that the physiologic regulation of body temperature can be markedly influenced by hypothalamic thermal or chemical stimulation, and that there are concomitant behavioral changes following these treatments. One inference that can be drawn from these studies is that the preoptic and anterior hypothalamic region is an important site for both physiologic and behavioral temperature regulation. The second inference is that behavioral and physiologic responses are wired in parallel; if the physiologic response is an activation of heat-loss mechanisms, then the behavioral response will be in the same direction. In addition, if physiologic responsiveness is impaired by preoptic or anterior hypothalamic lesions, then behavioral responses increase in order to compensate for this loss in the face of heat (Lipton, 1968) or cold stress (Carlisle, 1969b), and in spite of an impaired accuracy of behavioral regulation.

BEHAVIORAL DATA

This section will discuss the response characteristics of rats on an ad libitum reinforcement schedule in an ambient temperature of −5° C. There are two primary variables the subject can control under these conditions: the duration of heat-lamp activation (burst duration) and the occurrence of these bursts (burst frequency). Average burst frequency is relatively constant when heat intensity is varied, with roughly one burst being obtained each minute, except at the lowest intensities (Carlisle, 1968a). Burst duration, on the other hand, varies systematically with thermal intensity, as shown in Figure 5. Short-duration bursts are obtained at high intensities, and long-duration bursts at low intensities. A plot of these data on log-log coordinates for intensities of 100 to 400 watts yields a straight line, indicating that burst duration can be described by a power function of the form $BD = aI^{-b}$, where BD is burst duration in seconds, I is intensity in watts, and a and b are constants. The intercept of the line, a, has little meaning in this case since the lamps are left on continuously at intensities greater than 0 but less than 100 watts. The value for the slope of the line, b, is −1.7 for the burst-duration data shown in Figure 5. The exponent is negative because burst duration and intensity are inversely related. Data for the highest intensities, 450 and 500 watts, were excluded from calculations for the equation of the line since the thermal rise-times for these stimuli are comparable to that of the 400-watt stimulus. Note that the data points for these two high intensities deviate from the straight line, as they should if the effective heat reaching the subject is comparable to that of the 400-watt stimulus. The lower panel of Figure 5 shows that less heat is obtained per minute as thermal intensity is increased. These data also fit a straight line in log-log coordinates for intensities of 100 to 400 watts, indicating that the amount of heat received per minute can also be described by a power function.

The behavioral control of heat intake can be illustrated by the record of a test for one rat shown in Figure 6. The first hour of the test was a warm-up period, and the data for this hour were excluded from the averaged values for the remainder of the test shown at the bottom of the figure. The intensity of the heat lamps was varied randomly at hourly intervals. The record of hypothalamic temperature shows that the warm-up period was quite literally that, while temperature was relatively constant thereafter. Hypothalamic temperature is typically maintained within the narrow range of 1° C under these conditions. The cumulative burst-duration record was obtained by advancing the pen of a cumulative recorder at one step per second as long as the lever was depressed.

A different look at these data can be obtained by plotting the individual functions for five rats at intensities of 100 to 400 watts, as shown in Figure 7. Each point is the average of two 1-hour tests at the specified intensities. The individual

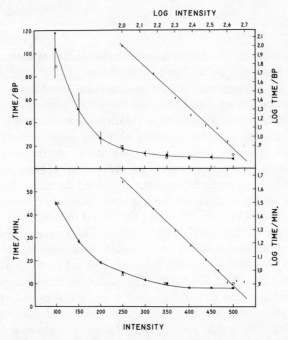

Fig. 5. Mean burst duration (time/BP) in sec, and sec of heat received per min (time/min) for five rats working for radiant heat of the specified intensities in an ambient temperature of −5° C. (From Carlisle, 1968a. **J. Comp. Physiol. Psychol.**, 66:507–510. Copyright 1968 by the American Psychological Associations, and reproduced by permission.)

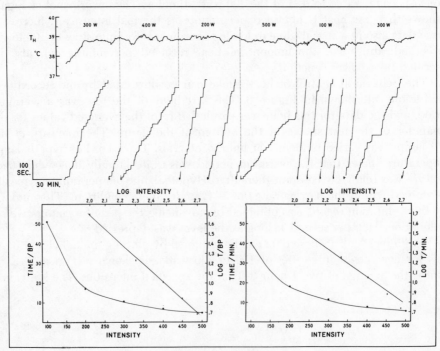

Fig. 6. (Legend on page 221.)

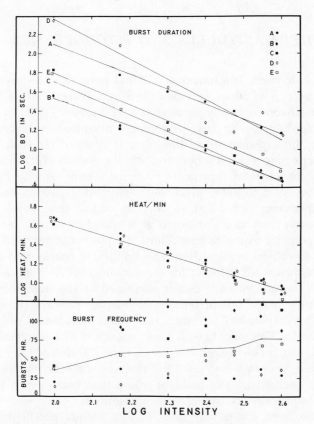

Fig. 7. Individual burst-duration (BD) distributions, heat intake, and burst frequencies for five rats as a function of the intensity of radiant heat in watts.

lines for the burst-duration distributions were obtained by the method of least-squares. The fit is quite good for subjects A and B, less so for C and E, while the data for D are very variable. The greatest slope is −2.1 for subject D, and the least is −1.4 for B. Note that the curves are diverse. Burst-frequency data also are diverse, but animals with long average burst-duration distributions (A and D) have low burst-frequency distributions, while subjects with short burst-duration distributions (C and B) have high burst-frequency distributions. A plot of the amount of heat received per minute, however, reveals no such divergent lines. Thus, at any given intensity, the burst-duration distributions for each animal are different, but the net effect is the same: a constant amount of heat is received each minute. This must mean that the strategy of reinforcement varies for individual subjects. That is, an animal could adopt a strategy of frequent short bursts or infrequent long bursts and still obtain the same amount of heat during a specified period of time.

Fig. 6. A 6-hr test for one rat, showing hypothalamic temperature (**Th**) and the cumulative burst-duration record. (From Carlisle, 1968a. **J. Comp. Physiol. Psychol.,** 66:507–510. Copyright 1968 by the American Psychological Association, and reproduced by permission.)

THE PERIPHERAL STIMULUS AND PSYCHOPHYSICS

Since the behavioral adjustment of thermal burst duration as a function of thermal intensity can be adequately described by a power function, the applicability of the well-known psychophysical law of Stevens (1962) is immediately suggested. According to this law, psychologic magnitude (ψ) grows at a rate determined by the exponent (n) of the physical stimulus (I), such that $\psi = kI^n$. Although perhaps suggestive, it is doubtful that the present experiments constitute any form of psychophysical experiment for a number of reasons. First, the subject is not being asked to judge psychologic magnitude. Second, the stimulus in the present experiment varies both in intensity and in time. Psychophysical experiments typically vary one dimension of a stimulus, usually intensity, while maintaining a constant exposure time. Third, the present experiment might better be considered a problem in regulation. This implies, of course, that sensory information must be processed in order for regulation to occur; there must be a cue associated with thermal intensity that is monitored by the animal. If we suppose that the cue is the magnitude of sensory stimulation, then the present work can be deemed "psychophysical" in that the subject is being asked to judge sensory magnitude. This might, with some stretch of the imagination, be considered a matching problem with the instructions: "Different intensities of heat will be presented; your task is to leave the lamps on until the sensation of warmth is the same on each trial." The problem would thus be to match lamp on-time with intensity to provide a constant (sensory magnitude).

Perhaps the basic reason why these studies are not psychophysical experiments is that the subject is not *required* to make a discrimination between a thermal stimulus and its absence, or between two thermal stimuli. On the other hand, this *is* a sensory experiment and deals with an organism's behavior with respect to sensory stimulation (see Malott and Malott, Chapter 17). The point here is that the behavioral adjustment of heat intake is accurate, which implies that the animal is using sensory information efficiently. The relevant cue for turning the lamps on or off must therefore be some temperature-dependent signal either in or on the animal. Our assumption is that peripheral temperature changes provide the relevant cue when the hypothalamus is not experimentally manipulated. For example, the behavioral adjustment to a change in the parameters of reinforcement occurs very fast and prior to any change in hypothalamic temperature, which implicates peripheral temperature changes as the relevant aspect of the stimulus attended to. These temperature changes are not simple, since the frequency of reinforcement is not the same for two stimuli in which the rate of change of temperature is different even if the increment in skin temperature or the caloric density of each is similar. The radiant thermal stimulus contains information about the rate of change of temperature as well as its physical magnitude, and both variables appear to influence rate of reinforcement (Carlisle, 1966a).

The literature on the nature of cutaneous temperature receptors makes many of the above observations understandable, but it does not offer any ready explanation for a power function relation between stimulus intensity and either the observed burst-duration distributions of rats or human psychophysical estimates of magnitude. Cold and warm fibers clearly exist in the periphery, but the nature of their response to thermal stimulation is not logarithmic. The steady-state firing rate of a warm fiber, for example, increases up to a point with an increase in temperature, and then decreases beyond this point. Cold fibers also show a peak frequency of firing at some temperature, with a decrease in rate above and below this peak (Hensel, 1963). These fibers also respond to the rate of change of temperature as well as the absolute level of temperature. A warm fiber shows an overshoot in frequency during sudden warming, and a suppression of firing during cooling. The converse holds for cold fibers. There is therefore no paucity of information in peripheral warm and cold fibers, but it is difficult to generate a simple formulation for the afferent signal that is consistent with a power law.

Although a power function cannot describe the characteristics of peripheral warm and cold receptors, at least at this time, it is a perfectly adequate description of the overall characteristics of the sensations of warmth and cold. J. C. Stevens and S. S. Stevens (1960), using conductive thermal stimulation, found that warmth and cold obeyed the psychophysical law; the exponent for warmth was 1.6, while that of cold was 1.0. The exponent was much lower when warmth was studied using radiant energy. In this case, the sensation of warmth was related to absorbed irradiance by a power function with an exponent of 0.7 (Stevens and Marks, 1967). It is interesting to note that Kenshalo et al. (1967) found that the *threshold* for warmth is the same for both conductive and radiant heat. Marks and Stevens (1968) studied perceived warmth with different durations of radiant stimulation. They found that warmth grew as a power function of irradiant flux with an exponent of 0.84 for durations of 2 to 6 seconds; the exponent increased with longer durations, and was 1.04 for 12-second exposures. Warmth varied little if the irradiant flux was constant, even though skin temperature was increasing with increasing durations of exposure, which suggested to them that adaptation may have offset the effect of a rising skin temperature.

The problem of adaptation is a significant one in studies of thermal sensation. Kenshalo and Scott (1966) found that complete adaptation could be obtained between skin temperatures of 28 and 37.5° C. The greatest effect of adaptation was noted during the first few minutes of stimulation, and was virtually complete in 20 to 25 minutes. Kenshalo et al. (1968) found that warm and cool thresholds were constant if the rate of change of the stimulus was 0.1° C per second or greater; the threshold increased rapidly for slower rates of change. They suggested that the effect of the rate of change of the stimulus was mediated primarily by its influence on the rate of adaptation of warm and cold receptors.

MEASUREMENTS

THE STIMULUS

Specification of the thermal stimulus might appear to be a simple problem at first glance. Radiant heat produces an increment in skin temperature, and the magnitude of this increment should therefore be the relevant property of the stimulus that is measured as close to the receptors as possible. This is actually quite difficult since the receptors are buried in the skin, and radiant heat is absorbed primarily at the skin surface with penetration to deeper layers decreasing sharply with depth (Hendler et al., 1963). The first problem, then, involves deciding whether to measure subcutaneous temperature or skin surface temperature, or both. The assumption here is that if the increment in temperature produced by some combination of duration and intensity of reinforcement is known, and the number of such reinforcements during a specified period of time is known, a useful estimate of the heat received by the subject can be obtained by multiplying these two measures. This has been done for the rat and squirrel monkey (Carlisle, 1966a; Weiss and Laties, 1960), but the generality of this procedure is questionable since the index is based only on the increment in temperature (ΔT) and therefore ignores the rate of change of the stimulus (dT/dt), the rate at which the rate changes (d^2T/dt^2), and the gradient within the skin.

The increment in skin temperature, then, will not be a good index of the heating effect of reinforcement when stimuli vary in duration and in intensity since this measure need not reflect the absolute quantity of absorbed energy. An estimate of the heating effect of reinforcement which does not depend on the form of the stimulus is an expression of the amount of energy absorbed per unit area per unit time: incident radiant flux. Some estimates of heat intake for the rat and squirrel monkey have been obtained using this caloric measure (Carlisle, 1966a).

A further problem is introduced in operant studies when the subject is free to move within a limited environmental enclosure. Estimates of heat intake based on the heating effect of reinforcement or its caloric value could be in error if the position of a subject with respect to a fixed energy source were not constant. Measures of the change in total body heat content, fortunately, can be used to check on calculated heat intake, thereby verifying that the subject is gaining or losing heat at a rate predicted by the caloric density of reinforcement (Carlisle, 1966a). The problems involved in specifying the stimulus for a moving animal with respect to a fixed stimulus source are not unique to thermal studies (see Dalland, Chapter 2; and Yager and Thorpe, Chapter 12). These problems can be circumvented by restraining the subject (see Stebbins, Chapter 3), although this may not always be feasible or desirable.

The usual procedure in studies of behavioral temperature regulation has been to specify the stimulus in terms of the duration of reinforcement and the power dissipated in the heat lamps. This procedure is quite inadequate since the heat reaching the animal will depend upon the distance from the lamps to the subject, the angle of incidence, emission characteristics of the particular lamp, and characteristics of the animal (reflecting properties of the skin, presence or absence of fur, and the geometry of the surface exposed to the radiation). Given these considerations, it would seem that multiple measures of the stimulus, such as the change in subcutaneous and skin surface temperature, as well as radiant flux, would be useful. The measurement of radiant flux is especially necessary since this measure allows the replication of experimental procedures with the least ambiguity. Finally, continuous measures of central and peripheral temperature provide much useful information.

THE RESPONSE

Response frequency and response duration are straightforward characteristics to measure, and these have been the only measures used with behavioral temperature studies. A more penetrating analysis is possible, however, with both CRF and ad libitum reinforcement. The heat lamps are either on or off, so that it should be possible to measure interresponse times (IRTs—the distribution of "off" periods), burst-duration distributions ("on" periods), and the dependencies as well as probabilities that obtain between these events. This type of analysis has been used with other behaviors (Anger, 1963; Wertheim, 1965), but no information is available at this time for temperature-dependent behavior.

TEMPERATURE

As noted previously, it is important to measure hypothalamic and skin temperature. Of these measures, hypothalamic temperature is the more difficult since the sensing element must be small enough to be implanted in the brain, yet sturdy enough to be useful in long-term behavioral studies. Thermistors, in contrast to conventional thermocouples, have been found to be quite useful for the measurement of brain temperature in moving subjects. The advantages of thermistors are

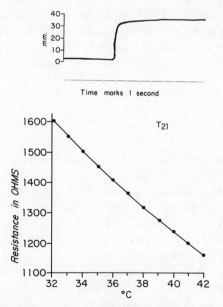

Fig. 8. Top: temporal record of a thermistor response to a step change in temperature. Deflection in mm. Bottom: calibration curve for a thermistor.

their small size, simplicity of operation as resistors in a circuit, high sensitivity, and freedom from noise during recording. These advantages are counterbalanced by the necessity for accurate calibration.

A thermistor is a semiconductor characterized by a negative temperature co-efficient; resistance therefore varies inversely with temperature. If the element is calibrated in a constant-temperature bath so that resistance as a function of temperature is known, an unknown temperature can subsequently be determined by measuring resistance. The usual procedure in this laboratory has been to use the calibrated thermistor as one arm of a Wheatstone bridge. A change in the resistance of the element produces an imbalance in the bridge which can be made proportional to voltage and displayed on a conventional strip-chart recorder.

A wide variety of types and sizes of thermistors are commercially available. We have used a small, 0.33-mm diameter bead-type thermistor (VECO 32A7) for measurement of hypothalamic temperature. The 0.001-inch diameter platinum leads are soldered to 40-gauge Teflon-insulated constantan wire, and the exposed leads are then coated with an electrical insulation. The constantan wire is soldered to a miniature electrical connector, and the thermistor is affixed to the tip of an electrode for support.

The temporal response characteristics of a thermistor are specified by the time-constant, which is defined as the time to reach within $1/e$, or approximately 37 percent, of the final value of a step change in temperature. The time-constant for commercial elements is determined by moving the thermistor rapidly from one air temperature to another, and measuring the time to reach 63 percent of the final value. For biologic work it is more useful to specify a measurement based on moving the element rapidly from one water bath to a second of a different temperature. A high-frequency recording system, such as the Offner Dynagraph, is necessary for this measurement. A sample determination of the time-constant for a thermistor is shown in Figure 8. The time to reach 63 percent of the final level of the change in temperature was 0.2 seconds. The bottom part of the figure shows the temperature-resistance calibration curve for the same thermistor.

SUMMARY

The analysis of temperature regulatory behavior with operant techniques is a relatively new field, the earliest reports dating from 1957. It should not be surprising, then, that the area offers more promise than substance at this time. It is quite probable that the rate of growth of interest in the field will accelerate, for it seems to be uniquely suited for an analysis of behavioral and physiologic variables and their interaction. This may be especially true in the field of animal psychophysics since conditions of deprivation, drive, and reinforcement all are on the same energy continuum—temperature or the displacement of temperature from some norm. The thermal stimulus can be specified, and responses to that stimulation studied under conditions in which important environmental and physiologic variables are either measured or controlled. Some of the interesting and unique features of thermal reinforcement have been noted in the preceding pages, and perhaps also some of the pitfalls involved in its use. It may be trite to say that much remains to be learned, but this is true. The promise of the thermal system is that it offers an opportunity to get at some of the central factors that produce response variance in the face of the most assiduously rigorous stimulus control. It may even be possible, as a first approximation, to specify not only the stimulus and the response, but perhaps the significant transformations that intervene.

REFERENCES

Anger, D. 1963. The role of temporal discriminations in the reinforcement of Sidman avoidance behavior. J. Exp. Anal. Behav., 6:477–506.

Baldwin, B. A., and D. L. Ingram. 1967a. Behavioural thermoregulation in pigs. Physiol. Behav., 2:15–21.

———— and D. L. Ingram. 1967b. The effect of heating and cooling the hypothalamus on behavioural thermoregulation in the pig. J. Physiol. (London), 191:375–392.

———— and D. L. Ingram. 1968a. The effects of food intake and acclimatization to temperature on behavioural thermoregulation in pigs and mice. Physiol. Behav., 3:395–400.

———— and D. L. Ingram. 1968b. Behavioural thermoregulation in mice. Physiol. Behav., 3:401–407.

———— and D. L. Ingram. 1968c. Factors influencing behavioral thermoregulation in the pig. Physiol. Behav., 3:409–415.

———— and D. L. Ingram. 1968d. The influence of hypothalamic temperature and ambient temperature on thermoregulatory mechanisms in the pig. J. Physiol. (London), 198:517–529.

Barofsky, I. 1968. Deprivation and radiant heat reinforcement. Psychol. Rep., 23:19–23.

Beckman, A. L. 1968. The effect of intrahypothalamic application of norepinephrine on behavioral and physiological thermoregulation in the rat. Unpublished doctoral dissertation, University of California, Santa Barbara.

———— and H. J. Carlisle. 1969. Effect of intrahypothalamic infusion of acetylcholine on behavioural and physiological thermoregulation in the rat. Nature, 221:561–562.

Bligh, J. 1966. The thermosensitivity of the hypothalamus and thermoregulation in mammals. Biol. Rev., 41:317–367.

Carlisle, H. J. 1966a. Heat intake and hypothalamic temperature during behavioral temperature regulation. J. Comp. Physiol. Psychol., 61:388–397.

———— 1966b. Behavioural significance of hypothalamic temperature-sensitive cells. Nature, 209:1324–1325.

———— 1968a. Peripheral thermal stimulation and thermoregulatory behavior. J. Comp. Physiol. Psychol., 66:507–510.

———— 1968b. Initiation of behavioral responding for heat in a cold environment. Physiol. Behav., 3:827–830.

———— 1969a. Effect of fixed-ratio thermal reinforcement on thermoregulatory behavior. Physiol. Behav., 4:23–28.

———— 1969b. Effect of preoptic and anterior hypothalamic lesions on behavioral thermoregulation in the cold. J. Comp. Physiol. Psychol., 69:391–402.

Carlton, P. L., and R. A. Marks. 1957a. Heat as a reinforcement for operant behavior. USA MRL Tech. Rep. No. 229. Fort Knox.

———— and R. A. Marks. 1957b. Heat reinforced operant behavior as a function of prolonged cold exposure. USA MRL Tech. Rep. No. 325. Fort Knox.

———— and R. A. Marks. 1958. Cold exposure and heat reinforced operant behavior. Science, 128:1344.

Corbit, J. D. 1970. Behavioral regulation of body temperature. *In* Hardy, J. D., ed. Physiological and Behavioral Temperature Regulation, Springfield, Illinois, Charles C Thomas, Publisher.

Cowles, R. B., and C. M. Bogert. 1944. A preliminary study of the thermal requirements of desert reptiles. Bull. Amer. Mus. Nat. Hist., 83:265–296.

Epstein, A. N., and R. Milestone. 1968. Showering as a coolant for rats exposed to heat. Science, 160:895–896.

Hainsworth, F. R. 1967. Saliva spreading, activity, and body temperature regulation in the rat. Amer. J. Physiol., 212:1288–1292.

Hamilton, C. L. 1959. Effect of food deprivation on thermal behavior of the rat. Proc. Soc. Exp. Biol. Med., 100:354–356.

———— and W. Sheriff, Jr. 1959. Thermal behavior of the rat before and after feeding. Proc. Soc. Exp. Biol. Med., 102:746–748.

Hammel, H. T. 1968. Regulation of internal body temperature. Ann. Rev. Physiol., 30:641–710.

———— F. T. Caldwell, Jr., and R. M. Abrams. 1967. Regulation of body temperature in the blue-tongued lizard. Science, 156:1260–1262.

Hardy, J. D. 1961. Physiology of temperature regulation. Physiol. Rev., 41:521–606.

Hendler, E., J. D. Hardy, and D. Murgatroyd. 1963. Skin heating and temperature sensation produced by infrared and microwave irradiation. *In* Hardy, J. D., ed. Temperature—Its Measurement and Control in Science and Industry, New York, Reinhold Publishing Corp., vol. 3, part 3, pp. 211–230.

Hensel, H. 1963. Electrophysiology of thermosensitive nerve endings. *In* Hardy, J. D., ed. Temperature—Its Measurement and Control in Science and Industry. New York, Reinhold Publishing Corp., vol. 3, part 3, pp. 191–198.

Kenshalo, D. R., and H. A. Scott, Jr. 1966. Temporal course of thermal adaptation. Science, 151:1095–1096.

———— T. Decker, and A. Hamilton. 1967. Spatial summation on the forehead, forearm, and back produced by radiant and conducted heat. J. Comp. Physiol. Psychol., 63:510–515.

———— C. E. Holmes, and P. B. Wood. 1968. Warm and cool thresholds as a function of rate of stimulus temperature change. Percept. Psychophys., 3:81–84.

Laties, V. G., and B. Weiss. 1959. Thyroid state and working for heat in the cold. Amer. J. Physiol., 197:1028–1034.

———— and B. Weiss. 1960. Behavior in the cold after acclimation. Science, 131:1891–1892.

Lipton, J. M. 1968. Effects of preoptic lesions on heat-escape responding and colonic temperature in the rat. Physiol. Behav., 3:165–169.

Marks, L. E., and J. C. Stevens. 1968. Perceived warmth and skin temperature as functions of the duration and level of thermal irradiation. Percept. Psychophys., 4:220–228.

Nakayama, T., H. T. Hammel, J. D. Hardy, and J. S. Eisenman. 1963. Thermal stimulation of electrical activity of single units of the preoptic region. Amer. J. Physiol., 204:1122–1126.

Olds, J. 1962. Hypothalamic substrates of reward. Physiol. Rev., 42:554–604.

Panuska, J. A., and V. Popovic. 1963. Learning in hypothermic rats. J. Appl. Physiol., 18:1016–1018.

Pliskoff, S. S., J. E. Wright, and T. D. Hawkins. 1965. Brain stimulation as a reinforcer: intermittent schedules. J. Exp. Anal. Behav., 8:75–88.

Revusky, S. H. 1966. Cold acclimatization in hairless mice measured by behavioral thermoregulation. Psychon. Sci., 6:209–210.

Rozin, P. N., and J. Mayer. 1961. Thermal reinforcement and thermoregulatory behavior in the goldfish, *Carassius auratus*. Science, 134:942–943.

Satinoff, E. 1964. Behavioral thermoregulation in response to local cooling of the rat brain. Amer. J. Physiol., 206:1389–1394.

Stevens, J. C., and S. S. Stevens. 1960. Warmth and cold: dynamics of sensory intensity. J. Exp. Psychol., 60:183–192.

———— and L. E. Marks. 1967. Apparent warmth as a function of thermal irradiation. Percept. Psychophys., 2:613–619.

Stevens, S. S. 1962. The surprising simplicity of sensory metrics. Amer. Psychol., 17:29–39.

Weiss, B. 1957a. Pantothenic acid deprivation and thermal behavior of the rat. Amer. J. Clin. Nutr., 5:125–128.

———— 1957b. Thermal behavior of the subnourished and pantothenic-acid-deprived rat. J. Comp. Physiol. Psychol., 50:481–485.

———— and V. G. Laties. 1960. Magnitude of reinforcement as a variable in thermoregulatory behavior. J. Comp. Physiol. Psychol., 53:603–608.

———— and V. G. Laties. 1961. Behavioral thermoregulation. Science, 133:1338–1344.

———— and V. G. Laties. 1963. Effects of amphetamine, chlorpromazine, and pentobarbital on behavior thermoregulation. J. Pharmacol. Exp. Therap., 140:1–7.

———— V. G. Laties, and A. B. Weiss. 1967. Behavioral thermoregulation by cats with pyrogen-induced fever. Arch. Int. Pharmacodyn., 165:467–476.

Wertheim, G. A. 1965. Some sequential aspects of IRT's emitted during Sidman-avoidance behavior in the white rat. J. Exp. Anal. Behav., 8:9–15.

Yeh, S. D. J., and B. Weiss. 1963. Behavioral thermoregulation during vitamin B_6 deficiency. Amer. J. Physiol., 205:857–862.

MARK A. BERKLEY [1]

10

VISUAL DISCRIMINATIONS IN THE CAT *

INTRODUCTION

For all their popularity as pets, cats have been conspicuously neglected as experimental animals by behavioral scientists. Yet there are many advantages and even strong reasons for using the cat as a behavioral animal. He is of a convenient size, is easy to maintain, and generally speaking, has a reasonable disposition so that he can be easily handled in the laboratory. Perhaps a more important reason is that a great deal of research has been done by physiologists and anatomists on his nervous system.

Anyone who has attempted to do a behavioral experiment with a cat is soon aware that this animal cannot be trained as easily as a monkey, a rat, or a pigeon. Some of the problems encountered in training cats are: (1) certain responses are preferred to others; (2) certain foods are highly preferred (high protein foods for the carnivorous cat); and (3) they interact with the experimenter probably to a greater extent than any of the other widely used experimental animals. With these things in mind, it can be seen that attempting to place a cat in a situation devised for a pigeon or a monkey is not appropriate; yet this has been the most common approach in behavioral experiments with this animal. For example, many experiments used runways or mazes (Smith, 1936; Kennedy and Smith, 1935; Sperry et al., 1955; Baden et al., 1965; and others), which have been used widely with rats. The monkey testing apparatus developed at Wisconsin (WGTA) was also modified for use with cats, particularly by Warren and his associates (e.g., Warren and Baron, 1956). The shuttle box was another of the more popular types of apparatus that have been adapted for use with cats (e.g., Butler et al., 1957), and appears to be particularly suitable for auditory experiments. Only a few investigators used methods specifically devised for the cat. Guthrie and Horton (1946), for example, made use of a throttlestick device which the animal had to move in order to escape from a cage. A similar operandum has been described recently by Symmes (1963) in which the playful pawing of kittens was used as the response. All these devices have been used more or less successfully by many investigators, but most

[1] PSYCHOLOGY DEPARTMENT, FLORIDA STATE UNIVERSITY, TALLAHASSEE, FLORIDA.

* This research was supported by PHS Research Grant MH15035 from the National Institute of Mental Health, Grant NB08282 from the National Institute of Neurological Diseases and Blindness, and a grant from the Florida State University Research Council. The author would like to acknowledge the assistance of D. S. Warmath in the collection of the data.

workers using cats as experimental subjects—regardless of the type of apparatus —report that training is lengthy and difficult. With the WGTA and runways, for example, the number of trials per day is small, requiring weeks and even months to reach criterion performance.

Among the behavioral methods so far applied to the cat, the powerful operant methods have been the least used. One reason for this lack is the apparent difficulty in obtaining steady rates of responding with cats pressing a lever or making some other type of simple operant response. The few studies (e.g., Mello and Peterson, 1964; Mello, 1968) which used operant paradigms required lengthy training to achieve stable performance. We wished to train cats to make a variety of visual discriminations rapidly and, in addition, to make use of several of the current operant behavior paradigms. This meant that the animals should generate moderate rates of responding or complete a large number of trials (greater than 30 to 40) per session. A further requirement was that the system be completely automated. The following discussion is a brief description of such an apparatus and training method. Most of the discussion deals with two-choice simultaneous discriminations and visual stimuli. A number of the dimensions of visual stimuli have been examined, including form, brightness, and movement, and data illustrative of the testing procedures and stimulus dimensions are presented below. We have also modified the behavioral apparatus for use with other types of stimuli and training paradigms. For example, thermal sensitivity of the cat's nose is being tested and we are using the apparatus in conditioned suppression paradigms (see Smith, Chapter 6).

REINFORCEMENT

To achieve the first goal of rapid training, it was necessary to find a reward that was appropriate for the cat, one that is highly preferred and easily dispensed. There are a number of suggestions available in the literature, none of which are completely satisfactory. The foods are either difficult to prepare and keep (Hodos et al., 1963; Crawford and Kenshalo, 1965), or cannot be easily dispensed automatically (pieces of beef—spleen, heart, kidney, and so forth). Using a technique worked out for monkeys by Glickstein (personal communication) and the School of Pharmacy at the University of Washington, pellets of varying constituents were manufactured for use with cats. The ingredients that were tried included dried gravy mixes, beef extracts, and pulverized dry cat chow. The latter appeared the most preferred by cats and we finally settled on a mixture of the dry cat chow and binders. Pellets of the proper consistency to withstand ejection by pellet dispensers must have a low fat content. To achieve the low fat requirement, however, meant that only 40 to 50 percent of the pellet could be made of the chow, with the remainder of the pellet made up of binders. This combination turned out an excellent pellet from the standpoint of automation, but the animals would not eat them in sufficient quantities to make them really adequate for use as a reward. They were, however, a great improvement over the liquids and meat tidbits. Pellets were used in the early experiments but recently a system using beef baby food as a reward was developed.[1] The baby food dispenser consists of an air-operated piston and a food reservoir. The piston extrudes a small amount of baby food each time a solenoid valve is operated. The advantage of this latter method is that the animals do not have to be severely food-deprived to work for this reward, and all animals thus far tried have been successfully trained. The success rate with pellets was about 80 percent.

APPARATUS

A number of attempts to teach cats to press a lever (operandum) for milk and then for food pellets were made using an enlarged rat testing chamber. It required considerable patience and a few "tricks" to train them. A typical "shaping" procedure was used in that a reward was delivered by the experimenter to the animal in the test chamber each time a response was made that approximated the desired lever-press. In order to speed this process, the lever was moved from the front wall of the chamber (the typical position in a rat or monkey test chamber) to a position on the test cage floor, close to one of the forepaws of the animals. This greatly decreased the amount of time necessary to train the animals to depress the pedal and produced good rates of responding on high-density reinforcement schedules; that is, when rewards were delivered at frequent intervals during pedal pressing. Visual stimuli were presented on the front wall of the chamber above the food cup and response pedal. Although several animals were successfully trained to press the pedal, not one was brought under the control of the visual stimuli. Different stimuli which when presented signaled the availability (positive stimulus) or the unavailability (negative stimulus) of food for a pedal press did not control pedal pressing. Observation of the animals disclosed that they never looked away from the food cup except when attempting to escape from the test chamber. Changing the level of the test cage illumination, however, could be used as a stimulus to control responding. For the types of visual discriminations we wished to teach the cat, however, this system was clearly not adequate. These observations led to the design and construction of a new testing apparatus which placed the stimuli, operandum, and food terminal in close proximity. This not only shortened training time but assured that the animals would observe the test stimuli.

The details of the apparatus are shown in Figure 1. The stimuli, reward terminal, and operanda are located at the end of a short Plexiglas cylinder which is mounted on the outside of the test chamber. The animal sits in the test chamber and thrusts its head into the cylinder (see Fig. 1, A) through a hole in the wall of the chamber. The operanda, consisting of two nose keys, the visual stimuli, and the food terminal are located at the outer end of the cylinder. This

[1] The piston pump feeder was modified from a system designed by T. Crawford and G. Oliff, Department of Psychology, Florida State University.

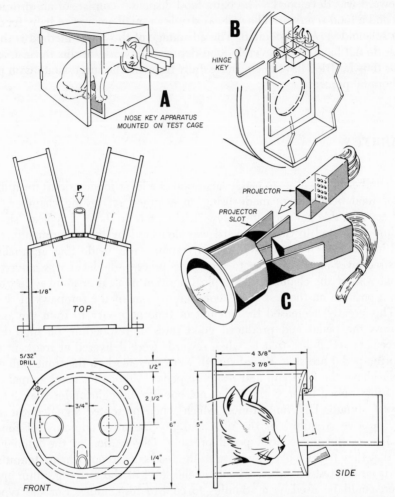

Fig. 1. A-test chamber with test apparatus mounted on outside; B-rear view detail of nose-key showing quick-disconnect hinge; C-cradles for in-line projectors are shown mounted on the back of the test cylinder. The remainder of the figure lists the dimensions and shows construction details. All parts are made of Plexiglas and are cemented together with chloroform.

arrangement quickly orients the animals to the stimuli, reward terminal, and operanda at the same time. Responses consist of pressing the key with the nose.

Figure 1 shows the apparatus set up for use with pellet rewards, but recently the baby food delivery tube has replaced the pellet dispenser tube (see Fig. 1, P). Projectors or other stimulus generators are placed behind the nose keys. In the early stages of training, the animals may attempt to operate the keys with their forepaws or attack the keys when they do not receive a reward. To minimize the ability of the animals to place their paws in the cylinder, a Plexiglas disc was made which has a 3- to 4-inch aperture. This annulus is screwed to the inside of the test chamber over the opening to the plastic cylinder, reducing its effective diameter. With this plate in place, the animal cannot place both its head and forepaws in the tube simultaneously. The annulus is removed when training has progressed to a stable level, and the cat is no longer attempting to paw the keys.

The nose keys (see Fig. 1, B) are made of thin, clear or frosted Plexiglas with a quick-disconnect hinge which facilitates removal for cleaning. None of the dimensions appear to be critical, but those shown in the figure have proven to be very convenient.

TRAINING PROGRAM

The program devised for use with the apparatus is a modification of a program devised by Glickstein et al. (see Chapter 11) for use with monkeys. All programming of stimuli and recording of responses is automatic. A discrete trial procedure is used which consists of presenting two visual stimuli simultaneously, one on each key. If the cat depresses the nose key displaying the correct (positive) stimulus, a reward is delivered and the stimuli are turned off for a short time period before the next trial is presented. If the incorrect (negative) stimulus is chosen, no reward is delivered and the stimuli are turned off until the next trial.

The stimuli appear in a random left-right sequence, with the restriction that the positive stimulus does not appear on more than four consecutive trials in the same left-right position. The intertrial interval (ITI) is adjustable, but short intervals (2 to 4 seconds) seem to work best. The ITI after an incorrect response is 4 seconds and after a correct response is 2 seconds. In early training stages, rapid responding is maintained using a 2-second ITI, regardless of stimulus choice. The animal is required to withhold responding during the ITI; responses during the ITI recycle the ITI timer. Thus, the animal must wait out the full time interval counted from his last response, not from the last trial. To eliminate position habits—responding to one side only regardless of stimulus position—a further restriction in the programmer limits the number of consecutive responses on the same key to eight. Beyond that number, the circuit generating random left-right positions is disabled and the correct stimulus appears only on the side opposite the position habit. The correct stimulus remains in this position until the animal responds to the nonpreferred side.

TRAINING PROCEDURE

After the animal has been reduced to 80 percent of ad lib weight, it is placed in the test chamber and observed through a small window. When the cat places its head in the plastic cylinder (Fig. 1, A), a reward is delivered to the food terminal (Fig. 1, P). Within a few minutes, the animal is holding its head in the cylinder for periods lasting several seconds. At this point, head movements that approach one nose key are rewarded, and finally, only depression of the nose key with the nose is rewarded. This procedure of rewarding successive approximations to the desired response ("shaping") is extremely rapid and usually requires only 5 to 10 minutes. Occasionally, an animal will require as many as two or three "shaping" sessions, but much of the rapidity of training appears to depend on the technique of the trainer; some people are better at it than others.

Usually 25 to 50 reinforcements are sufficient for food terminal and nose key training. When the cats have learned the response, they are permitted to make 200 to 400 responses on a single key before the random left-right position circuit is activated. The animals are then given several daily sessions of training to learn to discriminate between an illuminated key and a dark key which vary in position. Responses on the lighted key (positive stimulus) are rewarded and responses on the dark key (negative stimulus) are not (a simple "brightness" discrimination). Figure 2 shows the rapidity with which the animals are able to learn this simple discrimination with food pellets as the reward. In several cases, the "brightness" discrimination was learned (criterion of greater than 90 percent correct) on the first training day (e.g., see PG, CF7, CF9, and CF12 in Fig. 2).

Figure 3 (upper portion) shows the same simple problem, but with animals rewarded with beef baby food instead of food pellets. Only 3 to 4 days were required from the first exposure to the apparatus to when most of the animals reached a high level of performance on this discrimination problem. The total time invested in each animal to this point (excluding feeding, cleaning, weighing, and so forth) is approximately one hour. In Figure 3, the first number on the abscissa for each animal indicates the number of days the animals were "shaped" in the apparatus before being given the light-dark problem.

The lower portion of Figure 3 shows a similar discrimination problem, but in this case a line oscillating at 25 cycles per second was the positive stimulus. A dark or blank key was the negative stimulus. The moving lines were produced by miniature cathode ray tubes placed behind the nose keys. A further descrip-

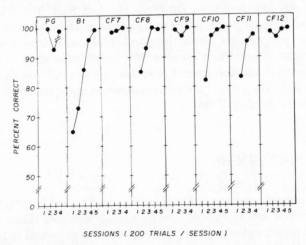

SESSIONS (200 TRIALS / SESSION)

Fig. 2. Simple light-dark discriminations with cats rewarded with food pellets.

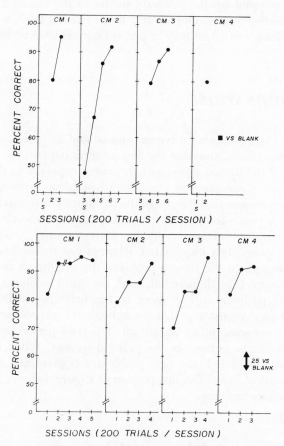

Fig. 3. Upper: Simple light-dark discrimination behavior of cats rewarded with beef baby food. The first number on the abscissa for each animal notes the number of days needed to key-train the animal. Lower: Early stages of real-movement discrimination training in which the positive stimulus was a line oscillating vertically at 25 cps and the negative stimulus was a blank key.

tion of the stimulus display is given in the last part of this chapter.

A criterion of 90 percent correct for three consecutive days was at first required before the next discrimination problem was presented. Frequently, however, the animals' performance was clearly above chance (50 percent correct) for a considerable time but below 90 percent correct, and it was necessary to adjust the criterion accordingly. For example, several animals performed at 85 percent correct or better for several days (see Fig. 7), but did not appear to be improving. They were performing consistently above chance, so a modified criterion was used. In these cases, the animals were advanced to the next discrimination problem when they had three consecutive daily sessions on which they scored between 87 and 90 percent correct. These difficulties are typical of discrete trial procedures and serve to point up the arbitrary nature of the choice of a criterion. In some difficult discriminations, animals may never reach a level of 90 percent correct but may perform consistently at 75 percent correct or even lower.

FORM DISCRIMINATIONS

The data in Figure 4 shows a typical animal and its performance on a series of pattern discriminations. Note that the first problem (square versus blank) is also shown in Figure 2 (CF9) and represents the initial exposure to the testing situation for this animal. Learning was rapid on all problems with a high degree of transfer from one problem to the next. In the first form discrimination problem, an inverted triangle is presented on one key and an upright triangle on the other. A brightness difference is correlated with the correct triangle orientation. The inverted triangle is completely illuminated, whereas just the outline of the upright triangle is illuminated. In the second problem, the brightness cue is absent with both triangles completely illuminated, and the third problem is just the reverse of the first problem with respect to the brightness difference. This sequence of problems demonstrates that the animals are responding to the shape of the stimulus and not some other dimension. The poor performances on days 14, 22, and 46 were due to failures in the pellet dispenser. When the triangle discriminations were completed, the next problem was presented and consisted of horizontal and vertical lines. The last portion of Figure 4 shows the performance of this animal on this problem.

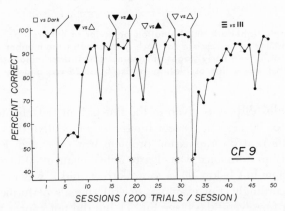

Fig. 4. The performance of cat CF9 on a series of form discriminations. The small figures at the top of the figure depict the pair of stimuli that were presented simultaneously to the animal. In all cases, the left figure of the pair was the positive stimulus.

"FADING" AND BRIGHTNESS MATCHING

When an animal is having difficulty making a discrimination, it is sometimes helpful to add a cue to the correct stimulus to aid in the discrimination. In addition to a distinctive pattern (e.g., circle versus a square), a brightness cue might be added to the correct stimulus (e.g., Terrace, 1963; Sidman and Stoddard, 1967). The situation confronting the animal might be a circle and a square presented simultaneously, with the circle (positive stimulus) being brighter (greater luminance) than the square. In the early stages of training, the brightness is correlated with the correct pattern. Each time the animal presses the key displaying the correct pattern (the circle which has the greater luminance of the two stimuli), the intensity of the incorrect stimulus is increased by a small increment. If the animal makes an incorrect choice, the intensity of the incorrect stimulus is decreased by a small increment. The animals first respond to the stimuli on the basis of brightness (luminance) differences. As training progresses, the brightness cue is "faded out" leaving only the shape or form of the stimulus as the cue for making a correct response (see Chapter 11). The brightness of the correct stimulus is usually recorded with a recording milliammeter and produces records simular to those shown in Figure 5 (also see Luschei and Saslow, 1966). The data shown in Figure 5 were obtained from a modification of the system described above.

The modification was the use of a luminance difference without the pattern cue. In this case, the stimuli on both nose keys have the same form (shape), but one stimulus is set at some constant intensity and is the correct (rewarded) stimulus. The negative stimulus is a lower light intensity. Each time the animal responds to the dimmer or incorrect stimulus, the incorrect stimulus intensity is decreased, increasing the luminance difference between the two stimuli. Responses to the positive stimulus increase the intensity of the negative stimulus by a small amount, decreasing the luminance difference between the two stimuli. The intensity is adjusted by changing the voltage to the bulbs with a potentiometer which is rotated by a bidirectional motor. The use of a potentiometer to control intensity, of course, also results in chromatic changes in the lamps, and this procedure, therefore, is usable only as a rough evaluation of the brightness matching abilities. A recording milliammeter records the position of the potentiometer and hence, the intensity of the incorrect stimulus. When the two are equal in intensity, responses to each are equally probable and an oscillating horizontal line will be produced on the recording milliammeter as shown in Figure 5. The horizontal dashed line shows the intensity of the negative stimulus which would be an intensity match to the positive stimulus. The figure shows the records of an

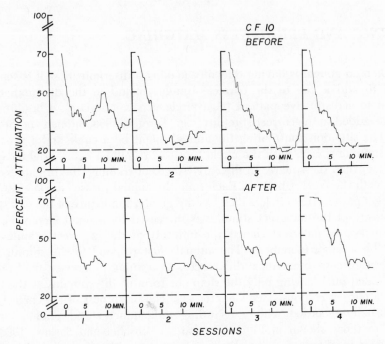

Fig. 5. Brightness matching in a cat (CF10) before and after a massive striate cortex lesion was made. See text for details.

animal in this brightness matching situation on four consecutive daily sessions. The top portion of the figure shows that on the first day the animal does not do well in matching the brightness of the two keys, but on subsequent days he closely approximates a brightness match. The lower portion of the figure shows the same situation with the same contingencies for brightness matching, but these measurements were taken after striate cortex lesions were made in this animal. When this animal was tested on a simple brightness discrimination—an illuminated versus a dark key—no impairment was seen when compared to pre-surgery performance. The brightness matching paradigm, however, showed that presurgical levels of matching brightness were not reached. It is likely that this animal had a large region of blindness in the center of his visual fields and was using peripheral vision in attempting to match brightness. These data demonstrate the usefulness of making a variety of measurements in animals with brain lesions. If brightness matching abilities had not been evaluated, we would not have seen any impairment in intensity discrimination. In many studies, the training procedure is so lengthy and difficult that the investigator is content to be able to make one or two tests of each animal's abilities. With the apparatus and training program described, many different tests may be used with relatively little time needed for testing each animal. (The use of the fading procedures in teaching brain-damaged animals different pattern discriminations is discussed in detail by Glickstein et al., in Chapter 11.)

DISCRIMINATION OF REAL MOVEMENT

It is clear from the experiments of Hubel and Wiesel (1965) and others that movement is a very potent visual stimulus. Except for the early experiments of Kennedy and Smith (1935), very little behavioral work has been done on visual movement detection in the cat (Berkley, 1969). In order to study this particular aspect of vision, the discrimination apparatus previously described was modified in a simple way. The pattern projectors behind the nose keys were replaced with 1-inch cathode ray tubes (CRT). The keys were changed to clear Plexiglas so that the tube displays could be seen through the keys. Lines or dots were produced on the CRTs, and were made to oscillate at a linear rate by the application of a triangular wave form to the vertical deflection amplifiers of the CRT. The rate of movement was controlled by changing the frequency of the triangle wave, and the extent of movement was controlled by adjustment of the amplitude of the wave. In the experiments reported, the extent of the movement was limited to 1 cm on the face of the CRT. Using 7 cm as an estimate of the position of the cats' eyes relative to the CRTs, a movement of 1 cm is equivalent to approximately eight degrees of visual angle. Since the heads of the animals are not fixed in any way, this is just an approximation; however, after being trained in the apparatus for several weeks, the cats do maintain a relatively fixed head position.

The training program was the same as described earlier. In order to present

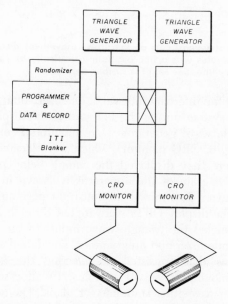

Fig. 6. Block diagram of movement programming apparatus. Cylinders at bottom of figure represent one-inch cathode ray tubes.

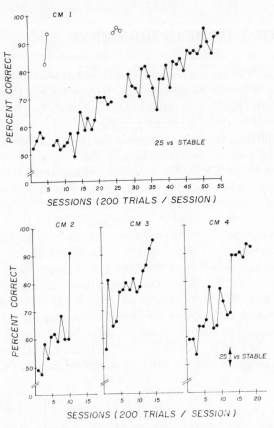

Fig. 7. The performance of several cats on the initial movement discrimination problem. In all cases the positive stimulus was a line oscillating vertically at 25 cps and the negative stimulus was a stationary line. See text for further details.

blank displays during the intertrial interval, a dc offset voltage was applied to the vertical amplification system during the ITI so that the display was deflected off the CRT. The triangle wave generators were monitored continuously on slaved oscilloscopes (see Fig. 6, CRO monitor), which were located near the programming equipment where they displayed the stimuli being presented in the test chamber. A general diagram of the apparatus is shown in Figure 6. The programmer and randomizer determined the left-right position of the displays and the input signals to the display CRTs were routed through a special switch box. The switch box channeled the triangle wave inputs to the appropriate CRT as determined by the randomizer and programmer. The data that follow involve only simple discriminations that consisted of selecting the key in front of the CRT that had the moving (positive) stimulus. In all cases, only one display was moving; the other was either stationary or blank. The next two figures show the results of training animals to press the key in front of a line moving at a rate of 25 cm per second (200 degrees per second). The animal's task was to choose the oscilloscope tube which had this stimulus on it. The bottom portion of Figure 3 shows the rate at which the animals learned this simple problem. The next problem in the sequence was to present a stationary line on the previously blank CRT. The animal was presented with one oscilloscope tube which had a line moving at a rate of 25 cm per second and another CRT on which there was a line which was stationary. The position of these two stimuli varied randomly as previously described. Figure 7 shows the performance of animals on this problem. All animals started with a low percentage of correct choices but improved rapidly. Generally, within 10 or 12 days the animals reached criterion. CM1 in Figure 7 took 55 sessions (approximately 2 months) to learn this simple problem. On day 5 of this problem, the previous problem (25 versus the blank key) was introduced to see if the apparatus was functioning properly (open circles, Fig. 7). On the first day of the rerun, the animal produced 82 percent correct choices, and on the next day, 93 percent. The 25 versus the stationary problem was then presented again. The open circles later in the curve (days 26 to 28) represent another rerun of the simpler problem. We then returned him again to the 25 cm per second versus stationary line problem and continued training another 25 or 30 days until the criterion was achieved. Of the 8 or 10 animals we have trained on these problems, this particular cat, CM1, is by far the slowest. The next figure (Fig. 8) shows the performance of two animals on a number of movement discriminations involving different rates and meridians. The arrows on the figure indicate the meridian in which the line stimulus moved. A dot next to the arrows indicates that the moving stimulus was a dot rather than a line. The numbers beneath the arrows (e.g., 5 versus S, 3 versus S) indicate the rate of stimulus movement in centimeters per second. Note that with one exception, all animals are performing well above chance early in training but require a relatively long time to reach a 90 percent correct criterion. The original criterion of 2 consecutive days performance at better than 90 percent correct was eased, as described earlier. Any behavior that is significantly different from chance is adequate and the arbitrary choice of 90 percent may, under some circumstances, be inappropriate. For example, some animals performed for weeks in the 80 to 90 percent correct range. When slower rates of movement are presented, an even lower percentage of correct choices may be seen consistently. By presenting slower and slower rates and getting lower and lower percentages, thresholds may be obtained in this way. The last figure (Fig. 9) shows the behavior of two other animals making movement discriminations. The lower right-hand portion of the figure is the behavior of subject CM4 in response to a line stimulus moving at 3 cm per second in the horizontal meridian. The open circles indicate days on which the animal was presented with the same stimuli but moving in the vertical meridian. Note the slight improvement the first time this was done. The problem of "attention" is worth mentioning here. Frequently, the dimension of a stimulus that is being investigated is not the same dimension to which the animal is responding (Reynolds, 1961). In the case of movement detection, a stimulus dimension that may confound the results is position. That is, it is possible that the animals were making the discrimination on the basis of difference in position of the moving stimulus (line or dot) from one trial to the next rather than to the dimension of movement. Two findings, however,

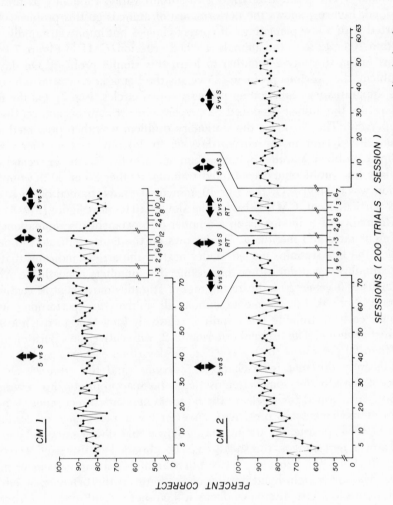

Fig. 8. The performance of two cats (CM1 and CM2) on a series of movement discrimination problems. The arrows indicate the direction of movement of the positive stimulus. The negative stimulus was a stationary line (S). The number below the arrows indicates the rate of ... ... See text for further details.

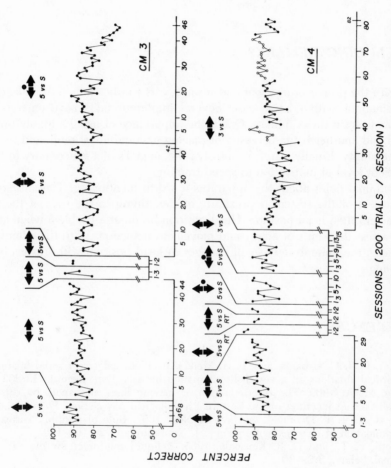

Fig. 9. The performance of two cats (CM3 and CM4) on a series of movement discrimination problems. The arrows indicate the direction of movement of the positive stimulus. The negative stimulus was a stationary line (S). The number below the arrows indicates the rate of movement in cps. See text for further details.

245

tend to rule out this explanation. The first is that there is a very high degree of transfer when the movement meridian is changed from vertical to horizontal, and second, we have changed the position of the stationary stimulus on the CRT from time to time without observing any decrement in performance. It is possible that the small decrement in performance seen in some animals (e.g., CM2 and CM4) when the meridian is changed from vertical to horizontal is due to a slight position effect and is a subject for future study.

CONCLUDING REMARKS

With the proper equipment and reward, cats can be trained to make difficult discriminations with relative ease. Several important facts have emerged from attempts to train these animals. One is the importance of using a highly preferred reward and another is the necessity of placing operandum, stimuli, and reward in close proximity. Finally, careful control of the animal's diet is necessary to achieve a sufficient level of motivation to speed training.

One final point about the apparatus is worth mentioning. The most troublesome aspect of the system is proximity of the stimuli to the eyes of the animal and uncontrolled head position. Head position becomes a problem when attempting to assess the limits of acuity and movement detection. With the stimuli being so close to the animals, any small changes in head position will drastically affect visual angle.

REFERENCES

Baden, J. P., J. C. Urbaitis, and T. H. Meikle, Jr. 1965. Effects of serial bilateral neocortical ablations on a visual discrimination by cats. Exp. Neurol., 13:233–251.

Berkley, M. A. 1969. The discrimination of moving lines and spots by cats. Paper delivered at meetings of the Eastern Psychological Association, Philadelphia.

Butler, R. A., I. T. Diamond, and W. D. Neff. 1957. Role of auditory cortex in discrimination of changes in frequency. J. Neurophysiol., 20:108–120.

Crawford, F. T., and D. R. Kenshalo. 1965. A liquid reinforcer for the cat. J. Exp. Anal. Behav., 8:29–30.

Guthrie, E. R., and G. P. Horton. 1946. Cats in a Puzzle Box, New York, Holt, Rinehart & Winston, Inc.

Hodos, W., A. M. Laursen, and T. Nissen. 1963. A reinforcer for cats. J. Exp. Anal. Behav., 6:162.

Hubel, D. H., and T. N. Wiesel. 1965. Receptive fields and functional architecture in two nonstriate visual areas (18 and 19) of the cat. J. Neurophysiol., 28:229–289.

Kennedy, J. L., and K. U. Smith. 1935. Visual thresholds of real movement in the cat. J. Genet. Psychol., 46:470–476.

Luschei, E. S., and C. A. Saslow. 1966. Automatic stimulus attentuator for rapid discrimination training. J. Exp. Anal. Behav., 9:249–250.

Mello, N. K. 1968. Color generalization in the cat following discrimination training on achromatic intensity and on wavelength. Vis. Res., 6:341–354.

———— and N. J. Peterson. 1964. Behavioral evidence for color discrimination in the cat. J. Neurophysiol., 27:323–333.

Reynolds, G. S. 1961. Attention in the pigeon. J. Exp. Anal. Behav., 4:203–208.

Sidman, M., and L. Stoddard. 1967. The effectiveness of fading in programming a simultaneous form discrimination for retarded children. J. Exp. Anal. Behav., 10:3–15.

Smith, K. U. 1936. Visual discrimination in the cat: IV. The visual acuity of the cat in relation to stimulus distance. J. Genet. Psychol., 49:297–313.

Sperry, R. W., N. Miner, and R. E. Myers. 1955. Visual pattern perception following subpial slicing and tantalum wire implantations in the visual cortex. J. Comp. Physiol. Psychol., 48:50–58.

Symmes, D. 1963. Operant manipulandum for kittens. J. Exp. Anal. Behav., 8:29–30.

Terrace, H. S. 1963. Discrimination learning with and without "errors." J. Exp. Anal. Behav., 6:1–27.

Warren, J. M., and A. Baron. 1956. The formation of learning sets by cats. J. Comp. Physiol. Psychol., 49:227–231.

MITCHELL GLICKSTEIN [1]
SUSAN BARROW [1]
ERICH LUSCHEI [2]

11

VISION IN MONKEYS WITH LESION OF THE STRIATE CORTEX *

INTRODUCTION

Recent studies have made major advances in the methods and techniques for determination of sensory capacities of animals. Our confidence in the results of such studies is strengthened by the replicability of thresholds from animal to animal, and the frequent similarity between measures of animal and human sensory functions. One natural application of animal psychophysics is to use the same methods for evaluation of sensory capacities in animals with lesions, in the expectation that such studies may help towards understanding the nature of sensory processing by the brain. For example, if a sense organ projects independently to two or more places in the brain, we might learn more about possible differential functions of these central structures by ablating one or the other, and testing residual sensory capacity. In the case of vision, we might destroy the striate cortex or the superior colliculus and attempt to determine the nature of the visual loss. Along with anatomic and physiologic data, behavioral study of lesion effects would help in analysis of the functional capacity of these two parallel visual pathways. We might determine the effects of such lesions on photopic and scotopic brightness thresholds, visual acuity, and the ability of the animals to discriminate form, color, and movement, and thus evaluate the capacity of the surviving visual structures. We must recognize, of course, that in the example given, the geniculocortical and collicular circuits are not completely independent. There is clear evidence for connections from striate cortex to the superior colliculus (Wickelgren and Sterling, 1969).

In the present experiments, we have applied some of the methods of animal psychophysics to the study of visual function in monkeys after lesions were made in the striate cortex. We shall discuss here the nature of residual vision in striate-

[1] DEPARTMENT OF PSYCHOLOGY, BROWN UNIVERSITY, PROVIDENCE, RHODE ISLAND.
[2] DEPARTMENT OF PHYSIOLOGY AND BIOPHYSICS, USPHS REGIONAL PRIMATE CENTER, UNIVERSITY OF WASHINGTON SCHOOL OF MEDICINE, SEATTLE, WASHINGTON.

* This research was supported by Grant 15385 of the United States Public Health Service. We are grateful to Eileen LaBossiere who prepared the histologic material.

249

lesioned monkeys with special reference to behavioral techniques which have helped determine the sensory capacity of such animals.

ABSENCE OF FORM AND PATTERN DISCRIMINATION IN STRIATE-LESIONED MONKEYS

Behavioral techniques have advanced in the past 25 years. Stimuli can be more precisely controlled and responses more precisely measured than in earlier studies, and more is now known about the effects on behavior of various reinforcement contingencies. Even with older behavioral methods, however, Klüver (1941) had already determined many aspects of visual impairment caused by striate cortex lesions in monkeys. In Klüver's experiments, the monkey's test cage faced a table on which there was a pair of transilluminated stimulus boxes. Animals were trained to pull a wire connected to one or the other box, only one of which contained a food reward. Either or both of the test stimuli could be lit, and the luminance and distance of each stimulus could be varied independently. Monkeys readily learned to choose the more luminous of two cues and could perform this task even after they had been subjected to bilateral ablation of the striate cortex.

Detailed analysis of the animal's performance suggested that discriminations were not made on the basis of luminance as such; a small, brightly lit pattern was confused with a larger, dimmer one. Because of the apparent trade-off between luminance and area, Klüver concluded that when the striate cortex was removed, monkeys could solve visual discrimination problems only on the basis of a difference in total luminous flux; they could respond to different amounts of total light energy in the stimuli, but seemed to be unable to solve visual problems on any other basis. Form or pattern vision appeared to be totally absent after the lesions. Klüver also noted that although visual detection thresholds were relatively normal when the test cage was dark, increasing the ambient light in the apparatus severely impaired performance of monkeys with striate cortex lesions. Threshold measurements to lights of different wavelength in Klüver's experiment and in a subsequent study by Malmo (1966) suggested that the striate animal's luminous efficiency curve was scotopic.

Recently, Weiskrantz (1963) has studied residual visual capacity in a young monkey after bilateral striate removal. In his initial tests, Weiskrantz confirmed the major conclusion of Klüver: The monkey was incapable of solving form discrimination problems (e.g., horizontal versus vertical stripes) but readily discriminated differences in luminance. If, however, the test patterns differed greatly in amount of contour, the monkey could solve the problem despite equivalence in luminous flux. Moreover, under some conditions the animals performed such discriminations with ambient illumination at photopic levels.

EXPERIMENTAL TECHNIQUES

We have been studying the ability of monkeys with lesions of the striate cortex to perform visual problems after large lesions are placed in the striate cortex. The experiments are not yet completed. Although some conclusions may have to be modified, a few major points are clear. We will discuss here the visual capacities of monkeys with near-total lesion of striate cortex with special reference to behavioral techniques which we have found useful in assessing residual visual capacity.

Monkeys were trained to press one of two keys for a food reward. Solid state logic circuits were used to order the presentation of stimuli and the reinforcement. The contingencies are very similar to those used in discrimination training in the Wisconsin General Test Apparatus. Stimulus pairs are projected onto two keys by in-line projectors. The stimuli may differ in size, color, shape, or luminance. The positive cue appears randomly on the left or right key, but no one side is positive for more than four successive trials. Responses to the positive cue are reinforced each time; responses to the negative cue initiate the intertrial delay without reinforcement. A coincidence-detecting circuit is so arranged that if the monkey

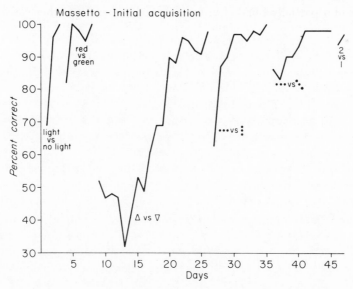

Fig. 1. Normal rhesus monkey (**Macaca mulatta**): Acquisition curves for first six discrimination problems. 35 more discrimination problems were subsequently trained prior to first operation.

were to press both keys simultaneously or within a short interval, the response would not be reinforced even if the correct key happened to be the first one pressed. Additional circuits automatically correct for the tendency of monkeys to form position habits. If the monkey should respond to either key for eight times in a row, the positive stimulus is then presented only on the opposite key until two correct responses are made. Intertrial delays are continuously variable.

Under these conditions of training, normal monkeys readily learn to choose the correct cue. Moreover, after animals are trained on several discrimination problems, the number of trials required to master each successive problem tends to be less; animals can acquire discrimination learning sets under these conditions of training.

Figure 1 shows the performance of a normal monkey when first tested in the apparatus after being trained to press either key for food reward. The individual acquisition curves are similar to those seen in traditional hand-training methods, and after several discrimination problems are mastered, criterion performance is achieved within a few trials on subsequent problems. In Figure 1 and subsequent figures, breaks in the curves indicate a change in training procedure (for example, changing the positive or negative cue).

When tested after unilateral occipital lesion (Fig. 2), monkeys show near perfect retention for simple luminance and color problems, but are initially impaired on pattern discrimination. The observed impairment in pattern discrimination is consistent with the scotoma that might be expected to follow unilateral striate lesion. Animals must presumably learn to reorient themselves to overcome the effects of a partially blinded visual field. In this and all other cases, however,

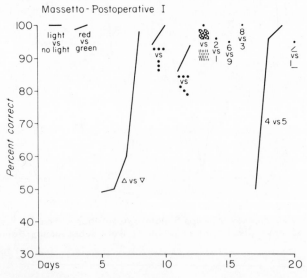

Fig. 2. Rhesus monkey (**Macaca mulatta**): Unilateral striate lesion. Performance on visual discrimination problems.

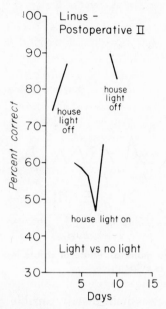

Fig. 3. Rhesus monkey (**Macaca mulatta**): Bilateral striate lesion. Performance on light/no-light problem when first tested.

animals were eventually quite good at relearning form discrimination problems with further training after unilateral striate lesion.

Figure 3 shows the performance in a brightness task of the first animal of our series after the second striate cortex lesion was made. When first tested after bilateral occipital lesion, this animal appeared to behave almost precisely as

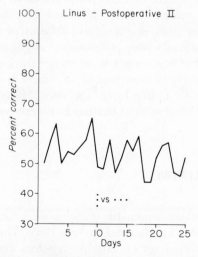

Fig. 4. Rhesus monkey (**Macaca mulatta**): Bilateral striate lesion. Initial performance on form discrimination task. No learning is evident.

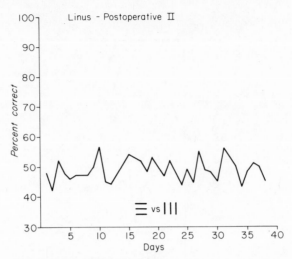

Fig. 5. Rhesus monkey (**Macaca mulatta**): Bilateral striate lesion. Performance on form discrimination task. No learning is evident.

Klüver had described. He was immediately capable of solving a light–no-light simultaneous discrimination. Moreover, successful performance initially appeared to be contingent on low ambient illumination. When the cage lights were switched on, performance fell to a near chance level and quickly returned when these lights were dimmed. The animal initially appeared totally incapable of learning a form problem despite thousands of testing trials. Figure 4 shows this animal's performance on 3,000 trials of a horizontal-vertical discrimination without evidence of learning. Figure 5 shows performance on another pair of similar patterns with 5,000 testing trials. Despite a total of 8,000 training trials, there was no apparent improvement of the animal's performance in form discrimination.

There was limited evidence in the literature (Weiskrantz, 1963) that some capacity for form discrimination might survive ablation of the striate cortex. Hence we suspected that the animal's poor performance might not necessarily represent its true visual capacity but was somehow mirroring the inadequacies of our training procedure. Accordingly, we attempted to slowly train this animal to form discrimination by gradually fading brightness cues. Moreover, initially we used a pair of stimuli which differed in total contour but were equal in flux.

ATTENUATOR TRAINING

One of us had used an automatic stimulus attenuator to help train rats in visual discrimination tasks (Luschei and Saslow, 1966). The attenuator is a bidirectional motor which drives a set of variable resistors arranged in parallel. The direction and amount of shaft rotation can be externally controlled, thus adding to

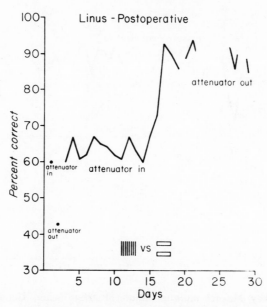

Fig. 6. Rhesus monkey (**Macaca mulatta**): Bilateral striate lesion. Performance on form discrimination task with attenuator. Note suddeness of acquisition of form discrimination.

or decreasing resistance in an external circuit. In these experiments, the resistor was placed in series with the filament of the bulb in the negative cue. Initially, the resistor is set high enough so that the bulb illuminating the negative cue is turned off. Thus the problem becomes one of simply selecting the illuminated cue. Each time the animal makes a correct response, the resistance is lowered by a given amount, thus slightly brightening the negative cue. Each time an error is made, the resistance is raised, thus dimming the negative cue. The ratios of dimming to brightening are controlled by the external circuits. In this case the ratio was two to one: Hence, random performance would quickly cause the negative cue to be completely attenuated. Another resistor changes the voltage input to a recording device, thus providing us with a record of the position of the shaft, hence of the animal's performance. The fading procedure is used in a way very similar to that described by Blough (1956) (see also Chapter 7 by Rosenberger) for measurement of visual thresholds in animals.

Figure 6 shows the performance of our first animal when tested with the attenuator after the second striate lesion was made. When the attenuating resistance is high the negative cue is totally blanked, hence the animal can solve the problem on the basis of luminance. The apparatus is so arranged as to automatically decrease luminance differences when performance is successful, hence the negative cue begins to appear after several correct trials. With continued training, the animal attenuated the luminance difference until it reached a difference threshold. In this case, the animal fluctuated near its brightness threshold for several training sessions until one day (Fig. 6) when it suddenly gave evidence of solving the problem on the basis of differences in form. Our conclusion that the animal had truly

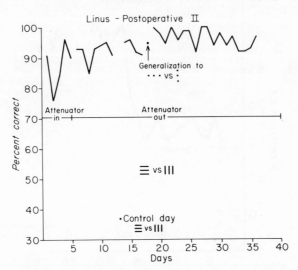

Fig. 7. Rhesus monkey (**Macaca mulatta**): Bilateral striate lesion. Generalization tests for previously learned form discrimination.

learned a visual form discrimination was strengthened by the fact that the initially learned form was readily generalized to other similar forms (Fig. 7). In the control day shown in Figure 7, both positive patterns were presented to the animal at the same time. Preference between these two patterns was random, even though one of the projectors was now controlled by the circuit formerly activating the nega- tive cue. Performance appeared slightly lower than chance on this control day, since when the stimuli were identical, the monkey rapidly adopted a position habit which led to a high percentage of responses being scored as incorrect. This control serves to rule out differential brightness cues or fortuitous auditory cues as the basis for the previously observed performance. In two other animals we also saw initial deficits in visual function. These animals were immediately placed on the attenuator and both rapidly developed the ability to learn and to discriminate visual forms, and generalize such discriminations to other similar forms.

Contrary to our initial findings, animals with bilateral striate lesions were taught to discriminate patterns. They had to relearn such discriminations and they did this with some difficulty. We feel that the use of the fading procedure was valuable and perhaps essential for establishing the fact that the animal had surviving form vision.

It is important to discuss some of the anatomic findings in these cases. The caudal portion of striate cortex which contains the foveal projection (Daniel and Whitteridge, 1961) is easy to ablate since it lies on the lateral surface of the hemispheres. However, the peripheral portions of the visual fields are projected onto the most anterior portion of striate cortex (Daniel and Whitteridge, 1961) which lies in the banks and depths of the calcarine fissure. In both animals which

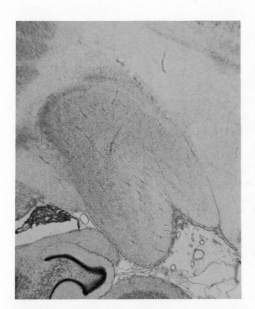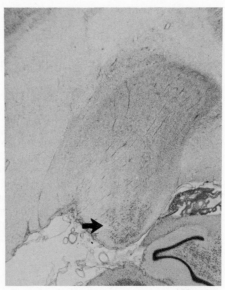

Fig. 8. Lateral geniculate bodies of monkey whose discrimination performance is illustrated in Figures 4 through 7. Note surviving cells (arrow) in right lateral geniculate body.

have come to autopsy, the striate cortex was totally removed on only one side. In each of the two cases, a small portion of the most rostral part of the calcarine fissure remained intact on one side and a few cells in the lateral geniculate body remained undegenerated (Fig. 8). An estimated 5 percent or less of the geniculo-striate system remained in both of these animals, hence the question must be asked as to which structures in the brain mediate form vision. Indirect evidence suggests that these few remaining cells were sufficient and necessary for learning to discriminate forms.

A third animal was fully capable of brightness discrimination after bilateral lesion, but seemed totally incapable of form vision even after several thousand trials of discrimination training with the automatic attenuator, suggesting that a complete striate lesion may abolish all form vision. A word of caution is necessary here since we have as yet no histologic verification of the lesion of this animal.

Stimulus attenuation has proved to be a powerful method for studying residual sensory capacity in a brain-lesioned animal. In initial training, animals appeared totally incapable of responding to form cues. The method of stimulus fading tended to maintain the animal's performance in a brightness task, which it could do, and consistently provided it with the opportunity to solve the same discrimination on the basis of form cues. We feel that without this behavioral procedure, we would not have drawn the correct conclusion as to visual capacity in the cases with near-total lesion of striate cortex.

REFERENCES

Blough, D. S. 1956. Dark adaptation in the pigeon. J. Comp. Physiol. Psychol., 49:425–430.

Daniel, P. M., and D. Whitteridge. 1961. The representation of the visual field on the cerebral cortex in monkeys. J. Physiol. (London), 159:203–221.

Klüver, H. 1941. Visual functions after removal of the occipital lobes. J. Psychol., 11:23–45.

Luschei, E., and C. Saslow. 1966. Automatic stimulus attenuator for rapid discrimination training. J. Exp. Anal. Behav., 9:249–250.

Malmo, R. 1966. Effects of striate cortex ablation on intensity discrimination and spectral intensity distribution in the rhesus monkey. Neuropsychologia, 4:9–26.

Weiskrantz, L. 1963. Contour discrimination in a young monkey with striate cortex ablation. Neuropsychologia, 1:145–164.

Wickelgren, B., and P. Sterling. 1969. Influence of visual cortex on receptive fields in the superior colliculus of the cat. J. Neurophysiol., 32:16–23.

DEAN YAGER [1]
SYLVIA THORPE [1]

12

INVESTIGATIONS OF
GOLDFISH COLOR VISION *

INTRODUCTION

There is abundant evidence to suggest that fish have color vision. Early behavioral experiments (von Frisch, 1912, 1913; Wolff, 1925) provided a foundation
for subsequent work on the color vision of fish. In 1959, McCleary and Bernstein
used classical conditioning of heart rate to demonstrate that goldfish could discriminate colored paper panels of red, green, and blue, independently of brightness. More recently, instrumental "go"–"no-go" and forced-choice discrimination
procedures have been employed. These investigations have provided a wavelength
discrimination function (Yarczower and Bitterman, 1965), photopic spectral
sensitivity functions for different conditions of adaptation (Yager, 1967; 1969), a
scotopic spectral sensitivity function (Yager, 1968), and a spectral saturation
discrimination function (Yager, 1967). In some of these experiments, brightness
has not been properly controlled—a hazard to guard against in assessing the color
vision of any species—but recent data demonstrate color vision in goldfish unequivocally.

We are fortunate to have physiologic data from several levels of the goldfish
visual system. In considering these data we will proceed from distal to proximal
layers through the retina to the highest visual projection area of the fish brain,
the optic tectum.

The absorption spectra of single goldfish cones have been determined by the
method of microspectrophotometry (Liebman and Entine, 1964; Marks, 1965).
Three pigments, with maximal absorption at 455 ± 15 nm, 530 ± 5 nm, and $625
\pm 5$ nm, have been found and their spectral absorption spectra are shown in
Figure 1.

Electrophysiologic recordings from the retina reveal an opponent organization of neural processes at more proximal levels. This type of organization was

[1] PSYCHOLOGY DEPARTMENT, BROWN UNIVERSITY, PROVIDENCE, RHODE ISLAND.

* The research reported here, and the preparation of this chapter, were supported principally
by Grant EY-00400 from the U.S. Public Health Service.

We gratefully acknowledge those discussants whose comments were helpful in writing
the final draft of this chapter.

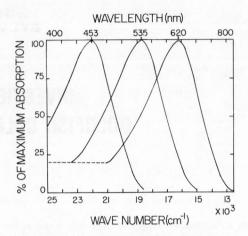

Fig. 1. Goldfish cone photopigment absorption functions.

first suggested by Hering (1964) and developed by Hurvich and Jameson (1957) as the opponent-process theory of color vision. This theory postulates that chromatic sensations are coded in the nervous system in two independent subsystems, red-green and yellow-blue. The spectral responses of these opponent color systems

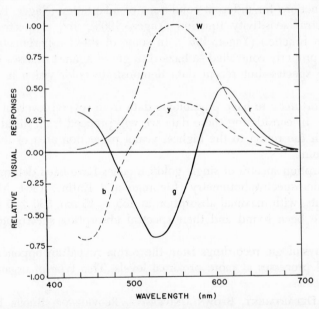

Fig. 2. Theoretical chromatic and achromatic response functions for the average human observed, r = red, g = green, y = yellow, b = blue, w = white. (From Hurvich and Jameson, 1957. **Psychol. Rev.**, 64:392. Copyright by the American Psychological Association, and reproduced by permission.)

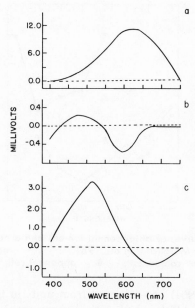

Fig. 3. Spectral responses of "S" potentials from the goldfish retina. (After Wagner et al., 1960.) See text for explanation.

for humans, along with the achromatic system, are illustrated in Figure 2 for comparison with the physiologic data from fish. The curves can be derived as linear combinations of cone absorption spectra (Jameson and Hurvich, 1968), and have been measured psychophysically in the human.

Wagner et al. (1960) recorded graded potentials from isolated goldfish retinas. These S potentials are shown in Figure 3. The L potential (Fig. 3a) is hyperpolarizing to all wavelengths, and is reminiscent of the achromatic function of Figure 2. The C potentials (Fig. 3b, c) show either hyper- or depolarization, depending on the wavelength of the stimulus light. They correspond roughly to the opponent chromatic functions in Figure 2.

Color-sensitive units are also found in the retinal ganglion cells of goldfish (Wagner et al., 1960; MacNichol et al., 1961). For example, a unit that gave a short burst of responses to the *onset* of short wavelength stimulation ("on" response) would respond only immediately after the *offset* of long wavelength illumination ("off" response). The transition from "on" to "off" responses could be made within 10 nm, and the spectral sensitivity of each type of response could be determined. Figure 4 shows the spectral sensitivity for a "red-green" unit, whose pattern of discharge seems to follow the pattern of polarization seen for the C potentials. This figure also illustrates a nonopponent unit which gave the same type of response at all spectral wavelengths. The peak sensitivity of such units occurs in the same spectral region as the maximum hyperpolarization of the L potential.

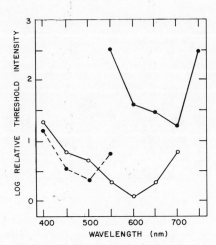

Fig. 4. Spectral sensitivity curves of an opponent (on-off) and a non-opponent ganglion cell in the goldfish retina. (After MacNichol et al., 1961.) ——O——: non-opponent "on-off" cell; ——●—— opponent cell, "on" component; - - -●- - - opponent cell, "off" component.

Finally, Jacobson (1964) has recorded from units in the superficial layers of the optic tectum of the goldfish, which is the primary projection area of the visual system in the fish brain. Several types of spectral sensitivity curves were recorded, including both "on-off" spectrally opponent cells and "on" or "off" spectrally non-opponent cells.

There exists, then, a large body of evidence suggesting color vision mechanisms in the goldfish: from three types of cone photopigments we have proceeded to an opponent type organization, as evidenced in the S potential and in recordings from ganglion cells and the optic tectum. The experiments and theory described in this chapter are an attempt to relate this known physiology to the actual color discriminating abilities of the intact organism.

EXPERIMENTS

SUBJECTS

Common goldfish (*Carassius auratus*), 15 to 20 cm in length, served as subjects. They were maintained in individual tanks at a water temperature of 24.5° C, located in a room with a controlled 18-hour light, 6-hour dark cycle. Subjects obtained all of their food in the experimental situation, and were therefore approximately 21 hours deprived at the beginning of each experimental session.

APPARATUS

The apparatus used in our experiments is diagrammed in Figure 5. The experimental chamber is a glass tank 35.6 by 17.8 by 23.8 cm, on either side of which is a box containing a 150-watt tungsten bulb and 35 by 18 cm sheets of heat-absorbing glass, an appropriate Wratten color filter, and diffusing material. Also included in each box is a low amperage (0.15 ma) cue light. One end of the experimental tank is aligned with an optical system such that a homogenous spot of light 13 mm in diameter may be projected onto a diffusing patch behind either of two 4 by 2.5 cm pieces of clear Plexiglas placed 7 cm apart. Each Plexiglas rectangle is attached to a mechanical fish lever (Hogan and Rozin, 1962), and these are the "choice keys." Figure 6 illustrates the stimulus situation and manipulanda. At the opposite end of the tank an opaque target is attached to such a lever, and this is the "observing key." All of the manipulanda are 7 cm above the floor of the tank. An electromechanical feeder (Ralph Gerbrands Co., Arlington, Mass.) provides 20 mg Noyes (Lancaster, N.H.) fish food pellets for correct responses. All equipment is controlled automatically by conventional electromechanical relays. In the early experiments different spectral bands were produced with interference filters (Balzers, Liechtenstein), but a Bausch and Lomb monochromater is now used. Intensity control is provided by thin-film (Bausch and Lomb) and Wratten (Kodak) neutral density filters.

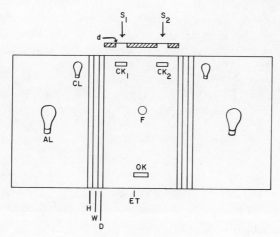

Fig. 5. Diagram of apparatus. ET–experimental tank, S_1 and S_2–stimulus channels, CK_1 and CK_2–choice keys, OK–observing key, F–feeder, AL–adapting lights, CL–cue lights, H–heat-absorbing glass, W–Wratten filters, D,d–diffusers.

Fig. 6. View of the subject in the experimental tank, illustrating the response keys and stimulus patches. (Photo by James Gordon.)

CALIBRATIONS

Calibrations of stimuli were made with a Photovolt photomultiplier instrument which had been calibrated against a thermopile. The relative spectral output of the optical system was measured through a cell consisting of aquarium glass, an inch of aquarium water, and a piece of the same clear Plexiglas which was used for the response targets; thus the sensitivity measures could be expressed in terms of relative energy at the cornea at threshold. The spectral distributions of adapting and diluting lights were measured with an ISCO model SR spectroradiometer.

For a general treatment of the problem of calibration of visual stimuli, the reader is referred to Boynton (1966).

PROCEDURE

TRAINING. Goldfish are surprisingly easy to train for operant discrimination studies. We have found that the following steps in training are quite successful:
1. Deprivation: Deprive the fish of all food for about one week.
2. Magazine training: Place the fish in the experimental tank and deliver up to 50 pellets per day at irregular intervals for several days with the automatic feeder. Continue this procedure until the fish eats the pellets rapidly after delivery into the tank. Vibrations in the water produced both by the operation of the feeder and by the pellet striking the surface are thus established as cues that food has been delivered. In addition, a small cue light should be illuminated for a few seconds with each pellet delivery.[1]
3. Operant training: Program the apparatus such that striking either choice key, both of which are equally illuminated, always produces a food pellet (continuous reinforcement—CRF). When first placed in the apparatus the hungry fish randomly strikes one of the choice keys and receives a food pellet (reinforcement). Within a few hours the fish will be making well-defined "pecks" at the choice keys and responding several times a minute. Continue this procedure with about 50 pellets a day for several days.
4. Observing response: When the fish is placed in the experimental tank, the stimulus lights are now off and the choice keys inoperative. The apparatus is programmed such that striking the observing key at the back of the tank sets the apparatus as it was in step 3 (CRF on both illuminated choice keys). After the fish has obtained a pellet, the choice keys are again made inoperative, the stimulus lights are extinguished, and the adapting lights come on again until another observing response is made. The use of an observing response has at least two advantages: (1) the fish presents the stimuli to himself, and thus makes a choice only when he is ready to attend to the stimuli; (2) the fish has both stimulus patches in his field of view, since the observing key is placed far from the choice keys. In an analysis of observing behavior, Kelleher (1958) has noted that if either the choice stimuli or the differential reinforcement associated with them is eliminated, an observing response extinguishes. The conclusion is that the animal does in fact attend to the choice stimuli when an observing response is made. It seems reasonable to assume in our experiments that the fish is attending to both choice keys.
5. Discrimination training: Program the apparatus such that only one of the

---

[1] The cue light is not *necessary* to maintain the behavior, but is an added conditional stimulus for the delivery of food. Yager (1968) obtained a dark-adapted spectral sensitivity function in which food reinforcement was delivered in complete darkness.

choice keys is illuminated and operable on a 50–50 random schedule. Because of the previous training on illuminated keys the fish almost always responds on the illuminated key. Responses on the nonilluminated choice key simply turn on the adapting lights and do not deliver reinforcement.

6. Variable ratio (VR) training: In order to obtain a greater number of trials before the fish is satiated with food, it is advantageous not to deliver reinforcement with every correct response. We have found that reinforcing on the average every third correct choice (VR 3 schedule) maintains the behavior adequately. The cue light should be illuminated on all correct trials, including those when reinforcement is not delivered.

7. Correction procedure: To prevent the establishment of position habits, when an incorrect response is made, the stimulus remains on the same key for subsequent trials until a correct choice is made; then the stimulus switches randomly on the next trial. Of course, following an incorrect response, no responses are counted for psychometric functions until after the next correct response.

The details of time intervals, number of trials, choice stimuli, etc. will be introduced with specific experiments.

THRESHOLD DETERMINATIONS.   Our experimental procedure is diagrammed in Figure 7. A constant state of adaptation is maintained by diffusely illuminating the adapting lights behind the large Wratten filters on either side of the experimental tank (Fig. 5) for at least 30 seconds between trials. An observing response after this time extinguishes the adapting lights and illuminates one of the stimulus patches behind the Plexiglas keys. The fish must then swim to the other end of the tank within 15 seconds and strike one of the choice keys. In the spectral sensitivity experiments, if the fish hits the choice key which is illuminated, a correct

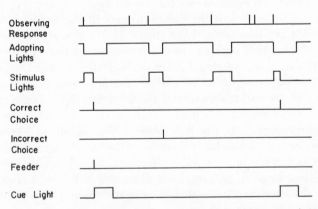

Fig. 7. Diagram of experimental procedure. The adapting lights must be on at least 30 sec before an observing response extinguishes them and simultaneously illuminates a choice key with the stimulus light; the fish must hit one of the choice keys within 15 sec after making the observing response. Four types of trials are illustrated: Correct and reinforced response; Incorrect response; No choice response after 15 sec; Correct unreinforced response (VR3 schedule of reinforcement).

response is recorded and a food pellet may be delivered on the VR 3 schedule; only one choice response is allowed per trial. If he strikes the choice key which is not illuminated, then an incorrect response is recorded and the correction procedure is put into effect. For the saturation discrimination experiment, a correct response is recorded when the key illuminated with "white" light (2,850° K tungsten) plus monochromatic light is struck; the other key is illuminated with "white" light only. In both types of experiments, whenever a correct response is made the stimulus light is extinguished and the cue light comes on; after 15 seconds [2] the cue light is extinguished and the adapting lights come on. If the fish does not respond within 15 seconds of making his observing response, the trial is terminated and the adapting lights are turned on again.

A modified method of constant stimuli is used to determine thresholds. First, levels of energy of the monochromatic light required for a range of 50 to 85 percent correct performance are roughly determined. Four to six energy levels approximately 0.3 log unit apart are necessary to cover this response range. (With the method of constant stimuli an intermediate stimulus step size should be chosen such that percent correct responding neither goes from 100 percent to 50 percent correct with one stimulus step, nor remains about the same over several steps.) Within an experimental session, these. stimuli are presented in a descending order in blocks of 25 trials at each energy level. A descending rather than a random order of stimulus presentation is used to avoid the possibility of many consecutive blocks of trials at stimulus energies near or below threshold; this could lead to a decline of attention and establishment of severe position habits.

Psychometric functions can be constructed from the data obtained, and the interpolated 75 percent correct energy level is chosen as threshold. In general, the psychometric functions are changing most rapidly near the 75 percent correct point, and thus the choice of the energy level required for 75 percent correct responding as the threshold results in the smallest error of measurement. Each daily session is devoted to one wavelength, and at the end of the session the subject is returned to an 85 to 90 percent correct level of responding to a stimulus which is well above the threshold. Several determinations are made at each wavelength.

The essential features of our procedure are the requirement of an observing response and the use of a forced-choice situation. In contrast to the "go"–"no-go" method, the forced-choice method gives the animal two behavioral alternatives, thereby always providing a "yes" response. It also minimizes the importance of motivation. By using discrete trials we avoid the time-consuming process of gathering response rate data for fish, and also the problem of interpreting such rate data (see Blough and Yager, in press, for a discussion of the interpretation of different kinds of response measures and a general treatment of procedures to use in animal psychophysics).

---

[2] We have found that intense adapting lights may be aversive, and if they are illuminated immediately after both correct and incorrect responses, choice responding may be inhibited. Observing responses may continue to be emitted because they are reinforced by turning off the adapting lights.

EMPIRICAL FINDINGS AND THEORETICAL ANALYSIS

Our experimental plans include the determination of spectral sensitivity, saturation discrimination, and wavelength discrimination functions under several conditions of light adaptation. We have developed a quantitative model of the fish visual system derived from the opponent-process theory (Hurvich and Jameson, 1957) which will be tested by its ability to account for these psychophysical functions in terms of physiologic responses from the fish visual system. It is beyond the scope of this chapter to present the theoretical treatment in detail, and the reader is referred to Yager (1967; 1969) for more complete derivations.

SPECTRAL SENSITIVITY.   So far we have determined the photopic spectral sensitivity function for three states of adaptation: slightly yellowish tungsten, long wavelength (red, Wratten #26), and short wavelength (blue-green, Wratten #75) light (Yager, 1967; 1969).

Log spectral sensitivity functions for the two states of chromatic adaptation (Yager, 1969) are shown in Figure 8. Maximal sensitivity for the long-wavelength-adapted function is near 475 to 500 nm, and for the short-wavelength-adapted function, around 600 to 625 nm. There is clearly a large effect of the adapting light

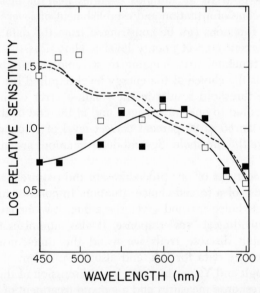

Fig. 8. Geometric means of the log relative sensitivity for two fish and two states of chromatic adaptation. Filled squares: Wratten #75 adaptation. Open squares: Wratten #26 adaptation. The smooth curves are best-fitting photopigment summation functions. Solid curve is fitted to the filled squares. Dashed curve is fitted to the open squares. Dotted curve is the best-fitting photopigment summation function following tungsten light adaptation. Data are in terms of an equal quantum intensity spectrum at the retina. (From Yager, 1969. **Vision Res.**, 9:183.)

on the shape of the photopic spectral sensitivity function in goldfish.[3] It is interesting to note the similarity between the spectral sensitivity function for the long wavelength adaptation and that same function under broad-band (2,400° K) tungsten light adaptation in the earlier study (Yager, 1967). Apparently, tungsten light looks very "red" to the goldfish because the visual adapting effects are very similar. Great care must be taken in specifying the adaptation conditions in both behavioral and physiologic investigations; an adapting light that looks white to the experimenter is not necessarily perceptually neutral for the fish.

Spectral sensitivity must be related to the spectral absorption curves of the visual pigments found in the retina. The light absorbed by the pigments in some way triggers neural responses which are combined at some point in the visual system to produce "brightness," or at least some perceptual quality that enables the fish (or human) to make a discrimination. The following analysis relates the spectral sensitivity functions shown in Figure 8 to the goldfish cone photopigments (Liebman and Entine, 1964; Marks, 1965; Fig. 1). In particular, the question asked is: How do the relative contributions of the photopigments change with changes in chromatic adaptation? For comparison with the absorption spectra of visual pigments, the data in Figure 8 have been corrected for preretinal absorption using Burkhardt's (1966) measurements; thus, the sensitivities are expressed in retinal terms. Also, the retinal sensitivities have been converted from energy units to measures of the relative number of quanta required for threshold discrimination; this is necessary because the absorption of light by the retinal photopigments is quantal in nature.

The simple additive model of the visual system assumes that the achromatic response is due to the weighted sum of the three cone pigment responses, a, β, and γ (see Fig. 1). Thus:

$$S_\lambda = k_1 a_\lambda + k_2 \beta_\lambda + k_3 \gamma_\lambda \tag{1}$$

where S_λ is the behaviorally-measured sensitivity, and k_1, k_2, and k_3 are weighting factors which are estimated with a least-squares fit to the data. The photopigment functions adjusted for the two states of chromatic adaptation are shown in Figure 9, and the sensitivity functions calculated by equation 1 using the estimated k factors are shown in Figure 8 along with the behavioral data. The photopigment summation functions describe smooth curves which fall fairly close to the means of the measurements for the two subjects.

---

[3] Even though variability within and between subjects is often a problem in animal psychophysical data, it is still possible to obtain reliable psychophysical functions. For example, there is a very pronounced effect of chromatic adaptation conditions on the shape of the goldfish photopic spectral sensitivity curve, and this effect is much larger than within-conditions variability. To minimize variability and thus to sharpen such effects, one might try such procedures as: (1) obtaining thresholds for at least two stimuli (e.g., wavelengths, auditory frequencies, odors) within a single session, (2) assuring constant stimulus conditions by requiring the animal to position himself always in the same way with respect to the stimulus (observing response), (3) choosing an instrumental procedure which reduces response bias for that particular species and stimulus (see Blough and Yager, in press), and (4) employing a correction procedure so that the animal is forced to respond appropriately and is reinforced for it.

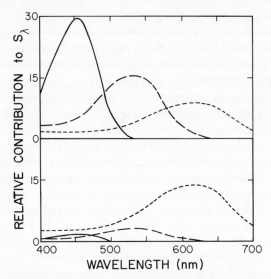

Fig. 9. Adjusted photopigment functions for two states of chromatic adaptation. Upper graph: Wratten #26 adaptation. Lower graph: Wratten #75 adaptation. Solid curves: $k_1 \, \alpha_\lambda$. Dashed curves: $k_2 \, \beta_\lambda$. Dotted curves: $k_3 \, \gamma_\lambda$. (From Yager, 1969. **Vision Res.**, 9:183.)

SPECTRAL SATURATION. Spectral lights of equal brightness usually differ not only in hue but also in saturation. For example, a color-normal human looking at a stimulus of 585 nm under daylight adaptation sees a yellow of low saturation, while 410 nm of equal brightness gives a violet sensation of very high saturation. Estimates of degree of saturation are very difficult to make, even for a human observer. However, a monotonically related psychophysical measure of saturation is "least-colorimetric-purity," or the least amount of spectral light that must be added to white light to make it just detectably different in color from the white alone. This function is usually plotted as the logarithm of the reciprocal of the least-colorimetric-purity, so that the top of the graph indicates high saturation. The form of this function is strongly dependent on the specific characteristics of the color vision mechanisms. If saturation is at zero for all wavelengths, then the animal is a monochromat. If the animal can discriminate most wavelengths from a white stimulus except for one or two points in the spectrum where saturation approaches zero, then it is probably a dichromat, like the red-green– or yellow-blue–blind human. If the animal can discriminate all wavelengths from white, and there are no points in the spectrum where saturation approaches zero, as with the normal human, then the animal probably has trichromatic vision.

The saturation discrimination function has been determined in the goldfish for tungsten adaptation only. Conditions were the same as in the spectral sensitivity experiment except that there was a constant amount of white light on each stimulus patch. When the fish pressed the observing target, monochromatic light was added to the white light on one stimulus patch and additional white light (broad-band tungsten) was added to the other to keep the brightness on the two stimulus patches equal. The method of constant stimuli was used in this experiment also, and the fish was rewarded with food for pressing the target illuminated with the mixture of white and monochromatic light. Psychometric functions for the determination of the energy spectral lights required for 75 percent correct responding in this experiment were similar to those obtained in the spectral sensitivity experiment. These chromatic threshold energy values were converted to luminance units by the equation:

$$Lo_\lambda = \frac{E_{o_\lambda}}{E_{t_\lambda}} \qquad (2)$$

where E_{t_λ} is the threshold energy from the spectral sensitivity experiment, E_{o_λ} is the chromatic threshold energy, and L_{o_λ} is the luminance of the chromatic threshold stimulus in units of threshold energy. This method of expressing stimulus luminance is similar to the decibel scale *re* measured threshold (sensation level) in audition, and is a standard photometric convention.

The same operations were carried out for the diluting light, *w*. Then the ratio:

$$\frac{L_w + L_\lambda}{L_\lambda} \qquad (3)$$

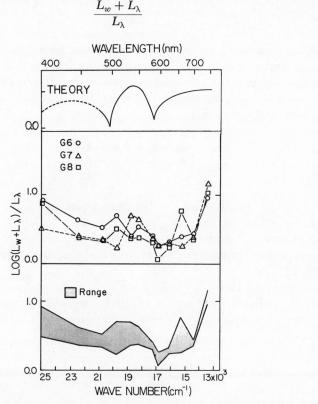

Fig. 10. Top, theoretical saturation discrimination function from the opponent-colors theory. Middle, spectral saturation discrimination functions for three fish. Bottom, range of the measurements across subjects. Tungsten adaptation. (From Yager, 1967. **Vision Res., 7:**717.)

was computed for each wavelength. This is the reciprocal of the least-colorimetric-purity required for detection of a saturation difference.

Figure 10 is a plot of this expression for each of the three fish used in this experiment. It is obvious that saturation discrimination for all three fish is maximal at the spectral extremes, and there is a secondary maximum in the midspectral region between about 510 and 535 nm. There is a well-defined minimum at around 600 nm, and a shallower one at 490 to 500 nm. None of the monochromatic lights used in this experiment were confused by any fish with a tungsten light. The evidence suggests that all spectral wavelengths elicit color responses that differ from the response to the broad-band tungsten distribution and, therefore, that goldfish vision is trichromatic.

Spectral saturation must also be related to the spectral absorption curves of retinal visual pigments. Two types of evidence suggest that the opponent-process theory of Hering, as developed quantitatively by Hurvich and Jameson (1957), describes most accurately the way in which the responses from the cones are combined to mediate color discriminations: *First*, Hurvich and Jameson have had a good deal of success in accounting for several human visual functions with the use of this model. *Second*, as pointed out in the introduction, opponent-type chromatically-coded responses have been discovered at several different levels of the fish visual system.

This theory assumes that the paired chromatic response processes (Fig. 2) are determined by positive and negative interactions among three fundamental processes, a, β, and γ. If a, b, c, and d are names for hypothetical chromatic responses for the fish and w is the achromatic response, then the equations for the goldfish visual response functions which correspond to the human functions in Figure 2 are as follows (Yager, 1967):

$$a_\lambda - b_\lambda = k_2\beta_\lambda - k_1a_\lambda \qquad (4)$$
$$c_\lambda - d_\lambda = k_2\beta_\lambda - k_3\gamma_\lambda \qquad (5)$$
$$w_\lambda = k_1a_\lambda + k_2\beta_\lambda + k_3\gamma_\lambda \qquad (6)$$

where k_1a, $k_2\beta$, and $k_3\gamma$ are the best-fitting photochemical absorptions for the spectral sensitivity function for a particular state of adaptation. When plotted as a function of wavelength, these expressions bear a striking similarity to the spectral response functions for the S potentials and ganglion cell recordings in Figures 3 and 4.

Jameson and Hurvich (1955) have shown that saturation discrimination is accurately predicted by the ratio of total chromatic response to achromatic response at each wavelength.[4] This expression, based on equations 4, 5, and 6, is as follows:

$$\frac{|k_2\beta_\lambda - k_1a_\lambda| + |k_2\beta_\lambda - k_3\gamma_\lambda|}{k_1a_\lambda + k_2\beta_\lambda + k_3\gamma_\lambda} \qquad (7)$$

[4] This is similar to the model used by DeValois and Jacobs (1968) in their study of the relations between lateral geniculate cell responses and saturation discrimination in several species of monkeys.

This theoretical function is also shown in a logarithmic plot on Figure 10 along with the saturation discrimination data. The opponent-process function bears a close relation to the behavioral data. Two minima are clearly present and correspond closely to the behavioral minima. The theoretical function also rises toward the spectral extremes and at the middle wavelengths, which is also characteristic of the behavioral function.

The next step in this analysis will be to determine spectral saturation discrimination functions for the two states of chromatic adaptation described above. Here, a psychophysical procedure can be used to provide a direct test of the appropriateness of a particular mathematical theoretical model. If the model is correct, the behavioral functions will have the general shapes of the theoretical functions in Figure 11, which are calculated from equations 4 to 7, using the two sets of k values determined in the spectral sensitivity experiment with chromatic adaptations.

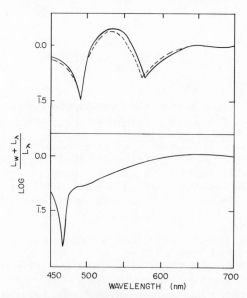

Fig. 11. Theoretical saturation discrimination functions for two states of chromatic adaptation, calculated from the opponent-process theory (solid lines). Upper graph: Wratten #26 adaptation. Lower graph: Wratten #75 adaptation. Also shown in the upper graph is the theoretical saturation discrimination function following tungsten light adaptation (dashed line).

SUMMARY

Isolated information is found in the literature about cone photopigment absorption functions and physiologic responses from several different levels of the goldfish visual system. Precise discrimination measures are required to integrate this information into a synthesized account of visual response in the intact organism.

In this chapter, an operant-method is described which has been used to obtain discrimination measures in a two-choice situation. To measure photopic spectral sensitivity, the energies of spectral lights required for 75 percent correct choice responding were determined. To measure spectral saturation, the reciprocal of the least-colorimetric-purity required for 75 percent correct choice responding to a mixture of spectral light and broad-band tungsten light was determined for the same range of spectral stimuli. On the basis of the measured saturation discrimination function, the data indicate that goldfish probably have trichromatic vision. The form of the saturation function is accounted for by a model of the visual system that postulates: (1) a summation of responses from different types of cone photopigments of known absorptions to yield a brightness response, and (2) interactions between activities initiated in the different types of cones to yield opponent chromatic responses at the neural level. This is consistent with the available electrophysiology.

REFERENCES

Blough, D. S., and D. Yager. In press. Visual psychophysics in animals. *In* Hurvich, L., and Jameson, D., eds. Visual Psychophysics, Handbook of Sensory Physiology, Berlin, Springer-Verlag, vol. VII, part 3.

Boynton, R. 1966. Vision. *In* Sidowski, J., ed. Experimental Methods and Instrumentation in Psychology, New York, McGraw-Hill Book Company, pp. 273–330.

Burkhardt, D. 1966. The goldfish ERG: Relation between photopic spectral sensitivity functions and cone absorption spectra. Vision Res., 6:517–532.

DeValois, R., and G. Jacobs. 1968. Primate color vision. Science, 162:533–540.

Frisch, K. von. 1912. Sind die Fische farbenblind? Zool. Jahrb. Abt. allg. Zool. Physiol. Tiere, 33:151–164.

———— 1913. Weitere Untersuchungen über den Farbensinn der Fische. Zool. Jahrb. Abt. allg. Zool. Physiol. Tiere, 34:43–68.

Hering, E. 1964. Outlines of a Theory of the Light Sense. Translated by Hurvich, L. and Jameson, D. Cambridge, Harvard University Press.

Hogan, J., and P. Rozin. 1962. An improved mechanical fish-lever. Amer. J. Psychol., 75:307–308.

Hurvich, L., and D. Jameson. 1957. An opponent-process theory of color vision. Psychol. Rev., 64:384–404.

Jacobson, M. 1964. Spectral sensitivity of single units in the optic tectum of the goldfish. Quart. J. Exp. Physiol., 49:384–393.

Jameson, D., and L. Hurvich. 1955. Some quantitative aspects of an opponent colors theory. I. Chromatic responses and spectral saturation. J. Opt. Soc. Amer., 45:546–552.

———— and L. Hurvich. 1968. Opponent-response functions related to measured cone photopigments. J. Opt. Soc. Amer., 58:429–430.

Kelleher, R. 1958. Stimulus-producing responses in chimpanzees. J. Exp. Anal. Behav., 1:87–102.

Liebman, P., and G. Entine. 1964. Sensitive low-light-level microspectrophotometer: detection of photosensitive pigments of retinal cones. J. Opt. Soc. Amer., 54:1451–1459.

MacNichol, E., M. Wolbarsht, and H. Wagner. 1961. Electrophysiological evidence for a mechanism of color vision in the goldfish. *In* McElroy, W., and Glass, B., eds. Light and Life, Baltimore, Johns Hopkins Press, pp. 795–813.

McCleary, R., and J. Bernstein. 1959. A unique method for control of brightness cues in the study of color vision in fish. Physiol. Zool., 32:284–292.

Marks, W. 1965. Visual pigments of single goldfish cones. J. Physiol., 178:14–32.

Wagner, H., E. MacNichol, and M. Wolbarsht. 1960. The response properties of single ganglion cells in the goldfish retina. J. Gen. Physiol., 43:Suppl. 2, 45–62.

Wolff, H. 1925. Das Farbenunterscheidungsvermögen der Ellritze. Z. vergl. Physiol., 3:279–329.

Yager, D. 1967. Behavioral measures and theoretical analysis of spectral sensitivity and spectral saturation in the goldfish, *Carassius auratus*. Vision Res., 7:707–727.

———— 1968. Behavioral measures of the spectral sensitivity of the dark-adapted goldfish. Nature, 220:1052–1053.

———— 1969. Behavioral measures of spectral sensitivity in the goldfish following chromatic adaptation. Vision Res., 9:179–186.

Yarczower, M., and M. Bitterman. 1965. Stimulus generalization in the goldfish. *In* Mostofsky, D., ed. Stimulus Generalization, Stanford, Stanford University Press, pp. 179–192.

DAVID B. MOODY [1]

13

REACTION TIME AS AN
INDEX OF SENSORY FUNCTION *

INTRODUCTION

It is probably quite apparent from the contents of this book that there are many techniques which can be used to determine either the minimum levels of stimulation or the minimum difference in levels of stimulation necessary to produce behavioral consequences. These techniques all produce a measure of sensitivity conventionally called the *threshold;* they all determine something about the fineness with which an organism can discriminate certain elements of his environment from other similar elements.

The data on a subject's acuity provided by threshold techniques are important to our understanding of sensory processes, but they are by no means the only behavioral data necessary. Data are also required on responses to stimuli which are well above threshold levels in the range to which the organism usually responds. The present chapter discusses a behavioral procedure which can be used to deal with such stimuli. The next chapter concerns techniques which have been used to correlate the behavioral data obtained with this procedure with concurrently measured neurophysiologic events.

Specifically, the present chapter deals with a procedure which can be used to determine psychophysical intensity equivalences of qualitatively different stimuli. Examples of such equivalences are tones of various frequencies which sound equally loud even though their physical intensities differ, or lights of different wavelengths which look equally bright even though they contain different amounts of radiant energy. Such data indicate the relative sensitivity of the particular sensory system involved, and are clearly important in the understanding of how these systems function.

Very few psychophysical procedures have been developed for use with suprathreshold stimuli with animal subjects. An understanding of why this statement

[1] Kresge Hearing Research Institute, University of Michigan Medical School, Ann Arbor, Michigan.

* The work reported in this chapter was supported by National Institutes of Health grants HD-00930 and MH-12021 to Columbia University and NB-05077 and NS-05785 to the University of Michigan.

should be true is important for an appreciation of the advantages of the present method. Human subjects can be verbally instructed to scale suprathreshold stimuli or to equate stimuli which differ in several attributes on the basis of only one of these attributes. With sufficient practice, most subjects become quite reliable observers, and when their responses are appropriately treated, psychophysical scales of suprathreshold stimuli can be derived. Examples of such scales are the mel scale for pitch (Stevens and Volkmann, 1940), the bril scale for brightness (Hanes, 1949), and the phon (Fletcher and Munson, 1933) and sone scales (Stevens, 1936) for loudness.

The psychophysical methods used with humans to study suprathreshold stimulus functions essentially measure the probability of some response as a function of the conditions of stimulation. For example, in a magnitude estimation experiment in which the subject responds with some number as an estimate of his perception of stimulus intensity, the probability of his giving any particular number is a function of the physical value of the stimulus. Similarly, in a loudness matching experiment, the verbal response "equal" is more probable for certain intensities of comparison tone than for others.

The relative probability of any particular response under a given set of stimulus conditions is only partially determined by the subject's perception of the stimulus. The instructions given the subject also have some influence on the response, and therefore instructions must be used which maximize the influence of perception while minimizing the influence of the instructions themselves. If the instructions are too specific, the influence of the subject's perception of the stimulus is reduced. For example, a subject might be shown two different monochromatic lights, and told they are equal in brightness. When he is then asked to adjust the second light to be equal in brightness to the first, he will probably be influenced by the "standard" match which he was shown. The point to be made here is that the experimenter cannot tell the subject that two differently colored lights are equally bright, because to the subject, they may be quite unequal.

The same thing, of course, is true with animal subjects, but with the added problem (discussed in the opening chapter) that all instructions must be translated into contingencies of reinforcement and/or punishment. Such contingencies imply decisions by the experimenter of the stimulus conditions under which reinforcement or punishment should be delivered. An animal subject could be reinforced when he reports that two different monochromatic lights are equal in brightness, but the equal point must be defined by the experimenter, and such definition presupposes knowledge of the equivalence which the procedure is attempting to determine. The effect on the animal would be similar to what we would observe with a human subject who is given instructions that are too specific; the subject becomes biased towards responding according to the "instructions" rather than according to his perception of the stimulus.

On the other hand, contingencies of reinforcement which are not specific produce behavior which is not reliable enough to determine psychophysical data. Discriminative behavior can be influenced by many factors other than the stimulus and as many of these factors as possible must be controlled by the experimenter. One reason for the availability of many procedures for the determination of thresholds is that specific contingencies can often be established which do not introduce unwanted biases. In a threshold experiment, for example, we want the animal to discriminate the "I see it" situation from the "I don't see it" situation. ("See" may, of course, be replaced by "hear," or "smell," or whatever is appropriate; the "it" may refer to the presence of a stimulus or to a difference between two stimuli.) In these cases, we can specifically train the animal to discriminate between stimulus present and stimulus absent by only reinforcing when the stimulus is physically absent. We know that the animal cannot see a stimulus which is not there, and therefore, a report of "I do not see it" when the stimulus is absent is always correct, and may be reinforced without the danger of introducing inappropriate response biases.

Let us consider the problems of dealing with suprathreshold stimuli. We want our subjects to report that a single attribute (e.g., brightness) of a complex stimulus is "the same" or "different," but we have no stimulus condition which can be established as always being the same in that attribute, or always being different, and thus are unable to specify when reinforcement should be delivered. If, as a first approximation, we reinforce our subject for responding "different" to some widely separated stimuli which look quite different to us, we will probably discover that he learns to discriminate this particular pair of stimuli from others, and responds "different" to it. It is highly likely, however, that stimuli to which he does not respond "different" actually look different, but because he has learned to discriminate the particular pair which is reinforced from nonreinforced pairs, his responses do not reflect his perception of the stimulus. The problem, again, is that the instructions determine the subject's report of the stimulus more than does the sensory input.

It may appear difficult, if not impossible, to study the perception of suprathreshold stimuli in animal subjects. Fortunately, such is not the case. Certain features of behavior tend to covary with parameters of external stimulation without specific training. An outstanding example is the variation in response latency when the intensity of the stimulus is changed. Low stimulus intensities yield long latencies, and vice versa. Since no differential reinforcement with respect to the value of the stimulus is necessary to produce this behavior pattern, it is probably reasonable to assume that latency is an indicator of sensory function which is not distorted by arbitrary choices of stimulus-response pairings.

The use of response latency, or more familiarly, reaction time, is not a new idea in psychophysics. The systematic study of reaction time began in Wundt's Leipzig laboratory in the late 19th century and was continued by Cattell and his students at Columbia University. Cattell felt that response latency was an indicator of the intensity of sensation and that: "When differences (in stimuli) require equal times for discrimination, the discriminations are equally difficult, and the differences are equal for consciousness" (Cattell, 1902; see 1947, p. 356).

Cattell's suggestion that those stimuli which produce equal response latencies can be considered psychophysical equivalents hints at the beginnings of the present method. Since Cattell's time, several human studies have been done using equal reaction times as an indication of equal sensory effect. These studies lend validity and interpretability to the animal studies which will be considered later in this chapter. Steinman (1944) used the method to determine functions which related $\Delta I/I$ to I for increments in intensity of a visual stimulus. The functions obtained were directly comparable to functions obtained in the same situation with more classical psychophysical methods. Chocholle (1940) found substantial agreement between equal loudness curves obtained using the equal reaction time method and the Fletcher-Munson (1933) curves for verbally instructed loudness matching. Pollack (1968) found that visual stimuli of different wavelengths which were matched for luminance by the method of flicker photometry produced equal reaction times. Pollack also demonstrated that classical scotopic and photopic sensitivity functions could be derived by the equal latency method. These data leave little doubt that the reaction time method can produce data which reflects sensory function as reliably as more classical methods. It seems reasonable, therefore, to use names such as brightness and loudness, which are usually operationally defined by other procedures, to describe the data obtained using the equal reaction time method.

ANIMAL REACTION TIMES:
AN ANALYSIS OF THE PRESENT METHOD

The first suggestion that the human reaction time procedure could be adapted for use with animal subjects was provided by Skinner (1946). By providing pigeons with a "ready" signal which indicated the approaching onset of the "respond" stimulus, and by differentially reinforcing only short latency responses, he was able to obtain stable latencies of about 200 to 300 msec. These are about half as long as latencies reported by investigators not using the ready signal or the differential reinforcement of short latencies.

Stebbins and his collaborators took the basic features of Skinner's procedure, the ready signal and differential reinforcement, and added many refinements which eventually led to the method we now use. The procedure is probably best explained by first giving the details of the current procedure, and then considering the variations of the procedure which have been used in the past. The present behavioral procedures have been used in slightly different forms for the determination of both the equal loudness function of the monkey (Stebbins, 1966) and the equal brightness function of the pigmented rat (Moody, 1969). Since there is a considerable difference in the instrumentation necessary for the different sense modalities and the different organisms, a discussion of some general problems of instrumentation will be presented later in this chapter.

The heart of the present procedure was first suggested by Stebbins and Lanson (1961). The method uses a single response bar and two stimuli, usually drawn from separate modalities. Although only a single bar is involved, a procedural distinction is drawn between bar press and bar release, so that the procedure actually involves two responses, the second of which (bar release) is physically contingent on making the first (bar press). The procedure is organized in a trial-by-trial fashion. A cycle starts with the beginning of the intertrial interval (ITI).

When the ITI elapses, the first stimulus (S_1) comes on. This serves as the "ready" signal which indicates to a well-trained animal that bar press is the appropriate response. Most animals learn to press the bar very shortly after the onset of the S_1, but if for any reason the animal stops responding, the S_1 will remain on until the session is terminated. We have experimented with terminating the S_1 after some fixed period of time, and then recycling to the start of the ITI, but found no particular advantage in doing so.

When the animal presses the bar, a timer is started which determines the time from bar press to the onset of the second stimulus (S_2). In human reaction time studies, this interval is called the foreperiod. When the foreperiod has elapsed, the S_2 is presented and a clock is started which measures the latency of bar release. As soon as the animal releases the bar, the reinforcer is delivered, the S_1 and S_2 terminate, the latency clock stops, and the cycle starts again at the beginning of the intertrial interval.

To review the procedure for a normal trial: the subject must wait, without responding until the S_1 is presented; he then must press the bar and hold it down until the S_2 is presented and then release it to obtain a reinforcer. A diagrammatic representation of this procedure is shown in Figure 1. An important difference between this procedure and Skinner's (1946) procedure is that the animal must make a specified, preparatory response to the "ready" signal. This response enables him to release the bar very quickly after the onset of the S_2 since it insures that he will be in a specified place (holding down the bar) when the S_2 is presented. This feature proved to be especially important in adapting the method for use as a psychophysical procedure with rats, since it made it possible to accurately specify the location and orientation of the receptors without the necessity of physically restraining the animal.

Obviously, the above cursory description of the procedure leaves out important details such as optimal temporal parameters and special contingencies for incorrect responding. Since these may vary considerably from situation to situation, each will receive special attention.

We have used intertrial intervals of from 5 to 30 seconds. Several factors en-

NORMAL TRIAL

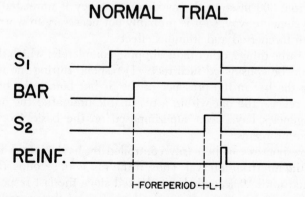

Fig. 1. A schematic representation of the behavioral procedure in effect on a normal trial. "L" is the latency.

ter into the choice of this value, and at least one of them has a direct bearing on the nature of the psychophysical data which are obtained. Since stimuli can be used which are well above threshold, the possibility exists that intense enough stimuli might produce changes in receptor characteristics on successive trials. This is especially true when visual stimuli are involved, since relatively low intensity levels are required to produce significant light adaptation and therefore lower the sensitivity of the eye on successive trials. The possibility of a threshold shift produced by intense auditory stimuli also exists, but our preliminary data indicate that the sound levels and durations are such that temporary threshold shift would be very unlikely to occur in the reaction time situation. With visual stimuli, however, if it is desired to maintain the animal in a dark-adapted state, a safe rule would be to use as long an intertrial interval as possible. In general, intertrial intervals of less than 5 seconds are not desirable since at least that amount of time is usually necessary for the reinforcer to be consumed. Since the intertrial interval is a substantial part of the total cycle length, it largely determines the rate of data acquisition. Thus the advantages of long intervals must be weighed against the slow data acquisition which results.

The foreperiod value may be either fixed or variable within a session. Fixed foreperiods are easier to implement, but have the inherent disadvantage that the animal may learn certain "timing behaviors" (e.g., Laties et al., 1965) which enable him to anticipate the onset of the S_2, thus giving unrealistically low reaction times which are unrelated to the value of the stimulus. In the remaining discussion, we will consider only procedures using variable foreperiods. The choice of a range over which the foreperiod will vary is usually determined by such practical considerations as the maximum time the particular subject will reliably hold down the bar. We have used values up to 3 seconds in the rat and up to 4 seconds in the monkey without any problem. Longer foreperiods could be used, especially in the monkey, but no gain is apparent in doing so. The minimum foreperiod should not be less than about 300 msec. We have data which indicate that values less than 300 msec tend to produce slightly longer latencies, possibly due to response competition between components involved in the recently completed response of pressing the bar and the newly required response of releasing the bar. In the foreperiod range from 300 msec to the maximum, latency is unrelated to foreperiod value in any systematic way, so it is probably not necessary to worry about interactions between foreperiod and stimulus effects.

There are three things, other than stopping completely, which the subject can do which should be considered incorrect: (1) respond during the intertrial interval, (2) release the bar in the presence of the S_1 but before the onset of the S_2, and (3) fail to release the bar within a reasonable time after the onset of the S_2. Special contingencies have been superimposed on the basic procedure to deal with these three problems.

Intertrial responses can be easily controlled by having them reset the cycle to the start of the intertrial interval. Thus, if the ITI is 10 seconds, the next S_1 will not be presented until 10 seconds have elapsed since the last response. This contingency has been a universal feature of all versions of the procedure because it is extremely effective in eliminating intertrial responses.

The number of bar releases before the onset of the S_2 (anticipatory responses) is an important indicator of the degree of stimulus control. This number can be likened to the "false alarm" rate in a signal detection experiment; it is a report of a signal which is not really there and is therefore an indication of guessing by the subject. Several contingencies are possible to attempt to control the number of anticipatory responses. In the early rat work, Stebbins and Lanson (1961) simply reset the cycle to the beginning of the ITI, which was fairly long (27 seconds). Later, the same authors (1962) added a 2-minute time-out which was accompanied by a nonaversive clicker. Although the time-out is slightly more effective in controlling anticipatory responses in the rat, it substantially lowers the rate of data acquisition. For the purposes of obtaining large amounts of psychophysical data, therefore, we either use the earlier cycle reset contingency or else simply reset the foreperiod duration to its programmed value without terminating the S_1 or resetting the cycle. With monkeys, the cycle reset contingency maintains anticipatory responses at a satisfactorily low level, and with rats, the foreperiod reset contingency is only slightly less effective than the cycle reset or time-out contingencies, but results in the fastest data acquisition rate. The possibility of punishing anticipatory responses with a mild shock exists and would also result in a high data acquisition rate providing the animal did not stop working altogether. Data are not currently available on the use of shocks to punish anticipatory responses except in the context of a shock maintained version of this procedure which will be discussed briefly later in this chapter.

The third problem—failure to "respond as quickly as possible" after S_2 onset—has been the subject of a considerable amount of research. The treatment of this problem first requires defining what we mean by "as quickly as possible," and then deciding what contingencies should be employed if this limit is exceeded. The decision about the actual temporal value involves many interacting factors, and so is best postponed until the contingencies are decided.

Miller et al. (1966) used a contingency which, after a set period from the onset of the S_2, canceled reinforcement availability for bar release and terminated the S_1 and S_2, but did not stop the latency timer. They were investigating the possibility of using this procedure, which they called the differential reinforcement of brief latency responses (DRB) but which is more conventionally referred to as a limited hold procedure, to obtain minimal reaction times from monkeys. By progressively reducing the value of the limited hold, Miller et al. were able to reduce median latencies from about 350 msec to about 210 msec. Equally as significant was the reduction in semi-interquartile range which also occurred with the limited hold procedure. However, since any procedure which reduces the density of reinforcement may initially tend to *increase* variability and the overall median latency (Stebbins and Lanson, 1962), several training sessions may be required for the limited hold procedure to have the desired effect. A troublesome feature of the Miller et al. procedure is that it results in a stimulus change (S_1 and S_2 both terminate) when the limited hold is exceeded. Thus, latencies longer than the value of the limited hold are not comparable to shorter latencies as psychophysical data. We have had considerable success with a limited hold procedure in which S_1 and S_2 remain on, and only reinforcement availability is canceled when the limited hold value is exceeded. With this procedure, median latencies to pure tone auditory stimuli of about 200 msec have been obtained with semi-interquartile ranges

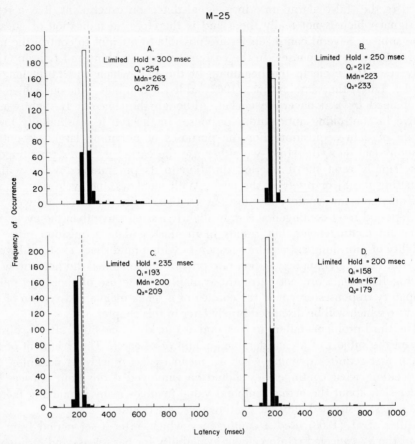

Fig. 2. Frequency distributions of response latencies under various limited hold values and conditions for one monkey. A, B, and C were obtained during sessions when there was no feedback; D was obtained during a session when the light and tone terminated when the limited hold was exceeded. The vertical dashed lines represent the limited hold value.

of about 8 msec (Fig. 2, A to C). It should be noted, however, that changing to the Miller et al. procedure with this animal resulted in even shorter median latencies (Fig. 2D).

Using a modification of a procedure developed by Snodgrass et al. (1967) for use with humans, Saslow (1968) extended the limited hold procedure even further by introducing what she called "payoff bands." Saslow's monkeys had to respond to a flash of light paired with a click with latencies which fell between two limits to be reinforced. If they did not respond appropriately, they were given feedback as to whether their latencies were too long or too short. Saslow demonstrated that she could train monkeys to place from 60 to 80 percent of their responses in a 50 msec band and that the location of this band could be moved between 200 and 600 msec.

Several features of the behavior resulting when limited hold procedures are used commend them as aids in training psychophysical subjects. One such feature is the reduction in the variability of the latency measure. Obviously, the smaller the variability in the latency data, the stronger the statement that can be made about psychophysical functions derived from these data. However, when the value of the limited hold. is reduced beyond a certain point, variability will begin to increase, presumably as a result of an attempt on the part of the subject to anticipate the onset of the S_2. It has been suggested that the optimum value for the limited hold is that duration which produces minimum variability in the latency distribution. However, since such a value might tend to restrict the effects of S_2 intensity on the latency measure, it is probably not optimum for the purpose of determining psychophysical functions. For this purpose, a value should be used which allows latencies falling in the ranges expected from variation in S_2 intensity to be reinforced but does not allow extremely long latencies, indicative of lack of stimulus control, to be reinforced. We generally use a limited hold value of 1 second.

A second desirable feature of limited hold training is that it increases the degree of stimulus control. When animals are initially trained to hold down the bar, they seem to learn the rule, "If no reinforcement on this trial, hold the bar longer on the next trial." When an animal behaves according to this rule, he need not attend to the S_2, and therefore may not be under its control. The purpose of limited hold training is to teach the rule, "If no reinforcement on this trial, respond faster to S_2 onset on the next trial," or in other words, to train the animal to attend to the S_2.

There is a danger inherent in the limited hold procedure; namely, the possibility of accidentally reinforcing the animal less in one particular qualitative stimulus dimension than in the others, and therefore producing a response bias (see Nevin, Chapter 18). We think we have been successful in avoiding this problem by selecting S_2 intensities such that the animal misses approximately equal numbers of reinforcements at all qualitative values of the S_2.

We have occasionally used one additional feature in our procedure: catch trials. A catch trial is identical to a normal trial except that the S_2 is never presented and no reinforcer is delivered for bar release. Catch trials are best implemented by operating all of the apparatus that would function on a normal trial, but turning off the source (light bulb or oscillator) of the S_2. The "latency" is then measured from the time the shutter or tone switch is operated until the animal releases the bar, and indicates whether the animal is attending to the S_2 or to some extraneous stimulus related to S_2 onset. An extremely short catch trial "latency" might, for example, mean that the subject was using auditory cues from the operation of a shutter rather than visual cues from the appearance of a light. Long catch trial "latencies," on the other hand, provide assurance that the latencies measured on a normal trial are really related to the stimulus being investigated. The proportion of catch trials to be included in a given session depends on the particular experiment, but too large a proportion not only reduces the rate of data acquisition, it may also bias the animal toward making longer latency responses on normal trials.

INITIAL TRAINING. Little has been said so far about the initial training required for this procedure. The training is fairly simple and straightforward. It begins with standard bar press training by the method of successive approximation. Shaping is carried out with the S_1 turned on all the time, the bar press producing the S_2 (which should be well above threshold), and bar release producing the reinforcer. It is probably a good idea to introduce the variation in the qualitative aspect of the S_2 (wavelength, frequency) at this point in training to increase generalization between values of the S_2. After the animal is working reliably, a brief intertrial interval can be introduced, and gradually increased to full duration. The cycle reset contingency for intertrial responses can be introduced at this stage. The rate of increase in ITI duration, of course, is determined by the rate with which the animal learns the discrimination between S_1 on and S_1 off. Most animals learn very quickly not to respond during the ITI, so this stage of training does not take very long (1 or 2 sessions).

Once the S_1 discrimination is established, the foreperiod duration can be gradually increased to differentiate bar holding. The contingency for anticipatory responses which will be used in the experiment can be instituted at this stage, but if a time-out is used, it should be brief. The increase in foreperiod duration must usually be done fairly slowly so that the animal does not extinguish completely. Hold differentiation training is probably the most difficult stage of initial conditioning, and requires careful monitoring of the progress of training. In the event that the animal begins to miss many reinforcements, it is necessary to reduce the foreperiod to avoid complete extinction. Several sessions may be required to get the animal to hold the bar for the maximum foreperiod duration, but having completed this stage, the animal is essentially completely trained.

When behavior has stabilized in terms of low numbers of intertrial and anticipatory responses, the limited hold procedure can be started. By gradually decreasing the limited hold, as discussed above, significant reductions in the variability of the latency distribution can be achieved. Catch trials, if they are to be used, can also be introduced at this stage of training. As soon as a satisfactory level of variability is attained, and intertrial and anticipatory responses are at a low level, the limited hold can be set at its final value, and variation in the intensity of the S_2 can be introduced. In our experience, the relative times at which the various contingencies are introduced are not too critical. We have tried many variations of the above training procedure, and all have been reasonably successful. The above procedure, however, seems logically to be the most simple and straightforward.

STABILITY CRITERIA.   A word should be included about what can be considered an acceptable proportion of intertrial responses, anticipatory responses, etc. We have found considerable differences in these measures between rats and monkeys, and even between individual members of the same species. Monkeys usually emit no more than 1 percent intertrial responses and 3 percent anticipatory responses after they are well trained. With rats, there may be as many as 5 percent intertrial responses and 15 percent anticipatory responses in even the best subjects. Early in training, of course, these proportions will be higher.

If catch trials are used, a good rule of thumb is that the average "latency" measured should be greater than the maximum foreperiod minus the average foreperiod. This would indicate roughly that the animal was holding the bar for at least the longest foreperiod value. The more the catch trial "latency" exceeds the calculated value, the greater the control by the S_2.

A brief mention was made earlier about a version of this procedure in which the animal works to avoid an electric shock rather than to obtain a food reinforcer. This procedure, which has been developed in our laboratory by Swayzer Green for use with squirrel monkeys, is essentially a mirror image of the positive reinforcement procedure. If the animal successfully completes a trial, he will not be shocked. Any deviation from the specified behavior results in electric shock. Examples of times at which shock would be administered are for intertrial responses, for premature releases, for failure to respond in the presence of the S_1, and for latencies to the S_2 which are greater than the value of the limited hold.

The data from this procedure are in substantial agreement with those from the positive reinforcement procedure. This procedure has the advantage of being able to maintain behavior over the course of extremely long sessions, as might, for example, be necessary to follow the time course of some drug.

DATA AND ITS TREATMENT

It may be quite apparent by now that since a latency is obtained on every trial in a session, which may last for over 400 trials, a substantial amount of data is produced by this method. The latencies can be grouped according to the value of the S_2 stimulus for the purposes of analysis, and a measure of central tendency can be calculated. The measure traditionally used with latencies is the median, with the semi-interquartile range being used as the measure of variability. Medians are not as easy to calculate as means, but the skewed nature of latency distributions demands a measure which is not sensitive to extreme values.

When median latency is plotted as a function of the intensity of the S_2, functions such as those shown in Figure 3 and Figure 4 are obtained. The curves in Figure 3 were obtained from a study which determined the equal brightness function of the pigmented rat (Moody, 1969). The curves were fitted to the data points by eye. The curves in Figure 4 were obtained from a study (Stebbins, 1966) which determined the equal loudness function of the monkey. Those curves were produced by simply connecting the data points. The reason for fitting smooth curves to the rat data was to eliminate the ambiguity in the determination of equal latency points which results when the latency-intensity (L-I) functions are not monotonic. When nonmonotonicity occurs, several S_2 intensities result in the same latency value, and special rules have to be established to determine which S_2 intensity should be considered the correct one to enter into the equal latency function.

The small interquartile ranges evident in Figure 4 are another desirable feature of L-I data. The variability in the rat data (Fig. 3) is greater than the monkey data but it is not prohibitively large. The increase in variability with an increase in median latency is a typical feature of all latency data including human reaction time (e.g., Pollack, 1968). The implication of this change in variability on the derivation of equal latency functions will be discussed later.

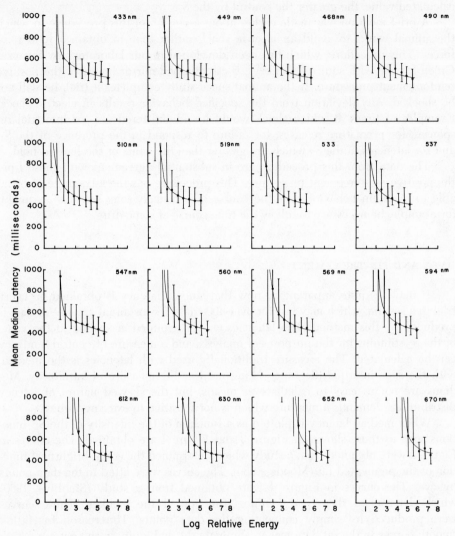

Fig. 3. Functions relating median latency of bar release to the relative intensity of a visual S_2 at various wavelengths. Data are average values from 7 rats. Smooth curves were fitted by eye.

One of the most important features of the L-I data in Figures 3 and 4 is the extremely large dynamic range of the functions. One would logically expect that as a stimulus approached threshold values, response latencies would increase, just as in a threshold experiment, subjects go from detecting a stimulus 100 percent of the time to not detecting it at all. But in monkey data reported by Stebbins (Chapter 3), for example, subjects go from almost complete failure to detect auditory stimuli to 100 percent detection in a range of about 15 dB. Stebbins' latency data (Fig. 4), however, varies over a range of as much as 70 dB, and furthermore,

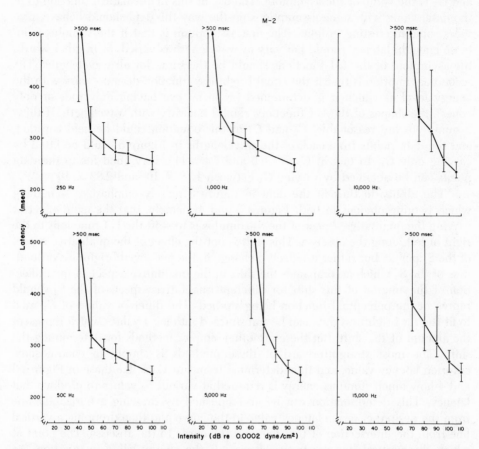

Fig. 4. Functions relating median latency of bar release to the intensity of an auditory S_2 at various frequencies. Data are from a single monkey. (From Stebbins, 1966. **J. Exp. Anal. Behav.,** 9:140. Copyright 1966 by the Society for the Experimental Analysis of Behavior, Inc.)

this variation is still occurring 100 dB above threshold. Clearly, more is involved in the latency measure than a simple threshold effect. This large dynamic range, occurring at such high stimulus intensities, is the feature of L-I data which makes it useful in determining suprathreshold stimulus equivalences.

The shape of both the visual and auditory L-I functions can be generally described as exponential decay functions. In attempts to actually determine mathematical equations to fit the visual functions of the rat, we have found a *power* function of the form:

$$L = C_1 I^{C_2} + C_3$$

(where L = latency and I = S_2 intensity) provides the best fit. In this equation, C_1 is a constant which determines the displacement of the function along the abscissa, C_2 is a negative constant which determines the shape of the functions, and C_3 is the value of the asymptote. The use of this mathematical function to fit the data, along with some assumptions on the way the data should behave, provides some interesting insights. The first assumption is that if the stimulus is intense enough, latency should not vary as wavelength is varied; or in other words, the asymptote of the L-I functions should be the same for all wavelengths. The second assumption is that if the equal brightness function does *not* vary with the energy level at which it is determined (as in an eye having only rods or only cones), the shapes of the L-I functions should not vary with wavelength. If these assumptions are reasonable, C_2 and C_3 of this equation could be held constant, and the data points from each of the wavelengths in Figure 3 could be fitted by varying only C_1. In fact, if $C_2 = -0.6$ and $C_3 = 445$, very good fits to the data points can be obtained by varying C_1 between 1.78×10^3 and 2.82×10^5.

The ability to thus fit the data in Figure 3 merely emphasizes something which is quite obvious in both Figures 3 and 4; namely, that the main effect of varying the qualitative aspect of the S_2 stimulus is to shift the L-I functions to the right or left along the abscissa. This shift is not the effect of the qualitative aspect of the S_2 per se, but rather it reflects a change in the perceived brightness or loudness of the S_2 which accompanies the shift in the qualitative aspect. A quantification of the amount of this shift for different qualitative aspects of the S_2 should represent the perceptual function being studied. The different values of C_1 used to fit the rat brightness data can be transformed into log I values which represent the amount of the shift, but there are other simpler methods for determining the shift. The most straightforward of these methods is simply to choose some criterion latency value, and then determine from functions like those in Figures 3 and 4 how much stimulus energy is required at various S_2 values to produce that latency. This determination can be accomplished by drawing a horizontal line from the desired criterion latency value to the curve and then dropping a vertical line from the intersection of that line and the curve to the abscissa. The point at which this vertical line meets the abscissa is the energy value in question. An obvious restriction must be placed on the criterion latency value chosen: it must be within the range of latencies at which all of the functions are defined. If it is too low, it will be below the asymptote of the L-I functions, and if it is too high, it may be higher than the latencies produced at even the lowest stimulus intensities. If a limited hold contingency is used which results in a stimulus change, the criterion latency also cannot be greater than the limited hold value.

Equal loudness functions for the monkey determined by this graphical method from the data in Figure 4 are shown in Figure 5 (Stebbins, 1966), and equal brightness functions for the rat derived from the data of Figure 3 are shown in Figure 6. Since low S_2 energies produce long latencies, the contours are arranged from bottom to top in order of decreasing latency criterion values. Note that the equal latency (equal brightness) functions for the rat in Figure 6 are roughly parallel to one another (aside from certain discrepant points) while the loudness contours in Figure 5 flatten out at higher intensity levels. This difference brings to mind one of the assumptions which was made in mathematically fitting the rat data; namely, that all the L-I functions could have the same shape. Clearly in the monkey data they could not, since forcing the same shape in L-I functions

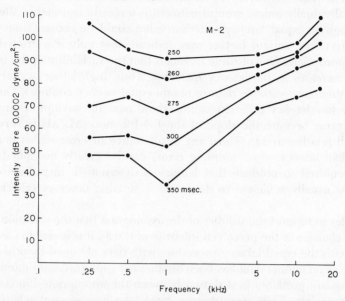

Fig. 5. Equal loudness functions for the monkey determined graphically from the data in Figure 4. The criterion latency is indicated above each contour. (From Stebbins, 1966. **J. Exp. Anal. Behav.**, 9:140. Copyright 1966 by the Society for the Experimental Analysis of Behavior, Inc.)

would mask the intensity effect evident in the flattening of the contours. Since the rat brightness contours are roughly parallel, this assumption was reasonable in

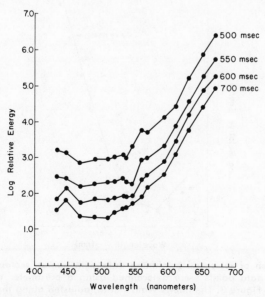

Fig. 6. Equal brightness functions for the rat determined graphically from the data in Figure 3. The criterion latency is indicated to the right of each contour.

that case. The point, however, is that the best course to follow is to treat each L-I function individually unless group treatment is a clearly reasonable alternative.

Although an equal latency criterion value could be chosen from any point on the L-I curves, certain factors may indicate that only a restricted range of values is appropriate. One of these factors is that the variability of the latency distributions increases as the latency increases. Thus, high latency criterion values result in using more variable data to obtain equal latency contours. On the other hand, very low latency criterion values—those near the asymptote—may also be subject to error because the slope of the L-I function ($\Delta L/\Delta I$) is very low (i.e., ΔL is small relative to ΔI). Thus, any small source of error which enters into a given median latency (e.g., sampling error) can be greatly magnified when the intensity required to produce that latency is determined. Inspection of the L-I functions is usually sufficient to determine a suitable range of criterion latency values.

In order to support the validity of the assumption that the variation in latency represents changes in the perceived intensity of the S_2, it is useful to compare data obtained with the equal latency procedure with data obtained by other methods. Since little or no animal data has been obtained at suprathreshold intensity levels, comparisons are probably best drawn between the appropriate human data and equal latency data. These comparisons must take into account whatever differences are known to exist between the human sensory system and that of the particular animal being studied. Since, for example, the rat eye is composed almost entirely of rod receptors, the appropriate comparison is probably between human scotopic luminosity data and the rat equal brightness contours. This

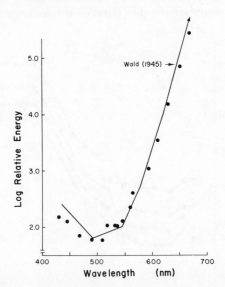

Fig. 7. A comparison of rat equal brightness data with human scotopic luminosity data (Wald, 1945). The data points were determined using a parameter of power functions fitted to the data in Figure 3. The line is Wald's data, adjusted along the ordinate to allow comparison.

comparison is shown in Figure 7 where Wald's (1945) luminosity data are shown as the line superimposed on equal latency data points which were determined by the mathematical fitting procedure mentioned earlier. Since the functions can be superimposed, it seems quite reasonable to suppose that the equal latency measure represents the spectral sensitivity of the subject. This supposition is further supported by comparison of the present data with luminosity data from the white rat's electroretinogram (Graham and Riggs, 1935), and with behaviorally determined threshold luminosity data from the pigmented rat (Muntz, 1967).

In comparing monkey equal loudness data with the human data (Fletcher and Munson, 1933) shown superimposed on monkey data in Figure 8, it should be remembered that the monkey threshold function extends up to at least 45 kHz and has a slightly different shape between 1 and 15 kHz (see Stebbins, Chapter 3). The tendency of both the human and monkey data to flatten out at high stimulus intensities is evident, but the monkey equal loudness functions are all shifted to the right, presumably because of the increased sensitivity of the monkey to high frequencies. The human data do not make it seem unreasonable, however, to believe that equal latency contours reflect equal loudness.

A word might be said about relations between equal latency data and "threshold" data, and about using the equal latency method to determine thresholds. Since threshold stimulus values lie on the same continuum as the stimuli dealt with by the equal latency method, it seems reasonable that some latency criterion could yield functions equivalent to threshold functions. Thresholds are

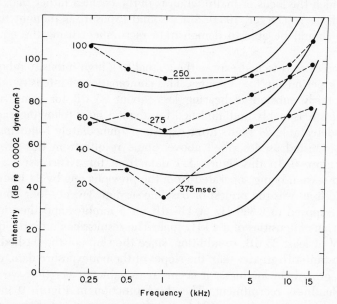

Fig. 8. A comparison of monkey (Stebbins, 1966) and human (Fletcher and Munson, 1933, redrawn from Weaver, 1949) equal loudness contours. The numbers to the left of the human contours (solid lines) represent the loudness level in phons. The numbers near the monkey data (dashed lines) represent the latency criterion at which the contour was determined.

usually defined as the 50 percent occurrence of the "I see it" response; equal latency points are the 50 percent occurrence (because of the use of *median* latency) of latencies equal to or less than the criterion latency. Varying the criterion latency may be thought of as roughly equivalent to a threshold subject varying the criterion of when he will say "yes." A high enough criterion latency should approximate this "yes" criterion. If catch trials are included as part of the procedure, the median "latency" measured on them will give some indication of what criterion latency might be used to define threshold. The threshold latency criterion should probably be less than the median catch trial "latency" in order to make the thresholds comparable to thresholds obtained by other methods. Equal latency contours obtained using this criterion should then be equivalent to threshold functions. The problem, however, is that catch trial latencies may run as high as 4 seconds, and in this range, latency data are so variable as to be difficult to interpret.

We are currently beginning to use the equal latency procedure to study changes in the loudness function of the monkey produced by exposure to high intensity pure tone stimuli. Clinically, measurement of the perception of loudness, or more specifically of the phenomenon called loudness recruitment, has proven to be a valuable diagnostic tool in assessing and localizing hearing disorders. Loudness recruitment may be defined as a greater change in the increment of loudness in relation to the increment in the stimulus observed in certain diseased ears as compared to normal ears (Fowler, 1963). Recruitment is observed mainly in ears in which the locus of malfunction is in the cochlea rather than the middle ear or eighth nerve (Jerger, 1962). Since sound exposure is thought to affect the cochlea, we should be able to demonstrate recruitment using the equal latency technique.

Our procedure is to first expose the animal to a high intensity (about 110 dB) pure tone for periods up to 5 minutes. This combination of intensity and duration produces a fairly substantial hearing loss (about 35 dB for some frequencies) which remains reasonably undiminished for about 1 hour following exposure, but which is undetectable 24 hours after exposure. Immediately following exposure, the animal is tested as described above. Some results from this procedure are shown in Figure 9. In this figure, L-I data from three successive sessions are shown, each session being separated from the previous one by 24 hours. The first session (solid line) was the pretest or baseline session. Twenty-four hours later the animal was exposed to 2,800 Hz at 113 dB for 5 minutes and then immediately tested at various intensities of a 4 kHz tone. The result, shown by the dashed line, was a loss of at least 35 dB. In addition, since the slope of the dashed line above 40 dB is substantially greater than the slopes of the nonexposure data, indicating a more rapid growth in loudness, it seems reasonable to say that we are indeed measuring loudness recruitment. The third function in Figure 9 indicates the data obtained from a session run 24 hours after exposure and shows complete recovery of normal hearing.

One of the parameters of the sound exposure situation which we have investigated is the frequency difference between the exposure and test tones. Some sample results for a test tone of 4 kHz are shown in Figure 10. The shaded area

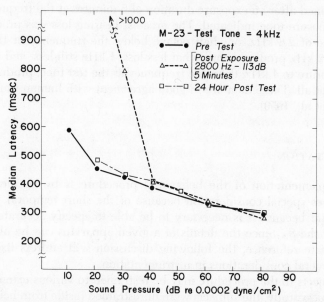

Fig. 9. Auditory latency intensity functions to a 4 kHz test tone illustrating the effect of 5 minute exposure to 2800 Hz.

in the figure indicates the range of median latencies measured on days when there was no sound exposure given. This includes data from sessions run 24 hours

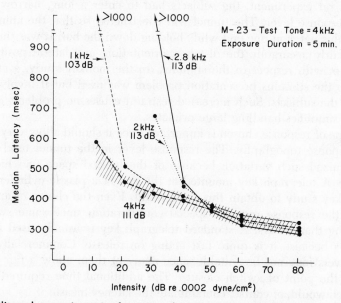

Fig. 10. Auditory latency intensity functions obtained following 5 minute exposure to pure tones of the frequencies and intensities indicated. The hatched area represents the range of normal data.

before and 24 hours after exposure sessions. Each of the functions shown in the figure was obtained after an exposure duration of 5 minutes at the frequency and intensity of exposure tone indicated. The greatest hearing loss was produced by an exposure tone of 2.8 kHz, one-half octave below the frequency of the test tone. Exposure to 2 kHz produced somewhat less loss, 1 kHz still less, and interestingly enough, exposure to 4 kHz, the same frequency as the test tone, produced no measurable loss at all. These data are in good agreement with human sound exposure data (Davis et al., 1950).

INSTRUMENTATION

The implementation of the behavioral procedure is by no means difficult, but it requires special consideration because of the short temporal values being measured, and because it is necessary to be able to specify accurately the value and onset of the S_2. Since the details of a given apparatus can be obtained from the appropriate reference, the following discussion will address itself to points regarding general considerations in instrumentation.

The subjects in the procedure may be restrained to various extents. In the rat equal brightness study, the subjects were unrestrained (aside from being restricted to a standard operant conditioning chamber for rats). The monkeys in the equal loudness experiment were run in primate restraining chairs and their heads were further immobilized to permit earphones to be mounted over the external auditory meatus. The important consideration in deciding on the amount of restraint necessary is the degree of control which can be exercised over stimulus presentation. In the rat experiment, the subjects had to enter a long, narrow tunnel to reach the response lever. The tunnel was constructed so that the animal had to face a stimulus patch at one end while holding down the bar. It was thus possible to specify fairly accurately the distance, orientation, and lateral position of the subjects' eyes with respect to the stimulus. In the monkey study, a more direct approach to the stimulus presentation problem was used but it involved greater restraint of the subjects. Such increased restraint causes no problems in training, and greatly simplifies handling large primates.

The type of response chosen is important since it should allow very little variation in response topography. The response lever in the tunnel used in the rat study minimized such variation because of the limited space in which the rat could move. A telegraph key mounted at the end of a plastic cylinder was used in the monkey study to obtain this same result. Even the choice of an electrical switch for the response requires special consideration since some switches are slower acting than others. A standard telegraph key is usually used in reaction time studies because it is quite fast acting on release. Commercially available response levers may not be suitable since many of them allow a fair amount of travel past the point of switch closure. The additional time required to release such a switch would, of course, contaminate the latency measure.

Since latencies are measured from S_2 onset, it is necessary to be able to specify exactly when the S_2 turns on. Visual stimuli are usually controlled by electromagnetically operated shutters, which, depending on their construction, may have a delay of 40 msec or more from the time the magnet is energized until the S_2 actually appears. Similarly, most electronic tone switches have an inherent delay in this same range. Special circuitry can be devised to compensate for this delay, or the delay can simply be measured and subtracted from the latencies.

Related to the problem of specifying S_2 onset time is the problem of the rise time of the S_2. To avoid clicks at the onset of an auditory stimulus, for example, it is necessary to turn it on gradually: allowing it to go from zero amplitude to maximum over a period of at least 5 msec. Even longer rise times are often desirable, but at high intensities, the animal may initiate his response before the S_2 has reached the maximum intensity. Thus latency of response would be unrelated to the specified intensity of the S_2. In any event, it is necessary to specify exactly when during the rise time the latency measurement is begun. In the monkey loudness study, for example, the latency timer was turned on just at the beginning of the rise time. A similar situation exists with visual stimuli, but since instantaneous onset can be used, rise time need not be a problem.

The calibration of the energy content of the S_2 is extremely important, but such calibrations are so specialized that a given procedure might be totally inapplicable in a different situation. An example of the type of calibration procedure used in the monkey study can be found in Chapter 3 by Stebbins. In the rat experiment, the visual stimuli were calibrated in relative units by calculations based on known and measured characteristics of the light source and optical system. (See Riggs, 1965, for suggestions on visual calibration procedures.)

The choice of programming and recording equipment for use in this procedure can also have some effect on the data obtained. Since this choice is frequently made on the basis of what is available, several of the alternatives will be considered. The procedure has been implemented with both relay type logic and solid state logic, including the use of an on-line digital computer.

The use of relay equipment has many obvious disadvantages, and is not recommended. Electromagnetic switching is simply not fast enough to provide reliable control and recording. The operate time of relays can run as high as 20 msec, and this might be increased even further by the logic configuration involved. Where there is absolutely no alternative, the use of high speed relays (reed or mercury-wetted) in the critical timing circuits will minimize the problem.

The measurement of the latencies should be done in milliseconds, or at least in 1/100th seconds. This is probably done with least investment in equipment by using a high speed clutch-type timer (Standard Electric), but doing so requires having someone transcribe each latency, and still involves many inaccuracies. Electromagnetic printing counters have been used to automate the transcription task, but generally cannot be operated at high enough speeds. Electronic counters are available which are compatible with both relay and solid state equipment, and some of these can provide a permanent printed record of both latencies and stimulus conditions by connecting them to a digital recorder.

Solid state control is by far the simplest, most reliable method of implementing this procedure. Not only is it fast enough to eliminate the timing errors inherent in relay equipment, but binary counters to record latencies can also be constructed from the same modules used to perform control functions. Our own experience has been that the solid state modules are also much more reliable than relay components. Digital recorders are compatible with the logic levels usually used by these components, and can be used to provide printed records.

An alternative method of obtaining a permanent record of latencies is to produce some computer compatible copy, usually punched paper tape. A fair amount of additional logic may be required to produce punched tape, but it substantially reduces subsequent data analysis efforts.

The most satisfactory all-around method of implementing this procedure is with the use of an on-line computer for both control and data recording. Because of the versatility of these machines, and also because of recent advances in computer technology, this approach is rapidly becoming the most economical as well. By providing the computer with a 1 kHz real-time clock and minimal additional interfacing, it can easily be programmed to run the entire procedure with any contingencies desired. The nature of the timing operations done by computer software is such that temporal parameters can be specified and controlled to the nearest millisecond. Complex stimulus presentation devices such as programmable oscillators can also easily be controlled by a computer, where other control systems would be almost impossible to use. The paper tape input-output devices usually sold with these machines can simultaneously provide a permanent, trial-by-trial record of a session which is suitable for later detailed analysis by other programs. It is also possible to program the computer to run several different experiments simultaneously (time sharing), but this alternative may require certain sacrifices because of the extreme complexity of the programs involved. For example, a slower clock rate may be necessary, meaning that latencies in milliseconds cannot be measured by computer software nor can temporal values be exact to the millisecond. The use of external timing circuits is necessary to maintain these capabilities. In spite of these added complexities, the computer provides advantages of which no other instrumentation is capable. The use of the same machine for high-speed data reduction is probably the greatest of these advantages for the equal latency procedure. The actual computation of medians for all of the S_2 stimuli used in any session takes only a fraction of a second, not including input and output. The time involved in having an assistant do so would probably be at least an hour for every hour animals are being run.

SUMMARY

No procedure is completely without faults, so perhaps some review of the problems, limitations, and possible sources of error will simplify comparison of this procedure with others. Many of the problems are common to all psychophysical procedures, so an attempt will be made to indicate what effects certain of the problems may have on the data obtained from this particular procedure.

The first thing to consider is the soundness of the basic assumption that latency of a motor response is a reliable indicator of sensory effect, and that equal latencies indicate equal sensory effects. The primary justification for this assumption is that equal latency data are in substantial agreement with data obtained by other procedures. Furthermore, human data indicate that we are measuring what we say we are measuring. It might be argued that many things, other than sensory input, affect the latency measure. This is true, but the advantage of the present procedure is that all of these other variables (or at least as many as possible) can be held constant while only the S_2 stimulus is varied. Thus, the bias which might be introduced by inappropriate reinforcement contingencies is minimized because the contingencies are always the same no matter what the value of the S_2 stimulus. It is my contention, furthermore, that as long as identical contingencies are maintained, and appropriate control is exercised over response topography, receptor orientation, etc., it is not necessary to require minimum latencies. An equal response is an equal response, regardless of its absolute level, providing all responses are measured under identical conditions.

Differences in terminal performance might be produced by differences in initial training on this procedure. The danger is not so much one of overall differences in performance between subjects, but rather differences which are peculiar to one or more of the several different stimuli used as S_2s for a given subject. If, for example, initial training is carried out at only one particular S_2 value, subsequent testing at this stimulus might produce different results (e.g., shorter latencies) than at other stimuli even though the perceived intensity might actually be the same. This is the reason for suggesting earlier that during training the subject should be exposed to all values of the S_2.

A problem frequently encountered in psychophysical procedures with animals is that behavior "breaks up." The animal may simply stop working or may take excessive time to complete a session. During the course of extended testing, this "break up" may be indicated by a rise in the number of anticipatory responses (guessing). There are several possible methods for dealing with this class of problem. One is simply to move the animal back to an earlier stage of training to make the task easier. Another is to change the deprivation level: increase it if the animal is stopping, decrease it if the animal is guessing. Alternatively, the amount of reinforcement per correct response might be varied. The problem with these procedures is that they would all probably make it impossible to combine "pretreatment" latencies with "posttreatment" latencies because latency is affected by reinforcement parameters (Stebbins and Lanson, 1962; Stebbins, 1962). Even though some data might have to be discarded, these treatments should at least make it possible to obtain additional data.

There is always the problem of day-to-day reproducibility of the latency-intensity functions even though conditions are kept constant. This can be maximized by controlling as many extraneous factors as possible, but when these controls fail, about all that can be done is to establish stability criteria, and only use data which meet these criteria. An example of such a criterion might be that median latencies obtained on different days under identical conditions be within x milliseconds of each other to qualify for inclusion in the sample. The value of x will, of course, depend on the particular experiment. This criterion might also be extended to include limits on the amount of variability which would be allowed in a given day's latency distribution.

There is one rather severe limitation of the present method: it is restricted to animals who can be trained to make the holding response. It has proven to be extremely difficult, for example, to train a pigeon to hold a pecking key (Gollub, personal communication). It might be possible to condition some other kind of holding response, a foot pedal for example, but then other measures would have to be taken to insure receptor orientation.

Another limitation of the latency procedure concerns the fact that it does not result in a metric scale of perception. Equal latency contours specify only that, for example, a certain intensity of one frequency of a pure tone sounds as loud as some other intensity of a second pure tone. These data are equivalent to the phon scale (Fletcher and Munson, 1933) of loudness. What these scales do not tell us is what intensity is twice, or half, etc., as loud as a given reference tone. They do not, in other words, produce scales equivalent to the sone scale of loudness (Stevens, 1936). An attempt to construct such a scale based on latencies (Stebbins, 1966) was not entirely successful, but some encouraging work (Honig and Shaw, 1962; Boakes, 1969) on the bisection of sensory intervals does not make it seem impossible to construct such scales.

As yet, there are no data on the use of the method in modalities other than vision and audition (with the exception of central stimulation of the visual and auditory systems; see Chapter 14, by Miller). One problem with the study of other senses has been the control of stimuli. It is not yet possible, for example, to specify exactly when an odor "turns on," and it is therefore impossible to measure the latency to onset. The possibility of studying x-ray stimulation of the olfactory system, which is effectively instantaneous in onset, with the latency procedure remains to be explored (see Chapter 6, by Smith).

The procedure also has yet to be used on other than intensive dimensions. It should be possible, however, to determine equal discriminability contours on other dimensions through the use of a modified choice or discriminative reaction-time situation. The equal latency procedure in humans was, in fact, originally used for this purpose (see Cattell, 1947).

It is also suggested that this method may be of interest to pharmacologists wishing to separate the sensory effects of some drug from motor effects. Although we as yet have no data on pharmacologic effects, it is reasonable to assume that pure sensory effects would result in a shift of the L-I functions along the abscissa, while motor effects would produce either an increase in variability or a shift in the functions along the ordinate.

As has already been indicated, the most successful application of the equal latency procedure has been in the equation of stimuli which are well above absolute threshold. The ability to deal behaviorally with these stimuli has enabled neurophysiologists to study the functioning of sensory systems in awake, behaving animals. The adaptation of the procedure for this application will be discussed in Chapter 14 by Josef Miller.

REFERENCES

Boakes, R. A. 1969. The bisection of a brightness interval by pigeons. J. Exp. Anal. Behav., 12:201–209.

Cattell, J. M. 1947. The time of perception as a measure of differences in intensity. *In* James McKeen Cattell: Man of Science, 1860–1944, Lancaster, Pa., Science Press.

Chocholle, R. 1940. Variation des temps de réaction auditifs en fonction de l'intensité à diverses fréquences. Année Psychol., 41:65–124.

Davis, H., C. T. Morgan, J. E. Hawkins, R. Galambos, and F. W. Smith. 1950. Temporary deafness following exposure to loud tones and noise. Acta. Otolaryng. (Stockholm), Supp. 88.

Fletcher, H., and W. A. Munson. 1933. Loudness, its definition, measurement, and calculation. J. Acoust. Soc. Amer., 5:82–108.

Fowler, E. P. 1963. Loudness recruitment: definition and clarification. Arch. Otolaryng. (Chicago), 78:748–753.

Graham, C. H., and L. A. Riggs. 1935. The visibility curve of the white rat as determined by the electrical retinal response to lights of different wavelengths. J. Gen. Psychol., 12:279–295.

Hanes, R. M. 1949. The construction of subjective brightness scales from fractionation data: a validation. J. Exp. Psychol., 39:719–728.

Honig, W. K., and J. Shaw. 1962. The bisection of spectral intervals by pigeons: a first attempt. Paper read at meetings of the Eastern Psychological Association.

Jerger, J. 1962. Hearing tests in otologic diagnosis. Asha, 4:139–145.

Laties, V. G., B. Weiss, R. L. Clark, and M. D. Reynolds. 1965. Overt "mediating" behavior during temporally spaced responding. J. Exp. Anal. Behav., 8:107–116.

Miller, J. M., M. Glickstein, and W. C. Stebbins. 1966. Reduction of response latency in monkeys by a procedure of differential reinforcement. Psychon. Sci., 5:177–178.

Moody, D. B. 1969. Equal brightness functions for supra-threshold stimuli in the pigmented rat: a behavioral determination. Vis. Res., 9:1381–1389.

Muntz, W. R. A. 1967. A behavioral study of photopic and scotopic vision in the hooded rat. Vis. Res., 7:371–376.

Pollack, J. D. 1968. Reaction time to different wavelengths at various luminances. Percept. Psychophys., 3:17–24.

Riggs, L. A. 1965. Light as a stimulus for vision. *In* Graham, C. H., ed. Vision and Visual Perception, New York, John Wiley & Sons, Inc., pp. 1–38.

Saslow, C. A. 1968. Operant control of response latency in monkeys: evidence for a central explanation. J. Exp. Anal. Behav., 11:89–98.

Skinner, B. F. 1946. Differential reinforcement with respect to time. Amer. Psychol., 1:274–275 (Abstr.).

Snodgrass, J. G., R. D. Luce, and E. Galanter. 1967. Some experiments on simple and choice reaction time. J. Exp. Psychol., 75:1–17.

Stebbins, W. C. 1962. Response latency as a function of amount of reinforcement. J. Exp. Anal. Behav., 5:305–307.

———— 1966. Auditory reaction time and the derivation of equal loudness contours for the monkey. J. Exp. Anal. Behav., 9:135–142.

———— and R. N. Lanson. 1961. A technique for measuring the latency of a discriminative operant. J. Exp. Anal. Behav., 4:149–155.

—— and R. N. Lanson. 1962. Response latency as a function of reinforcement schedule. J. Exp. Anal. Behav., 5:299–304.

Steinman, A. R. 1944. Reaction time to change compared to other psychophysical methods. Arch. Psychol. N.Y., Monogr. #292.

Stevens, S. S. 1936. A scale for the measurement of a psychological magnitude: loudness. Psychol. Rev., 43:405–416.

—— and J. Volkmann. 1940. The relation of pitch to frequency: a revised scale. Amer. J. Psychol., 54:315–335.

Wald, G. 1945. Human vision and the spectrum. Science, 101:653–658.

Weaver, E. G. 1949. Theory of Hearing, New York, John Wiley & Sons, Inc., p. 307.

JOSEF M. MILLER [1]
In collaboration with
JOSEPH KIMM [1]
BEN CLOPTON [2]
EBERHARD FETZ [2]

14

SENSORY NEUROPHYSIOLOGY AND REACTION TIME PERFORMANCE IN NONHUMAN PRIMATES * †

INTRODUCTION

It was clear from the conference that information is rapidly accumulating on sensory behavior in animals. Psychophysical relationships between stimulus and response parameters recently derived from animal subjects have been shown to be as reliable and precise as those obtained from man. Moreover, through analysis of these stimulus-response functions we are acquiring a better understanding of the influence of various stimulus parameters on behavior. One of the basic themes of the conference concerned the extension of our understanding of sensory functions to include the role of afferent neural structures in behavior. Contemporary behavioral procedures yielding psychophysical functions in animals provide a vehicle for such an extension. Simply stated, this approach suggests that we begin to study afferent neural activity in behaviorally trained animals from which precise measures of psychophysical relationships may be concurrently obtained.

Classical sensory neurophysiology is based upon techniques and measures of neural function which may be extended and applied to behaving animals. When appropriately employed, these electrophysiologic measures are stable, based upon known principles of neural function, and backed by a baseline of observations necessary for the evaluation of such data. However, just as the precision and

[1] Departments of Otolaryngology, Physiology and Biophysics, and Regional Primate Research Center, University of Washington Medical School, Seattle, Washington.

[2] Departments of Physiology and Biophysics, and Regional Primate Research Center, University of Washington Medical School, Seattle, Washington.

* This work was supported in part by PHS grants NB 08181, FR 00166, and NB 05077 from the National Institutes of Health.

† We wish to acknowledge our appreciation to Dr. Dwight Sutton for reading this manuscript and for his helpful comments.

stability of behavioral measures are based upon restricted sets of procedures, these electrophysiologic measures are only appropriately employed with a restricted set of methods.

In the past, methods that have yielded precise and stable measures of electrophysiologic activity have been incompatible with behavioral experimentation. Factors involved in many electrophysiologic studies include anesthesia, paralysis, artificial respiration, pneumothorax, some reduction in cerebrospinal fluid volume, and exposure of neural structures. A behavioral analysis of sensory function under such conditions is impossible.

A dichotomy in the approach and methodology for analyzing "sensory functions" in behavioral and physiologic studies has evolved and endured as a consequence of the difference in immediate objectives of these disciplines. We suggest that an approach to the study of sensory function which embodies but one of these viewpoints is unnecessarily limited. Moreover, such a traditional attitude has resulted in an artificial division of the available knowledge of sensory functions into two categories: (1) knowledge of neuronal response properties, and (2) knowledge of behavioral function. This division can and should be eliminated. The student of psychophysical behavior often wishes to explain the "mechanism" underlying a particular behavioral response. Similarly, students of central neural function often feel compelled to speculate on the behavioral implications of their observations. These parallel but independent approaches do not presently permit unqualified translation between electrophysiology and behavior. A better understanding of sensory processes will be based upon elimination of this dichotomy.

EXPERIMENTAL APPROACHES TO THE PROBLEM OF COMBINING ELECTROPHYSIOLOGIC AND BEHAVIORAL DATA

Recent attempts to bridge this division have taken several forms. Three different approaches will be considered. The first approach is based upon attempts to compare electrophysiologic data from animal experiments directly with behavioral data obtained from man; the second has evolved from the simultaneous evaluation of electrophysiologic and behavioral activity in man; and the third consists of simultaneous studies of electrophysiologic and behavioral responsiveness in animals.

RELATION OF ANIMAL ELECTROPHYSIOLOGIC DATA TO HUMAN BEHAVIORAL DATA

The first approach, utilized in many cases by physiologists, attempts to relate animal neurophysiologic data to behavioral observations made on humans by other investigators. For example, comparisons have been made showing that neurophysiologic functions relating latency or frequency of firing of single afferent cells to stimulus intensity have parallels with behavioral functions relating latency of motor response or rate of response to stimulus intensity. Moreover, extension of this approach has led to comparisons between intensity of neural responses from animals and behavioral functions based upon verbal magnitude estimations in man.

It is difficult at this time to justify the comparison of very diverse measures of neuronal and behavioral responsiveness suggested by some investigators (e.g., the rate of cell firing in animals and verbal magnitude estimations in man; Mountcastle et al., 1966; Werner and Mountcastle, 1965). Even though some strikingly similar relations have been observed, the disparate procedures involved in the neural and behavioral observations greatly restrict the validity of these comparisons. Any conclusion based upon a similarity in neuronal and behavioral activity observed from two such different procedures and preparations must be based upon the assumption that the neuronal activity observed in the acute animal preparation is similar to activity existing unobserved in the behaving human. Evidence is available which indicates that neuronal activity is dependent upon the physiologic state of the preparation, as might be induced by a particular type and dose of anesthetic. Moreover, neural responsiveness will vary with levels of attentiveness and wakefulness. Such differences are represented in the extreme by acute animal studies of physiologic function and human behavioral studies such as those referenced above.

ELECTROPHYSIOLOGIC AND BEHAVIORAL DATA IN HUMANS

A second approach in psychophysiology is provided by attempts to record electrophysiologic data simultaneously with behavioral responses in humans. Aside from social and moral limitations on the physiologic techniques that can be employed and the mechanisms which can be explored with humans, the technical difficulties encountered in attempting to record minute potentials from the nervous system through overlying tissue imposes major restrictions on this approach. In one respect, these difficulties have been overcome through the use of computer-summing devices (Barlow and Brazier, 1954; Clark et al., 1961; Brazier et al., 1961). Thus, through repeated observations of episodes of neural activity immediately following a stimulus, digitizing the voltage changes and arithmetically summing them, time-locked changes in voltage add, whereas random changes in voltage tend to average out. Hence, presumably such devices allow us to greatly increase the signal-to-noise ratio of our final record.

There are, however, some major physiologic problems of interpretation introduced by the use of such instruments. It is currently difficult to independently specify properties of observed summed or averaged responses that are neurophysiologically significant. Thus, it is difficult to determine which properties of the summed response to evaluate and compare to our measure of behavioral performance. These difficulties result from observations that: (1) this procedure may introduce distortion into the physiologic record; (2) it is sometimes difficult

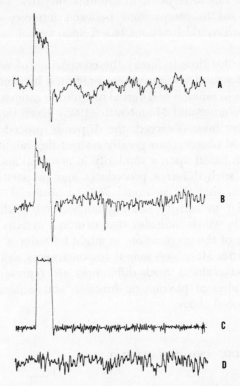

Fig. 1. Summed responses (500 trials) recorded across the third digit of the ipsilateral (A) and contralateral (B) hand to a 1-volt square pulse (C) applied unilaterally across the first digit. Amplitude of record C printout reduced by 10:1. (D) Control record from contralateral hand, with resistor across active lead.

or impossible to specify the origin of the averaged electrophysiologic response; and (3) there is little basis for evaluating long latency potentials usually observed from humans with this procedure.

The procedure of averaging physiologic potentials includes mechanisms for distorting or masking characteristics of the neural response. Given any variability in the response, the process of summing can produce an averaged response with amplitude, latency, or wave form different than any individual evoked response. As a consequence of such treatment, confusion arises in regard to the evaluation of characteristics of the response.

Furthermore, these devices are capable of summing very small time-locked potentials generated far from the recording electrodes. Figure 1 illustrates such a summed recording generated in response to repetitive 1-volt pulses applied across one finger. Responses were recorded from an adjacent finger of the ipsilateral hand (A) and from the contralateral hand (B). There is little amplitude difference between the summed responses. The major reduction in voltage probably occurs across the skin. This example illustrates some of the difficulties that may be encountered in specifying the origin of potentials recorded with such instruments.

Moreover, the analysis of the long latency neural responses commonly studied in human preparations introduces problems of interpretation. In many studies, analyses have been made showing evoked responses with initial latencies from 80 to 800 msec. From purely behavioral considerations, the immediate role such responses may play in overt performance is questionable. We know that behavioral responses reflecting parameters of the sensory stimulus may be elicited in less time than that necessary to evoke neural activity of such latencies. The physiologic basis for such long latency potentials is poorly understood. Again, it is difficult to provide an adequate independent justification for selecting a particular property or set of properties of the neural response as relevant to a behavioral response.

ELECTROPHYSIOLOGIC AND BEHAVIORAL DATA IN ANIMALS

Many of these difficulties of interpretation of neural activity may be overcome by using techniques for recording neural activity in unanesthetized animals with chronic indwelling electrodes and by studying short-latency evoked potentials with physiologic properties which are better understood. Combining chronic electrophysiologic techniques with behavioral conditioning procedures for deriving precise measures of sensory performance in animals provides a third, and perhaps most effective, alternative approach for the study of afferent neural processes involved in stimulus-dependent behavior.

BASIC PROBLEMS IN NEURONAL AND PSYCHOPHYSICAL ANALYSIS

It is evident that in the design of an experiment aimed at recording precise, concurrent measures of neurophysiologic and behavioral responsiveness we must consider factors which are specifically relevant to a combined behavioral and neurophysiologic investigation. We must also consider more traditional factors relevant to each area separately.

BEHAVIORAL ANALYSIS

Behavioral considerations were discussed throughout the conference. The procedures and principles of behavioral analysis described there and in this book are indeed applicable to chronic electrophysiologic-behavioral studies of sensory function. The unsophisticated application of behavioral techniques in electrophysiologic studies is of questionable value.

An obvious but often overlooked point is that the measures of performance selected must be clearly identified as a meaningful measure of sensory behavior. As a case in point, the isolated observation of responses following repeated onset of a light does not necessarily allow us to assume that the light was exerting a controlling influence on the performance. Behavioral analysis is necessary for the demonstration of specific stimulus control. Such an analysis may take one of a number of directions; the level of evaluation depends upon the precision of the measure of behavior we wish to obtain.

In general, we wish to demonstrate the modification of the behavioral response with variation in stimulus parameters. For example, we may evaluate the changes in the probability of a response following specific changes in stimulus conditions. Sufficient information of basic principles of behavior currently exists to allow the measurement of changes in behavior and the evaluation of the relevance of these changes—the specification of stimulus control.

In studies where a careful analysis of behavior and its relation to experimentally produced changes in stimulation has been ignored in favor of more casual observation, any contribution to an integrated electrophysiologic-behavioral analysis is not possible. Such informal observations of behavior have in the past appeared as an afterthought appended to a physiologic study. They may be of some value to the physiologic findings but their functional interpretation is as difficult for the psychologist as the long latency summed gross potential is for the physiologist.

PHYSIOLOGIC FACTORS

This illustration raises questions relevant to physiologic factors which must be considered in such studies. At this time, the most meaningful measures of neural activity are those obtained with single cell recording techniques. Since our understanding of current generation and volume conduction in the central nervous system is limited, interpretation of gross potentials in general is somewhat difficult. Of the gross potentials resulting from afferent stimulation, perhaps the best understood is the primary evoked potential. Extensive research has been performed on this potential regarding its origin and generation (Purpura, 1959; Towe, 1966; Biedenbach and Stevens, 1969a, 1969b; C. F. Stevens, 1969). In addition, extensive baseline information exists on the characteristics and properties of primary evoked responses in acute preparations (i.e., anesthetized and surgically prepared animals). Studies have dealt with changes in evoked responses accompanying changes in the physiologic state of the preparation, recording site, stimulus parameters, and so forth. Such basic information on the characteristics of physiologic measures is essential for the adequate interpretation of data obtained with these measures and their appropriate use in the study of sensory processes.

Concurrent analyses of physiologic and behavioral measures require careful consideration of the entire range of procedures employed. Techniques from each area can be powerful when properly used. To stress one at the expense of the other may produce confounding interactions. For example, spurious changes in electrophysiologic activity may well result from such unmonitored or unconsidered changes in a behavioral situation as a variation in the state of deprivation or satiation of a subject during an experimental session. Such interactions handicap our evaluation of the data as they relate to physiologic function, to behavioral function, or to combined functional processes.

Aside from the interactions stressed above, technical problems are introduced in electrophysiologic-behavioral investigations due to the physical interaction of the different procedures and technology employed. For example, electromechanical behavioral equipment produces transient voltage pulses which are often amplified and recorded along with the physiologic signals of interest. Wires leading to and from implanted electrodes limit movement of the subject. Another problem, which at times is more subtle and difficult to recognize and control, results from the fact that muscle potentials may be recorded over large distances. This is the case even when differential electrodes implanted deep in the brain are used. A behavioral response which requires minimal movement of the subject or which occurs at a time separated from the measures of neural activity is indicated in such cases.

THE REACTION TIME TASK

The behavioral situations and techniques discussed in this conference would seem eminently appropriate for a concomitant physiologic-behavioral study of sensory processes. However, many have been directed at the investigation of behavior related to threshold levels of stimulation. Physiologic information available to date and our current views of neuronal function suggest that stimuli near threshold or small changes in the values of stimuli produce minimal changes in neural activity. The recording and analysis of such small changes in an unanesthetized preparation is technically difficult if not currently impossible.

In Chapter 13 by Dr. Moody, "threshold studies" were distinguished from "suprathreshold studies." As an example of a "suprathreshold study," Dr. Moody described the reaction time (RT) task. This task, designed for the study of sensory behavior with respect to suprathreshold stimulation, seems appropriate for the study of electrophysiologic correlates of behavior. Moreover, a number of characteristics of this task make it particularly suitable for a behavioral-physiologic study.

Let us briefly consider this behavioral task; the training procedures are relatively easy. The performance elicited is stable and quantifiable. The task is relatively simple; hence, it may be hoped that the neural circuits involved in performance of this task are also simple. Furthermore, a variety of stimulus intensities may be studied. In fact, the intensity range of stimuli employed may cover the dynamic range of the system investigated. Many characteristics of RT performance, such as latency-intensity relations, have been shown to be comparable across the mammalian species up to and including man. Thus, both general properties of sensory function and specific relationships that we obtain in regard to sensory processes involved in performance of this task may apply to man. Finally, and of great importance, it may be noted that the measure of the animal's performance and neural activity are temporally quantifiable. This provides a meaningful basis for comparison and may eventually provide a basis for the establishment of causal relationships between neural activity and behavior (Evarts, 1966).

The RT paradigm has an extensive history of use in studies of neural processes related to sensory behavior. Early work related to RT and its neurophysiologic processes varied over a wide range bearing on questions extending from the velocity of conduction in peripheral sensory nerves (Helmholtz, 1853) through the analysis of biophysical properties of neural excitation (Woodrow, 1915).

Following the observations by Maskelyne, the Royal Astronomer at Greenwich, of differences between observers' estimates of the time of stellar transits, the suggestion was made by Nicholi (Herman, 1879) that these discrepancies might be due to differences in conduction velocity in the individuals' nervous systems. Helmholtz (1853) attempted to use the RT technique to measure conduction velocity in human sensory nerves, and he reported RTs to stimulation of "the great toe" to be about 20 msec longer than those to stimulation of the "ear or the face." Cattell and Dolley (1895), however, failed to confirm Helmholtz's observations. Cattell's results indicated that the RT situation was ineffective for measuring neural conduction time in man. Although he attempted to control all possible variables in the experimental situation, he repeatedly found large variations in the time of the reaction. Cattell suggested that the variability was due to the central connections involved as well as the qualitative differences in the sensations aroused at the different points of stimulation.

The differences in the data derived by these early investigators are not too surprising since many factors are now known to influence RT. It is well known that RT depends on stimulus intensity. Froeberg (1907) was one of the first to report this experimental relationship. More recent investigators (Bartlett and Mac-Leod, 1954; Stebbins and Miller, 1964) have confirmed these findings by Froeberg and extended these observations to animals: with attenuation of intensity of the stimulus to near threshold values, response latency and variability increase. This latency-intensity (L-I) relationship, and the psychophysical functions which may be derived from it, are discussed in detail in Chapter 13 by Dr. Moody.

Recent physiologic studies using the RT task have relied on the observation of averaged cortical evoked responses in humans. Dustman (1965) has reported that wave component latencies of the averaged evoked potential are positively correlated with RTs; shorter averaged evoked potential latencies tended to be related to shorter RTs. Haider et al. (1964) reported that as the subjects' vigilance (as indicated by detection of dim flashes) diminished, RTs increased and amplitude of visual evoked long latency potentials decreased. Morrell and Morrell (1966) reported that amplitudes of visual evoked responses were correlated with RTs; the more intense the photic stimulus, the larger the evoked potential and the shorter the RTs. As previously discussed, technical and theoretical difficulties related to the observation of long latency computer-averaged evoked potentials make interpretation of these results difficult. However, these findings do support the suggestion that the use of the RT task in animals, coupled with more direct electrophysiologic procedures for monitoring neural activity, may indeed provide a fruitful approach for the study of neural processes involved in sensory behavior.

REACTION TIME IN NONHUMAN PRIMATES

The research to be discussed is based upon the study of certain central neural processes involved in RT performance in nonhuman primates. Observations of visual and auditory neural function and behavior will be described below.

EXPERIMENTAL METHODS

Behavioral aspects of this preparation were detailed in the preceding chapter. For the study of visual processes, monkeys restrained in chairs were trained to press a telegraph key to the onset of a clearly audible 1-kHz tone, to hold down the key for a variable foreperiod, and to release the key to the onset of a neon light. Release of the key in the presence of the tone and light was followed by delivery of a 190 mg banana flavored pellet (Ciba). Both light and speaker were mounted on the upper plate of the restraining chair, approximately 10 cm in front of the monkey's eyes. The light was mounted behind a ground glass diffusion filter and viewed through a 1 cm hole in the stimulus display box. In the auditory situation, the animals' heads were further restrained and Permoflux earphones (PDR-600) were fitted directly over the external auditory meatus. The behavioral preparation is similar to that illustrated in Figure 2 of Chapter 3. The animals were trained to press a key following onset of the light and to release the key upon presentation of a pure tone delivered through the earspeakers. In the visual experiments, the intertrial interval was 30 seconds and the foreperiod varied from 0 to 5 seconds. In the later auditory experiments, the foreperiod range was changed to vary between 1 and 4 seconds and the intertrial interval was reduced to 10 seconds. In both cases, initiation of a trial was dependent upon the absence of key presses for a period equal to the minimum intertrial interval. All subjects were trained with a contingency for differential reinforcement of brief latency responses (Miller et al., 1966).

A diagrammatic representation of the arrangement of the behavioral and electrophysiologic equipment is shown in Figure 2. In the visual experiments, relay and solid-state (BRS) logic units were used to program automatically the conditioning procedures and to record behavioral performance. For the auditory studies, solid state circuitry and a Digital Equipment Corporation (PDP-8) computer were used to program the conditioning procedures and to measure behavior. This means of control permitted automatic variation of the parameters of the tone stimulus during each experimental session. The latency of key release following tone onset was punched on paper tape by the computer for off-line analysis.

Details of the stimulus generation and calibration procedures are given elsewhere. (For visual experiments, see Miller, 1965; Miller and Glickstein, 1967; for the auditory experiments, see Stebbins et al., 1966, and Chapter 3.) Visual stimuli

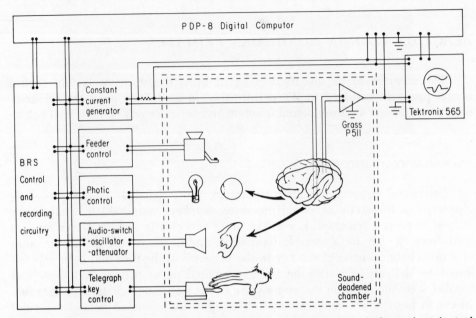

Fig. 2. Diagrammatic representation of arrangement of behavioral and electrophysiological apparatus.

were varied in log units from a maximum intensity of 8 ft-c. The tone was electrically switched with a rise and fall time of 5 msec. Intensities of all tones were measured with a calibrated probe tube and a condenser microphone. Tone intensities are given in dB re 0.0002 dynes/cm^2.

After preliminary training, platinum-iridium bipolar electrodes were implanted in the CNS of monkeys under aseptic conditions. In the visual experiment, electrodes were implanted stereotaxically in the lateral geniculate nucleus (LGN) and, under direct visualization of the fissural pattern, in the macular area of the visual cortex (Talbot and Marshall, 1941; Daniel and Whitteridge, 1961). Monkeys in the auditory experiment received electrodes directed at the auditory cortex (Ades and Felder, 1945). In addition, control electrodes were implanted in cortical sites outside primary sensory areas.

Figure 3 shows the electrode assembly placed in visual cortex of one monkey. The electrodes projected 1.5 to 2.0 cm into visual cortex. The exposed tips (1 mm^2) were separated by approximately 2 mm. Other cortical implants, including those for association cortex and auditory cortex, were similar to those pictured in Figure 3. Electrodes for auditory cortex projected 4 to 5.5 mm from the stabilization plate of the assembly. These electrodes were introduced into the primary auditory area from the lateral surface of the superior temporal gyrus. As many as nine electrodes were included in one auditory cortex assembly. Paired bipolar electrodes, with exposed tips separated by 1.5 mm in the dorsal-ventral plane, were used for thalamic placements.

These electrodes were used to deliver direct electrical stimulation to, and to

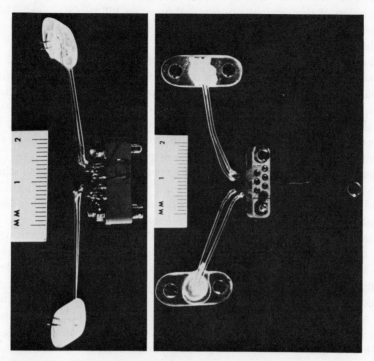

Fig. 3. Electrode assembly for bipolar, bilateral stimulation and recording in visual cortex. The assembly is a modified design of one described by Doty et al., (1956).

record from, structures along the classical auditory and visual pathways. Intracranial stimulation was provided by a constant current generator designed in our laboratory. The output was a 60-Hz sine wave, continuously variable from 1 to 1,000 μa (rms). The system provided isolation of 1×10^{12} ohms to ground and a minimum output impedance of 2×10^5 ohms. We have used this stimulation in monkeys being tested over a 2-year period and have found no obvious histologic changes in the tissue between the tips of the stimulating electrodes attributable to the use of this stimulation. (See Fig. 12a, Miller and Glickstein, 1967.) All neural potentials were recorded differentially with standard electrophysiologic equipment, including Grass P511 preamplifiers and a 565 Tektronix oscilloscope. Frequency response of the system was limited by low and high half-amplitude filters set at 3 Hz and 2 kHz.

EXPERIMENTAL RESULTS AND DISCUSSION

Given an experimental preparation in which the subjects were trained to stable performance in the RT task and implanted with nonpolarizable bipolar electrodes in the afferent systems, a number of experimental questions pertinent to the role of afferent system control of this behavior could be answered. Our first questions took two forms. One concerned the effects of introducing direct electrical stimulation of the afferent sensory pathways on RT performance. The second concerned the relationship between afferent neural and behavioral responsiveness to peripheral stimulation.

Following recovery from surgery, the subjects were reintroduced into the behavioral situation. Determination was then made of appropriate current intensities to pass between pairs of the implanted bipolar electrodes. For animals in the visual experiment, this determination was not difficult. The intensity of manually presented stimulus pulses was increased to a point at which the monkey began to exhibit visual orientation responses. With cortical stimulation these responses were consistently directed to within a few degrees of the "foveal gaze." The subjects were then tested in the standard RT experiment with peripheral stimulation. Concomitant with the onset of the key release stimulus, electrical stimulation was delivered to the central nervous system. Like the peripheral stimulus, the electrical stimulation remained on until the key release occurred.

Observations made on the first visual RT monkey with electrodes in the macular cortex are representative of our findings. Over a period of approximately 40 trials following introduction of the central stimulation, intensity of the peripheral stimulation was decreased. At first, RTs increased as the intensity of photic stimulation decreased. However, by the time the intensity of the visual stimulus was reduced by 4 log units (though still at least 2 log units above threshold), RTs no longer increased but instead came under the control of the central stimulation. In other monkeys, using initially higher intensities of central stimulation, transfer was accomplished in fewer trials. In our most recent monkey trained in the auditory experiment and tested with electrical stimulation of the auditory cortex, transfer from peripheral to central stimulus control was completed in fewer than 10 trials presented over a 2-minute period.

On the other hand, maximum intensity electrical stimulation of frontal and parietal association cortices (1,000 μa) was ineffective in eliciting a key release response, with over 500 trials, in monkeys trained in the visual RT experiments. In one visual RT animal, an electrode pair directed at the LGN was later found to have one pole near the capsule of fibers medial to and surrounding the LGN and one pole 3 mm medial in the thalamus (across part of the medial geniculate nucleus). Stimulation between these points was ineffective in eliciting an RT response.

Characteristics of the RT response to effective central stimulation were similar to those observed with peripheral stimulation. General behavior was similar in the RT situation with either peripheral or central stimuli in all but one monkey. This one subject, with electrodes in the LGN, demonstrated an increase in variability of response latency at high intensities of central stimulation. The subject's behavior became generally unstable and the monkey stopped performing in the RT task with high intensity central stimulation. On the basis of the anatomy of the base of the brain in the region of the LGN, it is likely that high intensities of stimulation resulted in current spread to pain receptors in the dura underlying the LGN, thus eliciting behavior incompatible with stable RT performance.

The similarity in the behavioral responsiveness to peripheral and central

stimulation and the rapidity of transfer to central stimulation of the afferent pathway may be interpreted to suggest that the primary afferent paths of the visual
and auditory system are indeed involved in this behavior, and further indicate
that there is at least some basic similarity between the effects of incoming neural
activity evoked by peripheral stimulation and that initiated by direct electrical
stimulation.

We next looked for measurable differences in the responses to peripheral.
versus cortical stimulation. Hopefully, with a relatively invariant behavioral measure such as response latency, small differences in performance may be demonstrated. It was necessary to equate behaviorally the intensities of the peripheral
and central stimulation if they were to be compared. Latency-intensity (L-I) functions to both classes of stimuli were examined in the visual and auditory RT task.
For peripheral and central stimulation in both systems at high intensities, the RT
function approximates a minimal latency asymptote and varies little over a wide
range of stimulus intensities. This finding justifies comparison of RTs to peripheral and electrical stimulation at high intensities.

Figures 4 and 5 illustrate the L-I functions obtained with peripheral and
cortical stimulation in the visual and auditory RT experiments. At high stimulation
intensities, a consistent reduction in response latency of 30 and 15 msec was observed with cortical stimulation in the visual and auditory experiments respec-

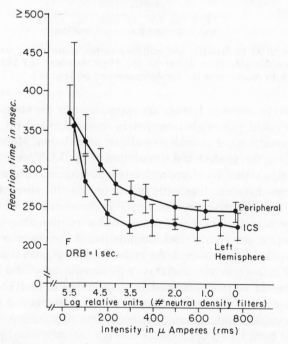

Fig. 4. Comparison of RT to photic and visual cortex stimulation. Medians and interquartile
ranges are plotted. Each point is based on at least 50 trials. (From Miller and Glickstein,
1967. **J. Neurophysiol.,** 30:399–414. Copyright 1967 by the American Physiological Society.)

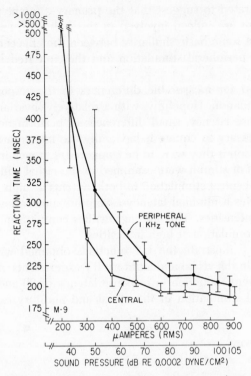

Fig. 5. Comparison of RT to acoustic and auditory cortex stimulation. Medians and interquartile ranges are plotted. (From Miller et al., 1969. **Science**, 163:592–594. Copyright 1969 by the American Association for the Advancement of Science.)

tively. These shifts in response latency are approximately the same as the latencies of the primary evoked potentials recorded in unanesthetized primates to photic stimulation and anesthetized animals to auditory stimulation. Moreover, in an animal in which RTs to direct electrical stimulation of the LGN were compared with photic stimulation, a reduction of approximately 20 msec was observed.

These findings are consistent with the view that the afferent sensory pathway is in series with the motor system in RT performance. Direct stimulation of LGN apparently acts to "short-cut" transmission of visually evoked impulses through retina, optic nerve, and tract. Stimulation of the macular cortex appears to result in a bypass of processes at the retina and eliminates transmission times to the cortex. Findings in the auditory experiments may also reflect general properties of afferent systems involved in determination of RT performance.

These latency shifts have been compared above to latencies of primary evoked potentials in the visual and auditory systems. This relationship would be more impressive had it been based upon direct observations of evoked potentials made in the same monkeys when performing the RT task. With this in mind, an attempt was made to record evoked potentials from the macular cortex through the electrodes used for stimulation in animals performing in the visual RT experiment.

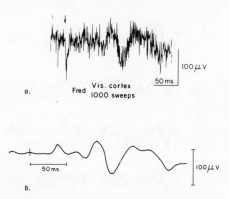

Fig. 6. Evoked potentials from visual cortex.
    a. Recording of neural activity summed by a computer of average transients during first 200 msec. after photic stimulation. Negative deflections upward. Sum of 1000 sweeps. Arrow indicates onset of visual stimulus. (From Miller and Glickstein, 1967. **J. Neurophysiol.,** 30:399–414. Copyright 1967 by the American Physiological Society.)
    b. Filtered, extended hand tracing of response in a.

Attempts to record evoked potentials from the visual system were somewhat less successful than originally hoped. With the use of a computer of average transients, a reproducible potential was obtained from one monkey (Fig. 6). The record is the sum of 1,000 trials. A major deflection occurred with a latency of approximately 80 msec. There was a small consistent potential (possibly equivalent to the primary) observed with a 30-msec latency. This finding, coupled with the findings of others (Hughes, 1964; Doty et al., 1964), suggests that visual evoked cortical potentials in the unanesthetized monkey may be demonstrable only with flash stimuli of very high intensities.

The indicated presence of an evoked potential with a latency of 30 msec supports our interpretation of the effect of cortical stimulation on RT performance. The use, however, of a summing device in recording this potential restricts the evaluation of this observation. Attempts to record evoked potentials from the stimulating electrodes in the auditory cortex were more successful. Figure 7 illustrates the potentials evoked by bursts of white noise and a 1-kHz tone at various intensities. Each record is composed of five superimposed traces. At high intensities of stimulation, the initial evoked response latency was approximately 15 msec. This correspondence between the latency of the evoked potential and the parallel changes in RTs with cortical and acoustic stimulation provides further corroborating evidence for the suggestion that the afferent pathways play a direct and perhaps controlling role in RT performance.

The question should be raised whether the application of cortical stimulation introduces unknown qualitative differences into the RT situation and whether such differences may affect a change in response latency independent of any spe-

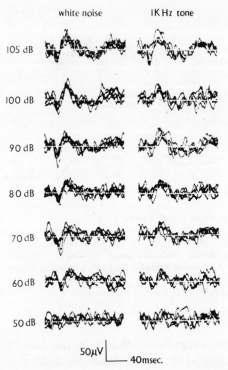

Fig. 7. Evoked potentials from auditory cortex to white noise and a 1 kHz tone at differing intensities. Each response represents the superposition of five traces.

cific sensory role of the afferent system in this task. Observations which oppose this interpretation are:

1. The ease of transfer of the behavioral response from peripheral to central stimulation of appropriate cortical sites.
2. The lack of transfer of the behavioral response to electrical stimulation of sites in association cortex.
3. The difference in magnitude of behavioral response latency changes with central stimulation in the auditory and visual systems.
4. The agreement of these RT differences with initial latency of the peripherally evoked cortical potentials.

   The form and time course of the evoked potentials (Fig. 7) are similar to those expected of acoustically evoked "primary" cortical potentials. The initial latency of this potential showed little if any consistent variation with changes in the intensity of the stimulation. If this potential is indeed the "primary" response, one questions this lack of change in initial latency. Such changes are a known property of cortical evoked primaries. A possible explanation for this finding follows from the observation that primary evoked responses show most rapid latency changes at or near threshold levels of stimulation; at higher intensity levels, latency changes may be minimal. It may be that the intensities employed in this

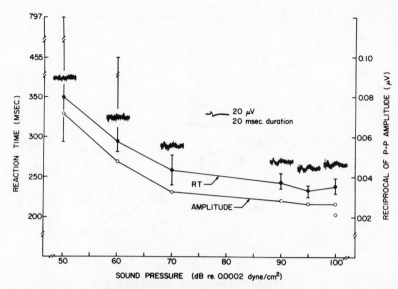

Fig. 8. Median RTs and reciprocals of the peak-to-peak amplitude of evoked potentials recorded simultaneously from one monkey. Each point is based upon 25 trials. An example set of five superimposed evoked responses is included for each stimulus intensity. Stimulus was a 1 kHz pure tone.

investigation are already at a level producing only minimal latency changes in the electrophysiologic response.

An additional property expected of the primary potential is that of change of amplitude with changes in stimulus intensity. Such changes are evident in Figure 7. Moreover, this variation in amplitude of the evoked potential may be examined in light of variations in behavioral response latencies observed with changes in stimulus intensity. Figure 8 illustrates the relation between reciprocals of the peak-to-peak amplitude of the evoked potential and RTs to a l-kHz tone in one monkey. Figure 9 illustrates a similar finding to a 250-Hz and an 8-kHz tone in another monkey.[1] In both Figures 8 and 9 it is evident that as intensity of auditory stimulation increases, peak-to-peak amplitude of the evoked cortical response increases and RT decreases.

A correlation between latency shifts of both the neural and behavioral responses was expected with changes in intensity of acoustic stimulation. The lack of such a relationship between latency of the neural response and stimulus intensity plus the observation of corresponding variation between neural response amplitude and behavioral response latency requires some consideration. First,

---

[1] During these experiments, electrophysiologic signals from the preamplifiers were also transferred to the analog-to-digital converter of the PDP-8 computer for on-line analysis. The computer was programmed first to sample (at 4 kHz) a 100-msec episode of cortical activity starting from the onset of the tone, and then to determine the latencies of the first positive-going peak and the first negative-going peak, and the peak-to-peak amplitude of the signal. This procedure was followed for each evoked potential. Statistics based upon these individual measurements were then calculated.

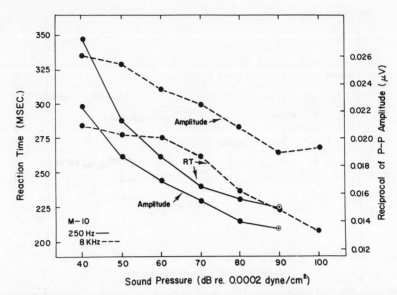

Fig. 9. Median RTs and reciprocals of the peak-to-peak amplitude of evoked potentials recorded simultaneously from one monkey. Measurements were taken to 250 Hz and 8 kHz pure tones at various sound pressure levels. (From Miller et al., 1969. **Science**, 163:592–594. Copyright 1969 by the American Association for the Advancement of Science.)

in regard to latency changes of the evoked potential, it has been suggested that the intensities employed in this investigation were at a sufficiently high level to produce only minimal changes in latency. As activity continues through the synaptic system involved in this behavior, latency dispersion would account for the latency changes observed in the RTs. Secondly, we know that the speed of conduction through a synaptic system is based upon, among other properties, synchrony of the neural activity (Towe and Kennedy, 1961). Thus, if amplitude of evoked potential reflects amount or synchrony of neural activity, one basic property of the synaptic system includes the mechanism for transforming such amplitude differences into latency differences. This property may reflect the basis for the observed close relationship between amplitude of evoked potential and the behavioral response latency, and may in part determine the role of sensory cortex in RT behavior.

FUTURE INVESTIGATION

ORGANIZATION OF AUDITORY CORTEX

Future investigation of the role of the afferent sensory path in behavior may take a number of directions. One question of some interest concerns the observed difference that exists between the slopes of the evoked potential amplitude-intensity functions in Figure 9. Such differences have been consistently observed

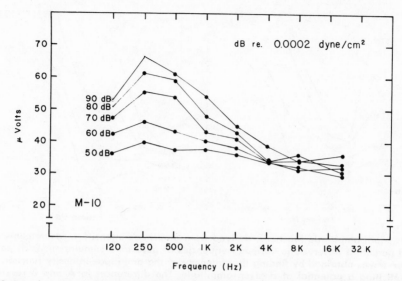

Fig. 10. Equal intensity function derived from amplitude-intensity measurements of evoked potentials observed to various frequencies of pure tone stimulation. Each point was obtained by finding that amplitude of the amplitude-intensity function elicited by a tone of a given intensity.

for all frequencies tested at all recording sites examined. They have been studied by comparing the amplitude of the responses evoked at the different frequencies with a fixed intensity of stimulation. From such an analysis, a family of curves has been obtained (Fig. 10). Each curve represents the amplitude function across frequency for a particular intensity of stimulation. These curves suggest that at this particular recording site, the cortical tissue was maximally responsive to a specific frequency of auditory stimulation.

This observation, illustrated in Figure 10, may be viewed from a different point. Rather than evaluating the response amplitude elicited by stimulation at a given intensity, we may determine the intensity of various pure tones necessary to produce a primary evoked response of a given amplitude. The results from such an analysis of the data are shown in Figure 11a. These curves suggest that at this recording site the tissue was maximally sensitive to a particular frequency of stimulation.

A similar analysis of evoked potentials recorded from adjacent tissue of the auditory cortex in the same animal has been made. The results of the analysis are illustrated in Figure 11b. In comparing this tissue with that represented in Figure 11a, one notes a clear similarity; however, this tissue appeared maximally sensitive to a lower frequency of stimulation.[2] The different curves illustrated in this figure were obtained at different recording sites. Each site appears to have a most effective frequency of stimulation. These observations appear to be in

---

[2] Our stimulating system did not permit examination of a response to a 30-Hz tone. Thus, from this data, it is not known whether the functions would have continued to decrease.

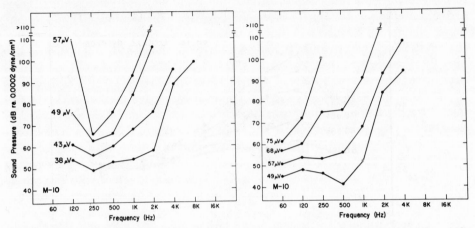

Fig. 11. Equal amplitude functions, derived from amplitude-intensity measurements of the evoked potentials observed to various frequencies of pure tone stimulation. Each point on each curve was obtained by finding that intensity of the amplitude-intensity function capable of eliciting a potential of a given amplitude. The differences in A and B result from different recording sites in the same monkey.

agreement with tonotopic maps of the primary auditory cortex in anesthetized monkeys (Kennedy, 1955), cats (Woolsey, 1961), and dogs (Tunturi, 1962).

On the basis of our current data this conclusion is not definite. Extensive study of this tissue and histologic determination of the specific loci of the electrode tips is certainly necessary. In addition, at most cortical sites examined to date, low frequencies (below 1 kHz) have been most effective in producing a primary evoked response. At one site in one monkey, a 2-kHz tone was found best. Note that all recordings discussed have been made differentially. This procedure was utilized to minimize artifacts from animal movements and from the acoustic stimulation system. This procedure imposes a restriction on the interpretation of such findings as a "most effective frequency" for different recording sites. One problem is the evaluation of the contribution of the tissue around each electrode tip to the evoked potential. With baseline information on the characteristics of this potential which, hopefully, will allow us to recognize and control artifacts, it is now possible to extend our observations to the properties of monopolar recorded potentials.

FREQUENCY DISCRIMINATION

This examination of monopolar recorded potentials is one of the current directions of work in our laboratories. This research, moreover, must include the analysis of this observation of a "most effective frequency" relative to behavioral performance. Human psychophysical studies have demonstrated that differential frequency discrimination thresholds are lowest at high intensities of stimulation. No direct findings from neurophysiologic investigations are available to explain this psychophysical relationship. In fact, the frequency-restricted responsiveness of single auditory cells which has formed a basis for speculation of neural mechanisms underlying frequency coding in the auditory system suggests, if anything, that individual cells should be most sensitive to changes in frequency at low intensity stimulation. (See, however, Hind et al., 1967.) A possible mechanism may be suggested on the basis of data illustrated in Figure 11. It is clear that as we examine the activity generated at either of these two cortical sites, the frequency range of tonal stimuli capable of eliciting high amplitude activity is less than the range capable of eliciting low amplitude activity. This observation is consistent with the suggestion that a particular point on the cortex may be more selectively responsive to particular frequencies of stimulation at high intensity levels than at low intensities of stimulation. This finding agrees with the behavioral observation in man on frequency discrimination at high intensities of stimulation.

This suggestion is, of course, quite speculative and falls into the class of neurophysiologic-behavioral analyses discussed earlier in this chapter; that is, the approach of comparing physiologic data from one experiment with behavioral data from another. The neurophysiologic observations alone are of some interest. The relationship of this data to behavior requires clarification through experiments comparing simultaneously recorded neural and behavioral measures.

An initial approach to this problem and the general question of the relationship of central auditory processes to frequency discrimination behavior is under way. Stebbins and Reynolds (1964) have demonstrated the effect of differential reinforcement on RT to photic stimuli. After initial training to two photic stimuli, the introduction of a differential reinforcement contingency resulted in an increase in response latency to the unreinforced stimulus, while RTs to the reinforced stimulus remained unchanged. It would be interesting to examine the effects of such a procedure on the primary evoked potential. The behavioral observations with acoustic stimuli have been examined and similar changes in response latency to those found with photic stimuli were observed. Initial observations of auditory cortical evoked responses suggest that a decrease in evoked potential amplitude may occur to the unreinforced stimulus.[3] If this is the case, it would be important to examine various cortical sites for changes in "most effective frequency" organization. Such an investigation may be followed by analysis of lower auditory centers in an attempt to determine the level at which such modifications of the neural activity occur.

EFFECTS OF CENTRAL STIMULATION

An additional question pertaining to sensory processes which may be investigated with these procedures includes the further study of neural and behavioral responses to electrical stimulation at other sites along the afferent pathway. In the

---

[3] This observation, although very preliminary, receives some indirect support from the finding of a greatly reduced amplitude of the evoked potentials in our RT animals when they were relieved of the telegraph key and hence, not overtly responding to the acoustic stimulus. Until appropriate controls are investigated, however, it is clear alternative explanations for these observations are possible.

auditory system where it is possible to measure short latency activity, it would also be very useful to examine behavioral responsiveness to brief pulses of direct electrical stimulation introduced at lower auditory centers. The use of such pulses would permit a direct comparison of the cortical evoked response elicited by peripheral and central stimulation, which is impossible with 60 Hz central stimulation, and the examination of the relationship of these potentials to behavioral response properties. Moreover, Luschei (1968) has demonstrated a reduction in RTs to peripheral stimulation in primates receiving concomitant direct electrical stimulation of the brain stem. Such facilitation of peripheral stimulation by central excitation may be examined along the afferent pathway. This will yield a better understanding of the processes underlying the relationship of acoustically and centrally evoked activity to RT performance.

ANALYSIS OF SINGLE CELL ACTIVITY

Arguments have been presented for the use of measures resulting from the RT task and the observation of primary evoked potentials in this chapter. However, the analysis of single unit activity from individual cells yields a more precise and better understood measure of neural function than that resulting from analysis of gross potentials. We believe that the use of this measure in conjunction with RT performance will provide a more substantial basis for the eventual formulation of causal relationships between neural and behavioral functioning.

The all-or-nothing response of a single cell recorded from the primary auditory cortex in an unanesthetized monkey is illustrated in Figure 12. The ease of quantification of temporal characteristics of the single unit responses is readily apparent. Figure 12 is the result of an initial attempt to examine such activity in the unanesthetized primate. In this preliminary study, no attempt was made to

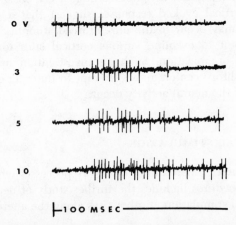

Fig. 12. Single cell activity recorded from auditory cortex of an unanesthetized monkey. Auditory stimuli were clicks of differing intensity. Voltage to speaker given at left of each trace. Vertical mark under bottom trace indicates presentation of stimulus.

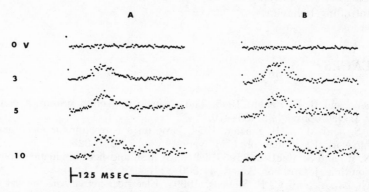

Fig. 13. Post-stimulus histograms of single cell activity from auditory cortex of unanesthetized monkey. Each histogram based upon 70 observed responses to single clicks of a given intensity. Click intensity, as voltage into speaker, is given at left of each trace. Histograms under A from observations made on cell shortly after it was isolated; those under B made four hours later.

control the behavior of the animal or to specify characteristics of the acoustic stimuli employed. The animal was seated in a primate chair placed inside a sound-deadened chamber. Clicks were delivered to the animal through a speaker mounted on the wall of the chamber. The only measure of characteristics of the clicks available is the amplitude of the voltage pulse delivered to the speaker. To date our findings are limited to observations that it is possible (1) to locate and isolate single cortical cells, (2) to evoke acoustic responses from them, and (3) to record from them long enough to study their behavior under a variety of conditions.

The observations illustrated in Figure 13 were taken from a cell that was isolated and studied for a period of 6 hours. This figure consists of poststimulus histograms generated on the basis of the response of this cell to 70 presentations of the click stimulus at four intensities. A 125-msec episode of activity was sampled following each click. Note that no time-locked change in activity was elicited when, as a control, the click intensity was set at zero volts. As the voltage increased, evoked activity increased. Concomitantly, a decrease in latency occurred with an increase in stimulus intensity. Changes in the evoked response of this unit with changes in intensity of stimulation correspond to those observed in classic electrophysiologic experiments. Stability of these observations is also illustrated in this figure. One series of measurements was taken shortly after the unit was isolated (A); the second measurement (B) was made approximately 4 hours later.

We believe that this extension of chronic neurophysiologic recording procedures and the incorporation of such techniques with concomitant measures of behavioral functioning provide a most fruitful direction for research on the role of central structures in behavioral performance. Moreover, the use of procedures and techniques that are firmly founded upon basic principles of physiology and psychology, coupled with measures of function that are precise, stable, and quantifiable, will provide an effective vehicle for the study of neural mechanisms controlling behavior.

REFERENCES

Ades, H. W., and R. E. Felder. 1945. The acoustic projection system: a comparative study. J. Neurophysiol., 8:463–470.

Barlow, J. S., and M. A. B. Brazier. 1954. Note on a correlator for electroencephalographic work. Electroenceph. Clin. Neurophysiol., 6:321–325.

Bartlett, N. R., and S. MacLeod. 1954. Effect of flash and field luminance upon human reaction time. J. Opt. Soc. Amer., 44:306–311.

Biedenbach, M. A., and C. F. Stevens. 1969a. Electrical activity in the cat olfactory cortex produced by synchronous orthodromic volleys. J. Neurophysiol., 32:193–203.

——— and C. F. Stevens. 1969b. Synaptic organization of cat olfactory cortex as revealed by intracellular recording. J. Neurophysiol., 32:204–214.

Brazier, M. A. B., K. F. Killam, and A. J. Hance. 1961. The reactivity of the nervous system in the light of the past history of the organism. In Rosenblith, W. A., ed. Sensory Communication, Cambridge, Mass., M.I.T. Press, pp. 699–716.

Cattell, J. M., and C. S. Dolley. 1895. On reaction times and the velocity of the nervous impulse. Mem. Nat. Acad. Sci., 7:391–415.

Clark, W. A., R. M. Brown, M. H. Goldstein, C. E. Molnar, D. F. O'Brien, and H. E. Zieman. 1961. The average response computer (ARC): a digital device for computing averages and amplitude and time histograms of electrophysiological responses. IRE Trans. Bio-Med. Electron., 8:46–51.

Daniel, P. M., and D. Whitteridge. 1961. The representation of the visual field on the cerebral cortex in monkeys. J. Physiol. (London), 159:203–221.

Doty, R. W., L. T. Rutledge, Jr., and R. M. Larson. 1956. Conditioned reflexes established to electrical stimulation of cat cerebral cortex. J. Neurophysiol., 19:401–415.

——— D. S. Kimura, and G. J. Morgenson. 1964. Photically and electrically elicited responses in the central visual system of the squirrel monkey. Exp. Neurol., 10:19–51.

Dustman, R. E. 1965. Phase of alpha brain waves, reaction time, and visually evoked potentials. Electroenceph. Clin. Neurophysiol., 18:433–440.

Evarts, E. V. 1966. Pyramidal tract activity associated with a conditioned hand movement in the monkey. J. Neurophysiol., 29:1011–1027.

Froeberg, S. 1907. The relation between the magnitude of stimulus and the time of reaction. Arch. Psychol., 1:1–38.

Haider, M., P. Spong, and D. B. Lindsley. 1964. Attention, vigilance, and cortical evoked potentials in humans. Science, 145:180–182.

Helmholtz, H. von. 1853. Über die Methoden. Kleinste Zeittheile zu Messen, und ihre Anwendung für physiologische Zwecke. Philos. Mag., pp. 313–325.

Herman, L. 1879. Handbuch der Physiologie. Leipzig, F. C. W. Vogel, vol. 2, p. 16.

Hind, J. E., D. J. Anderson, J. F. Brugge, and J. E. Rose. 1967. Coding of information pertaining to paired low-frequency tones in single auditory nerve fibers of the squirrel monkey. J. Neurophysiol., 30:794–816.

Hughes, J. R. 1964. Responses from the visual cortex of unanesthetized monkeys. Int. Rev. Neurobiol., 7:99–152.

Kennedy, T. T. 1955. An electrophysiological study of the auditory projection area of the cortex in monkey (Macaca mulatta). Doctoral Dissertation, University of Chicago. Ann Arbor, Mich., University Microfilms.

Luschei, E. 1968. Motor mechanisms and reaction time. Doctoral Dissertation, University of Washington. Ann Arbor, Mich., University Microfilms.

Miller, J. M. 1965. Neural circuits and reaction time performance in monkeys. Doctoral Dissertation, University of Washington. Ann Arbor, Mich., Ann Arbor Microfilms.

———— and M. G. Glickstein. 1967. Neural circuits involved in visuomotor reaction time in monkeys. J. Neurophysiol., 30:399–414.

———— M. G. Glickstein, and W. C. Stebbins. 1966. Reduction of response latency in monkeys by a procedure of differential reinforcement. Psychon. Sci., 5:177–178.

———— D. B. Moody, and W. C. Stebbins. 1969. Evoked potentials and auditory reaction time in monkeys. Science, 163:592–594.

Morrell, L. K., and F. Morrell. 1966. Evoked potentials and reaction times: a study of intra-individual variability. Electroenceph. Clin. Neurophysiol., 20:567–575.

Mountcastle, V. B., W. H. Talbot, and H. H. Kornhuber. 1966. The neural transformation of mechanical stimuli delivered to the monkey's hand. In deReuck, A.V.S., and Knight, J., eds. Touch, Heat and Pain, A Ciba Foundation Symposium, London, Churchill, pp. 325–351.

Purpura, D. P. 1959. Nature of electrocortical potentials and synaptic organizations in cerebal and cerebellar cortex. Int. Rev. Neurobiol., 1:47–163.

Stebbins, W. C., and J. M. Miller. 1964. Reaction time as a function of stimulus intensity for the monkey. J. Exp. Anal. Behav., 7:309–312.

———— and R. W. Reynolds. 1964. Note on changes in response latency following discrimination training in the monkey. J. Exp. Anal. Behav., 7:229–231.

———— S. Green, and F. L. Miller. 1966. Auditory sensitivity of the monkey. Science, 153:1646–1647.

Stevens, C. F. 1969. Structure of cat frontal olfactory cortex. J. Neurophysiol., 32:184–192.

Talbot, S. A., and W. H. Marshall. 1941. Physiological studies on neural mechanisms of visual localization and discrimination. Amer. J. Ophthamol., 24:1255–1264.

Towe, A. L. 1966. On the nature of the primary evoked response. Exp. Neurol., 15:113–139.

———— and T. T. Kennedy. 1961. Response of cortical neurons to variation of stimulus intensity and locus. Exp. Neurol., 3:570–587.

Tunturi, A. R. 1962. Frequency arrangement in anterior ectosylvian auditory cortex of dog. Amer. J. Physiol., 203:185–193.

Werner, G., and V. B. Mountcastle. 1965. Neural activity in mechanoreceptive cutaneous afferents: stimulus-response relation, Weber functions, and information transmission. J. Neurophysiol., 28:359–397.

Woodrow, H. 1915. Reactions to the cessation of stimuli and their nervous mechanism. Psychol. Rev., 22:423–452.

Woolsey, C. N. 1961. Organization of cortical auditory system. In Rosenblith, W. A., ed. Sensory Communication, Cambridge, Mass., M.I.T. Press, pp. 235–258.

ROBERT W. REYNOLDS [1]

15

THE USE OF REACTION TIME IN MONKEYS
FOR THE STUDY OF INFORMATION PROCESSING *

INTRODUCTION

Earlier chapters in this book by Drs. Miller and Moody have already provided an excellent historical background to studies of reaction time using animal subjects. Those discussions have admirably illustrated the advantages of this behavioral technique, particularly as it has been applied to an analysis of sensory processes. While my interest in the study of reaction time in monkeys also derives from my association with Dr. Stebbins during a postdoctoral year in the Department of Physiology and Biophysics at the University of Washington, I have been concerned with the use of reaction time in a more traditional sense, i.e., in the study of information processing.

Woodworth (1938) has discussed the early development of this type of investigation in human subjects. The basic paradigm was originally established by the Dutch physiologist Donders (1868). Donders categorized reaction times into three types as a function of the number of stimuli and responses involved. The simple reaction, called the a-reaction, involved only one stimulus and one response. The b-reaction involved two or more stimuli, each of which was paired with a unique response. The c-reaction involved two or more stimuli, but only one response, which was to be made only on presentation of one of the stimuli. Thus, the a-reaction required only the perception that a stimulus had been presented, without any discrimination of the exact nature of the stimulus, and the execution of a single, preselected response. The c-reaction differed in that while there was still only one overt response to be made, the nature of the stimulus had to be discriminated, and the response made only to the appropriate stimulus. This, therefore, would presumably involve the insertion of a finite period of time required for sensory discrimination. Donders proposed finally that the b-reaction would involve a finite period of time for motor selection, or the choice of the appropriate response, in addition to the simple and stimulus discrimination times. In agreement with this model, Donders found that the c-reaction was significantly

[1] DEPARTMENT OF PSYCHOLOGY, UNIVERSITY OF CALIFORNIA AT SANTA BARBARA, SANTA BARBARA, CALIFORNIA.

* This research was supported by Grant No. MH 11293 from the National Institute of Mental Health.

longer than the a-reaction, and the b-reaction longer than the c-reaction. By subtraction, the difference between the c-reaction and the a-reaction gave the sensory discrimination time, while the difference between the b-reaction and the c-reaction was considered to represent the time involved in motor selection or choice.

Wundt (see Woodworth, 1938) subsequently pointed out that the c-reaction was not really free of a motor choice component; for any particular stimulus, the subject had to choose between responding and not responding. Although not responding did not involve overt movement, it is actually an alternative response in this situation. It seems likely that a distinct electromyographic motor discharge should be observable as an implicit muscle response associated with not responding, although I do not know of any evidence to substantiate this directly.

Subsequent analyses of reaction time, particularly by Külpe's group (see Woodworth, 1938) at Würzburg, raised some doubts about the validity of the Donders-Wundt analytic dissection of reaction time components as representing different stages of central processing of information. However, the various recent models of choice reaction time (Smith, 1968) seem to involve, at least to some degree, the assumptions inherent in this early approach. The reason seems to be the acceptance as a basic datum that choice reaction time is longer than simple reaction time and, in addition, that there is some monotonic relationship between reaction time and the number of choices. However, Moray (1967) has recently observed that the differences in human choice or disjunctive reaction time between two, four, and eight choice situations disappear when the subjects are well trained. Although Smith (1968) makes note of this work, he discounts the rather disastrous effect such data would have on the elaborate formal reaction time models on the grounds that Moray's data are based on a relatively small number of subjects.

Over the past several years we have been developing a procedure for comparing simple and choice reaction times in very highly trained subjects. This procedure was derived from studies in which squirrel monkeys and macaques (speciosa, rhesus, and cynomolgus) were trained on a complex schedule which permitted concurrent observations of simple and disjunctive reaction time (Donders' a- and c-reactions).

BEHAVIORAL TRAINING PROCEDURES

The initial step was to train the animals to perform the experimental task: to press a lever only in the presence of a 1-inch diameter colored light and to release the lever upon presentation of a second stimulus, a ⅞-inch diameter white circle superimposed on the colored light. Monkeys were restrained in chairs and transported to an electrically shielded, sound-attenuated chamber for each experimental session. They were placed before an apparatus panel containing a multiple stimulus projector (Grason-Stadler E5704B) and a telegraph key. The experimental sessions constituted the only source of food (750 mg D & G monkey pellets) other than a supplement of fresh fruit twice a week and a weekly, 1 hour ad libitum access to Purina Monkey Chow in an exercise cage while their chairs were being cleaned. These supplemental feedings always occurred after the daily test trials. Except during the test situation, water was available ad lib.

In the first stage of training, depression of the key in the presence of a 1-inch diameter colored disk was followed immediately by the presentation of a ⅞-inch diameter white circle superimposed on the colored disk. Release of the key was followed by a food pellet and disappearance of the white circle. When responding reached a stable level, the colored light was turned off with the release of the key and the animal was then required to refrain from pressing the key until the colored light came on again. The time between the key release and the appearance of the colored light was gradually increased from 0 to 30 seconds. A key press in the absence of the colored light reset the interval and delayed the reappearance of the colored light. When the animal had learned to perform this task, the requirement for key press was changed. The key had to be held down in the presence of the colored light for a gradually increasing interval of time before the presentation of the white circle. Key release upon presentation of the white circle was followed by a food pellet. Key release before white circle presentation turned off the colored light and reinstated the 30-second waiting period. When the animal was consistently holding the key down for a 5-second delay before the onset of the white circle, the time interval was switched to an interval randomly varying from 0 to 7 seconds. The final correct sequence was then: colored light— key press in the absence of the colored light reset the interval and delayed the re-lent to a "ready" signal as used in reaction time experiments with human subjects. The period of time between key press and white circle served as the foreperiod. The reaction time was measured between circle onset and key release. When the response stabilized, a limited hold was instituted in order to depress the reaction time as far as possible. In this procedure, reaction times longer than a specified time were not reinforced (Miller et al., 1966).

This situation represents a simple (Donders' *a*-reaction) reaction time in that there is only one "triggering" stimulus—the white circle, and only one response— the key release. Such a situation requires only the detection of the triggering stimulus, and the response is always the same, i.e., a key release.

The animals were run on this schedule daily for anywhere from 6 months to 2 years for 100 reinforced trials per day. During this time, the RTs became highly stable at values considered to be representative of a true reaction time response. Training was then initiated on a choice or disjunctive reaction time problem (Donders' *c*-reaction). In order to provide a continuing basis of comparison with the simple RT, choice trials were randomly intermixed with simple RT trials such that approximately 50 reinforced simple trials, 50 reinforced choice trials, and 50 nonreinforced choice trials were presented each day.

The choice RT trials could be distinguished from the simple trials by the use of a different color for the "ready light." The significance of the color in designating either a simple of a choice trial was reversed for half of the monkeys in order to control for any brightness contrast effects between the colored ready light background and the superimposed white triggering stimulus. To facilitate presentation, I shall discuss the case where the simple ready light is green and the choice ready light is red. A key press in the presence of the green light is always followed by the white circle (Condition I) as described above. This sequence occurs randomly on one-third of the trials. On the other two-thirds of the trials, the ready light is red. A key press in the presence of the red light is followed half of the time by the appearance of the white circle (Condition II). As in the simple RT trials, rapid key release to the white circle is reinforced by a food pellet. On the other half of the choice trials, the key press is followed by a white square instead of the circle (Condition III). Initially, key release to the white square simply led to the 30-second intertrial time-out period. As has been reported by Stebbins and Reynolds (1964), this procedure leads to a clear discrimination, with the nonreinforced responses to the square of significantly greater latency than the reinforced responses to the circle. Figure 1 shows the very rapid development of this discimination in one of my squirrel monkeys; the median RT to the square had risen to above the upper limit of the timing system (750 msec) by the second day of testing. It should also be noted in Figure 1 that the Condition II (choice) RT was initially elevated above the simple Condition I RT, which remained essentially unchanged. This indicates that the monkey was also discriminating the Condition II from the Condition I situation, even though the triggering stimulus was the same in both cases. This discrimination, therefore, was presumably on the basis of the ready light color. Although the Condition III RTs stayed significantly high, after about a month of training the medians began to drift downward. This was to be expected, since although a key release was not directly reinforced in this condition, neither was there a reinforcement for a long response. In fact, holding the key down simply prolonged the time before the next trial. There was no reinforcement contingency built into this situation that would

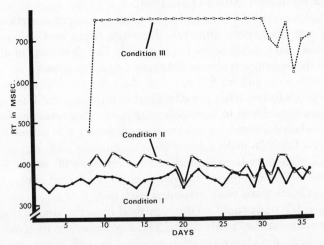

Fig. 1. Unadjusted median reaction times for squirrel monkey showing transition from simple reaction time schedule to concurrent choice and simple reaction time schedule. Condition I, simple RT; Condition II, reinforced choice RT; Condition III, non-reinforced choice RT.

necessarily prevent the choice *c*-reaction from eventually becoming a sort of simple *a*-reaction with partial reinforcement.

In order to prevent this from occurring, the program was altered such that a hold of greater than 750 msec for Condition III resulted in the immediate presentation of a new trial without a key release and without the 30-second time-out. The new trial could present any one of the three conditions. Initially, the monkeys were carefully shaped into holding the key down to the square by displaying the square for only 100 msec—too brief a time interval for a release to occur normally before the new ready light was presented. This time interval was then gradually increased up to the ultimate 750 msec. Quite by accident, however, we found that this careful shaping was unnecessary; my assistant once accidentally ran one of the monkeys on the concurrent simple and choice program with the full 750-msec hold requirement on Condition III. Up to that time, this monkey had only been given Condition I (simple RT) trials. Much to our delight and surprise, we found that the monkey began to hold after only six errors, and gave an essentially error-free performance from then on.

Monkeys trained on this procedure will perform essentially without errors, i.e., no anticipatory responses and no releases on Condition III trials, and have been run daily for periods of up to 2 years at 100 reinforced trials per day. Our present experimental setup includes programming hardware and subject stations for the simultaneous testing of five monkeys. RTs are punched out on paper tape in milliseconds along with a code identifying the animal and condition, and indicating whether the RT was longer than the limited hold for Conditions I and II or a correct hold for Condition III. The code also designates those Condition I and II trials that occur immediately after a Condition III trial. The data for each trial are contained in four characters on the tape. The first character contains the code. The animal number is contained in the first three channels. The fourth channel is punched on a Condition III and any Condition I or II that immediately follows a Condition III. The fifth channel indicates a hold. Channels six and seven designate the condition number. Channel eight is punched to discriminate data from spurious punches which occasionally occur, for example, when the equipment is turned on. The RT data for the trial are punched in BCD (binary coded decimal) on the following three characters. This is followed by a space. The tapes are analyzed on a computer (PDP-8) to give frequency distributions means, medians, standard deviations, and quartiles.

There are several possible sources of bias which must be taken into consideration. I have already mentioned the possible differential brightness of the white circle when viewed against a green background as against a red background. Although the psychophysical studies necessary to insure equal apparent brightness of the circle in the two conditions would not be difficult to do, as was indicated in other papers in the conference, they would be quite time consuming. We have attempted to minimize this possible source of error in two ways. First, the intensity of the colored lights has been reduced to 0.025 ft-c as measured by a Weston model 879 Low Level Illumination Meter at the face of the stimulus projector as compared to 1.60 ft-c for the white circle and white square. Second, we have controlled for this brightness effect between animals by reversing the significance of the colors for half of the animals.

A second possible source of error derives from the fact that the stimulus lights used are incandescent bulbs. While RT is measured from the time the pulse is applied to the bulb, full light intensity does not occur until approximately 120 msec later. The intensity curve (as measured by the resistance change of a Clairex 703L photocell in series with a 1-megohm resistor across 12VDC and placed on the face of the stimulus display unit) is an ogive which begins to rise 80 msec after application of the pulse and reaches maximum at approximately 120 msec. The use of neon bulbs, which have a very fast rise time, is unsatisfactory because of their relatively low intensity and the fact that introducing 115VAC into the experimental chamber could produce noise problems in future electrophysiologic recordings. In order to reduce the effect of the slow rise time, we have applied a constant voltage to the bulbs which is sufficient to keep them warm, but just below the point where they become visible to the dark-adapted eye. In addition, we have found that the rise curve is of constant shape provided that there is at least 5 seconds of dark time between successive illuminations. Since this is always the case with the white circle, the error introduced is constant, resulting in an equal positive error in the measurement of RT for Conditions I and II. The absolute magnitude of this error could only be determined by a psychophysical study of the point on the curve where the light first becomes visible to the animal. This would be rather complicated, since it is quite likely that this point would not only be a function of the absolute value of the intensity, but also the slope of the curve. An alternative procedure would involve the measurement of RT from the time of initiation of the evoked potential in visual cortex. To determine the total RT, the latency of transmission from retina to visual cortex could be added, although this also would be complicated by the dependence of this latency on the intensity of stimulation and also, presumably, the slope of the illumination curve.

We have considered alternative solutions to this problem, such as the use of glow modulator tubes or mechanical shuttering. The glow modulator tube would require a considerable amount of engineering to permit us to retain the advantage of using the in-line projector. With this projector, the ready light provides a constant fixation point so that there should be a relatively constant retinal projection of the circle or square stimuli. This, of course, will be of utmost importance when we begin to explore the evoked potentials and single cell responses to these stimuli. The use of mechanical shuttering was rejected because of the likelihood that it would introduce auditory cues.

Since our present interests are in comparisons of RTs under different conditions over which the shape of the light onset intensity curve remains constant, the determination of the absolute value of the RT is not essential. It should be remembered, however, that the values obtained are inflated by a constant error of 80 to 120 msec.

There are other possible sources of bias or variability that we have investigated, or are in the process of investigating. I have already reported (Reynolds, 1964) on the effect of changing from a variable to a fixed foreperiod in the simple RT procedure. Curiously, the median RT with a fixed foreperiod was significantly elevated over that obtained with a variable foreperiod. Since these observations were made on squirrel monkeys, we plan to extend them to the macaques we are currently running.

In the compound schedule, one-third of the Condition I and Condition II trials occurs on the average immediately after a Condition III trial, while the other two-thirds occur after a 30-second time-out. The question arises as to whether there is a carry-over of an effect such as "arousal" or change in relative dark adaptation from a Condition III trial to a trial immediately following which dissipates during a 30-second intertrial interval and which affects RT performance. The readout program was modified, therefore, to indicate those Condition I and II trials that occurred immediately following a Condition III trial. Preliminary analysis of the data, however, indicates that if such an effect does in fact exist, its magnitude is only on the order of 2 msec. In our consideration of this problem, another complicating factor was recognized. As I have indicated above, the foreperiod was programmed to vary randomly from 0 to 7 seconds. Normally, the monkey has an opportunity to observe the color of the foreperiod light during the time before he presses the key, and also during whatever foreperiod time occurs between key press and onset of the circle or square. However, on a trial following a Condition III trial during which the monkey has held the key down, it is possible that the circle or square could appear at the same time as the colored foreperiod light. This occurs because the monkey is already holding down the key when the colored foreperiod light comes on in this situation. There was, therefore, a range of foreperiod times possible on such trials when the monkey would not have time to discriminate the color of the foreperiod light. On such trials there would be no effective stimulus difference between Condition I and II trials. In order to eliminate this problem, the minimum foreperiod value has been increased from 0 to 1 second.

Finally, there appears to be a finite latency, which may be as much as 20 to 30 msec, that is a function of mechanical characteristics of the key, such as tension and contact travel. Fortunately, although this may introduce variability between animals over the five different experimental stations, it will not affect comparisons within any particular animal. We are trying to eliminate this variability, however, since it may be possible to relate individual differences in RT to individual physiologic characteristics.

BEHAVIORAL DATA

One of the reasons for my caution regarding the data obtained so far in these studies is that the determination and correction of the various sources of error have resulted in several modifications of our programming and recording equipment. Frequently, such changes required a period of "debugging" during which the monkeys unfortunately very quickly adapted their behavior to the "bugs" rather than ignoring them. This was helpful to us in the "debugging" process, but often required a period of retraining to get the monkeys back to the proper routines. Therefore the data we have obtained so far must be regarded as tentative until we can work up some naive monkeys through the completed system. Nevertheless, as I have indicated above, some of the data are quite provocative. A comparison of the median RTs for Conditions I and II for three of our most

TABLE 1

*Uncorrected data for one day session with rhesus monkey
on concurrent simple and choice RT schedule.*

CLASS MIDPOINT IN MSEC.	CONDITIONS		
	I	II	III°
+205.	0	1	0
+215.	0	0	0
+225.	0	0	0
+235.	0	0	0
+245.	0	1	0
+255.	5	7	0
+265.	11	10	0
+275.	21	19	0
+285.	6	11	0
+295.	5	4	0
+305.	0	2	0
+315.	0	0	0
+325.	2	0	0
+335.	0	0	0
+345.	0	0	0
+355.	0	0	0
+365.	0	0	0
+375.	0	0	0
+385.	0	0	0
> +395.	0	0	39
HOLDS =	0	0	39
N =	+ 50.00	+ 55.00	+39.00
M =	+275.58	+271.92	
SD =	+ 14.75	+ 18.74	
25P =	+266.81	+264.75	
50P =	+274.28	+274.47	
75P =	+280.83	+282.95	

° Note that monkey held successfully on all Condition III trials.

highly trained rhesus monkeys over a period of two and a half months of trouble-free testing shows that although the choice RT (Condition II) was appreciably longer than the simple RT (Condition I) when the monkeys began training on the compound schedule, the mean differences had dropped to 5.12, 4.23, and −0.27 msec after approximately 18 months of training. The standard errors of these differences, respectively, were 0.32, 0.54, and 0.90 msec. The overall median RTs for Condition I were 264.7, 254.1, and 312.4 msec, and for Condition II, 269.8, 259.7, and 312.1 msec. A frequency distribution of RTs for one day for the first animal is given in Table 1. These RTs must be corrected, of course, for the bulb rise times, as discussed above, so that the absolute median RTs presumably lie somewhere between 150 and 220 msec, which is quite respectable for visual RT with a variable foreperiod. Since these animals were run in different boxes, we do not know at this point whether the observed differences between animals are idiosyncratic to the monkey or the box.

These findings are consistent with results obtained on four squirrel monkeys, three speciosa, and four cynomolgus macaques, which had been trained on the compound schedule. These data must be regarded as only suggestive. The squirrel monkey data were obtained before I discovered the possible sources of error as described above. Indeed, it was because of the squirrel monkey data that my principal interest shifted from an investigation of the physiologic concomitants of RT to the psychophysical aspects. Although the speciosa monkeys were excellent subjects, their rather startling growth rate was such that they became too large for the restraining chairs before I could get sufficient data on them. The one on which I did obtain some data showed, over a period of 80 days, mean RTs of 361.0 msec for Condition I and 362.5 msec for Condition II with standard errors of the mean of 2.5 msec and 2.7 msec respectively. It should be noted that these data were taken before several of the modifications were made, and this may explain the fact that their latencies are considerably longer than for the rhesus. The cynomolgus were a little more difficult to train than the speciosa or the rhesus, although they eventually learned to perform the problem satisfactorily. Unfortunately, their behavior tended to be rather unstable, in that the slightest malfunction or alternation of the equipment or the program would produce a marked deterioration of their RT performance that would require weeks of retraining. Hopefully, such disruptive processes are now a thing of the past, since it would be worthwhile to be able to make comparisons across species. Although these data are only preliminary, in conjunction with Moray's (1967) data, they suggest that the elaborate formal models that have been developed for choice reaction time may have relevance only to the first stages of development of this behavior.

One of the most obvious advantages in using monkeys for these studies rather than humans lies in the fact that they may be tested daily over a period of years. The continuity, consistency, and amount of data obtainable from this kind of a subject would require from a human a devotion to science of heroic proportions. Of equal importance, however, is the fact that the use of animals permits exploration of the physiologic processes associated with the behavior. For example, assuming that our preliminary data are confirmed by replication, I strongly suspect that a different pathway or process is used in the execution of well-rehearsed choice behavior from that employed in the initial learning of the choices.

As I have pointed out in the introduction, most current theoretical formulations and models for choice reaction time are predicated on the proposition that choice reaction time is longer than simple reaction time (Smith, 1968). This implies some sort of sequential processing of information. While this may be accurate in the early stages of development of the choice behavior, the possibility that it is not true for the very highly trained response is quite significant not only for theories of reaction time, but also for any consideration of behavior in general. It would be important, therefore, to determine this on the behavioral level for its psychophysical importance. In addition, the use of this very stable behavioral paradigm in monkeys lends itself quite nicely to electrophysiologic exploration. It is possible that in the very well-trained animal, parallel pathways are established for all of the probable stimulus-response sequences as a function of the discriminative components of the stimulus configurations. Each of these pathways could be as direct as and of comparable latency to the simple RT pathway, and would be triggered directly by the specific stimulus component. This route would bypass the sequential processes involved in perceiving and discriminating the whole stimulus and then selecting the appropriate response, which presumably function in earlier phases of choice behavior. It may be that the early behavior is mediated by cortical pathways, while later responses are "short-circuited" through brain stem structures.

Most of our behavior involves selective responding to specific components of a complex environment. The analog of the highly structured, experimental, simple RT situation probably occurs quite infrequently in normal behavior. Much of the choice behavior, however, seems quite automatic in the adult, and requires a specific act of "choosing" only to the degree that novel stimuli with which the individual has not had prior experience are introduced into the situation. It would be important, therefore, to be able to trace the developing pathways as they progress from the initial to advanced stages of training. Although our present knowledge of the simple pathways is far from complete, exploration of transitional changes as described above may also facilitate our understanding the more simple processes.

The advantage of being able to talk with human subjects is probably negligible in this situation since the millisecond time scale sharpens the intrusive and other types of artifact associated with introspective report. On the other hand, the attendant possibilities for direct physiologic exploration of pathways and the tremendously greater amount of data, both physiologic and behavioral, that can be obtained suggest that the use of animal subjects is potentially a much more fruitful approach, at least to this aspect of information processing. As a rather painful bonus, we might add that unlike the relatively docile and pliable college sophomore (at least in his role as an experimental subject), the monkey seems to delight in outwitting the experimenter by discovering the flaws in his experimental design, his apparatus, his program, and finally in his character—for we also talk to these subjects, if only in the form of occasional bursts of profanity. Perhaps we are better men for that. Hopefully our science also benefits.

REFERENCES

Donders, F. E. 1868. Die Schnelligkeit psychicher Processe. Arch. Anat. Physiol., 657–681.

Miller, J. M., M. Glickstein, and W. C. Stebbins. 1966. Reduction of response latency in monkeys by a procedure of differential reinforcement. Psychon. Sci., 5:177–178.

Moray, N. 1967. Where is capacity limited? A survey and a model. In Sanders, A. F., ed. Attention and Performance, Amsterdam, North-Holland Publishing Co., pp. 84–92.

Reynolds, R. W. 1964. Reaction time as a function of fixed versus variable foreperiod in the squirrel monkey. Psychon. Sci., 1:31–32.

Smith, E. E. 1968. Choice reaction time: An analysis of the major theoretical positions. Psychol. Bull., 69:77–110.

Stebbins, W. C., and R. W. Reynolds. 1964. Note on changes in response latency following discrimination training in the monkey. J. Exp. Anal. Behav., 7:229–231.
Woodworth, R. S. 1938. Experimental Psychology, New York, Holt.

THOMAS R. SCOTT
W. LLOYD MILLIGAN [1]

16

THE PSYCHOPHYSICAL STUDY OF VISUAL MOTION AFTEREFFECT RATE IN MONKEYS

INTRODUCTION

Visual aftereffect of motion is the apparent motion of an objectively stationary stimulus pattern induced by prior viewing of a moving pattern. The aftereffect is probably always in a direction opposite to that of the eliciting motion. Aristotle was the first to describe the phenomenon (see Hutchins, 1952). His example was the apparent motion of stationary objects observed after steady fixation of a swiftly flowing stream. Purkinje (1825) described the aftereffect, which he observed after viewing a cavalry procession, and suggested that habitual eye movements learned during the eliciting period continued during the viewing of the stationary object. Helmholtz (1867) and Wundt (1874) were among those who supported this explanation of aftereffect. Plateau (1850) introduced the rotating spiral as an eliciting stimulus. The rotating spiral appears to move in toward the center or out away from it, depending upon the direction of rotation. The aftereffect is one of expansion in the former case and contraction in the latter. Plateau's observation defeated Purkinje's theory since the eyes cannot move in all directions at once. There is a voluminous 19th century literature, which includes attempts to illustrate analogous effects in other senses, e.g., Dvorak (1871). Mach (1875) was the first to propose a retinal locus for the physiologic processes involved in the aftereffect. Several ingenious retinal theories were subsequently devised to account for the aftereffect (e.g., Exner, 1876). A good review of the older literature is to be found in Wohlgemuth (1911) who suggested that the aftereffect might be a useful index to central nervous system function. A more recent summary is given in an excellent book by Holland (1965).

In 1955, Price and Deabler presented evidence that brain damage, albeit very loosely defined, could be detected on the basis of failure to report aftereffect. Following this, numerous experiments were performed which variously seemed to refute, verify, or clarify the relationship between aftereffect and the presence or

[1] PSYCHOLOGICAL RESEARCH LABORATORY, VETERANS ADMINISTRATION HOSPITAL, COLUMBIA, SOUTH CAROLINA.

absence of gross brain lesions (e.g., Gallese, 1956; Holland and Beech, 1958; Scott et al., 1963a).

Although the earlier investigators, as previously noted, favored a retinal locus for aftereffect processes, more recent evidence suggests that the neural structures which are active during the aftereffect phenomenon are located in more central parts of the visual system. Many attempts to localize these structures using binocular transfer were at first quite inconclusive (Day, 1958; Terwilliger, 1963; Scott, 1964). Using a technique of pressure-induced retinal anoxia first used in aftereffect research by Pickersgill (1964), and an experimental design first suggested by Terwilliger (1964), Scott and Wood (1966) concluded that in humans, at least, the aftereffect process has a central locus. Stager (1966) also reached the same conclusion. In a now famous, though recent series of studies, Hubel (1963) and Hubel and Weisel (1963) illustrated, by means of a unit response technique, cells in the visual cortex of the cat which respond with sustained firing only to motion across the retina in particular directions. These results are consistent with the central locus hypothesis. Barlow and Hill (1963) have found direction-sensitive cells in the rabbit retina, but nevertheless they favor a central locus in humans because of their own observations using pressure induced retinal anoxia. The existence of such cells suggests that the visual aftereffect of motion may be, in Hubel's words, "a higher order afterimage" (personal communication, 1965). In passing, it should be noted, however, that the aftereffect occurs independently of attention—a finding first reported by Wohlgemuth and confirmed repeatedly by others. Wohlgemuth suggested that the locus may therefore be in the lower visual centers, although this interpretation can hardly be considered conclusive because of uncertainty as to the nature of "attention" and its relevance to processes in the centers involved. The persistent evidence that damage to the cerebral cortex has various effects on the aftereffect rate suggests that the aftereffect process cannot be described simply in terms of selective fatigue of direction-sensitive cells, but probably involves a more diffuse type of neural integration such as that recently proposed by Pribram (1969) or Grossberg (1969).

This brief review of the history of experiments and theory reveals that the aftereffect phenomenon lies at the intersection of several fields of interest. Contributions have been made by purely behavioral means as well as by purely physiologic experiments, and it seems inevitable that mathematical theory will soon make an important contribution. Studies which combine physiologic and behavioral data would seem to be especially likely to uncover interesting and important information. Also, the general level of complexity of neural functioning represented by this phenomenon seems favorable when considered against the background of rapidly advancing knowledge of brain function and behavior. Somewhere between the neuron and the ego important discoveries are waiting, and although they are likely to be found closer to the neuron, some reaching upward toward more complex systems is surely needed.

The following sections will (1) provide a general description of problems of measuring motion aftereffect; (2) illustrate the adaptation of one of these measurement methods to the rhesus monkey; (3) present results from a series of studies in the monkey, including one animal in whom cortical ablations were performed;

and (4) discuss some problems peculiar to the measurement of aftereffect, including a principle of psychophysical indeterminacy and its implications.

METHODS OF MEASUREMENT

The first and most obvious method is simple report of presence or absence of perceived movement. This method might be more appropriately called the method of detection rather than measurement. Clearly, a quantitative measurement would be superior for experimental purposes. A second common method involves measuring the duration of the aftereffect. This procedure, although simple and therefore appealing, is subject to rather serious errors. Uncertainty during the latter part of the test period as to the exact time when the aftereffect stops makes this method very susceptible to S's expectations, whether these are based on initial experience, demand characteristics of the experiment, or the S's own theories regarding what "ought" to happen. This problem is dramatically demonstrated in an experiment by Scott et al. (1966). A third method, invented by Wohlgemuth (1911), requires the S to compare the apparent speed of the aftereffect with an objectively moving comparison stimulus seen later, at a time when there is presumed to be no aftereffect. This method, involving a long delay between test stimulus and comparison stimulus, is not suited for use with animals and is relatively time consuming even with humans. It is also subject to systematic errors of the same type encountered in duration measurement. Carlson (1962) developed a fourth method in which the S estimates the time which would be required for an objectively moving test stimulus to arrive at a point in the visual field outside the area affected by the eliciting stimulus. Again, the method does not lend itself to use with animals because of the complexity of the task.

The method used in our laboratory has been called "neutralization" by Taylor (1963a). Here, the test stimulus moves to counteract or neutralize the aftereffect. This method was invented by Cords and von Brucke (1907), but was rejected by Wohlgemuth because it involved the assumption of algebraic additivity of objective and subjective motions. This assumption has since been tested (Scott et al., 1963b), and appears to be valid.

Three principal adaptations of this method have been used. In each of these a rotating spiral is placed in one arm of a two-field mirror tachistoscope, and a cathode ray tube is mounted in the other arm. S views alternately the spiral, or eliciting stimulus, and a circular trace, or test stimulus, produced on the cathode ray tube. The circular trace, which always appears the same initial size, can maintain a constant size or can expand or contract in a linear fashion at any preselected rate. Alternatively, the size of the circle can be controlled by a potentiometer. E (or S) seeks a rate of change in size of the circle which exactly cancels or neutralizes an aftereffect of the opposite direction. The three adaptations of this method are as follows:

Continuous Tracking. The S's task is to make continuous adjustment of the potentiometer so that the circle appears to remain stationary during the test period. The final position of the potentiometer represents the amount of change in size during the interval, and since the interval is known, the average rate of change may be obtained directly. This method is similar to that used by Cann (1961) and Taylor (1963a, 1963b), but is unsuited to animals because of task difficulty. It is different from the tracking procedures described elsewhere in this book (e.g., Stebbins, Chapter 3) in that it involves continuous adjustment of the stimulus by S.

DISCRETE TRACKING. S is furnished with two push buttons which operate a stepper switch connected to the radial velocity control of the circle generator. Pushing button A increases the rate of expansion or decreases the rate of contraction of the circle; pushing button B has the opposite effect. S's task is to push button A whenever the circle appears to contract and button B for apparently expanding circles. This method differs from method 1 above in that more than one trial is required to obtain an aftereffect measurement, but S's task is simpler, requiring only a judgment of expansion or contraction. This procedure resembles the "staircase method" of Anderson et al. (1946), and is similar to the tracking methods described elsewhere in this book.

CONSTANT STIMULI. S is presented with a series of trials in which the circle expands or contracts at randomly sequenced, preselected rates. S's task on each trial is to report apparent expansion or contraction of the test stimulus. The rate of aftereffect is obtained by computing the mean of the resulting ogive (Guilford, 1936).

This last method was selected for use with monkeys because the task seemed simple enough for the animals to learn with relative ease and because the method readily yields an estimate of the standard error. However, one should be cautious when beginning an investigation requiring the cooperation of animals in making assumptions about what the animal can and cannot do. We were undoubtedly influenced strongly by the kinds of tasks monkeys had been known to perform in previous experiments. To say that the task of methods 2 and 3 above is "simpler" than the task in method 1 has only face validity. We have not tried to teach a monkey to rotate a knob so as to hold the size of a circle constant. Quite often in the history of animal experiments, tasks which initially seem beyond the animal's abilities have been found to be well within his capabilities given a proper training procedure. In choosing method 3 over method 2, however, we were guided by some experience. We have observed that when all the discriminations a monkey makes in a series of trials are difficult ones, the animal is likely to respond erratically, respond in a stereotyped manner, or cease responding altogether. The method of constant stimuli circumvents this problem by presenting trials over a considerable range of difficulty. Some human Ss who have been tested with the discrete tracking procedure complain after the experiment that "the circle never really moved at all," and have the feeling that they were "only guessing." They often find it hard to believe that anything was being accurately measured by the procedure. Perhaps monkeys, too, like to feel they are accomplishing something worthwhile.

MEASUREMENT IN THE MONKEY

Figure 1 shows a trained 3-year-old male rhesus (Roscoe) seated in the restraining chair. He looks into the tachistoscope and steadily fixates a spot of light at the center of the spiral for 10 seconds. At the end of this fixation period, the spiral vanishes and is replaced immediately by the test stimulus. To make a "correct" response the monkey presses the right-hand lever when an expanding circle appears and the left-hand lever when a contracting circle appears. A food pellet is released into the food cup for every second "correct" response. The cup is located directly between the levers and at the same height. This placement was selected to avoid obstructing the animal's vision. A lever response turns off the circle and causes the spiral to reappear for the next trial. If the monkey does not press either lever the circle vanishes after 4 seconds and another trial is begun. Either an "incorrect" response during the test interval or a lever press during the spiral fixation results in shock. A lever press made during the presentation of a motionless circle results in neither shock nor food.

Any aftereffect produced by the rotating spiral thus influences the monkey's responses to circles having varying rates of shrinkage and expansion. Clockwise rotation of the spiral, which is drawn counterclockwise outward, would be expected to produce apparent shrinkage, while counterclockwise rotation would be expected to produce apparent expansion.

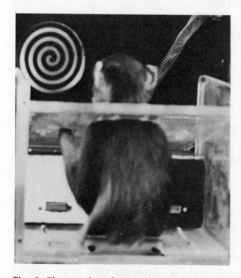

Fig. 1. The monkey fixates the clockwise-rotating spiral (left). When the circle appears (right) he presses the left lever signalling apparent contraction even though the circle is objectively of constant size.

CHOICE OF ANIMAL

Rats were initially considered as candidates for these studies. However, the complexity of organization of the rat's visual apparatus probably falls somewhat short for the kind of discriminations needed. Also, the considerable complexity of the task involved suggested that an animal somewhat higher on the phylogenetic scale might be more suitable. The monkey (*Macaca mulatta*) was chosen because of the excellence of his visual system and because it was believed that this animal possessed sufficient intelligence to learn the task. In retrospect, it would seem desirable for future study to choose a more docile species, or perhaps the chimpanzee. The rhesus monkey exhibits considerable nervousness and undesirable emotional behavior which result not only in loss of training time, but in increased complexity of problems regarding reinforcement and deprivation schedules. These problems are particularly severe during periods of training which give rise to frustration. It was also discovered, as has been reported by others, that some monkeys are not strongly motivated by food deprivation. Some animals (notably Agatha) in this series of studies would go for several days without eating and still sit apathetically in the experimental apparatus, ignoring the stimulus array. These problems occurred more often in adult females and seemed to be related to the menstrual cycle.

PRELIMINARY PROCEDURAL CONSIDERATIONS

Some initial attempts were made to train the animals in a free-cage situation. Here again, the nervousness of the rhesus monkey forced the use of a restraining chair. A monkey possesses such a large repertoire of task-irrelevant responses that unless some restraint is used, the asiduous, concentrated performance needed for these experiments probably could not be achieved in a reasonable length of time. Magazine training was no problem with these animals, but surprising difficulty was encountered in training the monkey to convey the food pellets from the cup to his mouth through the hole in the top of the restraining chair. Sometimes the first 2 or 3 days of training must be devoted to teaching this task.

SPIRAL-CIRCLE DISCRIMINATION TRAINING

After the animal has learned to press, for example, the right lever for food, the apparatus is set as follows. A recycling timer alternately presents the spiral and the circle. Initially, the spiral-on time is 5 seconds and the circle-on time is 5 seconds. The circle always appears as a dot in the center of the cathode ray tube and expands rapidly enough so that it is just at the edges of the screen at the end of the 5-second period. During this period of training, pressing the left lever has no effect. Pressing the right lever delivers food only when the circle is present, and mild shock when the spiral is present. The first introduction of shock often upsets the monkey. However, it was found impossible to force the animal to pay attention to the stimuli without the use of shock. The animal has already learned to press the lever for food. When no food is delivered during a spiral-on time the monkey nevertheless continues to press the lever. Soon the circle comes on and food is delivered. This is simply an example of fixed interval reinforcement, and the monkey will maintain a high rate of lever pressing under this schedule without ever paying attention to the spiral or circle. Under these conditions the animal will look around the room while pressing the lever repeatedly (and with a maddeningly casual air) until food is delivered. This pattern of behavior will continue for months without any evidence that lever presses are more likely during circle-on time. The spiral-on time can be manipulated to produce something which looks like discrimination. If the spiral-on time is increased to about 50 seconds, lever presses during spiral-on time become less frequent. However, this decrease in response frequency is not necessarily evidence for discrimination. It is characteristic of fixed interval reinforcement schedules that frequency of responding is low immediately after a reinforcement and gradually increases as the time for another reinforcement approaches. This pattern will occur with the discriminanda concealed, and monkeys on this schedule ignore the discriminanda anyway. We have not been able to eliminate responses during spiral-on time without using shock. To prevent temper tantrums, the shock was initially set at very low values and gradually increased. Monkeys differ greatly in their aptitude for learning this type of discrimination. Some animals require 2 or 3 weeks of daily practice before they reach the criterion of 100 consecutive correct responses. This criterion was not chosen arbitrarily, but was used because it seemed to be easily attainable and stringent enough for the purpose of the experiment. When the monkey begins to improve his discrimination noticeably, only a few days are required to reach this criterion. It is not likely, therefore, that difficulties encountered later in training the animal to shift to the other lever (see below) could be avoided by using a less stringent criterion.

SHIFT TRAINING

The next step in training is to change the contingencies so that the right lever now always delivers shock. The left lever delivers food during the circle-on time and shock during spiral-on time. To make the stimulus consistent with later parts of the training program, the circle now appears at its maximum diameter and shrinks rapidly to a point during the 5-second on-time. The monkey must now shift his responding to the left lever. This change constitutes a minor crisis for the animal, and sometimes several days are required for the animal to withhold his right lever response and establish a reliable pattern of responding to the left lever. The next problem is to shift the animal from one lever to the other each time he reaches the criterion of 100 consecutive correct responses. The objective is to teach the animal that if one lever does not work, the other will. This phase of training is completed when the animal shifts immediately after the first error.

After the third or fourth shift, the animal can usually be placed on a schedule so that after every 50 responses the apparatus automatically shifts to the opposite condition. During this part of training, the animal displays a string of errors after each shift, gradually changing his response to the correct lever. When the animal's errors occupy less than one-half the time period for each of the two conditions, the number of responses required before shift can be reduced gradually to a minimum of about five. Thus, at the conclusion of the shift training, the monkey makes one error immediately after a shift, followed by four correct responses, followed by an error which occurs on the next shift, followed by four correct responses, and so on.

EXPAND-CONTRACT DISCRIMINATION TRAINING

Up to this stage the animal gives no evidence of discriminating between the expanding circle and the contracting circle. As the number of trials per lever is decreased, however, the animal eventually discovers that a shrinking circle means left lever and an expanding circle means right lever. In some animals this does not occur for a number of days after the five trials per lever schedule has been reached. In one of these animals (Priscilla), it was necessary to randomize the number of trials for each lever since this monkey had learned an alternation pattern. Sometimes the intensity of the shock must be increased at this stage because some animals become adapted to a mild shock and may use it merely as a cue to change levers. The first correct discrimination occurs when the animal shifts from using one lever to the other without first making an error. After this first correct discrimination, the monkey very quickly gains an error-free performance within a day or two. To sharpen the animal's discrimination, the speed with which the circle expands and shrinks is gradually reduced. If this speed is made less than about ±1 minarc (minute of arc) per second the animal is apt to become neurotic, and this value is chosen as a working minimum. Few human Ss can make discriminations much finer than this.

FIXATION TRAINING

The study of many perceptual problems requires accurate fixation by S. This is particularly difficult when the S is an animal other than man. Over a period of several years, many methods have been tried in connection with the spiral aftereffect studies in monkeys. One such method involves placing some reflecting surface on the eyeball, usually in the form of a contact lens. A beam of light is then reflected against a prepared surface on the lens and the position of the reflected ray is used to determine the direction of gaze. We have tried this method and rejected it because the rhesus monkey lacks a prominent corneal bulge and we have not found it possible to affix anything to the eyeball in such a way that it does not shift. An additional disadvantage of this method is that a visible pencil of light in the periphery may interfere in an undesirable way with the process under study. Another method employs sensitive photocells which indicate changes in reflected light from the eyeball itself, resulting from the difference in reflectance of the iris and the surrounding sclera. This method requires rigid spatial location of the photoelectric cells with respect to the monkey's head—an almost impossible requirement in the rhesus monkey. Still another method involves the use of a retinascope. The *E* using this method directs a narrow pencil of light along the axis of the animal's regard while at the same time looking along this same pencil of light. When the animal looks directly down the light beam, his retina is clearly visible to *E* as a pinkish reflection seen only when the gaze is directed down the beam. This method makes possible quite accurate determination of the direction of gaze, but has the very significant disadvantages that the beam of light is aversive and also interferes drastically with the animal's ability to make fine visual discriminations. Some success has been obtained with a method in which *E* simply views the animal's face in dim illumination from some point behind the stimulus array and attempts to judge where the animal is looking. For some purposes this method is adequate, but the degree of accuracy is far from satisfactory for many perceptual experiments.

Another method in which the apparatus forces the animal to train himself to fixate has also been tried in this laboratory. A pip appears on an oscilloscope screen. At unpredictable intervals it begins to move to the left or right. The monkey can return it to center by pressing a lever. However, he must watch it closely at all times because if it moves more than a few millimeters from center, shock is administered. After extensive attempts to make this system work we have succeeded only in inducing severe behavioral disturbances, and the method has been abandoned. Some variation of the method may, however, be possible and would make an interesting and potentially very useful study.

Recently a very effective method has been devised. It was first suggested in principle by Weiskrantz (personal communication, 1963). Two accurately placed infrared light sources produce reflected images on the animal's eyes. The position of these images relative to the iris is monitored by the *E* by means of an infrared telescope or "sniperscope." The M-3 sniperscope containing a Farnsworth #6032 image tube operating at 20,000 volts is superior. This image tube provides more than sufficient resolution to allow the *E* to monitor the infrared reflections on the animal's iris and to administer differential reinforcement in order to bring about fixation behavior. Figure 2 is a plan view of the subject, *S*, viewing the perceptual field, *AB*, containing a small visible light source at point *P* which serves as a fixation point. L_1 and L_2 are infrared light sources which are accurately located in the same plane as the *S*'s line of regard, with angle L_1SP = angle L_2SP = approximately 30°. The infrared optical system at *O* and mirror at *M* are accurately located so that the principal axis of the telescope's optical system after reflection in *M* coincides with the animal's line of regard when fixating *P*. When the *S* fixates *P*, the reflected images of L_1 and L_2 appear at opposite edges of the iris. Deviation from *P* of less than 1° can be easily detected by *E*. As seen from the diagram, the animal is placed so that one of his eyes lies on the center line between the two light sources. The *E* focuses his attention on the centered eye.

The M-3 sniperscope is ordinarily focused for objects at a distance of 30 feet

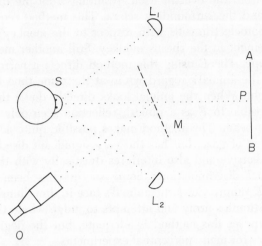

Fig. 2. Plan view of the apparatus for fixation training. The monkey, S, looks through mirror, M, at fixation point, P, centered in field AB. Infra-red lights at L_1 and L_2 form high-lights on monkey's eyes which can be seen in optical system, O.

or more. It is of course necessary to refocus the optical system to a distance of about 2 feet. Initially this was done with auxiliary lenses, but a preferable method is to unscrew the objective lens of the telescope until a proper focus is obtained.

This procedure places the animal in an unusual situation: whenever he fixates the spot of light, a reinforcement is administered either immediately or after a controlled delay. Although the animal is being viewed, he is not distracted by

Fig. 3. Immobile, trance-like state during fixation.

the appearance of the *E* in his visual field. Nor is there any distracting light source since the infrared filters render the light sources completely invisible (at least to humans). The monkeys rapidly learn to fixate very steadily. As the delay of reinforcement is increased up to 20 seconds, a pattern of rigid immobility develops, such that the animal appears to be in a trance during this period (see Fig. 3). Infrared movies show changes in facial expression which resemble the human frown upon presentation of the discriminative stimulus—particularly where the discrimination required is a difficult one.

A good procedure for training is as follows: the monkey, seated in a restraining chair, is in total darkness as far as visible light is concerned. *E* views the monkey through the infrared telescope, and when the animal is looking forward in the general direction of the desired fixation point, *E* presses a button which turns on the fixation light and also starts an electronic timer. The first time this occurs, the monkey will of course fixate the spot of light immediately since it is the only visible object in the field. Approximately one-half second after appearance of the light, the electronic timer automatically presents the discriminative stimulus, thus providing an opportunity for reinforcement. A delay of one-half second appears to be a good beginning value. After the first presentation, it may happen that the monkey will not fixate the spot of light when it appears. When this happens, *E* releases the button before the one-half–second period has ended. Releasing the button always zeroes the timer and turns off the fixation light. The *E* then waits until the animal is looking in the right direction before pressing the button again. After about 10 minutes of this procedure the monkey will make obvious fixation responses. The next step is to adjust the timer to produce longer periods of delay. A workable procedure is to double the delay; after the animal has learned to fixate for one-half second, a 1-second delay is easily learned. After the 1-second delay is learned, a 2-second delay can be introduced. During the training for longer delays, *E* becomes progressively more strict in requiring the animal to fixate accurately for the entire delay period. Any glancing away on the part of the animal results in *E*'s releasing the button, and the animal must begin all over again to fixate for the entire period before another opportunity for reinforcement can occur. The frequency of small eye movements is greatest at the beginning of the delay period. As delay continues, however, the animal becomes progressively more immobile. This can be understood perhaps by a consideration of the relative costs to the animal of looking away early in the delay period as opposed to later in the period. Glancing away after the first few seconds of a delay period results in a loss of only a few seconds until the next opportunity for reinforcement. However, after 18 seconds of a 20-second delay period, the animal has made a considerable investment toward receiving his next reinforcement, and looking away results in a long additional delay.

During training, superstitious behaviors are apt to develop. Some animals display lip smacking, vocalizations, and gross musculoskeletal responses such as shaking the head or grasping the sides of the chair. One animal developed an especially persistent habit of grasping the manipulandum box with both hands and shaking the monkey chair vigorously. These undesirable superstitious responses can be eliminated through the judicious administration of shock by *E*.

During measurement of aftereffect, the S must be observed carefully to see that fixation is maintained. When the bands of the rotating spiral move toward the center, fixation is readily maintained. But centrifugal motion sometimes induces visual tracking and disrupts fixation. An effective method of avoiding this difficulty has been to train fixation with the spiral illumination at zero and only the fixation point visible. Now if the illumination of the rotating spiral is gradually increased, it is easier to maintain fixation. However, as noted below, this problem was not successfully solved in one animal (Agatha) whose gaze always seemed to follow the spiral bands.

RESULTS

After training is complete, the animal has learned to avoid lever presses any time the spiral is present, to press the right lever for an expanding circle and the left lever for contracting circles, and to look steadily at the fixation point during presentation of the eliciting stimulus. Up to this point the animal has never seen a rotating spiral and no motion aftereffect is involved. From the E's point of view, reinforcement contingencies during training are clear since the animal is being trained to respond to objective changes in a visual stimulus. However, if the spiral has been rotating during the eliciting period, the E can no longer determine whether a lever press is "correct" or not. Before testing the first animal, no information concerning the magnitude of aftereffect in the monkey was available. Therefore, the first presentation of a rotating spiral was a problem for the E. A ratio of two responses per reinforcement had been used to increase response reliability during training. Therefore, the first rotating spiral was presented on a trial which would not have been reinforced and rapid objective circle motions were used in an attempt to zero in on the probable range of aftereffect to be encountered. This resulted in a plan involving nonreinforcement of circle speeds less than 4 minarcs per second. The experiment proper was carried out on 12 successive days. On odd-numbered days the spiral was stationary and only circle speeds of 1.7 minarcs per second were presented to keep up the desired sharpness in discrimination. On each even-numbered day the animal performed under three conditions: a stationary spiral, a clockwise rotation, and a counterclockwise rotation. These conditions were presented in the six possible orders on the six even-numbered days. Order of presentation of the different rates of expansion and contraction of the circle always followed the same counterbalanced program for each condition. During the conditions involving rotation of the spiral, shock was not administered for responses made to the 1.7 or 3.4 minarc per second rates, since this would have constituted negative reinforcement for responses indicative of aftereffect. This change in reinforcement schedule was trivial, since it resulted in no appreciable change in the proportion of shocked responses. In preliminary experiments, even complete elimination of shock was found to have no detectable effect on the animal's performance during runs of length similar to those of the experiment proper. The spiral was always presented for 10 seconds and the circle for 4 seconds.

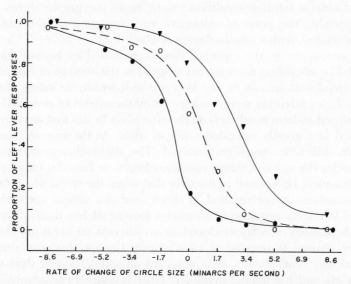

Fig. 4. Results obtained from Roscoe showing proportion of left lever responses to circles having different rates of expansion (+) and contraction (−), under three different spiral rotation conditions: counterclockwise (filled circles), stationary (open circles), and clockwise (triangles).

Figure 4 is based on the data obtained on the even-numbered days and shows the results of 1,442 presentations of the circle, in response to which 1,406 lever presses were made. Almost all of the 36 failures to respond occurred on difficult discriminations. The ordinate shows the proportion of responses made with the left lever. The abscissa represents the rate of change of circle diameter in minarcs per second. Contraction is indicated by the negative sign. The open circles and dashed line on the graph show the results from the stationary spiral condition.

It can be seen that when the spiral was not turning, the animal seldom made an error in judging circles whose rates of expansion or contraction were 8.6 minarcs per second or more. The nearly equal left and right lever responses to the motionless circle indicate that little if any lever preference was present. A rate of change to which the monkey responds equally often with the left and right levers is used as a measure of his point of subjective size constancy. This point on the ogive can be estimated by interpolation. The point of subjective size constancy when the spiral was not rotating was 0.17 minarcs per second, with an estimated standard error of 0.25. Thus, the monkey's subjective size constancy point is less than one standard error away from the objective size constancy point (0.00 minarcs per second). The means and standard error were computed as outlined in Guilford (1936, pp. 169–171).

Inspection of the results from the counterclockwise condition (filled circles on the graph) shows a systematic shift to the left. The point of subjective size constancy for this curve is at −1.62 minarcs per second, with a standard error of about 0.25. This means that a circle objectively contracting at 1.62 minarcs per second would be responded to as if it were motionless. Inspection of the results from the clockwise rotation condition (triangles on the graph) shows a marked shift to the right. The point of subjective size constancy for this curve is 3.25 minarcs per second, with a standard error of about 0.35.

These results are in the expected directions (based on human data) for the spiral used. The aftereffect rates are not as great as the average of 4.62 minarcs per second obtained with human Ss, but they are well within the range of individual differences. Later attempts were made to study the effects of drugs (D-amphetamine sulfate and sodium nembutal) on the aftereffect in this first monkey (Roscoe). This resulted in a greatly extended series of trials. As the animal gained experience certain difficulties were encountered. The slight change in reinforcement schedule under the spiral rotating condition began to have an effect on the animal's performance. He seemed to discover that when the spiral was rotating, difficult discriminations never resulted in shock, and the animal responded with a stereotyped left lever response to all circles moving at less than 1.7 minarcs per second. When shock was reintroduced in an attempt to break up this pattern, the monkey refused to respond at all whenever the spiral was rotating and the circle speed was slow. Finally, data obtained on spiral rotating days were completely useless and the animal made left lever responses exclusively. Increasing shock resulted in refusal to press the lever.

Several changes in the apparatus and procedure were made at this time in an attempt to correct some of the previous difficulties. For Roscoe, the spiral was 20 cm in diameter viewed at a distance of 1.5 meters. The circle was produced on a cathode ray tube having a moderate persistence green phosphor. The circle diameter was 7.6 cm. The new apparatus, which was constructed to extend the retinal area stimulated for studies in humans, employed a spiral 38 cm in diameter viewed at a distance of 1.1 meters. The circle, which appeared on the screen of a television picture tube, was 10 cm in diameter. The spiral used with Roscoe (see Fig. 1) was a 4-turn Archimedes spiral whose formula was $\rho = 0.398\ \theta$, with ρ in cm and θ in radians. The larger spiral was an 8-turn Archimedes spiral whose formula was $\rho = 0.378\ \theta$. Both spirals were drawn so as to have equal black and white areas. Speed of rotation was 180 rpm for the old apparatus and 160 for the new. Thus, the radial motions for the two spirals at the surface of the spirals were, respectively, 7.5 cm per second and 6.7 cm per second (see Scott and Noland, 1965). However, in the old apparatus the viewing distance was 1.5 meters while in the new apparatus it was 1.1 meters. In minarcs per second, then, the rates of radial motion in the old and new situations were 173 and 195 minarcs per second respectively. Based on work with humans (Scott et al., 1963b), the speeds are in the range producing the greatest aftereffects. If anything, the new apparatus would be expected to produce slightly more aftereffect.

A second monkey (Priscilla) was trained and the measurements obtained are shown in Figure 5. This time, spiral rotating trials were interspersed among spiral stationary trials in the hope that the problems encountered with the first monkey could be avoided. Much less aftereffect was obtained in the second animal partly because, as has been found in human Ss, during a series of rotating spiral trials the aftereffect tends to build up cumulatively from one trial to the next. The

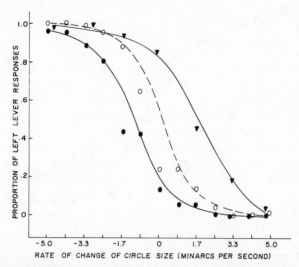

Fig. 5. Priscilla's results showing proportion of left lever responses to circles having different rates of expansion (+) and contraction (−), under three different spiral rotation conditions: counterclockwise (filled circles), stationary (open circles), and clockwise (triangles).

use of interspersed spiral rotating trials, therefore, considerably reduces the magnitude of the aftereffect. It was planned initially to perform some cortical ablations in Priscilla and to make a postoperative measurement. Unfortunately, this animal died due to accidental causes before postoperative measurements could be made.

A third animal (Agatha) was trained and every effort was made with this animal to avoid problems which had been encountered with the two previous Ss. The new fixation training method had been perfected and was the only method used for Agatha's fixation training. Each testing session was begun by presenting S with easy discriminations, i.e., circles expanding or contracting at a rate considerably greater than the aftereffect rate. These preliminary trials were used at the beginning of the session when the spiral was rotating as well as in sessions when it was stationary, thus the animal was accustomed to respond during spiral rotating conditions. The preliminary trials also had the effect of allowing the aftereffect to build up. As soon as the animal was responding reliably, a program of ordered trials, 30 at a time, was presented. The complete program utilized 13 evenly spaced circle rates, ranging from −6 minarcs per second through 0 through 6 minarcs per second. The different speeds were presented 10 times each in a random order. Nonreinforced trials were specified in the program, and an equal number of trials at each rate were not reinforced. Although this technique failed to overcome all of the previous difficulties, it led to more reliable results than any other procedure tried so far.

Figure 6 shows the results obtained with Agatha using this revised procedure. The most outstanding feature of these results is the apparent lack of any significant

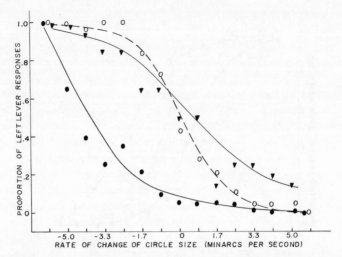

Fig. 6. Preoperative results obtained from Agatha showing proportion of left lever responses to circles having different rates of expansion (+) and contraction (−), under three different spiral rotation conditions: counterclockwise (filled circles), stationary (open circles), and clockwise (triangles).

aftereffect of apparent shrinkage. It is believed that this lack of aftereffect is the result of excessive eye movements induced by the centrifugal motion of the spiral bands. In spite of the improved fixation technique, this animal persisted in displaying tracking eye movements during clockwise rotation of the spiral. The rather large aftereffect in the other direction, however, was encouraging and

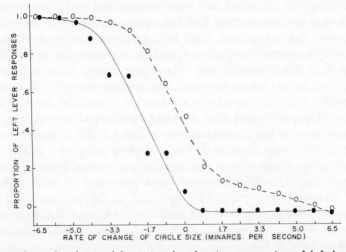

Fig. 7. Postmock results obtained from Agatha showing proportion of left lever responses to circles having different rates of expansion (+) and contraction (−), under two different spiral rotation conditions: counterclockwise (filled circles) and stationary (open circles).

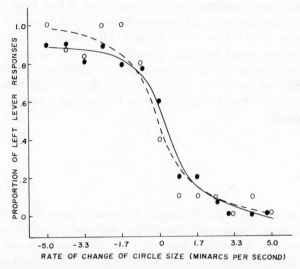

Fig. 8. Postoperative results obtained from Agatha showing proportion of left lever responses to circles having different rates of expansion (+) and contraction (−), under two different spiral rotation conditions: counterclockwise (filled circles) and stationary (open circles).

seemed to represent an effect of sufficient magnitude to be profitably studied before and after experimental brain surgery.

Two burr holes were placed bilaterally in the cranium just posterior to the coronal suture, about 1 cm from the midline. This procedure was carried out as a mock operation to control for any effects of trauma. Aftereffect was again measured 2 weeks after the mock operation. The results are shown in Figure 7. Clockwise rotation was not used in this series of trials. Toward the end of the postmock measurement series some of the animal's responses suggested slight adaptation. That is, the magnitude of the aftereffect obtained postmock was slightly less than that obtained premock, and the difference could be attributed to responses made in the last quarter of the series. Adaptation is known to occur in humans, and a slight decrease in aftereffect was therefore expected.

After the postmock measurement had been made, the animal was anesthetized and stainless steel electrodes were lowered into the parietal cortex through the burr holes made previously in the mock operation. Lesions were then induced galvanically, using a direct current of 1 ma for 30 minutes. The current was monitored through a milliammeter and a constant current circuit was used to prevent any fluctuations in current during this time. The small current and long time were chosen so as to produce lesions approximately 5 mm in diameter, having fairly regular spheroidal shape. These lesion sites were chosen without any specific rationale. Previous work with humans had shown reliable disturbances in aftereffect with a variety of cortical lesions. The parietal area was desirable in that it was accessible and the lesions could be easily verified and reproduced. Parietal lesions were not expected to produce paralysis, or visual deficit as some other locations would. Following the operation the animal recovered uneventfully. Her cage behavior was indistinguishable from what it had been preoperatively. When aftereffect measurement was resumed she seated herself willingly in the chair and performed as before. Her ability to discriminate expanding and contracting circles during spiral stationary conditions was unchanged.

Figure 8 shows the results of measurement of visual motion aftereffect beginning 2 weeks after the operation. Figure 8 differs dramatically from Figure 6 and shows that the strong aftereffect displayed by this animal preoperatively has been virtually obliterated.

DISCUSSION

Can it be argued that the difference between Figure 6 and Figure 8 is attributable to the brain lesions performed? Certainly this interpretation is not absolutely unequivocal. It has been observed that when animals are placed in the aftereffect measurement situation for a very long time they seem to learn to shift their reference point for choosing one lever over another from stationary circles to slowly moving circles. This is noticeable, for example, when running a series of trials with a stationary spiral. The animal sometimes seems to display an "aftereffect" opposite in direction to that normally associated with the direction of spiral rotation previously seen. Still later, the animal seems to choose a reference point depending upon whether or not the spiral is rotating. The important point is that in this last case the monkey's behavior is equally consistent with the interpretation that there is now no aftereffect. This ambiguity does not appear susceptible to resolution by current behavioral methods. We seem to have arrived at a point where it is proper to speak of a principle of psychophysical indeterminacy. As pointed out at the beginning of this chapter, the measurement of aftereffect is a measurement of subjective phenomenon, and it is a step further into the organism than the measurement of a threshold. Does it represent, then, an impassable boundary which will always resist the trespass of objective behavioral science? If so, deeper exploration will have to include more direct physiologic observations.

It may be revealing to approach this indeterminacy from a somewhat different perspective. The monkey's reliability as a source of information is comparable, motivationally at least, to that of the research scientist. Just as there is always a risk that a scientist will publish erroneous information, so is there the same risk for the monkey and for the same reasons. We want the monkey and the scientist both to tell us what is "really" happening, but we run the risk that they will instead tell us what they will be rewarded for. The human scientist usually realizes that honesty is the best policy in the long run and that although he may get his grant renewed by publishing some slightly altered data, eventually he will be found out. We must teach the monkey scientist the same lesson, but it is a lesson which requires a long time to learn if it must be learned by real experience rather than by vicarious symbolic rehearsal through language. If the process we are studying is time-independent, there may be no insurmountable problem. But some perceptual processes, and in particular the visual motion aftereffect, are definitely time-dependent. The first time we measure a human's aftereffect it will be greater than at any subsequent time. This reduction in aftereffect has been called adaptation (e.g., Scott et al., 1966), but its basis is not known. The fact of adaptation adds another ambiguity to the problem of communication between the animal and the experimenter. Even if adaptation does not occur in a particular phenomenon to be investigated in animals, if the time required for the animal to learn to communicate reliably is a considerable portion of that animal's life-span because of limitations of intelligence, still another limiting factor enters the situation.

On the other hand, if one accepts the monkey's honesty on faith, there still appear to be two possible interpretations. The apparent reduction of aftereffect may be attributable to adaptation. This does not seem likely because of the suddenness of the behavioral change, but it cannot be ruled out. The second interpretation is that the brain lesions interfered with the brain's processing of visual information in a way which resulted in a lessening of aftereffect. Our experience with humans having brain lesions has been that a lesion typically increases the aftereffect rate. In a current study we have found that in six out of seven patients examined who had strictly unilateral cortical lesions, aftereffect is greater in the damaged hemisphere than in the intact hemisphere. However, in some other patients, the aftereffect measured bilaterally (in the center of the visual field, as in the monkey studies) has been abnormally slight. Bilaterally symmetrical parietal lesions might just possibly have this effect, but further studies would be needed to answer the question. One might ask whether it is neurologically or physiologically reasonable that such an effect might result from such lesions. Michael (1969) has recently summarized the progress of physiologic work on visual information processing. He says, "It appears to be a general rule that the retinal processing of information involves a comparison by a ganglion cell of the signals from two sets of receptors" (p. 113). It may not be too great an extrapolation to suggest that in the higher centers a similar pattern is followed. Scott et al. (1967, p. 1270) has suggested that motion detection by the brain may be based on "a comparison between the firing rates of two populations of cells." The two populations would be those of Hubel's direction sensitive cells just stimulated and those sensitive to the opposite direction of motion. This comparison would presumably be carried out in some other portion of the brain than the primary projection area. It may not be surprising therefore that quite large areas of cortex may be involved in this complex perception.

It is interesting to view the problems the psychophysicist has with his animal Ss as a problem in communication. In studying complex processes such as the visual aftereffect of motion, one is at times strongly reminded of difficulties in communication between one human and another. John, age 16, spends hours of fruitless speculation as to whether Mary loves him. When he is 35 it will not be as hard for him to decide such questions. He will have had time to learn some difficult discriminations.

The other day as I was walking past the animal room I overheard a conversation between Agatha and a young monkey who was just beginning his discrimination training.

"Aunt Aggie, does the circle *really* expand?" asked the youngster.

"Child, you are too young for such questions," she replied.

REFERENCES

Anderson, T. W., P. J. McCarthy, and J. W. Tukey. 1946. "Staircase" Methods of Sensitivity Testing. NAVORD Report 65–46.

Barlow, H. B., and R. M. Hill. 1963. Selective sensitivity to direction of movement in ganglion cells of the rabbit retina. Science, 139:412.

Cann, M. A. 1961. Rate of aftereffect as a function of texture of the test field in the perception of the negative aftereffect of motion. Unpublished doctoral dissertation, Boston University.

Carlson, V. R. 1962. Adaptation in the perception of visual velocity. J. Exp. Psychol., 64:192–197.

Cords, R., and E. T. von Brucke. 1907. Über die Geschwindigkeit des Bewegungsnachbildes. Pfluger Arch. Ges. Physiol., 119:54–76.

Day, R. H. 1958. On interocular transfer and the central origin of visual aftereffects. Amer. J. Psychol., 71:784–790.

Dvorak, V. 1871. Versuche über die Nachbilder von Reizveranderungen. Sitz. Akad. Wiss. Wien, 61:257–262.

Exner, S. 1876. Über das Sehen von Bewegung und die Theorie des zusammengesetzten Auges. Sitz. Wiener Akad. Wiss., Bd 72, Abstr. III 156–190.

Gallese, A. J. 1956. Spiral aftereffect as a test of organic brain damage. J. Clin. Psychol., 12:254–258.

Grossberg, S. 1969. Embedding fields: a new theory of learning with physiological implications. Mimeographed preprint.

Guilford, J. P. 1936. Psychometric Methods, New York, McGraw-Hill Book Company.

Helmholtz, H. von. 1867. Handbuch der Physiol. Optik. Leipzig, L. Voss.

Holland, H. C. 1965. The Spiral Aftereffect, London, Pergamon Press, Inc.

——— and H. R. Beech. 1958. The spiral aftereffect as a test of brain damage. J. Ment. Sci., 104:466–471.

Hubel, D. H. 1963. The visual cortex of the brain. Sci. Amer., 209:54–62.

——— and T. N. Wiesel. 1963. Receptive fields of cells in striate cortex of very young, visually inexperienced kittens. J. Neurophysiol., 26:994–1002.

Hutchins, R. M., ed. 1952. Aristotle's Short Physical Treatises, The Essay on Dreams. Great Books of the Western World. Chicago, Encyclopaedia Britannica, Inc., vol. 1.

Mach, E. 1875. Grundlinie d'Lehre v.d. Bewegungsempfindungen, Leipzig, Engelmann, pp. 59–65.

Michael, C. R. 1969. Retinal processing of visual images. Sci. Amer., 220:105–114.

Pickersgill, M. J. 1964. After-effect of movement in the stimulated and opposite eyes during and after pressure blinding. Nature, 202:833–834.

Plateau, J. 1850. Vierte Notiz über eine neue Sonderbare Anwendung des Verweilens der Eindrucke auf der Netzhaut. Poggendorff's Annalen, Bd. 80, 287–92. Bulletin de Bruxelles, XVI, II p. 30 and p. 254. Inst., XVIII, no. 835, p. 5. Philos. Paguz., XXXVI, 434–6.

Pribram, K. H. 1969. The neurophysiology of remembering. Sci. Amer., 220:73–86.

Price, A. C., and H. L. Deabler. 1955. Diagnosis of organicity by means of the spiral aftereffect. J. Consult. Psychol., 19:299–302.

Purkinje, J. 1825. Beobachtungen und Versuche zur Physiol. der Sinne, Bd. II, Prague. p. 60.

Scott, T. R. 1964. On the interpretation of "Interocular Transfer." Percept. Motor Skills, 18:455–466.

—— and J. H. Noland. 1965. Some stimulus dimensions of rotating spirals. Psychol. Rev., 72:344–357.

—— and D. Z. Wood. 1966. Retinal anoxia and the locus of the aftereffect of motion. Amer. J. Psychol., 79:435–442.

—— R. A. Bragg, and R. G. Smarr. 1963a. Brain damage diagnosis with the MMG. J. Consult. Psychol., 27:45–53.

—— A. E. Jordan, and D. A. Powell. 1963b. Does visual aftereffect of motion add algebraically to objective motion of the test stimulus? J. Exp. Psychol., 66:500–505.

—— R. A. Bragg, and A. E. Jordan. 1967. Lack of effect of stimulant and depressant drugs on spiral aftereffect. Percept. Motor Skills, 24:1263–1270.

—— A. D. Lavender, R. A. McWhirt, and D. A. Powell. 1966. Directional asymmetry of motion aftereffect. J. Exp. Psychol., 71:806–815.

Stager, P. 1966. An integration of neurological factors in the spiral aftereffect. Canad. J. Psychol., 20:400–406.

Taylor, M. M. 1963a. Tracking the neutralization of seen rotary movement. Percept. Motor Skills, 16:513–519.

—— 1963b. Tracking the decay of the aftereffect of seen rotary movement. Percept. Motor Skills, 16:119–129.

Terwilliger, R. F. 1963. Evidence for a relationship between figural aftereffect and afterimages. Amer. J. Psychol., 76:306–310.

—— 1964. A reply to Scott. Percept. Motor Skills, 18:640.

Wohlgemuth, A. 1911. On the aftereffect of seen movement. Brit. J. Psychol., Monogr. Suppl., 1:1–117.

Wundt, W. 1874. Grundzuge der physiol. Psychologie, Leipzig, Engelmann.

RICHARD W. MALOTT
MARILYN KAY MALOTT [1]

17

PERCEPTION AND STIMULUS GENERALIZATION *

INTRODUCTION

A methodologic analysis (cf., Galanter, 1962; Goldiamond, 1962; Graham, 1958) will be used in an attempt to show how sensation and perception, along with a number of other traditional topics, can be placed under the general heading of stimulus control and made compatible with an experimental analysis of behavior (Malott, 1969).

A systematization or framework is being presented rather than a theory. This framework provides a way of interrelating a wide variety of experiments. Although such a framework satisfies many of the functions of a theory, predictions are not directly forthcoming and consequently evaluation may be more difficult. Perhaps a system is best evaluated in terms of the amount of data it can unify and the importance of the variables it emphasizes. Such an evaluation, however, is bound to be long term and highly subjective.

Much work in psychophysics (including that in this book) is concerned with studying particular receptor systems. Chapter 3 by Stebbins, for example, emphasizes relations of the behavioral data to the physiology of the auditory receptor system, although his method may be applied to other receptor systems. Chapter 18 by Nevin, on the other hand, deals with the theory of signal detection, where emphasis is placed on analyzing sensory processes without reference to particular receptor systems. An example of a behavioral law which attempts to transcend particular receptor systems is Weber's Law, which states that the size of the difference threshold is a constant proportion of the intensity level at which the difference threshold is determined. Like Nevin, we are more interested in an analysis of sensory and perceptual processes without emphasis on any particular receptor system. We will attempt to differentiate between the two processes and indicate our approach to them.

[1] PSYCHOLOGY DEPARTMENT, WESTERN MICHIGAN UNIVERSITY, KALAMAZOO, MICHIGAN.

* This work was supported by National Institute of Mental Health Grants 10755 to Denison University and 13178 to Western Michigan University. The help of the following undergraduate research assistants is gratefully acknowledged: Cornelia Dodd, Beverly Doe, James Gerry, Susan Orr, Janet Page, and Keneth Shaeffer. We are particularly indebted to the following graduate research apprentices for their participation in conducting experiments, analyzing data, and theoretical discussions: Fredrick Kladder, John Pokrzywinski, and John G. Svinicki.

Most of the chapters in this book deal with experiments on sensation. In sensory experiments using human subjects, the experimenter asks the subject whether or not the stimulus is present or whether or not there is a difference between a standard and a comparison stimulus differing along some physical continuum. He then tells the subject whether or not he is correct. Sensory research is concerned with absolute and difference thresholds. When the stimulus magnitude or the stimulus difference is below the threshold, the subject will be unable to respond appropriately when the stimulus is, in fact, present or the comparison stimulus different.

An absolute threshold may be obtained, using a subhuman species, by reinforcing responses when the stimulus is present and by extinguishing responses when the stimulus is absent. In order to obtain a difference threshold one could reinforce responses in the presence of one stimulus and extinguish responses in the presence of stimuli differing along some physical continuum. There are two important factors to note about such experiments. One is that the stimuli presented to the subject usually differ along only one dimension. The second is that the desired information about the threshold is obtained while maintaining a discrimination training procedure; the experimenter always knows when and when not to reinforce a response because he always knows which response is correct and which response is not correct.

In order to illustrate a perceptual experiment, let us consider the Mueller-Lyer illusion. Suppose a horizontal line of a particular length is taken as the standard stimulus. Horizontal lines of different lengths, with arrowheads placed on the ends, are comparison stimuli. To a human subject, the length of the comparison stimulus which "appears" equal to the standard stimulus will not be the same as the length of the standard stimulus; the arrowheads change the "apparent" length of the horizontal line. The length of the comparison stimulus which equals the standard is known as the point of objective equality. The length of the comparison stimulus which "appears" equal to the standard is called the point of subjective equality. The principal datum in perceptual research is not the threshold, but rather, the difference between the points of subjective equality and objective equality. When the point of subjective equality and the point of objective equality are different, we say that an illusion has been demonstrated. In the broadest sense, it may be that the main concern of perceptual research is the analysis of illusions. Note that this experiment on the Mueller-Lyer illusion differs from a sensory experiment in two ways. First, in the perceptual experiment, the standard and comparison stimuli differ along not just one but two dimensions: the length of the horizontal line and the presence of the arrowheads. Secondly, in the perceptual experiment, the experimenter cannot tell the subject when he is or is not correct because there is no way of knowing which of the comparison stimuli "appears" equal to the standard; this is, in fact, what the experimenter is trying to find out. These two factors are the crucial criteria for distinguishing between a perceptual experiment and a sensory experiment. In perceptual experiments, the stimuli vary over more than one dimension and differential reinforcement cannot occur while the points of subjective equality are being determined.

Unlike much work on perception, ours is an attempt to obtain parametric

Fig. 1. Training stimulus with vertical end-lines.

functions which are in line with previous work on sensation in psychophysics. In the past, many workers in perception have been content simply to demonstrate that an illusion exists or, at best, to determine points of subjective equality. Our approach has been to analyze perceptual phenomena, involving the interaction of two stimulus dimensions, in terms of multidimensional stimulus generalization. Variations in response rate are observed as a function of changes in stimulus parameters along two dimensions; points of subjective equality are then derived from these functions.

An example of our general procedure is to train pigeons to respond in the presence of a particular stimulus. This is done by presenting positive reinforcement contingent upon responses with the stimulus continually present. After the response has been established, a generalization test is conducted. During the test no responses are reinforced; the stimulus is varied along some physical dimension or dimensions and the rate of responding to different values is recorded. Experiments have shown that such a generalization test will usually produce response rates which decrease as a function of the difference between the training and test stimuli (e.g., Guttman and Kalish, 1956). The function relating response rate to the stimulus value is known as a generalization gradient.

For example, in the case of the Mueller-Lyer illusion, we might train the animal to respond in the presence of a horizontal 1.3-cm line with vertical end lines, as shown in Figure 1. Then we vary the length of the horizontal line with vertical end lines during a generalization test. The resulting generalization gradient usually

Fig. 2. Test stimuli with outward pointing arrowheads (top), vertical end-lines (middle), and inward pointing arrowheads (bottom).

has a peak at the training length, 1.3 cm. This is demonstrated in the middle gradient of Figure 3 where relative response rate is presented as a function of length of the horizontal line. Note that in this test, the stimulus varied over only one dimension, length of the horizontal line. In subsequent generalization tests we simultaneously vary another dimension, the angle of the end lines or arrowheads (e.g., we replace the vertical end lines with outward pointing arrowheads). Sample end lines are shown in Figure 2. We then see if there is a change in the location of the peak of the generalization gradient along the line length dimension. The top and bottom gradients of Figure 3 show gradients which would demonstrate the Mueller-Lyer illusion. When outward pointing arrowheads are placed on the ends of the horizontal line, the line might be expected to appear shorter and, thus, the peak should occur at a length longer than the training value. When the arrowheads point inward, the line would appear longer and the peak should occur at a value shorter than the training length. The location of the peak, obtained with the original vertical end lines, should be at the point of objective equality; the location of the peaks obtained with arrowheads are the points of subjective equality. If there are shifts in the peaks of the gradients from the point of objective equality, then we have demonstrated a perceptual illusion. In the generalization tests, reinforcement is withheld because, with the arrowheads, there is no way of knowing to which stimulus responses should be reinforced. If reinforcements are delivered in the presence of the training length with arrowheads, the peak of the generaliza-

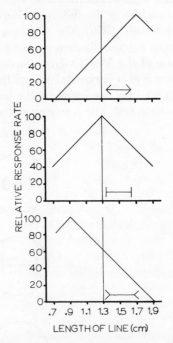

Fig. 3. Hypothetical relative generalization gradients over line length obtained with outward pointing arrowheads (top), vertical end-lines (middle), and inward pointing arrowheads (bottom).

tion gradient might quickly shift from the point of subjective equality to the training length where reinforcement are presently being received.

On the other hand, sensory research with animals consists essentially of a discrimination procedure in which correct responding is reinforced while incorrect responding is extinguished. A baseline which can be maintained over a long period of time is the principal datum. The stimulus varies over one dimension and differential reinforcement is always possible.

It is of considerable methodologic importance that a perceptual experiment requires a generalization procedure in which no differential reinforcement occurs. In perceptual research, discrimination procedures may be used to establish a baseline. In fact, it would be essential to use discrimination training over continua which do not ordinarily exert differential control over responding. For example, in the above experiment on the Mueller-Lyer illusion, differential responding to line length might not have been displayed after training on the 1.3-cm line with vertical end lines. In this case, training could then have consisted of reinforcing responses in the presence of a 1.3-cm horizontal line with vertical end lines and extinguishing responses in the presence of all other lengths of the horizontal line with vertical end lines. The question of primary interest, however, is how does the animal behave when novel stimuli are introduced in a generalization test probe; where will the peak of the gradient over horizontal line length be when novel arrowheads replace the vertical end lines? In such a probe, differential reinforcement is temporarily withheld for fear that it might eliminate the illusional behavior under study and replace it with veridical behavior. (One may either eliminate all reinforcement during the probe or deliver reinforcement in the presence of all stimuli presented; however, the former procedure of extinction would seem to be preferable since reinforcement in the presence of all stimuli would probably quickly eliminate all differential responding.) Consequently, the acquisition and baseline performance data collected in perception research are incidental to the main results obtained from the generalization test probes.

ACQUISITION AND BASELINE

The subjects in our research are barren hen pigeons maintained at 70 percent of normal free-feeding weight. They are inexpensive, easy to maintain, and have excellent visual capabilities (cf., Ferster, 1953).

The visual stimuli are projected behind a small plastic disc which serves as the pigeon response key. The response of pecking is conditioned and maintained by 3 seconds of access to grain presented via a feeder below the response key.

The basic procedure consists of first training the subject to eat from a food magazine and to peck the response key in the presence of the stimulus under consideration. The frequency of reinforcement for the response is then gradually decreased. The behavior is maintained with intermittent reinforcement until it is judged stable. Then a generalization test is given in extinction; responses are no longer reinforced during the test. Intermittent reinforcement is used prior to the generalization test in order to increase the resistance to extinction (i.e., the number of responses which will be obtained in the generalization test). Generalization tests consist of 20-second presentations of the various test stimuli separated by 10-second time-out periods of complete darkness during which the stimuli are changed and the numbers of responses are recorded.

The particular schedule of reinforcement is a variable interval schedule. This schedule has been chosen because it tends to result in a relatively orderly decrement in response rate during extinction and, therefore, a more reliable gradient should be obtained. The particular type of variable interval schedule we use is called a random-interval schedule; the distribution of the interreinforcement times can be described by a geometric distribution (cf., Farmer, 1963).

In many instances, we attempt to increase the amount of stimulus control obtained, i.e., the sharpness of the generalization gradient before the generalization test, by superimposing a discrimination procedure on top of the previously mentioned acquisition and baseline procedures. This may involve discrimination between an S+ (stimulus in the presence of which responses are reinforced) and an S− (stimulus in the presence of which responses are not reinforced). In some instances, the S− is simply the absence of the relevant stimulus dimension, e.g., 1.3-cm line versus no line; in some cases it is based on different values of the stimulus dimension, e.g., 1.3-cm line versus 0.7- and 2.1-cm lines.

The discrimination procedure is usually introduced immediately after the key peck response has been conditioned. The S+ is presented until a reinforcement is obtained and then the S− is presented. It remains present until 30 consecutive seconds have elapsed without a single key peck response; then the S+ is again presented. The procedure of prolonging the S− serves two functions. First, it prevents the possibility of presentation of the subsequent S+ functioning as accidental reinforcement for key peck responses near the end of S−. Second, if the animal does not pause for 30 seconds, it is indicative that more extinction in S− is needed and therefore the S− period is automatically lengthened (Snow and Uhl, 1969). Once an asymptotic discrimination has been established, the frequency of reinforcement in S+ is gradually decreased until the terminal baseline schedule is obtained (usually variable interval 64 seconds).

For ease of programming, we generally present the stimuli in a fixed order during training. It would be possible, therefore, for the animal to respond to the order of stimuli and not the actual stimulus values since the order is quite simple. However, subsequent generalization tests, using randomized presentation of stimuli, always indicate that a good visual discrimination is established when the baseline behavior also indicated the same.

In many of our experiments, we not only conduct discrimination training but also stimulus equivalence training; i.e., there may be a class of stimuli all treated the same, for example multiple S+s and/or multiple S−s. By holding the number of reinforcements constant in each stimulus we had hoped to be able to match the rate of the response in the various S+ stimulus values. However, we have found this difficult to do. The response rate in the presence of one stimulus value may be consistently high whereas the rate in a different stimulus value may be consistently low for several days. Usually, however, there are drifts in these rates so that their rank order shifts over a period of weeks.

In the next section, we will present data showing the effects of various training procedures on multiple-dimensional stimulus generalization. The stimulus dimensions are selected so as to provide information about the Mueller-Lyer illusion, stimulus matching, and sensory scaling.

BEHAVIORAL DATA

MUELLER-LYER ILLUSION

In the introduction to this chapter, we illustrated our approach to the analysis of the perceptual processes with a hypothetical animal experiment demonstrating the Mueller-Lyer illusion. A major part of our research, in fact, has involved that approach in the analysis of the Mueller-Lyer illusion.

EXPERIMENT A-1. TRAINING IN THE PRESENCE OF MEDIUM LINE LENGTH WITH VERTICAL END LINES. Pigeons were trained to peck a key in the presence of a 1.3-cm horizontal line with vertical end lines placed on the ends as shown in Figure 1. Responses were extinguished when neither the horizontal line nor end lines were present. A houselight was on at all times. The subjects were then given generalization tests in extinction over the length of the horizontal line. Figure 2 shows the endlines used in the tests: outward pointing arrowheads, vertical end lines, or inward pointing arrowheads.

The generalization gradients obtained using vertical end lines are presented in the middle row of Figure 4. The percentage of maximum responses (number of

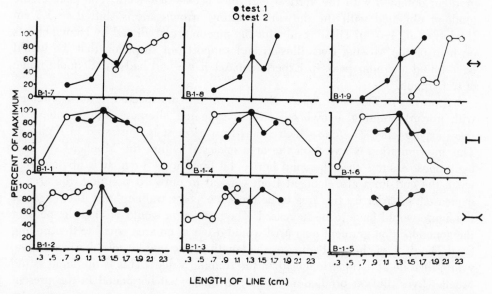

Fig. 4. Relative generalization gradients over line length obtained with outward pointing arrowheads (top row), vertical end-lines (middle row), and inward pointing arrowheads (bottom row). Each set of axes contains the gradients for one subject. Closed circles were obtained in the first test for the subject and open circles in the second test.

responses at the peak) is shown as a function of line length. For all three subjects, the maxima occur at the training length of 1.3-cm as predicted.

The outward pointing arrowheads were used in obtaining the top row of curves of Figure 4. In cases where subjects failed to respond enough to produce reliable gradients (a minimum of 50 responses at a maximum is required), no gradients are shown. Here the response rate increases as a function of length of the horizontal line and no maximum is shown; if there is a maximum it must occur at a longer length than used in the tests. The increase in rate is in the direction predicted.

The bottom row of gradients in Figure 4 was obtained when the arrowheads pointed inward. The gradients from the first test are variable and in no case are they as predicted. In the gradients from the second test, which used a range of shorter line length, the response rate increases as a function of line length in the direction *opposite* that predicted.

Subsequent tests were performed in which three different line lengths—one longer, one shorter, and one equal to the training length—were associated with each of the three types of end lines or arrowheads. The resulting gradients confirmed those previously found.

Experiment A-2. Training in the Presence of a Short Line Length with Vertical End Lines. In these experiments, the size of the display unit limited the size of the stimulus figure. In order to bring the range of our phenomenon with outward pointing arrowheads within the range of our equipment, we trained a new group of birds in the presence of a 0.7-cm horizontal line with vertical end lines. We then obtained the generalization gradients shown in Figure 5 with the flat end lines and outward pointing arrowheads. As was expected, the peak of the gradient obtained with the vertical end lines occurs at 0.7 cm. The peak of the gradient obtained with the outward pointing arrowheads is shifted to 1.3 cm (Malott et al., 1967a). These results for the pigeon are predicted by known effects on man of the Mueller-Lyer illusion and support our suspicion that we would have found a similar peak in Experiment A-1 if we had had an adequate range of test stimuli.

Analysis in Terms of Area. Because of the unexpected results obtained with inward pointing arrowheads, we investigated alternate interpretations of these experiments. The one which seems to work best is illustrated in Figure 6. This interpretation is based on the area enclosed within the Mueller-Lyer configurations. Assume that the solid horizontal lines are 1.3 cm. It is obvious that when the end lines are changed from vertical to outward pointing, the area is decreased; in order for the area to be the same as the training area, the length of the figure would have to be increased. The prediction would be that the peak of the generalization gradient over area would occur at an area equal to the training area. The peak of the gradient over the length of the middle solid horizontal line would then be at a value longer than the training values. This is the same as the Mueller-Lyer illusion prediction, and is, in fact, what happened in the present experiment.

Turning to the inward pointing arrowheads, it might at first glance seem that the area is enlarged as compared with the figure having vertical end lines;

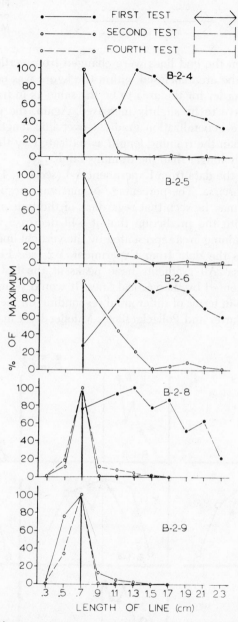

Fig. 5. Relative generalization gradients over line length obtained with outward pointing arrowheads (filled circles) and vertical end-lines (open circles). Each set of axes contains the gradients for one subject. Outward pointing arrowheads were used in the first test and vertical end-lines were used in the second (solid lines) and fourth (dashed lines) tests. (From Malott et al., 1967a. **Psychon. Sci.,** 9:55–56.)

however, this is not the case. Because the overall length of the end lines was kept constant regardless of the angle, the vertical distance between the butts of the end

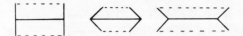

Fig. 6. Illustration of the area enclosed within the Mueller-Lyer figures.

lines decreased when the end lines were changed from vertical to inward point-ing. Consequently, the area enclosed within the figure was not increased but de-creased slightly. In order for the area to be the same as in training, the length of the figure would have to be slightly increased. Again, the prediction would be that the peak of the generalization gradient over line length should occur at a value, not shorter than the training length as indicated by the Mueller-Lyer illu-sion data, but slightly longer than the training value.

Figure 7 shows the data from Experiment A-1 (see Fig. 4) replotted with area appearing on the abscissa. The percentage of maximum responses is plotted as a function of area. It may be seen that regardless of the type of end lines, respond-ing is consistent with the prediction that it will decrease as a function of the distance from the training area represented by the vertical lines.

Figure 8 shows the data from Experiment A-2 (see Fig. 5) replotted with area on the abscissa. All gradients have peaks at the test area closest to the training area represented by the vertical lines. It would seem, then, that our data are best interpreted in terms of differential responding on the basis of area.

According to Carter and Pollack (1968), Mueller-Lyer made a similar analysis

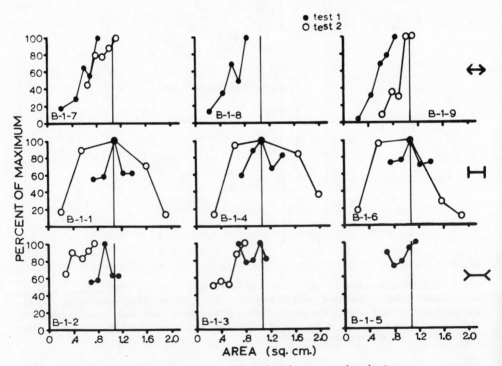

Fig. 7. The data of Figure 4 replotted with area on the abscissa.

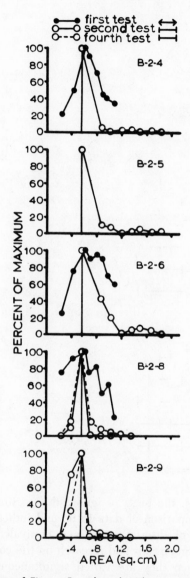

Fig. 8. The data of Figure 5 replotted with area on the abscissa.

of his original data; his subjects involuntarily took the space around the line into account in making their judgments. More recently, Erlebacher and Sekuler (1969) have found that their Mueller-Lyer data are best accounted for in terms of judgments based on the distance between the butts of the end lines on the Mueller-Lyer figures. This is true in spite of the fact that the human subjects were instructed not to use this distance in making their judgments. A review of the literature indicates that past experiments which have demonstrated the Mueller-Lyer illusion either discuss the possibility of such effects as responding on the basis of

Fig. 9. Training stimuli for a future experiment.

area or distance between the butts or ignore the possibility when it is, in fact, present. This makes comparison of data futile and indicates the need for future research on the effects of discrimination and equivalence training procedures along specific stimulus dimensions and research on the control exerted by various stimulus dimensions when they are varied simultaneously. Our own approach will be to attempt to eliminate differential responding to variations in dimensions such as area and distance between the butts of the end lines. We may, for example, use the stimuli shown in Figure 9 as training stimuli. Here a horizontal line of one intermediate length is S+ and shorter and longer horizontal lines are S−s regardless of the distance between the accompanying vertical "end lines." This discrimination training procedure should eliminate differential responding to area enclosed within end lines or distance between the butts of the end lines, but should produce differential responding to length of the horizontal line. If subsequent generalization tests, of the sort already reported, produced shifts in the peak of the gradient over line length as a function of the angle of the end lines, then we would be more convinced that a true Mueller-Lyer illusion was in operation. It seems safe to conclude at this point that there is more to the Mueller-Lyer illusion than meets the eye.

SUMMARY. In an attempt to demonstrate the Mueller-Lyer illusion, subjects were trained to respond in the presence of a horizontal line with vertical end lines. Generalization tests over horizontal line length were then conducted. The generalization gradients had peaks at the training length when the vertical end lines were used in the tests. When testing occurred with outward pointing arrowheads placed on the ends of the horizontal line, the gradients over horizontal line length shifted in a direction which demonstrated the Mueller-Lyer illusion. However, when inward pointing arrowheads were placed on the ends of the horizontal line, the gradients did not reveal the operation of the Mueller-Lyer illusion.

It was noted that this partial failure to demonstrate the Mueller-Lyer illusion might be due to differential responding on the basis of the area enclosed within the end lines of the Mueller-Lyer configurations. Past experiments which have demonstrated the Mueller-Lyer illusion have either discussed the possibility of such effects as responding on the basis of area or the distance between the butts of the end lines or have ignored the possibility when it is, in fact, present. There is a need for research on the effects of discrimination and equivalence training procedures along specific dimensions when they are varied simultaneously.

STIMULUS MATCHING AND NONMATCHING

Another area which fits into the category of multiple-dimensional stimulus generalization is that of matching and nonmatching. Consider a response key divided in half by a vertical black line. The colors on the two halves of the key may be varied independently of one another. Although the physical dimension varied is the same on the two halves of the key, two aspects of the stimulus are nevertheless varied independently of one another. Figure 10 shows stimuli which might be used to establish a matching discrimination. Responses are reinforced when both halves of the key are red (red-red) or when both halves are violet (violet-violet). Responses are extinguished when red is on the left and violet on the right (red-violet) or when violet is on the left and red is on the right (violet-red). If the subject responds at a higher rate when the two halves of the key

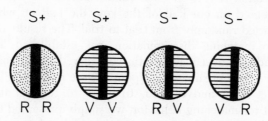

S+   S+   S-   S-

R R   V V   R V   V R

Fig. 10. Training stimuli for establishing a matching discrimination.

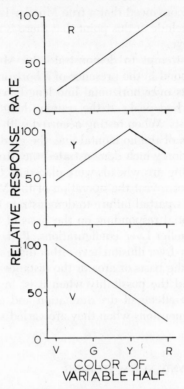

Fig. 11. Hypothetical relative generalization gradients demonstrating matching behavior with one half of the key held constant at red (top), yellow (middle), and violet (bottom).

match than when they do not match, he has a matching discrimination. Figure 11 shows the hypothetical generalization gradients obtained when a strong matching discrimination is generated. For any one gradient, one-half of the key is held constant at some particular color (e.g., for the top gradient, one-half of the key was always violet). Here the peak of each gradient is at the same color as the constant color.

Experiment B-1. Training in the Presence of Matching Stimuli. In one group of subjects responses were reinforced in the presence of one stimulus, red-red. No explicit discrimination training was given, and no houselight was present. Generalization tests were then conducted. In any one test, a particular color always appeared on one-half of the key; the half on which this constant color appeared varied randomly from trial to trial. The results of this experiment indicated that no matching discrimination was established; the peaks of the generalization gradients over wavelength were at red for all constant colors.

With another group of subjects, responses were reinforced in the presence of two stimuli: violet-violet and red-red. In order to conduct the most sensitive generalization test for matching behavior, we simply presented the four combinations of red and violet: red-red, violet-violet, red-violet, and violet-red. One would expect that if matching behavior were to be obtained with any colors, the training colors would be the most likely. Again, the data provided no consistent evidence that detectable matching behavior can be acquired as a result of stimulus equivalence training using only two different examples of matching stimuli.

With a third group of subjects, responses were reinforced in the presence of four matching stimuli: red-red, yellow-yellow, blue-blue, and violet-violet. Subsequent generalization tests produced statistical evidence for matching behavior (Malott et al., 1967b). However, we would prefer to have stronger evidence than was shown before closing the question of whether matching behavior may be reliably obtained without discrimination training. Perhaps training with a greater number of matching S+ stimuli would produce more dramatic evidence of matching behavior.

EXPERIMENT B-2. MATCHING DISCRIMINATION TRAINING—GENERALIZATION TO NOVEL COLORS. In this experiment, the S+s were violet-violet and red-red and S−s were violet-red and red-violet. For two subjects, when the discrimination was established, a generalization test was performed with the original training colors. The generalization gradients, shown in Figure 12, indicate that the response rate was higher in the presence of the matching stimuli than in the presence of the non-matching stimuli. Thus, we find that explicit training for a matching discrimination will, in fact, produce a matching discrimination.

For four other subjects, the question was asked: Will a matching discrimination established using two colors generalize to a situation in which novel colors are used? In order to answer this question, a generalization test was administered with the combinations of yellow and blue.

The results, seen in Figure 13, show that 3 out of 4 subjects demonstrated a matching discrimination; i.e., the rates in the two matching stimuli were above those in the two nonmatching stimuli. The fourth subject (A-2-10) had rates in the nonmatching stimuli intermediate between the rates in the two matching stimuli. The probability of 3 out of 4 subjects demonstrating a matching discrimination, when no matching discrimination exists, is 0.02. Thus we can conclude that the matching discrimination generalized to novel colors.

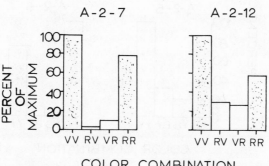

Fig. 12. Relative response rates for matching and non-matching combinations of red and violet. One histogram is shown for each of two subjects.

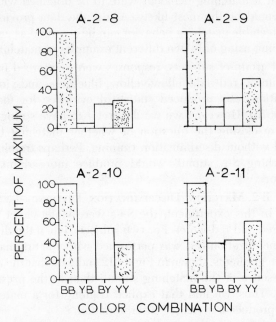

Fig. 13. Relative response rates for matching and non-matching combinations of yellow and blue. One histogram is shown for each of four subjects.

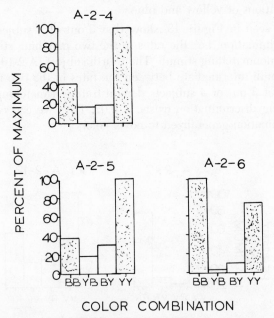

Fig. 14. Relative response rates for matching and non-matching combinations of yellow and blue. One histogram is shown for each of three subjects.

EXPERIMENT B-3. MATCHING DISCRIMINATION TRAINING—GENERALIZATION TO NOVEL COLOR COMBINATIONS. In this experiment, we attempted to equalize the rates in all of the matching stimuli in order to better observe matching behavior. The S+s were violet-violet, red-red, blue-blue, and yellow-yellow. The S−s were violet-red and red-violet. In other words, training was the same as in the last experiment except that the matching combinations of blue and yellow were added. There was no training with the nonmatching combinations of blue and yellow.

The results in Figure 14 shows that the matching discrimination established with red and violet did generalize to blue and yellow. In spite of the fact that the rates in the two matching stimuli were somewhat different, the rates in the two nonmatching stimuli were, for all three subjects, lower than the rates in the two matching stimuli. Again we see that the matching discrimination training generalized to novel stimulus combinations.

EXPERIMENT B-4. NONMATCHING DISCRIMINATION TRAINING—GENERALIZATION TO NOVEL COLORS. This experiment was similar to Experiment B-2 except that the S+s were the nonmatching combinations of red and violet and the S−s were the matching combinations of red and violet; e.g., a nonmatching discrimination was established. The subjects were tested for generalization of the nonmatching concept to novel colors using the various combinations of blue and yellow. The results are shown in Figure 15. Looking at the rates in the presence of the two nonmatching stimuli first, we see that they do not differ to any great extent. This is to be expected since both yellow and blue appear in both of the stimuli.

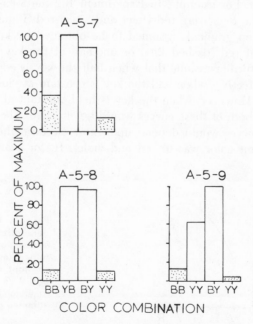

Fig. 15. Relative response rates for matching and non-matching combinations of yellow and blue. One histogram is shown for each of three subjects.

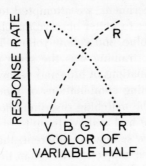

Fig. 16. Theoretical generalization gradients over wavelength assumed to be obtained keeping 1/2 of the key constant at red (dashed line) and 1/2 of the key constant at violet (dotted line).

Thus, it would seem that testing for generalization of a nonmatching discrimination should be more sensitive than testing for generalization of a matching discrimination. In fact, the results in Figure 15 show clear nonmatching behavior for each of the three birds. The rate in the two nonmatching stimuli is higher than in the two matching stimuli. This provides strong evidence for the generalization of a relational (in this case, nonmatching color) discrimination to novel colors.

EXPERIMENT B-5. MATCHING DISCRIMINATION TRAINING—GENERALIZATION TO NOVEL WAVELENGTHS OUTSIDE THE RANGE OF TRAINING WAVELENGTHS. In the preceding experiments, we might interpret the results in terms of generalization along the wavelength continuum. Training was frequently given with the various combinations of violet and red and testing was conducted with the combinations of blue and yellow. For example, in Experiment B-2 the S+s were red-red and violet-violet and the S−s were red-violet and violet-red. Figure 16 shows theoretical generalization gradients assumed to be obtained by keeping one-half of the key constant at red (dashed line) or one-half of the key constant at violet (dotted line). We further assume that when half the key is constant at red, only the red curve is effective; when half the key is constant at violet, only the violet curve is effective. However, when the key is held constant at another color, we might expect that both of these curves would be effective. The relative contribution of the two curves would depend upon how close on the wavelength continuum the constant color was to red and violet. If, for example, the constant

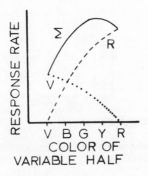

Fig. 17. Theoretical weighted generalization gradients over wavelength assumed to be obtained keeping 1/2 of the key constant at red (dashed line) and 1/2 of the key constant at violet (dotted line) and the summed gradient.

color were yellow, then the red curve might be dominant since yellow is closer to red than to violet. Figure 17 shows theoretical curves for red and violet with the red curve (dashed line) having a higher peak than the violet curve (dotted line). When the values of the two curves corresponding to each point on the abscissa are averaged, the resulting curve is that shown above those curves (solid line). This curve is seen to have a peak at yellow. Similarly, if we give the greatest weight to the violet curve, the peak could be made to occur at blue. Thus, by differentially weighting and averaging the two basic generalization gradients produced by discrimination training, one may predict peaks at new points on the wavelength continuum; e.g., matching behavior may be predicted on the basis of generalization over the simple physical continuum of wavelength.

Now we may reduce the possibility of such an explanation by using training with wavelengths on one end of the continuum and testing with wavelengths on the other end of the continuum. In the present experiment, the S+s were the matching combinations of bluegreen (501.3 nm) and green (538 nm) and the S−s were the nonmatching combinations of bluegreen and green. Generalization tests were subsequently conducted with the four combinations of red (605 nm) and yellow (576 nm). Figure 18 shows the results of these tests. Here again we see that three out of four subjects responded less in the nonmatching stimuli than in the matching stimuli. Since the probability of obtaining matching behavior in three out of four subjects is very low (see Experiment B-2), we can conclude that generalization of matching behavior may be obtained from bluegreen and green to yellow and red (Malott et al., 1968).

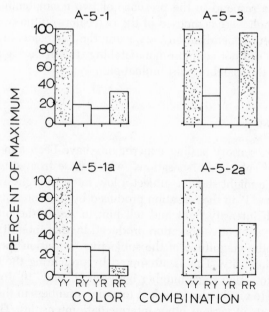

Fig. 18. Relative response rates for matching and non-matching combinations of red and yellow. One histogram is shown for each of four subjects.

Now the question is: Can generalization gradients like those shown in Figures 16 and 17 be used to explain generalization of matching from bluegreen and green to yellow and red? It can be shown that bluegreen and green constant gradients could be weighted and summed in the manner of Figure 17 to produce resultant gradients with peaks at yellow or red if: (1) the generalization gradient for bluegreen constant were higher at red than at yellow, and (2) the gradient for green constant were higher at yellow than at red. Though we do not yet have the relevant generalization data, it is unlikely that condition (1) will be met since yellow is physically closer to bluegreen than is red. It is more likely that both the bluegreen and green constant gradients are higher at yellow than at red, so that averaged gradients with peaks at yellow or red are unlikely. In any case, the present experiment has produced generalized matching behavior where the possibility of an explanation in terms of generalization over wavelength has been greatly reduced if not eliminated.

SUMMARY.   It was found that subjects trained to respond in the presence of one or two matching stimuli, with no discrimination training, did not exhibit matching behavior in subsequent generalization tests. Subjects trained to respond in the presence of four matching stimuli, without discrimination training, showed only slight evidence for matching behavior in subsequent generalization tests.

When subjects were trained to respond in the presence of two matching stimuli and not to respond in the presence of two nonmatching stimuli composed of the same colors, generalization of the matching discrimination was obtained to novel colors both within and outside the range of training colors.

Other subjects were trained to respond in the presence of four matching stimuli and not to respond in the presence of two nonmatching stimuli; the two nonmatching stimuli were composed of the two colors on the two ends of the continuum. Subsequent generalization tests, using the two colors in the middle of the continuum which did not compose nonmatching stimuli during training, revealed generalization of the matching discrimination.

SENSORY SCALING

Traditionally, sensory scaling experiments have been aimed at determining the magnitude of subjective "sensations" which arise from stimuli of known objective values. We might show a subject a low intensity light and instruct him to assign the number "1" to the sensation produced by that intensity. We would then show him a high intensity light and tell him to assign the number "10" to the magnitude of the subjective sensation produced by that intensity. Our goal would be to determine the magnitude of the subjective "sensation" produced by a light of intermediate intensity. This is attempted by presenting the intermediate light and asking him to assign some number between "1" and "10" to the magnitude of the "sensation." He would also be asked to assign numbers to the "sensations" produced by the lights of various other intermediate intensities. These results would then be summarized as a "sensory scale" like that shown in Figure 19. This will be

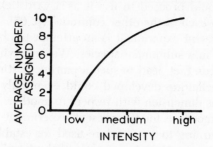

Fig. 19. Hypothetical results of a traditional magnitude estimation experiment. This represents a stimuli-response map.

called a stimulus-response map. (See Stevens and Galanter, 1957, for comparable examples.)

Since the days when sensory scaling experiments were first begun, we have learned that it is not too useful to talk in terms of "sensations." Nonetheless, the orderly data which result from such experiments raise some very interesting questions about stimulus control. What are the laws which describe the control exercised by the stimulus intensity over the subject's response?

In discussing the traditional sensory scaling experiment, we find ourselves not only dealing with a stimulus dimension but also with complicated response patterns such as saying the words "1" through "10." Graham and Ratoosh (1962) have pointed out that when doing psychophysical scaling with humans, the numerical assignments to stimulus values made by human subjects are generally treated as though they were the quantitative outcomes of a measuring operation. In reality, they are the qualitative outcomes of such an operation. If the outcome were quantitative, averaging the numbers assigned to a given stimulus would be permissible. However, since the outcome is qualitative, averaging cannot validly be done; rather the most frequent number assigned must be taken as the value attached to that particular stimulus.

In addition to these problems, it is difficult to determine what it "means" when a subject assigns a number to a stimulus. What is the nature of the subject's history which led to his assigning a particular number to a particular stimulus? It would seem that his history involved procedures such as requiring the subject to say "four" when four objects were present. If this is the case, then it may be that in the traditional sensory scaling experiment, the subject is, in essence, pairing at least two stimulus dimensions. One dimension is that presented by the experimenter, and the other is some dimension or dimensions associated, in the past, with his number responses; the response acts as a mediator for pairing the two stimulus dimensions.

Stevens et al. (1960) performed experiments in which the stimulus dimension associated with "force of hand-grip" was paired with various other stimulus intensity dimensions by human subjects. They state that, "Granted that squeezes can be matched to other sensations, the hand dynamometer provides a method for measuring sensory intensity in the sense of determining the *relative* form of the over-all operating characteristic of the sensory system," and "Furthermore, if we were willing to take any one of these sensory continua as a standard of reference, we could proceed to use it as a yardstick with which to measure sensory intensity on each of the other continua" (p. 65).

The present experiment is an attempt to obtain a similar pairing of stimulus dimensions in a subhuman species. We are trying to discover what training conditions will, in fact, lead to such a pairing of stimuli. If such a pairing is possible, then the technique developed could eventually lead to a comparable scaling of one stimulus dimension with respect to another.

The procedure for the present experiment may be more readily understood by first returning to a procedure used for establishing a matching discrimination in the previous section. An example of the training stimuli is shown in the top row of Figure 20. This is called conditional discrimination training, for whether or not one stimulus aspect (e.g., red on the left) is a part of an S+ is conditional upon the presence of another aspect of the stimulus (e.g., red on the right). It may also be called relational discrimination training because the reinforcement contingencies depend upon the relation between the two aspects of the stimulus. It was observed in the experiments on matching and nonmatching that the relational or matching discrimination generalized to novel colors.

The procedure in the present experiment is logically equivalent to that used to establish the previous matching and nonmatching discriminations. The difference is that the relevant stimulus aspects in this experiment are background color on the entire key and angle of a white line centered on the key. The bottom row of Figure 20 shows these training stimuli. The S+s were a red (605 nm) background with a superimposed vertical (90°) white line (red-90°) and a bluegreen (501.3 nm) background with a superimposed horizontal (0°) line (bluegreen-0°). The S−s were red-0° and bluegreen-90°. Given the matching and nonmatching stimuli in the top row of Figure 20, let the functions of red on the right be performed by a 90° white line centered on the key and violet on the right by a 0° white line. The color of the background will perform the function of the color on the left of the key with bluegreen substituted for violet. When this is done, red-

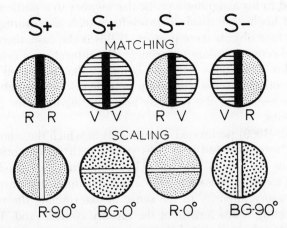

Fig. 20. Training stimuli for establishing a matching discrimination (top) and for establishing a relational discrimination for sensory scaling (bottom).

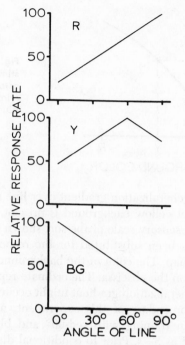

Fig. 21. Hypothetical relative generalization gradients over angle of line with the background constant at red (top), yellow (middle), and bluegreen (bottom), obtained after establishing a relational discrimination involving red, bluegreen, 0°, and 90°.

red is equivalent to red-90°, violet-violet is equivalent to bluegreen-0°, red-violet is equivalent to red-0°, and violet-red is equivalent to bluegreen-90°. The relational discrimination training involved with the two different sets of stimuli is logically the same.

If the formal equivalence is also a behavioral one, the results of the matching studies carry the implication that the relational discrimination established in the present experiment will also generalize to novel stimulus values. One might predict that generalization gradients similar to the theoretical gradients shown in Figure 21 would be obtained. When the background is held constant at red and the line angle is varied in a generalization test, one would expect to obtain a peak at 90° since red-90° was an S+ and red-0° an S− (top curve in Fig. 21). When the background is held constant at bluegreen and the line angle is varied, one would expect to obtain a peak at 0° since bluegreen-0° was an S+ and bluegreen-90° was an S− (bottom curve). When the background is held constant at a novel color, the peak of the generalization gradient over line angle might occur at a new value. The middle curve shows the gradient with a peak at the new line angle of 60° when the background is held constant at the new color of yellow (576 nm). This result would be equivalent to obtaining a peak at yellow when one-half of the key was held constant at yellow in the matching experiment.

On the basis of the above analysis, we have made the prediction that in the

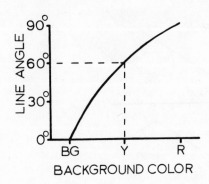

Fig. 22. Hypothetical stimulus-stimulus map obtained after establishing a relational discrimination involving red, bluegreen, 0°, and 90°.

present experiment, the generalization gradient over line angle will peak at a new line angle when the novel yellow background is present. The summary curve in Figure 22 is a theoretical sensory scale of the sort shown in Figure 19 except that a stimulus dimension has been substituted for the response dimension. We call this a stimulus-stimulus map. The color of the background held constant in a generalization test is shown on the abscissa. The ordinate represents the line angle at which the peak of the generalization gradient might occur.

To summarize the procedure of this experiment, nine pigeons were given conditional discrimination training with red-90° and bluegreen-0° as S+s and red-0° and bluegreen-90° as S−s. Prior to conditional discrimination training the subjects in groups a and c (C-3-1$_a$, C-3-2$_a$, C-3-3$_a$, C-3-1$_c$, C-3-2$_c$, and C-3-3$_c$) were trained to peck the key and received continuous reinforcement in the presence of a yellow key for four sessions. Group c was then placed directly on the conditional discrimination problem. Group a was first trained with the S+ of red-90°; then the S− of red-0° was added; next the S+ of bluegreen-0° was added; and finally the full conditional discrimination problem was in effect with the addition of the S− of bluegreen-90°. Prior to conditional discrimination training the subjects in group e (C-3-1$_e$, C-3-2$_e$, and C-3-3$_e$) were trained to peck the key and received continuous reinforcement in the presense of red-90° and bluegreen-0° for 3 days. Group e was then placed directly on the conditional discrimination problem. No houselight was present during the experiment.

After the conditional discrimination was established, all groups were tested for generalization over the angle of the line. The line angle was varied from 0° to 90° in 15° steps. The subjects in groups a and c were tested with the background constant at yellow. An example of one of the test stimuli is shown in Figure 23. Here a 45° line is superimposed on a yellow background. The test consisted of 14 blocks of 20-second stimulus presentations with each of seven line angles occurring once per block in random order. In the test for group e, both the red and bluegreen backgrounds were present. The test consisted of seven blocks of 20-second stimulus presentations with each of the 14 combinations of seven line angles and two colors occurring once per block in random order.

The results for the tests with the yellow background obtained with groups a and c are shown in Figure 24. The first row of generalization gradients are

Fig. 23. Test stimulus with yellow background and 45° line.

Y-45°

those obtained from the first four blocks of testing. The first column shows the gradients for group *a* and the second column the results for group *c*. Four of the six gradients have a peak at 60° (two in group *a* and two in group *c*), one at 45°, and one at 0°. The gradient with a peak at 0° has a secondary rise in the area of 45° to 60°. No consistent difference between the two groups appears to exist. Therefore the groups were combined and a median gradient was constructed. The median was first found for the absolute number of responses at each angle and then the percentage of maximum was calculated. The median gradient has a peak at 60° with the remaining points on the gradient near 50 percent.

The gradients for the last four blocks of testing are shown in the second row of Figure 24. Four of the gradients for individuals have peaks at 90°, one at 75°, and one is high and flat in the range from 0° to 45° with responding relatively low in the range from 60° to 90°. The median gradient has a peak at 90° with a secondary peak at 45°; the gradient is rather flat in the range from 45° to 60°.

These results indicate that at the beginning of testing with a yellow background, the peak of the gradient tends to be around the area of 60°. As testing continues, responding in the range from 45° to 60° still tends to be relatively high; however, the peak shifts toward a training value (in five out of six cases of 90°).

Figure 25 shows the red and bluegreen background generalization gradients for group *e*. The first row contains the gradients obtained with the red background in the first two blocks of the test. The first column shows the gradients for individual subjects and the second column the median gradient. All three of the gradients for individual subjects have peaks at 90°; the gradient for one subject is quite steep and those for the other two subjects are rather flat over the range from 60° to 90° with a secondary peak at 60°. The median gradient shows a monotonic decrease in percentage from 90° to 0°.

The second row in Figure 25 shows the gradients obtained with the bluegreen background in the first two blocks of the test. All individual gradients have a peak at 0° with no pronounced secondary peaks except possibly at 75°. The median gradient appears to decrease rather linearly from 0° to 90° with only slight irregularities.

The data indicate, as would be expected, that the gradients for the red and bluegreen backgrounds peak at the respective S+ line angles. However, when the novel color, yellow, is introduced, the gradient over line angle, obtained early in testing, peaks at a new value around the area of 60° (Svinicki, 1968).

One might ask if the gradient obtained with yellow is the result of summing the two basic gradients obtained with the red and bluegreen backgrounds since

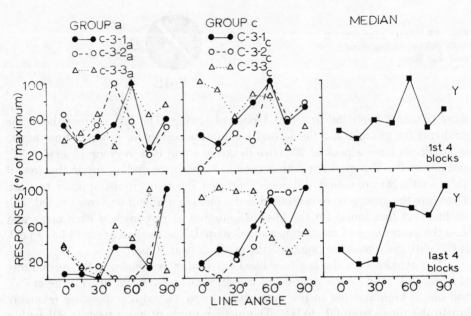

Fig. 24. Relative generalization gradients over angle of line obtained with a yellow background. The first column contains gradients for individual subjects in group a, the second column contains gradients for individual subjects in group b, and the third column contains median gradients. The first row contains gradients for the first four blocks of testing and the last row contains gradients for the last four blocks of testing. (After Svinicki, 1968.)

these were the training colors. To answer this, the curve in the third row of Figure 25 was obtained as follows: First, the median absolute numbers of responses at each line angle from the first two blocks of the test for the red and bluegreen backgrounds were summed; then the percentages were calculated. This summed gradient is rather flat across the continuum with a slight dip in the middle. If one of the basic gradients were given greater weight than the other gradient (e.g., by multiplying each absolute number of responses in the red gradient by two), it would still be impossible to obtain a summed gradient with a peak in the middle of the continuum. The implication is that the peak in the middle of the continuum obtained with the yellow background cannot be explained in terms of such a simple summation of the red and bluegreen gradients.

As indicated earlier, the fact that the generalization gradient over line angle showed a peak at a novel value for a novel background color leads to the possibility of constructing a sensory scale for wavelength. An empirical stimulus-stimulus map is shown in Figure 26. Wavelength appears on the abscissa and the line angle at which the peak of the median generalization gradient occurs is shown on the ordinate. It was found that the peak of the median generalization gradient occurred at 90° for the red background, at 0° for the bluegreen background, and at 60° for the yellow background (Svinicki, 1968).

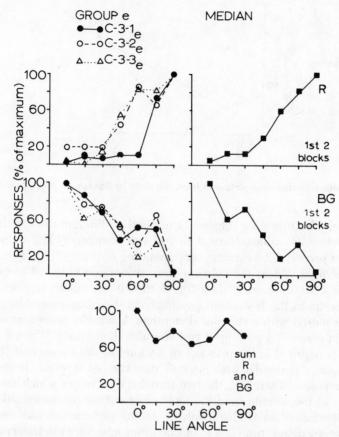

Fig. 25. Relative generalization gradients over angle of line obtained with a red (top) and a bluegreen (middle) background. Gradients for the individual subjects in group e are shown in the first column and the medians in the second column. The curve at the bottom is that obtained by averaging the median red and bluegreen gradients. (After Svinicki, 1968.)

One could compare this result with previous attempts to scale wavelength; however, we consider these data to be preliminary to the construction of sensory scales. This experiment is an attempt to specify what sensory scaling is and to devise a method for studying scaling in subhuman species. An actual attempt to scale wavelength, for example, should involve greater control over the stimulus dimensions (e.g., the brightness of the stimuli) and the gathering of more data points (e.g., testing with more background colors).

The increase in responding at intermediate line angles in the presence of an intermediate color (yellow) is in apparent conflict with some of the available data obtained with subhuman species; on the other hand, it seems to support other data. Svinicki (1968) has indicated why these discrepancies may exist. Three of

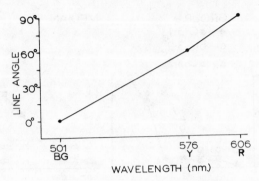

Fig. 26. Stimulus-stimulus map obtained from the data in Figures 24 and 25. (After Svinicki, 1968.)

the studies involved training subjects to respond at different rates in the presence of different stimulus values. Herrnstein and van Sommers (1962) trained pigeons to respond at several different rates corresponding respectively to several different intensities of light. When the subjects were subsequently tested in extinction at intermediate light intensities, they found that intermediate response rates occurred. Here, as in the traditional psychophysical scaling procedure, a response dimension is paired with a stimulus dimension. Again, the procedure would seem to involve, in essence, a pairing of two stimulus dimensions. When a specific response rate is required in the presence of a stimulus, this means that the response should occur at a particular time interval after the last response in order to produce reinforcement. Therefore, the two stimulus dimensions which are paired are the intensity of the stimulus and the interresponse time (or associated stimuli). A relational discrimination is also involved. In the presence of one intensity, one particular interresponse time is S+ and all other interresponse timers are S−s; in the presence of another intensity, another interresponse time is S+ and all other interresponse times are S−s.

Malott and Cumming (1965) obtained similar results when they tested in extinction with two S+s (each associated during training with the reinforcement of different interresponse times) and an intermediate test stimulus. Response rates were sometimes, although not always, intermediate for the intermediate stimulus, depending upon the values of the reinforced interresponse times.

In a study of Migler (1964), responses with no appreciable interresponse time were reinforced when one auditory click frequency was present and responses that were separated by 6 seconds or more were reinforced in the presence of another click frequency. Tests in extinction with intermediate stimulus values produced interresponse time distributions which had peaks at the training values; in no case was the peak at an intermediate value. This seems to conflict with the findings of Herrnstein and van Sommers and of Malott and Cumming. However, the results of the latter two experiments might have been due to the effects of averaging data from the generalization tests. Migler found that for intermediate click frequencies, the interresponse times which occurred most frequently were not intermediate but were either long or short or both. However, if median interresponse times were plotted for intermediate stimuli, these were found to be intermediate to the interresponse times that were reinforced in training. Therefore, any peak at intermediate interresponse times was an artifact of averaging data. Such a criticism cannot be made of the data obtained in the present study, but may explain the discrepancies obtained among the previous studies. It may be that *none* of the previous studies truly obtained peaks at intermediate stimulus values.

Cumming and Eckerman (1965) trained subjects to respond on one end of a linear series of keys in the presence of one intensity of light and at the other end of the series of keys in the presence of another intensity of light. Testing in extinction with intermediate intensities did not produce responding to keys at intermediate positions but instead to the training key positions. This is in agreement with the results of Migler.

The question of why the above results differ from those reported here still remains. The explanation would seem to lie in the training conditions. In the previous studies, the intermediate stimuli along one of the dimensions were necessarily presented during training. In Malott and Cumming's, in Migler's, and in Herrnstein and van Sommer's studies, intermediate times since the last response were present during training as were intermediate key positions in Cumming and Eckerman's study. These stimuli were S−s since responses were never reinforced in their presence. Consequently, it would be surprising if responding were obtained to these intermediate stimuli during testing.

In the present study, no intermediate wavelengths nor line angles were presented in training. Thus, no extinction occurred to these stimuli and a peak at an intermediate stimulus during testing is a plausible result.

Another approach to the problem of scaling is to be found in the bisection technique used by Boakes (1969) and by Honig and Shaw (1962). In Boakes' experiment, pigeons were trained to respond on a right key in the presence of a high intensity light and on a left key in the presence of a low intensity light. The subjective midpoint between the high and low intensity lights was found by withholding reinforcement and presenting intermediate intensity lights; the intensity at which the subject responded on 50 percent of the trials on the left key and 50 percent on the right key was taken as the midpoint. This experiment is quite similar to the experiment by Cumming and Eckerman (1965) discussed above; the main difference would seem to be that Cumming and Eckerman had a series of keys between the two training keys while Boakes used only two keys. In both cases, the two stimulus dimensions were intensity of light and position of the key; and in both cases, extinction to spots between the two keys could occur during training. Thus one would not expect responding to points between the keys during testing. Scaling for Boakes, however, did not depend on obtaining responding to intermediate spots between the two keys since his criterion measure was 50 percent responding to the two keys (Cumming and Eckerman could also have used such a measure).

It is interesting to note that Boakes' technique and ours involve logically identical training procedures. As in our experiment, Boakes' experiment establishes a relational discrimination: when the high intensity is present, the right key is S+ and the left is S−; when the low intensity is present, the left key is S+ and the right key is S−. One could obtain data similar to Boakes', using our procedures, by ignoring the data for angles between 0° and 90° and computing the percent of responding to the 0° and 90° angles in the presence of the yellow background. If other generalization tests had been conducted with new background colors, presumably the relative response rate to 0° and 90° would have shifted accordingly; some background color would have produced equal response rates in 0° and 90° and this would be taken as the midpoint. It is, of course, our assumption that this change in background color would also be accompanied by an appropriate shift in the peak of the generalization gradient over line angle obtained early in testing. We might expect that the following formula would predict the location of the peak from the relative rates at 0° and 90°: $Z = [(X \times 0°) + (Y \times 90°)]/(X + Y)$ where Z is the peak angle, X is the number of responses emitted to 0°, and Y is the number of responses emitted to 90°. When $X = Y$, the formula predicts that the peak of the gradient will be at 45°. Combining all of the subjects in groups a and c of the experiment we actually performed, the median number of responses to 90° in the entire generalization test with the yellow background was 90, and the median number of responses to 0° was 41. When these numbers are placed into the formula, we have $[(41 \times 0°) + (90 \times 90°)]/(41 + 90) = 62$. Since this is closer to 60° than any other test value and we, in fact, obtained a peak at 60° early in testing, the results provide some support for the theoretical analysis performed above.

Summary.   The relational discrimination training procedure of the present section was shown to be logically similar to the procedure for training a matching discrimination in the previous section. On the basis of this similarity, it was predicted and empirically demonstrated that generalization of the relational discrimination established in the present experiment does occur. This implies that the more general type of relational discrimination of the present experiment is behaviorally, as well as logically, related to the more restricted type of discrimination involved in stimulus matching.

Given the minimal training conditions for establishing a relational discrimination, early in generalization testing the subjects pair the stimulus dimensions involved such that the paired value of one dimension of the stimulus is a monotonic function of the value of the other dimension. (In other words, during generalization testing the peak of the generalization gradient over line angle occurs at 0° when the bluegreen background is present, at the new angle of 60° when a new yellow background is present, and at 90° when the red background is present.) Such a process allows us to construct a psychophysical scale of one dimension with respect to another. This may be, in essence, the process which occurs in traditional psychophysical scaling procedures using human subjects.

RELATIONSHIPS AMONG MUELLER-LYER ILLUSION, STIMULUS MATCHING, AND SENSORY SCALING

In order to emphasize the relations among the three research problems studied, it may be useful to point out that all of the types of experiments reported may be considered to be variations on the scaling experiment. Figure 27 shows hypothetical stimulus-stimulus maps which may be constructed from experiments in the three areas. The top function shows the hypothetical scale obtained from the scaling experiment just discussed.

The middle curve shows the stimulus-stimulus map which could be obtained from a matching experiment in which perfect matching was obtained. The abscissa represents the color of a section held constant in a generalization test and the

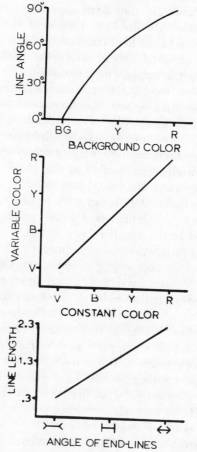

Fig. 27. Hypothetical stimulus-stimulus maps constructed from experiments on Mueller-Lyer illusion, stimulus matching, and sensory scaling.

ordinate represents the color at which the peak of the generalization gradient occurs during the test. It is true that the matching experiment seems different from the scaling experiment in the sense that in the matching experiment, we "know when to reinforce" responding to novel stimulus values, because we know when the stimulus aspects match. We don't know this for the scaling experiment. However, in another more important sense, we do not know when to reinforce responding in the matching experiment; we are interested in observing where the peak of the generalization gradient will occur without reinforcing responding in the presence of novel matching stimuli. If the general procedure used does, indeed, approach the problem of scaling, then we would expect that the generalization tests for the matching experiments would produce matching behavior and produce a function like the middle curve of Figure 27. Wavelength steps in one half of the stimulus would be expected to be subjectively equal to physically equal steps in wavelength on the other half of the stimulus.

The bottom curve shows a stimulus-stimulus map which might be obtained from an experiment on the Mueller-Lyer illusion if the illusion were demonstrated. The angle of the end lines held constant in a test appears on the abscissa and the length of the horizontal line at which the peak of the generalization gradient occurs during the test appears on the ordinate.

The training procedure, used in the experiments on the Mueller-Lyer illusion, involved no discrimination training over the dimensions varied during generalization testing. In that sense, it was similar to the procedure used in Experiment B-1 of the matching section, where responses were reinforced in the presence of one matching stimulus and no discrimination training was given. If this nondiscrimination procedure should produce an illusion in the Mueller-Lyer experiment, but not in the matching experiment, one would conclude that either the subjects came to the experiments with different histories with regard to the respective dimensions involved or that basic differences exist in the interactions of the dimensions.

The procedure used in the Mueller-Lyer illusion experiments differed from the procedure employed in most of the experiments on matching and scaling. In the majority of the matching and scaling experiments, a relational discrimination was established; in the Mueller-Lyer illusion experiments, responding was simply reinforced in the presence of one stimulus. It is interesting to speculate that without relational discrimination training, the Mueller-Lyer illusion may not be obtained if factors such as differential responding to area or to the distance between the butts of the end lines, are prevented from influencing the data. It may be that the Mueller-Lyer illusion, as it is usually considered, does not really exist. In that event, one might produce Mueller-Lyer illusion-like data by giving relational discrimination training similar to that used in the matching and scaling experiments. One could, for example, reinforce responding in the presence of a long line with outward pointing arrowheads and a short line with inward pointing arrowheads, and extinguish responding in the presence of the opposite combinations (with additional procedures to eliminate differential responding to area and distance between the butts of the end lines). The behavior thus generated should demonstrate the Mueller-Lyer illusion. Such stimulus and reinforcement conditions in the everyday environment may be what produces the illusional behavior in humans. The results of the scaling experiment, of course, have implications for this hypothetical Mueller-Lyer illusion experiment; testing over horizontal line length with vertical end lines should produce a peak in the generalization gradient at an intermediate value, as illustrated in the bottom stimulus-stimulus map of Figure 27.

OTHER PERCEPTION EXPERIMENTS

Scott and Milligan in Chapter 16 have successfully dealt with the spiral motion aftereffect illusion in the monkey. In their work, subjects were trained to press a right key in the presence of an expanding circle and a left key in the presence of a contracting circle. They obtained a function relating percent of left responses to rate of contraction (negative values) and expansion (positive values) when the subject was previously exposed to a stationary spiral. When the spiral was rotated in one direction, the function relating percent left responses to rate of contraction or expansion was shifted in one direction; when the spiral was rotated in the other direction the reverse occurred. This function is a type of generalization gradient for left responses; the gradient is shifted in one direction or the other, depending on the direction of rotation of the spiral. Instead of using peak of the gradient, as we do, they must use expansion or contraction rate which produces 50 percent responding to the left or right key as the point of subjective equality. This is necessitated by the use of two keys instead of one. As indicated in the section on sensory scaling, the use of two keys involves the use of an added stimulus dimension, position of the key. Responding to the middle positions is always extinguished. Therefore one would expect no responding to the middle positions during testing; but in the absence of responding in the middle, the related measure may be percent responding to the two outer positions which were S+s during training. In Scott and Milligan's case, a third dimension was manipulated and the change in the stimulus value which produced 50 percent responding (the "midpoint") was observed. In the experiments of Boakes (1969) and of Cumming and Eckerman (1965) (discussed in the section on sensory scaling), only two stimulus dimensions were involved: key position and one other stimulus dimension; unlike Scott and Milligan's work, no third dimension was involved.

The use of our own technique in the study of the spiral motion aftereffect illusion would involve only one key and two stimulus dimensions. We might train the subject to respond when the circle is stationary and not to respond when the circle contracts or expands. Generalization tests over rate of contraction and expansion should produce gradients with peaks shifted to one side of a zero rate of change in circle size after exposure to a spiral rotating in one direction and to the other side following the reverse condition.

Both Scott's study and our hypothetical study involve multidimensional stimulus generalization. Both involve the use of extinction when the point of subjective equality is being determined (in Scott and Milligan's case extinction was used near the values where the point of objective equality was located in order to avoid influencing the location of the point of subjective equality). In both Scott and

Milligan's and our study, we may plot a stimulus-stimulus map with spiral rotation on the abscissa. In the former case the rate of circle contraction or expansion which produced 50 percent responding on the training keys would appear on the ordinate; in our case the rate of circle contraction or expansion at which the peak of the generalization gradient occurred would appear on the ordinate.

Stebbins (1966) has taken another approach to a perceptual problem by obtaining equal loudness contours using a technique involving the measurement of latency of response as a function of variations in stimulus values over two continua: intensity and frequency. Moody (Chapter 13) reports the use of the latency technique in producing equal brightness contours. In Moody's experiments, short latency bar releases are reinforced upon the presentation of lights of various wavelengths and intensities. When no light is present the bar release is not reinforced. In spite of the fact that reinforcement occurs in the presence of all intensities of the stimulus, the latency of response varies over the functional range of the intensity continuum; there is a built-in gradient of responding over intensity with latency decreasing as a function of increases in intensity. The location of the latency gradient shifts as a function of changes in the wavelength of the light. Consequently, Moody is able to plot what we term a stimulus-stimulus map: wavelength appears on the abscissa and the intensity which produces a particular latency of response appears on the ordinate. He plots a group of stimulus-stimulus maps corresponding to different latencies; since it is assumed that latency does not vary as a function of wavelength, these functions are considered to be equal brightness contours.

We stated earlier that finding points of subjective equality is probably best done in extinction because reinforcement in the presence of all stimuli would be likely to eliminate differential responding. The latency technique used by Moody seems to be an exception to this rule, since latency varies as a function of intensity regardless of the fact that reinforcement is received in the presence of all intensities. The crucial fact, however, is that *differential* reinforcement, which would influence the points of subjective equality, is not given over intensity. In any case, it would seem that the latency technique is limited to experiments which involve the magnitude of a stimulus. We do not see, for example, how the latency technique could be applied to the dimensions of line angle and wavelength used in our section on scaling.

Our approach to the problem of obtaining equal brightness contours might be to train subjects to respond in the presence of a light of some particular wavelength and intensity. Generalization tests in extinction would be conducted over intensity. Different wavelengths would be used in various generalization tests. Shifts in the intensity at which the peak of the generalization gradient occurred as a function of wavelength would be observed. A stimulus-stimulus map (or equal brightness contour) would be plotted with wavelength on the abscissa and intensity at which the peak of the gradient occurred on the ordinate. We have, in fact, obtained pilot data on the use of this approach in obtaining equal loudness functions.

Thomas and Lyons (1966) used an approach, which is essentially the same as ours, in the investigation of an illusion. They trained pigeons to respond in the presence of a vertical white line projected on a pigeon pecking key. During training, the floor of the chamber was horizontal. Generalization tests over angle of the white line were conducted in extinction. The generalization gradients had peaks shifted to one side of the training angle when the floor was tilted in one direction; the gradients had peaks shifted to the other side of the training angle when the floor was tilted in the other directions.

INSTRUMENTATION

Most of our instrumentation is that frequently found in behavior analysis laboratories. Subjects are trained and tested in Lehigh Valley Electronics pigeon test chambers (#1519c). Only one response key is operative. Visual stimuli are projected behind the transparent key onto a translucent screen via Industrial Electronic Engineers, Inc. in-line read-out units. These are very convenient and readily programmed units into which a wide variety of commercially available gelatin, wavelength, neutral density, and pattern filters may be inserted.

We use BRS solid state digital logic for the automatic programming of our experiments. Cumulative recorders and electromechanical counters are used to record time, responses, and reinforcements.

SUMMARY

SOURCES OF ERROR

One problem with the use of the in-line read-out display is that of uncontrolled stimulus variability (e.g., the brightness of various stimuli). The importance of such variability depends on the nature of the particular experiment. Much of our research has been concerned with locating the peaks of generalization gradients and not with the specific shape of the gradients, so that precise stimulus specification is not always critical. The experiments in which this presents more of a problem are those on stimulus matching in which generalization to novel colors was obtained. During training, the subjects may have learned to match the brightness of the stimuli, rather than the color, as we presumed. If this were the case and if the novel colors used in the generalization tests matched the brightnesses of the training colors, then relevant novel stimuli were not, in fact, presented. In spite of the fact that it seems unlikely that the test stimuli were the same brightnesses as the training stimuli (they did not appear to be so to human observers), this remains a possibility. If the test stimuli were not the same brightness, then in any case generalization of matching to novel stimulus values was obtained, either to novel colors or to novel intensities.

One might consider the effects of amount of training as a possible source of error in our experiments. However, only under certain conditions of discrimination training would the location of peaks of generalization gradients be expected to be affected by the amount of training (Terrace, 1966); none of the discrimination training procedures used in our experiments would be expected to produce such changes in peak location. We are confident, therefore, that such a factor is not of importance for our purposes.

In general, our experiments should be considered as studies of a method and system; they are an attempt to determine if the approach is feasible in the study of the research problems described above. We are not, at this point, attempting precise quantitative analyses, but feel that we may now be in a better position to do so.

CRITERIA FOR RELIABLE GRADIENTS

Our experience with generalization gradients has led us to adopt the rough rule of thumb that gradients with less than 50 responses at the peak tend to be unreliable, whereas those with more than 50 responses tend to be reliable. While there are always exceptions, it has generally been found to be an acceptable criterion.

POTENTIAL APPLICATION TO OTHER AREAS

It is felt that some areas which have been primarily studied in terms of response differentiation and induction might be more fruitfully analyzed in terms of stimulus discrimination and generalization within the framework presented here and elsewhere (Malott, 1969). One example would be imitation. Imitation may be considered to be simply a stimulus matching problem where the two stimulus continua to be matched are typically the stimuli rising from the behavior of a model and those rising from the behavior of an imitator. An intermediate problem between a typical generalized imitation study and generalized matching studies, such as we have presented, would be one in which the subject responds positively when the behavior of one model matches the behavior of another model, thus eliminating the complex problem of response differentiation.

Language behavior might be similarly analyzed. Vocabulary acquisition can be studied in terms of symbolic matching where a symbol is arbitrarily matched with a particular picture. The exciting question of linguistic productivity may then be studied in terms of generalization of syntax, where a syntax or grammar is taught using one set of vocabulary items and then tested via a generalization procedure with a new set of vocabulary items. Such a procedure could, again, completely bypass the usual difficulties involved in response differentiation.

Needless to say, this approach may also be applied to essentially all of the classical illusions, though in some cases a fair amount of ingenuity is needed. One of the major problems in applying this to certain areas, such as the phi-phenomenon, is that the relevant stimulus parameters affecting the phenomenon have not been adequately specified and much basic work needs to be done to determine the relevant dimensions along which stimulus generalization tests should be conducted.

REFERENCES

Boakes, R. A. 1969. The bisection of a brightness interval by pigeons. J. Exp. Anal. Behav., 12:201–209.

Carter, D. J., and R. H. Pollack. 1968. The great illusion controversy: a glimpse. Percept. Motor Skills, 27:705–706.

Cumming, W. W., and D. A. Eckerman. 1965. Stimulus control of a differentiated operant. Psychon. Sci., 3:313–314.

Erlebacher, A., and R. Sekuler. 1969. An explanation of the Mueller-Lyer illusion: the confusion theory examined. J. Exp. Psychol., 80:462–467.

Farmer, J. 1963. Properties of behavior under random interval reinforcement schedules. J. Exp. Anal. Behav., 6:607–612.

Ferster, C. B. 1953. The use of the free operant in the analysis of behavior. Psychol. Bull., 50:263–274.

Galanter, E. 1962. Contemporary psychophysics. *In* Brown, R. Galanter, E., Hess, E. H., and Mandler, G., eds. New Directions in Psychology, New York, Holt, Rinehart, & Winston, Inc., vol. 1, pp. 87–156.

Goldiamond, I. 1962. Perception. *In* Bachrach, A. J., ed. Experimental Foundations of Clinical Psychology, New York, Basic Books, Inc., pp. 280–340.

Graham, C. 1958. Sensation and perception in an objective psychology. Psychol. Rev., 65:65–76.

———— and P. Ratoosh. 1962. Notes on some interrelations of sensory psychology, perception and behavior. *In* Koch, S., ed. Psychology: A Study of a Science, New York, McGraw-Hill Book Company, vol. 4, pp. 483–514.

Guttman, N., and H. I. Kalish. 1956. Discriminability and stimulus generalization. J. Exp. Psychol., 51:79–88.

Herrnstein, R. J., and P. van Sommers. 1962. Method for sensory scaling with animals. Science, 135:40–41.

Honig, W. K., and J. Shaw. 1962. The bisection of spectral intervals by pigeons: a first attempt. Paper read at meetings of the Eastern Psychological Association, Atlantic City, N.J.

Malott, R. W. 1969. Perception revisited. Percept. Motor Skills, 28:683–693.

———— and W. W. Cumming. 1965. A note on multiple schedules of IRT reinforcement. Psychon. Sci., 2:259–260.

———— M. K. Malott, and J. Pokrzywinski. 1967a. The effects of outward-pointing arrowheads on the Mueller-Lyer illusion in pigeons. Psychon. Sci., 9:55–56.

———— M. K. Malott, and J. G. Svinicki. 1967b. Generalization of stimulus matching without the use of non-matching stimuli. Psychon. Sci., 9:21–22.

———— M. K. Malott, and J. G. Svinicki. 1968. Generalization of stimulus matching outside the range of training stimuli. Paper read at meetings of the Psychonomic Society, St. Louis.

Migler, B. 1964. Effects of averaging data during stimulus generalization. J. Exp. Anal. Behav., 7:303–307.

Snow, M. E., and C. N. Uhl. 1969. Effects of time out and S+ postponement training procedures on free operant discrimination acquisition. Psychon. Sci., 14:218.

Stebbins, W. C. 1966. Auditory reaction time and the derivation of equal loudness contours for the monkey. J. Exp. Anal. Behav., 9:135–142.

Stevens, J. C., J. D. Mack, and S. S. Stevens. 1960. Growth of sensation on seven continua as measured by force of handgrip. J. Exp. Psychol., 59:60–67.

Stevens, S. S., and E. H. Galanter. 1957. Ratio scales and category scales for a dozen perceptual continua. J. Exp. Psychol., 54:377–409.

Svinicki, J. G. 1968. Generalization of a relational discrimination. Unpublished master's thesis, Western Michigan University.

Terrace, H. S. 1966. Stimulus control. In Honig, W. K. ed. Operant Behavior: Areas of Research and Application, New York, Appleton-Century-Crofts, pp. 271–344.

Thomas, D. R., and J. Lyons. 1966. The interaction between sensory and tonic factors in the perception of the vertical in pigeons. Percept. Psychophys., 1:93–95.

JOHN A. NEVIN [1]

18

ON DIFFERENTIAL STIMULATION
AND DIFFERENTIAL REINFORCEMENT * †

INTRODUCTION

Animal psychophysics occupies a special systematic position in psychology. On the one hand, it is obviously a close relative of psychophysical work with humans. Asymptotic performances are studied under precisely reproducible stimulus conditions, and interest centers on responding as a function of carefully specified parameters of stimulation. On the other hand, animal psychophysics must of necessity use information obtained in studies of animal discrimination learning and performance in order to establish and maintain behavior which is sensitive to stimulus variables. Much of the research in animal discrimination learning has been concerned with the effects of conditioning history and reinforcement variables on the acquisition of stimulus control over responding (e.g., Terrace, 1966). Asymptotic discrimination performance has also been studied as a function of the conditions of reinforcement (e.g., Nevin, 1967). Research in this area usually employs stimuli which differ grossly, and are specified in the experimenter's everyday language (e.g., red, green) rather than in the language of physics. It is widely assumed that the general character of the obtained relations is independent of the selection of particular stimuli.

Because animal psychophysics concerns itself explicitly with both stimulus and reinforcement variables, it may provide a link between the traditionally disparate areas of animal discrimination learning and human psychophysics. Although occasional efforts have been made at a unified conceptual framework (e.g., Bush et al., 1964), there is a distinct shortage of data on the interaction in animals of stimulus and reinforcement variables. Animal psychophysicists are concerned with careful selection and programming of differential reinforcement contingencies in the presence of different stimuli (as demonstrated by all chapters of this volume), but the conditions of reinforcement are rarely subjected to analysis once

[1] PSYCHOLOGY DEPARTMENT, COLUMBIA UNIVERSITY, NEW YORK, NEW YORK.

* The work reported in this chapter was supported in part by National Institute of Mental Health Grants 03673 to Columbia University, 08515 to Swarthmore College, and 16252 to Columbia University.

† I am indebted to Klaus Liebold, Suzanne Roth, Roberta Welte, and Gerald Zimmerman for their assistance in conducting experiments and analyzing the data.

satisfactory performance has been established. This chapter attempts to extend the domain of animal psychophysics by investigating the effects of differential reinforcement on responding in a psychophysical experiment.

The notion that psychophysical responding may depend on its consequences is certainly not new. Modern psychophysical research with human subjects routinely arranges explicit feedback, usually in the form of monetary payoffs and costs, for correct detections and false reports of a signal. Variation in these consequences, with signal strength constant, generates orderly functions relating the probability of correct detections to the probability of false reports. These functions, known as receiver-operating-characteristic or isosensitivity curves, may be characterized by a theoretical parameter which remains invariant as long as signal strength is fixed. In the theory of signal detection (Green and Swets, 1966), this parameter is known as d'. It is identified with the distance, in standard deviation units, between the means of two hypothesized normal distributions representing the internal effects of the signal and the background noise (external or internal) on which the signal is superimposed. The separation between distributions is assumed to depend on the ratio of signal plus noise to noise alone. The subject is presumed to report a signal when either signal plus noise, or noise alone, gives rise to an internal effect which exceeds a response criterion. The consequences of responding are presumed to affect the criterion, and therefore the probabilities of correct detections and false reports, without altering the separation between distributions.

It is important to understand that within this model the detectability parameter is not estimated directly by the probability of correct detections alone. Rather, it is necessary to measure both correct detections and false reports in order to derive a measure of differential responding to the signal. Because the model provides for an explicit separation of stimulus and reinforcement variables in a psychophysical experiment, it was adopted as a general frame of reference for the work reported here.

In human psychophysics, three standard techniques for generating isosensitivity curves are manipulation of the payoffs and costs, variation in the a priori probability of the signal, and the use of rating response categories (Green and Swets, 1966). Analogous methods have been used with animals. Hack (1963) has obtained detectability data with rats by varying the a priori probability of an auditory signal, and Blough (1967) has described a method analogous to ratings for transforming the response rates of pigeons to construct isosensitivity curves for wavelength difference. My own initial attempt in this area (Nevin, 1964) involved variations in reinforcement probability, with signal probability constant.

The subject was a single rat, with extensive experience in luminance discrimination procedures. It was trained to press one lever in order to produce a brief increment in the illumination of the chamber. In the presence of this signal, the rat could obtain water reinforcement by pressing a second lever. Signals were presented with probability 0.5 after an average of four consecutive responses on the first lever, given that at least 20 seconds had elapsed since the last trial. Signals terminated with the first response on the second lever, or after 2 seconds if no response occurred. If responding on the first lever met the schedule requirement but did not produce a signal, a "catch trial" was defined, and a response on the second lever within 2 seconds was scored as a false report. These catch trials are functionally equivalent to noise-alone trials in a signal detection experiment. They serve to assess the probability of pressing the second lever under conditions which are identical in all respects to signal trials, except for the absence of the signal itself. Second-lever presses occurring at other times reset the response requirement on the first lever to prevent the subject from obtaining reinforcement for simple alternation between levers or other performances not indicative of stimulus control.

This procedure is quite similar to those employed by Dalland, Stebbins, and Gourevitch (Chapters 2, 3, and 4) in that it requires the subject to engage in some explicit behavior to produce a signal, and then to report the signal with a different response. Detection is indicated not merely by the occurrence of the reporting response, but also by the interruption of the signal-producing behavior. This feature of interrupting an ongoing behavior has been cited as an advantage of the conditioned suppression procedure (see Chapters 5, 6, and 7), and the advantage is no less apparent here. Presumably, failures to detect a signal would be demonstrated both by absence of the reporting response and by continuation of the signal-producing response. Signal-producing responses were not recorded in the present study; rather, the experiment concentrated on the probability of the reporting response in the presence and absence of the signal.

In order to produce variations in the probability of correct detections and false reports, the probability of reinforcement was varied systematically, taking on values of 1.00, 0.50, and 0.20 over the course of 30 daily sessions. The ratio of signal intensity to chamber illumination was fixed at 0.24. This value was chosen on the basis of extensive preliminary work as moderately difficult for the subject to detect.

The results are shown in Figure 1, which indicates that the probabilities of both correct detections and false reports decreased as the probability of reinforcement was reduced. Although the range of the data is limited, the points approximate the upper portion of a theoretical isosensitivity curve of the sort predicted by signal detection theory. Along with the findings of Hack (1963), Blough (1967), and others, these results justify the use of signal detection theory in the analysis of animal psychophysical performances.

There is one distinct advantage to thinking about psychophysics from this point of view. Several of the chapters have been concerned with the treatment of responding at "subthreshold" values of a stimulus (e.g., Dalland, Chapter 2). Because the stimulus is physically present, the response is correct and should be reinforced. However, if the stimulus is truly subthreshold, does this not in effect reinforce the subject for guessing? Alternatively, in the conditioned suppression case, if the subject fails to detect a stimulus, it will receive an "unwarranted" shock (see Smith, Chapter 6). Either of these kinds of consequences could increase the rate of false positives: excessive responding in the absence of a signal in the former case, or interruption of responding in the latter case. But if such effects do occur, their treatment within this signal detection theory framework is straightforward. In the theory of signal detection, the notion of threshold is absent, and the

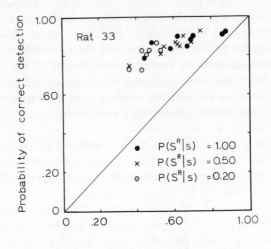

Fig. 1. Probability of responding with 2 sec of signal onset (correct detections) and probability of responding in the absence of signal (false reports) when probability of reinforcement for correct detections was varied. Each point represents the results of a single daily session of 300 to 400 trials.

subject does not guess. He is in a sense responding correctly whenever an observation exceeds his response criterion, even though the observation arises from noise alone. Using the signal detection model, one can attempt to partition the sources of control over responding into stimulus and reinforcement variables without attempting to partition positive responses into "true detections" and "guesses." As long as false reports are measured at least as accurately as correct detections, and are taken into account in estimating the detectability of the signal, the correlation of reinforcement with very weak signals raises no special problems.

Two experiments conceived within the general framework of signal detection theory are described here. Both employed the same general procedure. Stimulus-producing responses were followed by signals intermittently on interval schedules, and reporting responses sometimes produced food if they followed signals. Pigeons were chosen as subjects because of their long experimental life and because of the extensive information about their performances on various schedules of reinforcement.

The purpose of these studies was twofold. First, they were designed to provide information on methods for estimating the detectability of weak signals with animal subjects. The first experiment demonstrated that the detectability of a weak signal did not depend on the probability of reinforcement for detecting it, as long as the procedure included reinforcement for detecting a strong signal. Moreover, it showed that intersubject variability was minimized by arranging for reinforcement of every correct detection of the strong signal. These findings are essentially extensions of the rat data described earlier. The second experiment applied reinforcement schedules to develop a convenient method for obtaining isosensitivity functions from animal subjects.

A second aspect of these experiments is perhaps more relevant to a systematic analysis of behavior than to methods for studying particular animal sensory systems. The first experiment found that the difference in the detectability of two signals depended on the ratio of reinforcements obtained for detecting them, even though the signal intensities were constant. In the second experiment, the detectability of a signal was reduced by arranging for occasional reinforcement of false reports, in much the same way as by decreasing signal strength. These findings suggest that the separation of stimulus and reinforcement variables by signal detection theory may hold only for a limiting case.

EXPERIMENT 1

METHOD

SUBJECTS. Six male white Carneaux pigeons, with experience on a variety of luminance discrimination experiments, served as subjects. They were maintained at 80 percent of their free-feeding weights.

APPARATUS. The experiment was conducted in a two-key Lehigh Valley pigeon chamber. Translucent response keys, 1 inch in diameter, were located 6 inches apart on centers. A grain magazine was mounted centrally below the keys, and a dim houselight was located centrally above them. Continuous masking noise was provided by a small speaker.

The right key was continuously illuminated with white light provided by pilot lights behind a diffusing screen. Its usual luminance, S_0, was 1.50 mL. Increments in luminance (signals) could be presented by turning on additional lamps, each of which was provided with its own mask and diffusing screen to control its luminance. Two different signal intensities, S_1 and S_2, were selected on the basis of extensive pilot work. The luminance ratio S_1/S_0 was 0.20; for S_2/S_0 it was 0.75. The luminances were checked regularly throughout the experiment with a Macbeth illuminometer. The left key was continuously illuminated with a dim red light.

The experiment was programmed by standard relay equipment in a separate room. Data were recorded on counters, and response latencies were occasionally recorded with a Hewlett-Packard electronic counter and printer.

PROCEDURE. A 30-second cam timer ran continuously. The first peck on the white key, illuminated with S_0, in each 30-second cycle had one of three effects with equal probability: (1) S_1 was presented; (2) S_2 was presented; or (3) there was no change. These events were scheduled according to a quasi-random sequence with the restriction that they occurred equally often in blocks of 48 cycles. The sequence was changed several times in the course of the experiment. Only the first response in each cycle was effective; responding at other times had no programmed consequences.

If pecking the white key produced S_1 or S_2, the subject could receive food reinforcement for a single peck on the red key within 3 seconds. The white key returned to S_0 with the occurrence of the first peck on the red key, or after 3 sec-

TABLE 1

Sequence of Conditions in Experiment 1

CONDITION	$P(\text{RFT IN } S_1)$	$P(\text{RFT IN } S_2)$
1	0.5	0.5
2	1.0	0.5
3	0.0	0.5
4	0.5	0.5
5	0.5	1.0
6	0.5	0.0
7	0.5	0.5
8	0.5	S_2 not presented
9	S_1 not presented	0.5
10	0.5	0.5

onds if no peck occurred. In signal detection terminology, red key pecks within 3 seconds of onset of S_1 or S_2 were correct detections. If no signal occurred red key pecks were treated as false reports, since they occurred under conditions identical to those defining correct detections except that they did not follow a signal. The major dependent variables of the experiment were the probabilities of correct detections, S_1 or S_2, and the probability of false reports.

Premature pecks on the red key within the last 5 seconds of each 30-second cycle cancelled all contingencies for the next cycle, thus imposing at least a 30-second delay before the next possible presentation of reinforcement. This prevented the subjects from receiving reinforcement for performances such as simple alternation between the keys, and effectively ensured stimulus control by the signals.

The following features of the procedure should be noted. First, requiring pecking on the white key to produce S_1 or S_2 forced appropriate receptor orientation at the moment of onset of the critical stimuli. Second, random programming of an easy discrimination (S_2) and a difficult discrimination (S_1) provided for reinforcement of the entire sequence of behavior involving "looking for and reporting brightness changes," even if detecting S_1 was rarely reinforced.

Within this procedure, the probability of reinforcement for correct detections of S_1 or S_2 was varied systematically and the roles of S_1 and S_2 were assessed by eliminating one or the other from the procedure. Table 1 outlines the sequence of experimental conditions. Each condition remained in effect for 30 sessions. Each session lasted 75 minutes; the first 5 minutes were excluded from the analysis of the data. Sessions were run daily except for occasional interruptions of one or two days.

PRELIMINARY TRAINING.   Before the final procedure went into effect, the birds were trained to the terminal performance in a series of steps as follows. The pigeons had no experience with red keys. Therefore, they were first trained to peck the red key with food reinforcement for each peck. Next, the red key was turned off, the white key turned on, and production of the red key (and access to food reinforcement) was made contingent on pecking the white key. At first, every white key peck was effective, but after a few reinforcements, only the first peck in every 30 seconds turned on the red key. Finally, an easily detected signal was introduced, and reinforcement became available for responding on the red key only if the signal had occurred. As soon as there was evidence of control by the signal, the red key was turned on continuously. Because all subjects had been trained on luminance discriminations with intermittent reinforcement, it was possible to complete this phase of pretraining within a single session. If one were working with naive pigeons, a similar pretraining procedure might be followed, but it would probably take a number of sessions.

The next phase of pretraining involved variations in signal intensity. Over the course of some 40 sessions, the signal was made progressively weaker until performance deteriorated, and then made stronger until performance improved again. The values of S_1 and S_2 were chosen on the basis of information gathered during these sessions.

RESULTS

GENERAL CHARACTERISTICS OF PERFORMANCE. In general, all subjects performed appropriately on the procedure. After a correct detection, the birds would pause briefly, then begin to respond on the white key. Occasionally, they would stop to peck the red key once or twice, then resume pecking the white key. When a signal occurred, they usually pecked the red key within 3 seconds; red-key responses rarely occurred more than 3 seconds after a signal. If a signal was not detected, pecking simply continued on the white key at its usual rate. The average rate of responding on the white key differed considerably across subjects, but did not vary consistently with the experimental conditions.

DETECTION PERFORMANCE WITH EQUAL REINFORCEMENT PROBABILITY IN S_1 AND S_2. Minimally, a psychophysical procedure must provide repeatable measures of behavior which are sensitive to differential stimulation. Figure 2 shows the probability of a reporting response on the red key as a function of the stimulus change produced by the white key peck. All subjects except #18 exhibited high probabilities of detecting S_2, intermediate probabilities of detecting S_1 and low probabilities of false reporting in the presence of S_0 in Conditions 1, 4, and 7. Bird 18 apparently was not sensitive to the difference between S_1 and S_2 in these conditions.

Latencies of reporting given S_1 or S_2 were recorded for the last seven sessions on Condition 4. The conditional probability of response as a function of time from the onset of S_1 or S_2 was determined as follows. Latencies were pooled into 0.3-second class intervals, and the probability of response in each interval was computed by dividing the number of responses in that interval by the number of opportunities for responding in that interval. The number of opportunities to respond in an interval was determined by subtracting the number of responses in earlier intervals—which of course precluded an opportunity to respond later—from the number of times the stimulus was presented. The resulting conditional probability functions are given in Figure 3. For all subjects except #18, the conditional probability of responding to S_2 rose earlier and to higher levels than the probability of responding to S_1. This is consistent with the response probabilities shown in Figure 2.

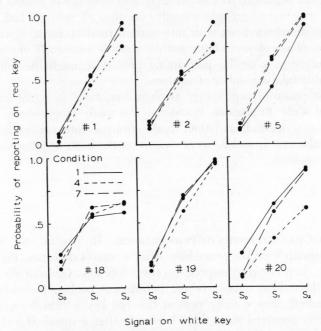

Fig. 2. Probability of responding within 3 sec of onset of signals S_1 and S_2, and in the absence of signal (S_0), when reinforcement was programmed with probability 0.5 in the presence of S_1 and S_2. Signals consisted of increments in illumination of a white key adjacent to the red, reporting key. S_1 and S_2 were increments of 0.20 and 0.75, respectively, relative to key illumination S_0. The data are taken from the final seven sessions of training on Condition 1, and from two subsequent replications.

It may be worth noting that S_1 lies very close to the conventionally defined difference threshold. The standard formula to correct for chance "guessing,"

$$P_c = \frac{P(S_1) - P(S_0)}{1.00 - P(S_0)}$$

was applied to these data, where P_c is the corrected response probability, $P(S_1)$ is the probability of detecting S_1, and $P(S_0)$ is the probability of false reporting in S_0. The resulting corrected probability of detecting S_1 ranged from 0.45 to 0.60 for the six birds, with a mean of 0.50 and a median of 0.50. Thus, the Weber fraction for pigeons in this luminance discrimination procedure, with $S_0 = 1.50$ mL, was 0.20. It is interesting to note that this is almost identical with the lowest values found by Mentzer (1966) using pigeons as subjects in various discrete trial procedures in which a dim spot was superimposed on a uniform field.

EFFECTS OF DIFFERENTIAL REINFORCEMENT FOR DETECTING S_1 AND S_2. When the probability of reinforcement for detecting S_1 or S_2 was changed, the probability of reporting those stimuli varied directly with the probability of reinforcement. There was no evidence of changes in the probability of reporting the

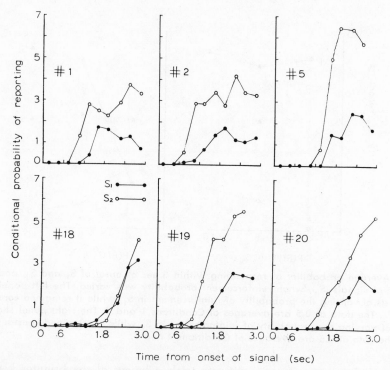

Fig. 3. Conditional probability of responding to S_1 and S_2 as functions of time from onset of signal. Data are pooled for the final seven sessions of training on Condition 4. Calculation of conditional probability is described in the text.

stimulus correlated with constant reinforcement probability. The effects averaged for all six subjects are shown in Figure 4, and are representative of all subjects. False reporting in S_0 covaried with responding in S_1 when the probability of reinforcement in S_1 was varied, but tended to vary inversely with responding in S_2 when the probability of reinforcement in S_2 was varied. There were wide individual differences in the latter relation. All subjects exhibited higher probabilities of false reporting in S_0 than detections of S_2 when reinforcement in S_2 was withheld.

The covariation in correct detections of S_1 and false reports in the presence of S_0, during Conditions 1 through 4, is shown for each subject in Figure 5. The average values across subjects for the data shown in Figure 5 are plotted in Figure 6, together with a theoretical isosensitivity curve with a detectability index $d' = 1.15$. This value was chosen by averaging the data of the final sessions on Conditions 1 and 4. The results are well approximated by the theoretical curve. This suggests that the detectability of S_1 is independent of the probability of reinforcement in S_1, and that detectability remains constant during extinction.

A similar result has been reported by Nevin (1967) for performance on a difficult simultaneous discrimination. Pigeons were presented with different intensities

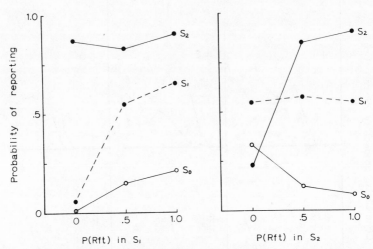

Fig. 4. Average probability of responding within 3 sec of onset of S_1 and S_2, and in the absence of signals (S_0), when reinforcement probability was varied. The left panel shows the effects of varying the probability of reinforcement in S_1, while it remained constant at 0.5 in S_2. The data at 0.5 are averages of Conditions 1 and 4. The right panel shows the effects of varying the probability of reinforcement in S_2 while it remained constant at 0.5 in S_1. The data at 0.5 are averages of Conditions 4 and 7.

of white light on two keys in discrete trials. Choices of the brighter key were reinforced with various probabilities. The accuracy of choice did not depend systematically on reinforcement probability, and accuracy remained constant while the overall probability of responding decreased during extinction.

The orderly covariation of responding to S_1 and S_0 was disrupted during Conditions 5 and 6, when probability of reinforcement for detections of S_2 was varied. For four of the six birds, false report rates decreased when the probability of reinforcement for detections of S_2 increased to 1.0, and increased markedly when detections of S_2 were never reinforced. There was no systematic effect on correct detections of S_1. As a result, the detectability of S_1 was altered for these subjects by the probability of reinforcement in S_2. To show this, the detectability index d' was estimated for S_1 from the probabilities of correct detections and false reports during the final seven sessions in each condition. The results are displayed in Figure 7. For all birds except #1 and #18, the detectability of S_1 was directly related to the probability of reinforcement in S_2. Perhaps more striking is the effect on intersubject variability, which was inversely related to the probability of reinforcement in S_2.

Now consider the effects of differential reinforcement in S_1 and S_2 on the difference in detectability of those signals. The analysis may be understood by reference to the hypothetical distributions presumed to correspond to these stimuli, and to S_0, sketched in Figure 8. The distributions and response criteria are

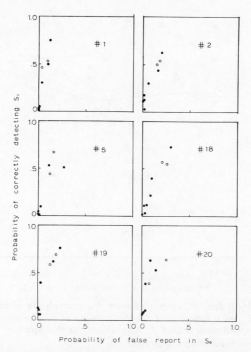

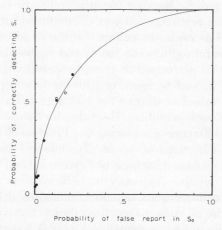

Fig. 5. The covariation of correct detections of S_1 and false reports in S_0 when the probability of reinforcement for correct detections was varied. The unfilled circles represent performance during the final seven sessions of Conditions 1 and 4, when reinforcement probability was 0.5. The filled circles represent performance during the final seven sessions of Condition 2 (reinforcement probability 1.0), five successive blocks of six sessions during Condition 3 (extinction), and the first six sessions of reconditioning on Condition 4.

Fig. 6. Averages of the data of Figure 5, together with an isosensitivity curve based on the assumptions of the theory of signal detectability, with $d' = 1.15$.

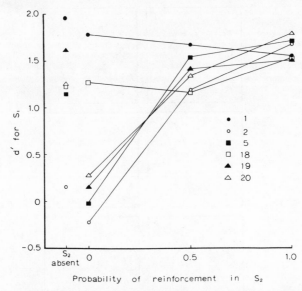

Fig. 7. The detectability index, **d'**, estimated from the probability of correct detections of S_1 and false reports in S_0, as a function of the probability of reinforcement in S_2. The data at 0.5 are averages of Conditions 4 and 7. Also shown at the left are the results for Condition 8, when S_2 was omitted from the procedure.

located to correspond to the average response probabilities for Conditions 1, 2, and 3. In order to account for the data, it is necessary to assume that increasing the probability of reinforcement for correct detections of S_1 in Condition 2 not only shifted the response criterion down, leading to higher probabilities of response to S_0 and S_1, but also decreased the separation between distributions corresponding to S_1 and S_2, because the probability of detecting S_2 remained roughly constant. When reinforcement was discontinued for correct detections of S_1 in Condition 3, it is necessary to assume that the response criterion shifted upward and that the separation between the S_1 and S_2 distributions increased. The same sort of analysis was performed on Conditions 4 through 7. The probabilities of correctly detecting S_1 and S_2, together with the false report probability, were used to estimate two values of d'—one for each signal—for each bird during the final seven sessions of each condition. The value for S_1 was then subtracted from the value for S_2. The difference was plotted as a function of the relative frequency of reinforcement for detections of S_2. In Conditions 3 and 6, the relative frequencies of reinforcement for detections of S_2 were 1.0 and 0, respectively. In the other conditions, the relative frequency of reinforcement in S_2 was calculated from the number of reinforcements actually obtained by detections of S_2, relative to the total obtained by all correct detections during those sessions.

Examination of the results, presented in Figure 9, suggests a systematic effect on the difference in detectability of S_2 and S_1 when relative frequency of rein-

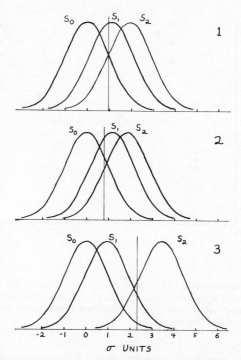

Fig. 8. Schematic representation of Conditions 1, 2, and 3, using unit normal distributions to represent the effects of signals S_1 and S_2, and their absence S_0. The locations of the S_1 and S_2 distributions and the response criterion have been adjusted to accord with average data for these conditions.

forcement varied. For every subject, the difference in detectability was greatest when only S_2 detections were reinforced, and least when only S_1 detections were reinforced. For all birds except #18, there was a positive relation between the difference in detectability and the relative frequency of reinforcement in the intermediate conditions. When the relative frequency of reinforcement was about 0.5, the difference was clearly above zero, demonstrating that the more intense signal was in fact more detectable when reinforcement frequency was equated.

EFFECTS OF REMOVING S_1 OR S_2. When S_2 was eliminated in Condition 8, one subject was clearly less accurate in detecting S_1 than in Condition 7, when S_2 was present and reinforcement available for detecting it. The other five birds performed about as well. These data are displayed at the left in Figure 7. When S_1 was eliminated in Condition 9, the probability of responding to S_2 remained about the same as in Condition 7 but false reporting in S_0 fell to near zero. This suggests that false report rates depended on reinforcement for detecting S_1: when that reinforcement was eliminated, or when S_1 itself was eliminated, there was virtually no false reporting.

The final replication with equal reinforcement in S_1 and S_2 (Condition 10)

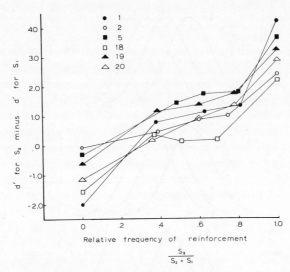

Fig. 9. The difference in detectability of S_1 and S_2 as a function of the relative frequency of reinforcement for detecting S_2. Conditions 1 through 7 each contributed one point, except that Conditions 1, 4, and 7 were averaged to obtain a single point for these identical conditions. See text for calculation of measures.

resulted in generally improved performances. False report rates were slightly lower, and detections of S_1 and S_2 slightly more probable than in Conditions 1, 4, and 7. It cannot be determined whether this improvement should be ascribed to the immediately preceding training with S_2 alone, or to additional exposure to the experimental situation.

To summarize: Experiment 1 indicated that detection performance in this situation was sensitive to signal intensity; that the detectability of a weak signal remained invariant when the probability of reinforcement for detecting it varied; that the variance across subjects in detectability of a weak signal was minimal when a strong signal was presented and reinforcement was given regularly for detections of the strong signal; and that the difference in detectability of the strong and weak signals depended on the relative frequency of reinforcement obtained for correctly detecting them.

Several objections may be raised against the analysis which led to the latter result. The first is at a theoretical level. The theory of signal detectability has been notably successful in isolating a measure of sensory sensitivity which is invariant with respect to nonstimulus variables, but it has been confined to the case of a single signal intensity. It is entirely possible that alternative applications of the theory, employing several values of the response criterion in experimental conditions involving two signals, would preserve the invariance of d'. To avoid further uncertainties in application of the theory, Experiment 2 used only one signal intensity in a given condition.

A second objection is at the level of measurement. Although the probabilities of correct detections and false reports in a single condition suffice to determine a value of d', it is more common to estimate d' from a complete isosensitivity curve (Green and Swets, 1966). To improve on estimates of d', and to minimize variance, Experiment 2 sought to work out a method for obtaining isosensitivity curves within a single condition.

The general procedure was to arrange a fixed interval between reinforcements for correct detections, during which signals were presented intermittently. Nevin (1967) found that the accuracy of choices in a difficult simultaneous discrimination remained invariant throughout a fixed period between reinforcement for correct choices, while the tendency to respond increased systematically as the interval elapsed. Therefore, fixed-interval reinforcement of detection should result in low reporting probabilities immediately after reinforcement, with increases as the next reinforcement approaches, but with no change in detectability of the signal. The covariation of correct detections and false reports within the interval should determine an isosensitivity curve.

EXPERIMENT 2

METHOD

Subjects.   After a year's inactivity, five of the six subjects in Experiment 1 were returned to 80 percent of their free-feeding weights and used in Experiment 2. Bird 5 died during the year between experiments.

Apparatus.   As in Experiment 1, except for changes in the luminance of the stimuli. S_0 was changed to 0.67 mL; the luminance ratio S_2/S_0 was 0.64, and S_1/S_0 was 0.32.

Procedure.   The sequence of events after each food reinforcement was as follows. The right-hand, white key was illuminated with S_0. The first peck at that key initiated a 5-second interval, and the first peck to occur at the end of that interval produced a 0.5-second signal with probability 0.5. Signals were scheduled by a probability generator; their duration was fixed to prevent the subject's latency from affecting exposure to the signal. A peck on the left-hand, red key within 3 seconds of signal onset was counted as a correct detection. If no signal was presented, and the bird pecked the red key within 3 seconds, the red-key peck counted as a false report. Whether or not a signal occurred and whether or not a red-key peck occurred, a new 5-second interval began, with identical contingencies at the end of the second interval. Five consecutive 5-second intervals of this sort were programmed. At the end of the fifth interval, the probability of a signal was 1.0, and correct detections always produced 3 seconds access to food reinforcement. If the bird failed to detect the signal, the fifth interval repeated until a detection occurred and food was obtained. For clarity, the term "cycle" will be used to designate the entire sequence of events between food reinforcements, and the term "interval" will refer to the individual 5-second periods composing the cycle.

In essence, this procedure superimposed a fixed-interval schedule of food reinforcement on the detection performance. During the first four 5-second intervals in the cycle, opportunities for correct detections and false reports were provided, but there was no contingency between reporting responses during these intervals and the eventual receipt of food. There was a contingency on stimulus-producing responses on the white key, however: the bird had to initiate the sequence of intervals with a key peck, and then had to peck once at the end of each 5-second interval in order to advance the sequence of intervals.

Anticipatory pecks on the red key—that is, pecks occurring within each interval—reset the 5-second interval timer. Red-key pecks after 5 seconds had no effect. Therefore, in the fifth interval, it was possible for the bird to pause 5 seconds, peck the red key, then peck the white key once, and then peck the red key again and obtain food. When it was discovered that some birds were doing this, resulting in marked increases in false report rates, it was arranged that *all* red-key pecks reset the interval timer, whenever they occurred. Under this arrangement, signals (and therefore reinforcements) could only occur 5 seconds after the beginning of an interval, or 5 seconds after a red-key peck.

The introduction of reinforcement for false reports was accomplished by scheduling the signal with some probability less than 1.0 at the end of the fifth interval, while reinforcement was always available at that time. Thus, the contingencies throughout the cycle were unchanged, and reinforcement still occurred only at the end of the cycle, but some reinforcements were obtained by reporting responses in the absence of signals. Initially, the probability of obtaining a signal at the end of the fifth interval was arranged by a probability generator which considered each such interval independently. If no signal occurred at the end of the fifth interval, and the bird did not report, the interval was repeated as before. If a signal then occurred, the bird could obtain reinforcement for a correct detection. The result of this procedure was that birds with low false report rates rarely made contact with the programmed reinforcement for responses in the absence of signals. This was remedied in the final experimental condition by scheduling signals at the end of the fifth interval with a randomly wired stepping switch which did not advance until reinforcement was obtained, ensuring that the subjects were exposed to the programmed relations between the absence of signals and reinforcement.

After brief retraining, the subjects were exposed to the signal intensities and reinforcement contingencies outlined in Table 2. Training on each condition lasted from 14 to 18 sessions, except Condition 10, which lasted only 8 sessions and served as a brief check on the recoverability of earlier performance. Sessions were conducted daily, except for occasional interruptions not exceeding two days, if the birds were within 15 g of their 80 percent weights. Sessions lasted about 75 minutes. Performance during the first eight cycles of each session was excluded from the data.

RESULTS

After a few training sessions, performance stabilized in the following pattern. After each food reinforcement, a period ranging from a few seconds up to about

TABLE 2
Sequence of Conditions in Experiment 2

CONDITION	SIGNAL	SIGNAL PROBABILITY IN FIFTH INTERVAL
1	S_2	1.0
2	S_1	1.0
3	S_2	1.0
4	S_2	0.9
5	S_2	0.7
6	S_2	0.5
7	S_2	1.0
8[a]	S_2	1.0
9	S_1	1.0
10	S_2	1.0
11	S_2	0.6

[a] The reset contingency described in the text was in effect in Condition 8 and all subsequent conditions.

one minute elapsed before initiation of pecking on the white key. Pecks at this key then continued at a roughly constant rate except for brief interruptions for pecks at the reporting key, while the tendency to switch and peck the reporting key increased as the subject progressed through the successive intervals of the cycle between reinforcements. The probability of reporting within 3 seconds of the signal at the end of the fifth interval was generally high, so that food was usually received after the completion of five intervals, as scheduled.

This sort of performance is in accord with the contingencies imposed by the procedure. The subject was required to respond on the white, stimulus-producing key in each interval in order to advance to the next interval. This is analogous to the contingencies of fixed-ratio schedules, in which eventual reinforcement is dependent on the occurrence of some prior number of responses. Schedules of this sort usually establish performances characterized by a pause after reinforcement, followed by a steady rate of responding until the next reinforcement is obtained. By contrast, the subject was not required to peck the red reporting key until the end of the fifth interval. This is analogous to a fixed-interval schedule, in which reinforcement is scheduled in time without regard for behavior during the interval. Fixed-interval schedules commonly result in a systematically increasing tendency to respond throughout the interval, even when the interval is interrupted by stimulus changes (Dews, 1962).

There was no systematic change in the average rate of responding on the white key throughout the various conditions of the experiment. However, behavior on the reporting key depended on the experimental conditions in effect.

To aid in understanding these data, the performance of Bird 1 will be considered in detail, and then summary data will be presented for all subjects. The probabilities of reporting given the presence or absence of signal at the end of each of the first four consecutive intervals of the cycle between reinforcements, and in the fifth interval, were calculated from data pooled for the final 10 sessions in each condition. As noted above, there was no contingency on reporting responses during the first four intervals, whereas a contingency existed during the fifth interval, which was repeated until reinforcement was obtained. Emphasis will therefore be placed on data from the first four intervals.

Figure 10 shows that the probability of reporting increased systematically within the sequence of intervals between reinforcements in all conditions. Reporting in the absence of a signal was always lower than in its presence. The reduction of signal intensity in Condition 2 resulted in flatter functions and higher false report rates than in Condition 1. In Condition 6, the signal intensity was the same as in Condition 1, but the bird obtained 40 percent of its reinforcements for reporting in the absence of a signal. The effects of this operation were similar to the reduction of signal intensity.

Conditions 8 and 9, during which the reset contingency was in effect for all red-key responses, appear to have replicated the results of the corresponding Conditions 1 and 2 satisfactorily, except for a slight elevation in false reporting in the fourth interval. Condition 11, during which the reset contingency was in effect and reinforcement for false reports was programmed differently, replicated Condition 6 quite well.

The performances of Birds 18 and 19 in these conditions were similar to those of Bird 1. Bird 2 maintained a very low false report rate in Condition 6, and consequently did not make contact with reinforcement in the absence of the signal. Its

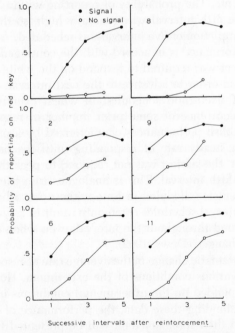

Fig. 10. Probability of responding within 3 sec of signal onset, and in the absence of signal, as a function of successive intervals after reinforcement. A strong signal was programmed in Conditions 1 and 8, a weak signal in Conditions 2 and 9, and a strong signal with 40% of the reinforcements obtained in the absence of signal during Conditions 6 and 11. All data are for bird #1.

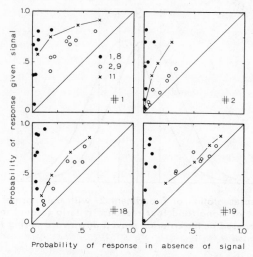

Fig. 11. Isosensitivity plots of responding within 3 sec of signal onset, and in the absence of signal, in the final ten sessions of training on the indicated conditions. The plots were constructed from data for the first four intervals after reinforcement.

performance in Condition 11, which guaranteed exposure to this variable, was like that of Bird 1. Bird 20 gave data like that of Bird 1 in Conditions 1 and 2. However, its Condition 1 performance was never recovered; even with the introduction of the reset contingency, its false report rate remained high throughout all subsequent conditions. There was no obvious reason why this bird differed from the others.

Isosensitivity curves were constructed from the probabilities of reporting given the presence and absence of signal in the first four successive intervals. Data from Conditions 1, 2, 8, 9, and 11 are presented in this form in Figure 11. No results are shown for Bird 20 because of the failure to recover its original performance. For the four remaining birds, data from Conditions 1 and 8, which involved the relatively easy detection of S_2 and never provided reinforcement for false reports, are given by the filled circles. The data points are concentrated along the left-hand edge of the plots, with no consistent differences between conditions. The data from Conditions 2 and 9, given by the unfilled circles, are typical functions for the detection of a weak signal. Performance in Condition 9, with the reset contingency, did not differ consistently from that in Condition 2. The results for Condition 11, employing an easily detected signal but providing 40 percent of all reinforcements for responses occurring in its absence, are given by the crosses. The data points are shifted to the right and downward, relative to those for Conditions 1 and 8. This is the same sort of shift as that produced by reducing signal intensity. In this sense, then, reinforcement for reporting in the absence of a signal was functionally equivalent to a reduction in signal intensity. Presumably, it would be possible to find some signal intensity and some schedule of reinforcement for responses in the absence of signal which would have quantitatively similar effects (as apparently occurred in the case of Birds 18 and 19).

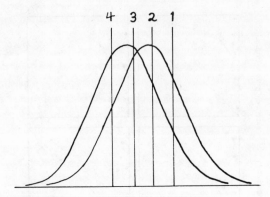

Fig. 12. Schematic representation of Experiment 2, with unit normal distributions for the presence and absence of signal and four response criteria located to suggest the way in which responding increased as the criterion moved downward during the first four intervals between reinforcements.

In terms of signal detectability theory, the results shown in Figure 11 may be viewed as arising from the situation schematized in Figure 12. The two distributions represent the presence and absence of signal, respectively. Four response criteria are located to correspond to the increases in the probability of reporting as a function of the ordinal number of the interval. According to this model, the relation between normalized response probabilities should be linear with a slope of 1.0 (Green and Swets, 1966). Response probabilities for Conditions 2 and 11 were transformed into z-scores and plotted in the form of isosensitivity curves in Figure 13. In all cases, the functions are approximately linear, and the

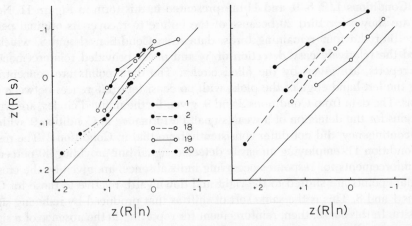

Fig. 13. Normalized isosensitivity curves for Condition 2 (left panel) and Condition 11 (right panel). $z(R/s)$ and $z(R/n)$ correspond to the probabilities of responding within 3 sec of signal onset, and in the absence of signal, respectively. Bird 20 was omitted from the right panel because of its failure to recover its Condition 1 performance on any of the intervening replications.

slopes do not differ consistently from 1.0. There is more variance across subjects in the slope and location of the line for Condition 11, which employed a strong signal with occasional reinforcement for responses in its absence, than in Condition 2, which scheduled reinforcement only for detection of a weak signal. These data are consistent with a signal detection model in which the separation between distributions is a joint function of signal intensity and the differential consequences of responding in the presence and absence of the signal. Evidently, there is more individual variation in sensitivity to differential reinforcement than to differential stimulation in this situation.

DISCUSSION

Under some of the conditions described here, reinforcement variables affected the probability of reporting but left signal detectability unchanged, whereas under other conditions, reinforcement acted to alter the measured detectability of the signal. A review of the present findings may indicate some crucial features of these conditions.

In Experiment 1, variations in the probability of reinforcement for detecting a weak signal (S_1) had little if any effect on the detectability of S_1 (see Fig. 6). Throughout this experiment, reinforcement was never scheduled for responding in the absence of a signal, so that the frequency of reinforcement for detecting S_1 relative to the frequency of reinforcement for reporting in the presence of S_0 was 1.0. Within these conditions, the differential detectability of S_1 and S_2 was systematically related to the relative frequency of reinforcement in their presence (Fig. 9), being greatest when the relative frequency of reinforcement for detecting S_2 was 1.0.

In Experiment 2, the detectability of a signal was invariant with respect to the proximity of reinforcement within a cycle (Fig. 13), a variable which did not affect the relative frequency of reinforcement for detecting the signal. However, detectability was reduced when reinforcement was scheduled for responding in the absence of the signal, a variable which altered the relative frequency of reinforcement correlated with the signal.

The relative frequency of reinforcement is a potent variable in operant discrimination and choice experiments (e.g., Herrnstein, 1964; Reynolds, 1963a, 1963b), so it is not surprising to find effects on psychophysical performance as well. However, it cannot be the sole variable responsible for the effects reported here. In Experiment 1, Conditions 5 and 6, the detectability of S_1 depended on the probability of reinforcement in S_2, even though the probability of reinforcement for detecting S_1 was constant and the frequency of reinforcement in S_1 relative to S_0 remained at 1.0. Also, the relative frequency of reinforcement is indeterminate during extinction, so that the effects of Conditions 3 and 6 are difficult to treat in this context. However, it is clear that when the relative frequency of reinforcement varied, the numerical index of signal detectability was systematically affected.

In the conventional detection experiment with humans, the definition of positive and negative outcomes seems quite clear. With animals, however, it is clear only if one feels confident about the identification and functional properties of positive reinforcers and punishers. The traditional categorization of events into positive, negative, and neutral has been severely challenged by work such as Premack's (1965) demonstrations of the relativity of positive reinforcement, and McKearney's (1969) findings that electric shock may function as either a positive or a negative reinforcer depending on its scheduled relation to responding and the history of the organism. The apparently neutral stimuli correlated with nonreinforcement may have aversive properties under some circumstances (Leitenberg, 1965) and reinforcing properties under others (Schaub and Honig, 1967). Thus, one cannot be sure, a priori, of the behavioral significance of the scheduled consequences of responding. This chapter has attempted to show that under some circumstances, variations in the consequences of responding are functionally equivalent to variations in the stimuli. Therefore, reinforcement effects must be specified and controlled with the same precision as that routinely used by psychophysicists in the specification and control of the stimuli.

A more general reason for studying the effects of reinforcement in psychophysical experiments follows from the special position occupied by animal psychophysics as a link between animal discrimination learning and human psychophysical performance. In the case of animal discrimination learning, there is a good deal of data suggesting equivalence between stimulus and reinforcement variables. For example, one method for studying discrimination is to establish a baseline performance with maintained reinforcement in the presence of one stimulus, S_1, and then introduce a second stimulus, S_2, correlated with extinction. An alternative method involves baseline training with equal reinforcement in both S_1 and S_2, and then discontinuing reinforcement in S_2. In both cases, S_1 and S_2 are presented successively and the S_1 reinforcement schedule remains constant throughout training. The former method involves a stimulus operation, and the latter a reinforcement operation, but their effects on behavior are at least qualitatively similar. Unless special training procedures are used, both operations produce decreases in S_2 response rate, and contrasting increases in S_1 response rate (Reynolds, 1961; Terrace, 1966). Also, both methods produce U-shaped gradients of extinction centered at S_2 on continua orthogonal to the $S_1 - S_2$ continuum (Honig et al., 1963; Nevin, 1968). Thus, there is no need to distinguish discriminations produced by changing a stimulus from those produced by changing a reinforcement schedule.

The standard discrimination learning situation with reinforcement in S_1 and extinction in S_2 has long been recognized as a limiting case of a large class of experiments in which different reinforcement schedules are correlated with S_1 and S_2. Over the past few years, accumulations of parametric data have suggested that the effects of extinction are continuously related to those of other schedules involving nonzero reinforcement frequencies in S_2 (e.g., Nevin, 1968). In like fashion, the standard signal detection experiment should be recognized as another limiting case of the general class, differing from discrimination learning experiments in its concern with asymptotic responding to physically similar stimuli. The present experiments begin to explore an experimental domain within which stimulus and reinforcement variables combine parametrically to determine the acquisition and maintenance of differential responding. Differential stimulation and differential reinforcement may function similarly within this domain. It remains to be seen whether theories which have been successful in dealing with the limiting cases can be extended to deal with a generalized psychophysics of stimulation and reinforcement.

REFERENCES

Blough, D. S. 1967. Stimulus generalization as signal detection in pigeons. Science, 158:940–941.

Bush, R. R., R. D. Luce, and R. M. Rose. 1964. Learning models for psychophysics. *In* Atkinson, R. C., ed. Studies in Mathematical Psychology, Stanford, Stanford University Press, pp. 201–217.

Dews, P. B. 1962. The effect of multiple $S^\triangle$ periods on responding on a fixed-interval schedule. J. Exp. Anal. Behav., 5:369–374.

Green, D. M., and J. A. Swets. 1966. Signal Detection Theory and Psychophysics, New York, John Wiley & Sons, Inc.

Hack, M. H. 1963. Signal detection in the rat. Science, 193:758–759.

Herrnstein, R. J. 1964. Secondary reinforcement and rate of primary reinforcement. J. Exp. Anal. Behav., 7:27–36.

Honig, W. K., C. A. Boneau, K. R. Burstein, and H. S. Pennypacker. 1963. Positive and negative generalization gradients obtained after equivalent training conditions. J. Comp. Physiol. Psychol., 56:111–116.

Leitenberg, H. 1965. Is time out from positive reinforcement an aversive event? Psychol. Bull., 64:428–441.

McKearney, J. W. 1969. Fixed-interval schedules of shock presentation: extinction and recovery of performance under different shock intensities and fixed-interval durations. J. Exp. Anal. Behav., 12:301–313.

Mentzer, T. L. 1966. Comparison of three methods for obtaining psychophysical thresholds from the pigeon. J. Comp. Physiol. Psychol., 61:96–101.

Nevin, J. A. 1964. A method for the determination of psychophysical functions in the rat. J. Exp. Anal. Behav., 7:169.

——— 1967. Effects of reinforcement scheduling on simultaneous discrimination performance. J. Exp. Anal. Behav., 10:251–260.

——— 1968. Differential reinforcement and stimulus control of not responding. J. Exp. Anal. Behav., 11:715–726.

Premack, D. 1965. Reinforcement theory. *In* Levine, D., ed. Nebraska Symposium on Motivation, Lincoln, University of Nebraska Press, pp. 123–180.

Reynolds, G. S. 1961. Behavioral contrast. J. Exp. Anal. Behav., 4:57–71.

——— 1963a. On some determinants of choice in pigeons. J. Exp. Anal. Behav., 6:53–59.

——— 1963b. Some limitations on behavioral contrast and induction during successive discrimination. J. Exp. Anal. Behav., 6:131–139.

Schaub, R. E., and W. K. Honig. 1967. Reinforcement of behavior with cues correlated with extinction. Psychon. Sci., 7:15–16.

Terrace, H. S. 1966. Stimulus control. *In* Honig, W. K., ed. Operant Behavior: Areas of Research and Applicaton, New York, Appleton-Century-Crofts, pp. 271–344.

Author Index

Complete references are given on pages indicated by italics

Subject Index

431